D0615609

# AFFAIRS OF PARTY

## The Political Culture of Northern Democrats in the Mid-Nineteenth Century

JEAN H. BAKER

*Affairs of Party*

BY THE SAME AUTHOR

*Ambivalent Americans: The Know-Nothing Party in Maryland*

*The Politics of Continuity: Maryland Political Parties from 1858 to 1870*

# *Affairs of Party*

## The Political Culture of Northern Democrats in the Mid-Nineteenth Century

JEAN H. BAKER

*Cornell University Press*

ITHACA AND LONDON

First published 1983 by Cornell University Press.
Published in the United Kingdom by Cornell University Press Ltd.,
Ely House, 37 Dover Street, London W1X 4HQ.

International Standard Book Number (cloth) 0-8014-1513-6
International Standard Book Number (paper) 0-8014-9883-x
Library of Congress Catalog Card Number 82-14283
Printed in the United States of America
*Librarians: Library of Congress cataloging information appears on the last page of the book*

*The paper in this book is acid-free and meets the guidelines for permanence and durability of the Committee on Production Guidelines for Book Longevity of the Council on Library Resources.*

For R. L. H. H. and F. B. H.

# *Contents*

# *Preface*

This book originated with the observation that the practice of American politics in the late twentieth century is dull and meaningless compared with that in earlier periods in the nation's history, when party affairs were the measure of public life. Although the reasons for this transformation appear to be well known, the nature of parties, their role as conveyors of American political culture, and the process by which they define public life remain less apparent. With the mid-nineteenth-century Democratic party as my focus point, I set out to examine the meaning of party experience.

Broadly speaking, this is a book about political culture and the ways in which a group of Americans thought and acted with regard to public affairs during the mid-nineteenth century. More narrowly conceived, it is a study of how northern children learned at school to be Americans and then, influenced by family and environment, became Democrats. To cover this process of induction, the first three chapters discuss the basic institutions of political training—the school, the family, and the party. Once established as partisans, mid-century Northern Democrats derived their evaluations of public affairs from their party, which besides developing programs and nominating leaders also provided a set of rituals and customary ways of thinking and acting. These practices conveyed the meaning of the Democracy to its following, and by a complex process of reinforcement the attitudes of this Northern Democratic fellowship simultaneously acted on and evolved from the activities of the party. To make these elusive aspects of political culture more concrete, the middle section of the book concentrates on the ruling expressions, convictions, and symbols of the Democracy, specifically its republicanism, racism, and Americanism. Finally, because the partisan culture of the Northern Democracy included behavior as well as ideals, the last section treats Northern Democrats in their public roles as soldiers and supporters of the Union during the Civil War, voters in the presidential elections of 1864 and 1868, and nationalists who in the 1870s sought the restoration of a "white America."

It is clear that Northern Democrats shared many (though not all) of their ideas and practices with other Americans—whether Whigs, Know-Nothings, Republicans, or nonpartisans—and in many respects there were only distinctions, never differences, between American political culture and the Democratic version of it. This is not surprising. After a civil cohabitation of decades, the Union had developed arrangements that, like the habits of long-married couples, provided established—though not unalterable—political patterns. These were retained even during the 1860s, when Northerners preserved their allegiant civic culture and, maintaining their two-party system, campaigned, wrote platforms, held elections, and accepted the winners. What the Democracy had created was a malleable version of American themes which, while easily distinguishable from that of its opponents, did not compete with national values. Accordingly, a great deal of what sometimes appears to be distinctive was not uniquely Democratic. This fact is one of the substantive themes of this book, for it is my intention to show the ways in which the Northern Democracy, for all its shrill sectarianism, nonetheless served as a nationalizing force.

Southern Democrats led quite different public lives, and for that reason they are not included here. Without entering into the perennial controversy over the differences and similiarities between the antebellum North and South, I believe that in matters relevant to this book, the South was qualitatively different from the North. Not only did the agents of socialization vary (the South had far fewer schools than the North, its party organization was more diffuse and decentralized, and it was never subject to popular influences such as ministrelsy), but its political culture was intimately affected by the existence of slavery and of a large black population. Increasingly, Southern Democrats were subjected to a regional culture that made their civic life diverge even further from that of their northern colleagues. It was not by chance that antebellum South Carolina, the first state to secede, did not hold popular presidential elections and thereby excluded its citizens from participating in a recurring allegiance-forming national ceremony. Certainly there were Southern Democrats before the war who shared many attitudes and types of behavior with their northern counterparts, and this common terrain needs further elucidation. But the failure of these Southerners to sustain their organization during the war reveals the qualitative differences separating Northern and Southern Democrats and justifies the latter's exclusion from any study of political culture that crosses the divide of secession, war, and Reconstruction.

A second goal of this book is to demonstrate the uses of culture as a means of explaining public concourse. Historians have tried various methods of understanding those elusive ordinary Americans of the past. One recent approach is to transform political history into what Samuel Hays calls "social analysis." This type of inquiry depends to a great extent on quantitative data and aggregate voting statistics. But given the data base available, I am convinced that the limits of such interpretation have been reached. For this reason, *Affairs of Party* is neither an event-filled party narrative nor an investigation of the ethnic, religious, and economic background of mid-century Democrats. Nor is it a study of their legislative positions. Not only have all these topics been researched, but no matter what the relative significance of these components in individual voting decisions, the answer represents only one aspect of the ways in which Americans led their civic lives. Insofar as practitioners of the "new political history" have persistently associated parties with ethnicity and religion, the existence of partisan cultures like that of the Northern Democracy has been obscured. In an effort to reverse this approach, the primary focus here is attachment to party—not class, occupation, residency, and religious denomination.

It is now appropriate to use political history as a tool for cultural analysis and to ask different questions: How did Americans learn their public roles? How did they view their government and what were their political ceremonies? What was the meaning of these rituals? Did they trust their government and the regime in power? How did they feel about their role in public life? In short, what was the political style of the country? For over thirty years these kinds of questions have inspired investigations of contemporary societies as diverse as China, Norway, and Indonesia. In most instances, the analysis has been comparative; cross-national evaluations have been the rule in works such as Gabriel Almond and Sidney Verba's *The Civic Culture: Political Attitudes and Democracy in Five Nations* and Lucien Pye and Sidney Verba's *Political Culture and Political Development*. This approach has somewhat impeded single-nation studies. Political parties, however, can serve as valid units of study because their principles may be tested against those of other partisan organizations. There is in fact a growing literature on American politics as culture, which includes Edgar Litt's *The Political Cultures of Massachusetts* and Daniel Howe's *The Political Culture of the American Whigs*.

In this book I have relied on Verba's definition of political culture as "the system of empirical beliefs, expressive symbols, and values which defines the situation in which political action takes place" and which encompasses, given its orientation to the subjective aspect of politics, not only the life histories of the individuals who make up the system but the public events and private experiences that become "the collective expression of a political system."[1] Political culture assumes that the attitudes, sentiments, and cognitions that inform and govern politics are not random arrangements, but represent (if only we could see them as an anthropologist does the tribal rites of Tikopia) coherent patterns that together form a meaningful whole. Thus, instead of investigating the election returns, legislative roll calls, and party nominations that made up the external world of Northern Democrats, I have concentrated on what formed the internal life of party members—their training and socialization at home and in school, the meaning of their campaign rituals, and the language of their party expression. In the last case, language—itself a form of action—is treated as a lens through which to view party values rather than as a disposable campaign mask used for voter manipulation. Many Northern Democratic sentiments, including support of Union and Constitution, remained abstractions best understood within their metaphoric, symbolic context. Viewed as culture, even the neglected episodes of traditional political history such as conventions and parades reemerge as sources.

Historians of nineteenth-century events and movements cannot make use of research surveys, which have become the principal resource in contemporary studies of political culture. Hence, in many cases but especially in Chapters 1, 3, and 5, I depend on individual biographies, on the assumption that partisan culture, like other customary behaviors, is embedded in human beings, some of whom successfully embody the general tendencies of the group. My concern here is not how representative the individual's ideas or behavior may have been, but rather the degree to which a particular Northern Democrat absorbed and summarized the group's sensibilities. What is sacrificed in universality is made up for by the accuracy and concreteness of individual examples. In a sense, the life history becomes the historian's completed questionnaire.

I have necessarily set my analysis in a generational framework. Thus, the first chapters concentrate on the early decades of the nineteenth century, during the childhood of the generation of Northern Democrats who reached political maturity at mid-century. Educated in certain

[1]Lucien Pye and Sidney Verba, *Political Culture and Political Development* (Princeton: Princeton University Press, 1965) pp. 513, 8.

kinds of schools and influenced by a particular understanding of their party, these Northern Democrats dominated party affairs by the 1850s and 1860s. Accordingly, it is necessary to treat political learning a quarter century before partisan ideals and behavior. Such a sequential framework violates current models of party systems, which, because they are oriented to electoral behavior, propose the existence of a new party system in the 1850s. This kind of chronological refinement, along with the requirement that parties be studied as dyads, obscures the generational perspective essential to understanding politics as culture. Instead, most students of political culture separate the political process into its cognitive aspects (in this case, what a Northern Democrat learned about politics through school, family, and party); its evaluative components (what a Northern Democrat thought about his government and the issues of the day as revealed through party symbols and expression); and finally, its affective factors (what a Northern Democrat felt about public affairs as revealed by his behavior). In a broad sense these divisions, which have been sequenced to follow the partisan history of one generation, form the structure of *Affairs of Party*. And although the chapters on becoming, believing, and behaving as Democrats are essential to an understanding of the party's culture, they may also be thought of as dealing with separate topics readily transferable to other parties and times.

Because this first generation of Democrats controlled party affairs during the 1860s, much of this book has to do with the Civil War and Reconstruction. This historical setting brought into vivid focus some aspects of partisan culture that remained latent in more placid times. Not only did the Civil War period affect Americans in a way that no other public event has before or since; it was also a time when events challenged national values, by destroying both the shared bonds of the past and collective anticipations for the future. Alfred North Whitehead once wrote of areas of general agreement too obvious to need expression: "like the air we breathe, such a form is so translucent, and so seemingly necessary, that only by extreme effort can we become aware of it."[2] Such a description applies to the early nineteenth century, but not to the Civil War, when, according to one Northern Democrat, "Peril gives the lessons of years in a day."[3] In normal times Democrats were less introspective and rarely considered such questions as the nature of the republic, the meaning of race, and the role of an opposition

[2]Alfred North Whitehead, *Adventures of Ideas* (Cambridge: Cambridge University Press, 1933), p. 14.

[3]*Congressional Globe*, 37th Cong., 1st sess., p. 132.

party. Whether investigating twentieth-century China or seventeenth-century England, students of political culture concentrate on critical episodes for the simple reason that such decisive events disclose otherwise opaque aspects of public life.

Northern Democrats are an admittedly awkward subculture, albeit a necessary one for any student of nineteenth-century politics. They are the first political organization having a sufficient history to permit any analysis of socialization. Other organizations—the Federalists, Jeffersonians, Whigs, and Know-Nothings—did not survive the requisite half-century, and the Republicans were much younger (a similar study of them would not be possible before the 1890s). And, as explained earlier, the Southern Democrats held different values and aspirations.

In this book Northern Democrats are defined as party supporters who lived in the twenty-two nonseceding states, the District of Columbia, and the Washington and Nebraska territories. Although political scientists often differentiate among leaders, activists, fellow travelers, and voters, for the most part such distinctions are avoided here. To make them would violate my understanding of party members as possessing a widely shared form of discourse that led them to say certain things, hold certain values, and behave in a particular way. Of course, there was nothing that exactly corresponded to the entity Northern Democrats. It is a fictive construction, as most generalizing terms are. Northern Democrats operated on different levels of ideological perception and interest, along a continuum of views and behavior. Yet because they had established a political community and had both a sense of themselves as an organization and a particular orientation to their nation's politics, they are presented here as a case study. The pronoun *they* as it refers to Northern Democrats is not used arbitrarily or capriciously; it designates the central tendency of a spectrum.

While writing this book, I have become indebted to a number of colleagues. Julie Roy Jeffrey of the Goucher history department read, talked about, and listened to various parts of it, both in and out of the classes we team teach. Gabrielle Spiegel of the University of Maryland department of history sharpened my understanding of political culture, although we continue to differ on its meaning. Herman Belz, also of the University of Maryland history department, scrupulously edited Chapter 3, and other chapters have benefited from the comments of R. Kent Lancaster and R. Robinson Baker. As is her custom, Joy Pankoff did excellent work with a difficult manuscript.

The initial research for *Affairs of Party* was supported by a fellowship from the American Council of Learned Societies and a sabbatical and summer fellowship from Goucher College. Although my family gave no leaves, I am grateful, as always, to my husband and children, who offered their own kind of support.

JEAN H. BAKER

*McDonogh, Maryland*

*Affairs of Party*

# *Introduction*

The year 1876 was a time for all Americans to remember the past, and Democrats were no exception. Throughout the year, at conventions, ward meetings, and especially during the presidential campaign, party leaders recalled the period before the Civil War when they had been the majority. Comforted by history, Democrats fused what they affectionately called "the Democracy" with their sense of nationhood and, holding American (and therefore partisan) principles to be eternal, considered their party "bound to live through all centuries, for it was founded in truth and truth will live forever."[1] Older members who had grown up with their party in power recalled the years between 1828 and 1860, when Democrats had won six of nine presidential elections, thereby reducing Whig and Republican victories to exceptions.

During this earlier period, besides the presidency, Democrats had controlled the House of Representatives for twenty-four of thirty-two years, and the Senate for twenty-eight. They had also maintained an enduring majority on the Supreme Court. Because their leaders so often ran public affairs and because party affiliation determined voting behavior in Congress, Democratic convictions informed what Stephen Douglas called "the great measures of the day."[2] Even in the 1850s, when sectional allegiance began to replace party membership as a voting cue, particularly in matters relating to the extension of slavery, Northern Democrats (more so than their southern counterparts and

[1]*Congressional Globe,* 37th Cong., 2d sess., 2467; Ibid., 44th Cong., 2d sess., 689.

[2]Stephen A. Douglas to Sidney Breese, 20 October 1840, Sidney Breese Papers, Illinois State Historical Society, Springfield. For information on party control of Congress, see Walter Dean Burnham, Jerome M. Clubb, and William Flanigan, "Partisan Realignment: A Systemic Perspective," in *The History of American Electoral Behavior,* ed Joel Silbey, Allan Bogue, and William Flanigan (Princeton: Princeton University Press, 1978), p. 65.

Northern and Southern Whigs) resisted these pressures. Their success before 1860 led one southern separatist to lament "the cursed bonds of party that paralyzed our strength and energy."[3]

This national power was duplicated at the local level. Although party support was diffuse, in some areas Democratic communities created by special historical and cultural circumstances dominated politics even in the 1860s, when the Republicans became the majority party. In states like California and Oregon, in regions like Little Egypt in Illinois and the tier of Ohio counties along the Ohio River, and in cities like New York, Democrats habitually ran community affairs. Whether the opposition was Whig, Know-Nothing, or Republican, its strength consistently fell below the benchmarks now used to define competitive politics.[4] Even after the electoral upheaval of the 1850s, Democrats retained control of either the statehouse or lower assemblies in fifteen of twenty-one northern states and elected two presidents and a majority of the representatives in the Thirty-fifth Congress. Although they lost large sections of the Northwest and New England to the Republicans, realignment did not end their influence; only the South's secession did that. But just as it is easy to exaggerate the importance of the party before the 1850s, so its decline in the 1860s and 1870s should not be overemphasized. In most elections in the latter years, a shift of one voter of every eight would have given the Democracy a majority and, translated into seats, increased the party's officeholders, state and federal, by 25 percent. Still, the party had not won the presidency for two decades, although it had, in what national leaders interpreted as a harbinger of the future, won control of the House of Representatives in 1871.

All of this Democrats remembered as they prepared for the presidential campaign, and they recalled as well that to achieve its earlier predominance their organization had depended on a stable party-in-the-electorate who usually voted their tickets. Although the realignment of

[3]Quoted in Joel Silbey, *Shrine of Party: Congressional Voting Behavior, 1841–1852* (Pittsburgh: University of Pittsburgh Press, 1967), p. 275, n. 1. Thomas Alexander, *Sectional Stress and Party Strength: A Computer Analysis of Roll-Call Voting Patterns in the United States House of Representatives, 1836–1860* (Nashville: Vanderbilt University Press, 1967); Silbey, Bogue, and Flanigan, *American Electoral Behavior,* p. 67; Glenn Linden, *Politics or Principle: Congressional Voting on Civil War Amendments and Pro-Negro Measures, 1838–1869* (Seattle: University of Washington Press, 1976); David Russo, "The Major Political Issues of the Jacksonian Period and the Development of Party Loyalty in Congress," *Transactions of the American Philosophical Society* 62 (May 1972): 3–49.

[4]Paul David, *Party Strength in the United States, 1872–1970* (Charlottesville: University Press of Virginia, 1972); Joel Silbey, *A Respectable Minority: The Democratic Party in the Civil War Era, 1860–1868* (New York: W. W. Norton, 1977), p. 26.

the 1850s shook the faith of some and brought fewer new voters into the ranks, a loyal, slightly smaller following reemerged before the Civil War.[5] Despite enclaves of special strength, Democrats were distributed throughout the country; hence the party had a national presence. Never rejected by any region, religion, or economic group, Democrats had earlier accused the Whigs of representing only the rich and well-born and the Know-Nothings of serving as the conspiracy of native-born Protestants. Now they indicted the Republicans for having no southern members and considered themselves, with some justification, the party of the American people.

To mobilize support and elect leaders who would put their principles into effect, Democrats after the Civil War continued to depend on state organizations loosely coordinated by a national committee. By the 1870s party affairs were arranged in an overlapping structure of ward and county conventions that encouraged participation among activists and held out for a few the possibility of patronage positions. Less well articulated was the relation between state and national politics, although in the copy-cat fashion of American public life Democrats, like Whigs, Know-Nothings, and Republicans, nominated their presidential candidates at a national convention. In the late 1840s the party also installed a national chairman and executive committee, along with a congressional committee. Although this partisan apparatus reflected the increasing centralization of the party, it was active only during congressional and presidential campaigns.[6] Still, by forcing local patronage holders to give up a portion of their salaries to elect Democrats to Congress, these mechanisms served to integrate national and local party affairs.

In this centennial year, the party looked forward to winning the presidency, keeping the House, electing as many as ten new senators, and controlling as many state governments as possible. But by 1876 there was more to the Democracy than its leaders, campaigns, and appeals; another significant factor was its meaning to generations of

[5]Silbey, *Shrine of Party,* p. 20; Silbey, Bogue, and Flanigan, *American Electoral Behavior,* pp. 86–93; Gerald Pomper, *Elections in America: Control and Influence in Democratic Politics* (New York: Dodd, Mead, 1968), p. 268.

[6]David Edward Meerse, "James Buchanan, The Patronage and the Northern Democratic Party, 1857–1858" (Ph.D. dissertation, University of Illinois, 1969), pp. 21, 32; Michael Holt, "The Democratic Party, 1828–1860," in *History of U.S. Political Parties,* ed. Arthur M. Schlesinger, Jr. (New York: Chelsea House, 1973), 1: 497–571; William J. Hartman, "Politics and Patronage: The New York Custom House, 1852–1902" (Ph.D. dissertation, Columbia University, 1952); Roy F. Nichols, *The Disruption of American Democracy* (New York: Macmillan, 1948), p. 57.

Americans. Over the years the party had come to offer a particular mode of public life—what might be called a subculture—and through it supporters defined the situations and circumstances in which their political actions took place. To be a Northern Democrat was to be part of a special culture; just as ethnicity, regionalism, and denominationalism framed the spiritual lives of Irish Catholics and Southern Baptists, so the Democracy established ways of acting and thinking about public matters.

One way to consider this partisan culture is to investigate the process by which a particular group, in this case Northerners in the first part of the nineteenth century, learned the attitudes and behaviors expected of them as Americans. In the United States, as in any postrevolutionary society, this was an especially crucial matter, for no part of the political system had tradition's blessing. Nor, as in the twentieth century, did established mediums for transmitting political information exist. Instead the family, the school, and the party inculcated public habits, and although these were not the only institutions involved in political socialization, they were the most influential. While the family taught partisanship, schools provided young males with their first training in submitting to authority, delegating power, commissioning leaders, and recognizing illegal coercion. In turn, Northerners who became Democrats were influenced by their party, which replicated expected behavior; thus, through their partisan activities, members learned roles that they repeated as Americans. Like the family and the school, the party reinforced loyalty to the regime because it offered ways to practice the political goals of the nation, and in the same way that a well-calibrated thermostat provides a constant level of temperature, the Democracy contributed to the stability of the system. The obvious first question is; how had some Northerners come to be Democrats? Chapter 1 attempts to answer this question for seven individuals and one community, while Chapters 2 and 3 focus on the preparations for partisan life learned in school and in the party itself.

For Northerners who became Democrats, the party provided training in how to behave as Americans—through participation in conventions, parades, and elections—and in how to think about public issues. Because older men controlled the party (nearly all the research on the nineteenth-century organization reveals its geriatric composition), novices learned from those already integrated into the system.

Traditionally, the views of the Democratic electorate have been studied through the opinions of these older party officials, although there is no way of knowing the extent to which leaders directed the ideas of their followers. Today we are rightly suspicious of using the visible opinion of political notables as a guide to mass feelings, and in modern canon to rely on such elite expression is to neglect the less privileged. But at the same time that an overdue commitment to history's disinherited has redirected scholarly attention, political scientists have uncovered the weak ideological focus of an electorate that only dimly perceives issues. "Most people," conclude two contemporary scholars, "exhibit little interest in public affairs and few participate actively. . . . It is just as well given the abominable state of popular knowledge and information about political issues."[7] For two contradictory reasons—the indifference of the masses and the independence of their judgments—measures of elite sentiment are considered a deficient gauge of public opinion. On either count, the historian's world of finely notched policy distinctions concerning slavery in the territories, confiscation, and Reconstruction was not inhabited by many Democrats.

There is considerable evidence, however, that nineteenth-century Americans gave closer attention to politics than is the case today, thereby guaranteeing a broader, deeper understanding of issues. Certainly there was less apathy among the electorate and more congruence among the visible opinion of political leaders, the formation of public agendas, and the invisible attitudes of followers. In part, the restricted size of the electorate and its sexual and racial homogeneity accounted for this, and, given the decline of competing organizations such as church and militia, it was easier for the party to shape policy preferences and forward its views to the elected than it would be one hundred years later.

Thus, party leaders shaped and articulated inchoate mass sentiments but did not create them. The nature of this relationship was acknowledged by candidates who, in large broadsides, called meetings to hear "an expression of opinion from the people."[8] Hence the relation between elite and mass, leader and follower, public issue and private concern, the one so visible, the other so obscured, was more that of a sculptor giving form to local materials than of a peddler hawking preformed wares. When leaders adopted the latter role and no longer

[7]Roger Cobb and Charles D. Elder, *Participation in American Politics: The Dynamics of Agenda Building* (Boston: Allyn and Bacon, 1972), p. 2. See also Angus Campbell, *et al.*, *The American Voter* (New York: John Wiley, 1960, pp. 171–76, 187; Eugene Burdick and Arthur Brodbeck, *American Voting Behavior* (Glencoe, Ill.: Free Press, 1959); Robert Axelrod, "The Structure of Public Opinion on Policy Issues," *Public Opinion Quarterly* 31 (Spring 1967): 51–60; Dale Baum, "Know-Nothingism and the Republican Party in Massachusetts: The Political Realignment of the 1850s," *Journal of American History* 64 (March 1978): 959–86.

[8]See, for example, "I consider it my Duty," 1859, Broadside Collection, Library of Congress; "Attention Honest Democrats," New York Public Library.

spoke for their following, they knew it. Twice Stephen Douglas suffered such rebuke: in 1848 after he voted agains the Wilmot Proviso, a Chicago crowd booed and hissed him; and six years later, after the Kansas-Nebraska Act had passed Congress, he wryly noted that he could have traveled from Boston to Chicago by the light of his burning effigy.[9]

Hence, that modern construct—the civic culture composed of an informed citizenry who participate in public affairs, weigh the issues, and make responsible judgments on personnel and policy—accurately described the mid-nineteenth century, a period when elected officials and voters listened to each other.

Chapters 4, 5, and 6 treat the ideological cues the Democratic party gave its followers, as these ideas developed from its liberalism and antistatism of the 1830s into the republicanism and racism of the mid-nineteenth century. Chapter 4 covers the revival of republicanism in party thought; Chapters 5 and 6 analyze its racism, first as expressed by three prominent Northern Democrats—Stephen Douglas, James Bayard, and Thomas Bayard—and then as conveyed through northern minstrelsy. By mid-century, the vital core of Democratic thinking was a firm commitment to a "white man's republic."

Being a Northern Democrat involved a great deal more than believing in certain ideals and feeling a particular way about the government and the country. It also entailed public activities that confirmed party attitudes. Through that process of reinforcement which converts some behavior into habit, these customs were built on selected abstractions from the party's past. Such circularity made it difficult to change the Democracy; hence, there was a static quality to partisan life and expression after 1840.

Chapters 7 and 8 discuss this behavior in three contexts: first, in the presidential elections of the 1860s, when the identities of being a Democrat and an American merged through the process of voting; second, in the roles played by Northern Democrats during the Civil War; and finally, in the party's relation to the South. As voters, soldiers, and supporters of a restored Union, Democrats were influenced by the instrumental needs of an organization that sought to elect its leaders and to install its policies. But these extrinsic purposes should not obscure the symbolic dimensions of partisanship so vital to nineteenth-century public life.

[9]Johannsen, *Stephen A. Douglas,* pp. 252–53, 451; Arthur Cole, *The Era of the Civil War, 1848–1870* (Springfield: Illinois Centennial Commission, 1919), pp. 71, 122, 131–32.

Part I

# LEARNING TO BE DEMOCRATS

# CHAPTER I

# *Partisan Roots*

> A man has come into the world, his early years are spent without notice in the pleasures and activities of childhood. As he grows up, the world receives him when his manhood begins. . . . He is then studied for the first time. This is if I am not mistaken a great error. We must begin higher up; we must watch the infant in his mother's arms; we must see the first images which the external world casts upon the dark mirror of his mind, the first occurrences that he witnesses; we must hear the first words which awaken the sleeping powers of thought, and stand by his earliest efforts if we would understand the prejudices, the habits, the passions which will rule his life.
>
> —Alexis de Tocqueville

No one, it is safe to say, was ever born a Democrat. Enthusiasts sometimes insisted that they would die such, but no genetic inheritance had determined their fate. On the contrary, they had learned to be Democrats, some unsuspectingly when they were children, others influenced later by friends and community. In different ways and at different times in their lives, the nearly two million Northern men who voted the party's ticket during the 1860s had acquired a behavior which, once instilled, became something of a habit. Even today, this persistence factor is hard to measure, but a reliable study of midwestern Democrats in 1860 indicates that nine out of ten of the party's voters turned out in subsequent presidential elections, eight of ten to repeat their Democratic ballot.[1] Although its effects are thus apparent, the process of partisan indoctrination remains uncharted, and neither traditional event-filled political history nor aggregate election analysis considers this dimension of being a Democrat.

One point has always held true: Americans did not learn their partisanship in school, for it has always been an unwritten canon that the

[1] Ray Miles Shortridge, "Voting Patterns in the American Midwest, 1840–1872" (Ph.D. dissertation, University of Michigan, 1974), pp. 1–94, 116, 157, 200.

schoolmaster's desk must never be a party stump. In service to the nation, schools were expected to instill allegiance to the whole, not to its parts, and to engender support of the system, not merely of the regime in power. Certainly formal education fulfilled this directive. Although election day was sometimes a school holiday, political campaigns passed without mention; current issues were rarely discussed; and lithographs of George Washington, not recent or sitting presidents, decorated pre–Civil War schoolrooms. Even Horace Mann, who found so much to criticize in the nation's schools, applauded this neutrality. "Let it be once understood," he wrote in 1848, "that the schoolroom is a legitimate theatre for party politics and with what violence will hostile partisans struggle to gain possession of the stage, and to play their parts upon it!" Accordingly, teachers were neither to read nor to comment on "controverted texts." Nor were colleges to be places, according to Princeton's Robert Patton, "for young men to squabble about politics."[2]

Enjoined to keep "the tender minds of the young free from the excitement of clashing doctrines," teachers were expected to be impartial, and, as James Ruckle discovered after his interview with the Hamilton County, Ohio, school committee, the surest way to lose a job was to reveal, as he did, "some party spirit." Others obeyed the unwritten rule, and many male teachers, because they were under twenty-one—as well as all female teachers—could not vote. Lacking a working attachment to an organization, they were less tempted to bring their party politics to class. Those who did were promptly fired, and a New Hampshire schoolteacher who was dismissed in the middle of Buchanan's 1856 campaign concluded that district committees would rather have "an ignoramus than a partisan."[3] The same nonpartisanship was expected of masters and apprentices, and one German immigrant learned not to bring his Jacksonian enthusiasms to his job.[4] Nor did children's readers and pleasure books inculcate preferences, and the

[2]Horace Mann, "Twelfth Annual Report," in Sol Cohen, ed., *Education in the United States: A Documentary History,* 5 vols. (New York: Random House, 1974), 2:1106; Robert Patton, *A Lecture on Classical and National Education* (Princeton, N.J.; D. A. Barrenstein, 1826), p. 6.

[3]Lawrence Cremin, *The American Common School* (New York: Bureau of Publications, Teachers College, Columbia University, 1951), p. 195; Cohen, ed., *Education in the United States) 2: 70;* Diary of Henry Van der Luyn, entry for July 30, 1832, Henry Van der Luyn Papers, New York Historical Society, New York City; "Papers on District Schools," Box of Miscellaneous Papers, Sturbridge Village Library, Sturbridge, Mass.

[4]*New York Teacher* 2 (July 1854): 295; Charles Reemlin, *The Life of Charles Reemlin* (Cincinnati: Weier and Deiker, 1892), p. 15.

catalyst for the reordering of nineteenth-century parties—Andrew Jackson—inspired despite, not because of, his contributions to the Democracy. Marcius Willson, the author of popular American histories for the young, omitted George Washington's service to the Federalists, as did Jacob Abbott. In the latter's *American History* the first president emerged in the 1790s "to guide the ship of state through stormy seas," not to direct it toward a Federalist port. Other writers lower cased party names as if this deflation would somehow render parties insignificant, leaving young minds free to make "untrammelled" choices.[5]

Not only were children given no formal partisan instruction; the role their parents should play in their political development was also avoided. By the 1830s, manuals such as Jacob Abbott's *The Duties of Parents* and periodicals such as the *Teacher's Guide and Parent's Assistant* had replaced the religious instruction of an earlier age, and instead of advising parents on the proper ways to raise Christians, domestic literature encouraged the guardians of the young to inculcate the habits of American republicanism. John Quincy Adams exhorted parents to "lay up these principles of the Constitution in your hearts and souls, bind them for signs upon your hands. Teach them to your children, speaking of them when sitting in your house, when walking by the way, when lying down, when rising up, write them upon your gates.[6]

This appreciation of the family's role in political socialization had a side effect: it increased the importance of mothers, who were considered responsible for their children's early political development and who therefore must understand, even if they could not participate in, public life. Northerners generally accepted the Swiss educator Pestalozzi's dictum that "the mother's book was the best book." By the Civil War the image of women as teachers in the home had become a power-

[5]Marcius Willson, *American History* (New York: Ivison, Phinney, Blakeman, 1856); Jacob Abbott, *American History* (New York: Sheldon, 1856), p. 271; Chauncey D. Jacobs, "The Development of School Textbooks in United States History from 1795 to 1885" (Ph.D. dissertation, University of Pittsburgh, 1939); Anne McLeod, *A Moral Tale: Children's Fiction and American Culture, 1820–1860* (Hamden, Conn.: Archon Books, 1975).

[6]John Quincy Adams, *The Jubilee of the Constitution* (New York: Samuel Colman, 1839), pp. 119–20. For examples of advice literature see *The Teacher's Guide and Parent's Assistant; A Parent's Friend;* Jacob Abbott, *The Duties of Parents in Regard to the Schools Where Their Children Are Instructed* (Boston: Title and Weeks, 1834); C. B. Taylor, *A Universal History of the United States of America* (Buffalo: E. Strong, 1833); Josiah Quincy, *An Address to Aldermen* (Boston: N. Hale, 1828); S. R. Hall, *Practical Lectures on Parental Responsibility* (Boston: Pierce and Parker, 1833); Warren Burton, *Helps to Education in the Homes of Our Country* (Boston: Crosby and Nichols, 1863); Marcius Willson, *The School and Family Primer* (New York: Harper Brothers, 1860); Sanford Fleming, *CHildren and Puritanism: The Place of Children in the Life and Thought of New England Churches, 1620–1840* (New Haven: Yale University Press, 1933).

ful argument for educating girls and using them before marriage as schoolteachers. Here the ideals of nineteenth-century domesticity and the "republican mother" converged. As a result thousands of middleclass northern women took on the task of raising sons to be virtuous citizens, accepting this as their contribution to building and sustaining the nation. "A mother who has had a good common school education will rarely suffer her children to grow up in ignorance," wrote a Massachusetts businessman to Horace Mann in 1841. Such attitudes acknowledged, according to Linda Kerber, "that political socialization takes place at an early age, and that the patterns of authority experienced in families are important factors in the general political culture."[7]

But how to instill the desired political habits was not made explicit, and while nineteenth-century parents were bombarded with specific counsel on inculcating proper eating and even sexual habits, the authors of prescriptive literature were silent about partisanship and vague about the proper way to raise a good American. Most encouraged parents to mold their sons into "upright obliging peaceable public-spirited men." But the particulars of how to inspire "the social duties of consanguinity" were ignored. A few manuals directed fathers, as a duty to their country, to avoid the overseverity that produced alienated adults ill suited for democracy, and in a slap at Andrew Jackson, Whig sympathizers warned parents not to make "heroes of leaders too near one's time." But for the most part the suspicion of parties and the fear of indoctrination forestalled any advice regarding the partisan training of the young, an omission that reflected continuing anxiety about national unity.[8]

Most authors of prescriptive literature presumed that family and society were mirrors, for, according to *Parent's Magazine*, "there can be no civil government without family government." This idea was not new;

[7]Henry Barnard, ed., *The Life of John Henry Pestalozzi* (New York: J. W. Schernerhorn, 1862), p. 251. H. Bartlett to Horace Mann, 1 December 1841, Massachusetts School Returns, Sturbridge Village Library; E. C. Wines, *Hints on a System of Popular Education* (Philadelphia: Hogan and Thompson, 1838), p. 119; Carl Kaestle and Maris A. Vinovskis, *Education and Social Change in Nineteenth-Century Massachusetts* (New York: Oxford University Press, 1980). For the concept of the republican mother, see Linda Kerber, "The Republican Mother: Women and the Enlightenment—An American Perspective," *American Quarterly* 28 (Summer 1976): 187–205 (the quoted sentence is on p. 204).

[8]Mary Cable, *The Little Darlings: A History of Child Rearing in America* (New York: Scribner's 1972) pp. 59, 79, Joseph Laurie, *Parent's Guide* (Philadelphia: Rademacher and Sheek, 1854), p. 110; John C. S. Abbott, *The Child at Home; or, The Principles of Filial Duty Familiarly Illustrated* (New York: Harper Brothers 1852); Enos Hitchcock, *Memoirs of the Bloomsgrove Family* (Upper Saddle River, N.J.: Literature House, 1970); Burton, *Helps to Education;* James Jackson, *The Training of Children* (Livingston, N.Y.: Danville, 1972).

Americans often paraphrased the seventeenth-century English manualist William Gouge's axiom that "the family is a little church and a little Commonwealth or rather a schoole wherein the first principles and grounds of government are learned." According to J. M. Mason, an early president of Dickinson College, "The father has a divine mandate to be head of the domestic establishment. His family is his Kingdom, his Children are his subjects and he is the governor in his own house and young subjects are submitted to his rule."[9]

In reality, young antebellum Northerners grew up in diverse family structures, few of which resembled the authoritarian ideal of the father acting as a domestic monarch. Certainly the influence of Northern parents was restricted, for, as the New England clergyman William Channing explained, "if it was not, children would be exact copies of past generations." A nation governed by replicas of their fathers would never accept the changes necessary for progress. Moreover, relationships that fostered a flaccid acceptance of authority were considered inappropriate training for those who must later combine obedience to law with assertion of rights. Although no one spoke in favor of insubordination, foreign travelers accustomed to more patriarchal families often found, as did Captain de Marryat, parents without control and sons who, at six, contradicted their fathers. From his travels in the 1830s Tocqueville concluded that the authority of American parents went "unopposed" only by the very young, and the French aristocrat described with distaste the faulty discipline that led to the independence of boys "who trace out their own path" at an early age.[10]

Avoided in school and overlooked in early nineteenth-century prescriptive literature, partisan training nonetheless began at home. Today's experts on political socialization agree that the family is—and has always been—the essential agency for determining party allegiance, a point documented in numerous surveys displaying the correspondence between the voting preferences of parents and children.[11] But the mech-

[9]Quoted in James Axtell, *The School upon a Hill: Education and Society in Colonial New England* (New York: W. W. Norton, 1974), p. 53; J. M. Mason, *Address Delivered at the Organization of Dickinson College* (Carlisle, Pa., 1822), p. 8.

[10]Quoted in Rush Welter, *American Writings on Popular Education in the Nineteenth Century* (Indianapolis: Bobbs-Merrill, 1971), p. 47; Alexis de Tocqueville, *Democracy in America* (New York, Vintage Books, 1960, 2:202; Captain Frederick Marryat, *A Diary in America with Remarks* (Philadelphia: Carey and Hart, 1839), pp. 3, 283, 286, 287; William Chace, "The Descent on Democracy: A Study of American Democracy as Observed by British Travellers, 1815–1860," (Ph.D. dissertation, University of North Carolina, 1941).

[11]For a review of this literature see Stanley Renshon, *Handbook of Political Socialization Theory and Research* (New York: Free Press, 1977).

anism of transmission is not clear, and whether children learn their party politics through imitation, instruction, psychological motivation, or because their social and economic position resembles that of their parents, has never been determined. To be sure, this replication does not include specific issues, for there have always been differences between fathers and sons on public policy. Presumably the lack of clear ideological definition in American parties has permitted sons to adopt their father's organization even while rejecting some of its political programs. Thus the conflicts of each generation have been different, although family attachments to a specific party have remained intact.

Before the Civil War, fathers were more important in partisan recruitment than they are today. With fewer competitors for a child's attention, the nineteenth-century family imprinted political behavior, and fathers were much more instrumental in defining partisanship than were nonvoting mothers, although at least one young American so adored his mother that he voted for her choice rather than his father's.[12] On the other hand, because nineteenth-century parties were newer and more ephemeral than those in the twentieth century, fathers could not exhibit for their sons the persistent alliances of some modern households. Such a legacy was apparent to Adlai Stevenson, whose grandfather apprised him, as a child, of his status as a fifth-generation Democrat, and throughout his life Stevenson acknowledged his "bad case of hereditary politics."[13] Nor could nineteenth-century fathers look to a tradition of two-party competition; the generation of Northerners who reached political maturity during the decline of the Federalists grew up during the Era of Good Feelings. Moreover, many nineteenth-century fathers were themselves first-generation voters, having received the vote as a result of naturalization or of their state's extension of the franchise.

Still, these differences should not obscure the family's influence not only over a son's choice of party, but also over the duration and intensity of his commitment.[14] What follows is an account of party behaviors

[12]"My father was a pronounced Democrat, my mother a pronounced abolitionist. . . . When the Buchanan-Fremont campaign of 1856 was in progress, I had attained an age that entitled me to be termed reasonable. . . . having faith in my mother, I took her side of the question. On the morning of election day, after father started for the polling place, I asked mother when she intended going. She smiled as she said: 'I have no right to, I am not a man and only men vote. . . .' I resolved to vote for my mother. . . ." Terence V. Powderly, *The Autobiography of Terence V. Powderly* (New York: Columbia University Press, 1940), pp. 11–12.

[13]John Bartlow Martin, *Adlai Stevenson of Illinois: The Life of Adlai Stevenson* (New York: Doubleday, 1976), p. 6.

[14]The essential works on political socialization are Kenneth Langton, *Political Socialization* (New York: Oxford University Press, 1969); Renshon, *Handbook of Political Socializa-*

based on the family histories of Northern Democrats who have left sufficient records to establish such a genealogy. Unlike aggregate analysis, these profiles record the partisan styles of men who, for the most part, held elective and appointive office; hence the material is biased toward political notables. Moreover, every man is by definition an exception; every partisan testament is unique. Yet the forms of behavior represented—the lifelong Democrat, the partisan of the old Jacksonian school, the switcher, the political vagabond, and the dropout—describe the political behavior of other Northern Democrats. Biography serves here not as a chronicle of great men, but as a means of illuminating the experience of others whose family histories varied but who acted in similar fashion.

## *The Loyalists*

William Steele Holman of Aurora, Indiana, spent thirty-two years in Washington as a congressman, but he was more comfortable at home where, feet up, tie undone, shoes unlaced, he talked with—and listened to—the people of his southern Indiana district. A Baptist, Holman never told off-color stories, but his constituents did, sharing with him familiar jokes of the times. One involved the man who, asked what his politics were, replied, "Democratic. My father was a Democrat"; asked what his religion was, replied, "Protestant. My father was a Protestant"; and, asked why he was a bachelor, stuttered, "My father was. Confound it. Don't bother me with your stupid questions."[15] Con-

---

*tion Theory;* Barne Stacey, *Political Socialization in Western Society,* (New York: St. Martin's Press, 1977); David Easton and Jack Dennis, *Children in the Political System: Origins of Political Legitimacy* (New York: McGraw-Hill, 1979); Fred Greenstein and Sidney Tarrow, *Political Orientations of Children: The Use of a Semi-Projective Technique in Three Nations,* (Beverly Hills, Calif.: Sage Publications, 1970); Judith Torney, A. N. Oppenheim, and Russell Farnen, *Civic Education in Ten Countries* (New York: John Wiley, 1975); Dean Jaros, *Socialization to Politics* (New York: Praeger, 1973); Fred Greenstein, *Children and Politics* (New Haven: Yale University Press, 1965); M. Kent Jennings and Richard G. Niemi, *The Political Character of Adolescence: The Influence of Families and School* (Princeton: Princeton University Press, 1974); Charles G. Bell, *Growth and Change: A Reader in Political Socialization* (Encino, Calif.: Dickenson, 1973); Jack Dennis, "Major Problems of Political Socialization Research," *Midwestern Journal of Politics* 12 (Feburary 1968): 85–114..

[15]The following sketch is based on Israel George Blake, *The Holmans of Veraestau* (Oxford, O.: Mississippi Valley Press, 1943); William S. Holman Papers, Indiana State Library, Indianapolis; Jesse Lynch Holman Papers, Franklin College Library, Franklin, Ind.; George Blake, "Jesse Lynch Holman, Pioneer Hoosier," *Indiana Magazine of History* 39 (March 1943): 26–51. The anecdote is in Henry Hupfeld, *Wit and Wisdom* (Philadelphia: Bradley, 1871), p. 778.

gressman Holman, like the man in the anecdote, inherited his religion and partisanship from his father, Jesse Holman, a farmer-lawyer-judge who migrated from Kentucky to Indiana in 1811.

Here in 1822 William Steele was born and lived all his life, on his father's original homestead overlooking the Ohio River. Many southern Indiana Democrats never voted for anyone else for Congress, and "the Great Objector," as he was affectionately called, became a living symbol of the Democracy. For Holman was a self-described "out and out party man," or, as one local paper put it, "a soldier of the Democrats with his armor ever buckled." As an office holder who was briefly considered for his party's presidential nomination, Holman was a special Democrat, but his style of politics resembled that of thousands of northern voters who never strayed from the party, never split a ticket, never defected, however briefly, to other organizations, and whose persistence frequently made nineteenth-century politics a standing decision. Like all Northerners, Holman faced temptations, but he did not desert to the Know-Nothing or Republican parties in the 1850s, and during the Civil War he did not work with Lincoln's fictive Union organization, which he labeled "black-washed Republicanism." Nor was he seduced into the postwar Union movement that attempted in 1866 to fuse Jackson Democrats, former Whigs, Conservative Republicans and Democrats into a new party. In 1872 Holman denounced efforts to incorporate Liberal Republicanism into his party, and he would have traded Horace Greeley for any "true" democrat (as indeed would many other party members after Greeley lost the election); ever loyal, he voted the official Democratic ticket. In 1890 Holman did not join the coalition of Democrats and Populists, although he agreed with the latter on most issues and incorporated their pledge "no monopoly of land for speculative purposes" into his campaign. With pride and accuracy, Holman referred to Democrats as "that great body of citizens with whom I have ever acted."[16]

Unlike some Democrats, whose faith strengthened over the years, Holman's was firm from the beginning. As a first-term congressman in 1859, the thirty-seven-year-old Indianan voted only for regular Democrats as candidates for Speaker of the House, and his refusal to support William Smith cost the North Carolinian the speakership and the House a lengthy delay. Criticized by less loyal colleagues, Holman insisted that Democrats, even when a minority, must preserve their independence and not just act as brokers between Know-Nothings and Republicans. Smith, according to Holman, was an anti-Democrat who had once described an election between the Democratic and Re-

[16]Blake, *The Holmans* p. 160; *Congressional Record,* 43d Cong., 2d sess., 274.

publican parties as similar to a choice between typhus fever and smallpox. In Holman's view, to withold a vote from such a man was cause for praise, not blame, and by refusing "to abandon my party principles, in an act of such political significance as the election of a Speaker of the House," he believed himself "correctly steadfast."[17]

Holman's convictions were as consistently Democratic as his behavior. "Economy, Retrenchment, and Reform" inspired fellow Democrats from Jackson to Cleveland, and Holman supported all three principles throughout his public career. During the 1860s he complained that Republican extravagance cost the people millions in taxes, and as an example he cited the White House, where expenses had tripled during Lincoln's administration. By the 1870s Holman had established a national reputation as "the watchdog of the Treasury," and although the controversies of these years—the Salary Grab Act, the Crédit Mobilier and Buena Vista scandals—were new, the Indiana congressman furnished familiar solutions from his party's old elixir of "an honest and frugal government" and "equal chance in the struggle for life by protecting all, granting favors to none." By the 1880s what Holman called "gigantic business enterprises and overgrown estates," encouraged by government subsidy, had replaced the United States Bank as instances of favoritism and monopoly. In an oft-repeated message Holman accused Republicans of

> taking land from the landless people of this nation, the laboring men of this nation—their rightful heritage—in order to build up excessive fortunes for a few favorites. You invest them with vast corporate powers and powers thus corruptly given, assail public virtue wherever it is found. It requires no prophet to tell that your policy must be challenged and these corporations shorn of their power or the free institutions of this Republic will perish.[18]

Appropriately, his last important speech, delivered to the House in 1893, conveyed the conception of the producer (but not working) class that had become Democratic habit. At this time the aging congressman still defined the party as he had during his youth:

> The Democracy is a sentiment not to be appalled, corrupted or compromised. It knows no baseness, cowers at no dangers, oppresses no weakness.

[17]Blake, *The Holmans,* p. 74; *Congressional Globe,* 36th Cong., 1st sess., 188, 191, 271, 295, 513, 614.

[18]Blake, *The Holmans,* pp. 205, 213, 227; *Congressional Globe,* 41st Cong., 3d sess., 1428; ibid., 42d Cong., 2d sess., 1305–06.

> Fearless, generous, humane, it rebukes the arrogant, cherishes honor and sympathizes with the humble. Destructive only to despotism, it is the only preserver of liberty, labor and prosperity. It is the sentiment of freedom, equal rights, and equal obligation.[19]

It could be argued that any organization devoted to such ideals deserved a lifelong commitment, and it is clear that by so defining his party Holman gave meaning to his life's work. The question remains why this particular Indianan was so faithful.

For one thing, Holman had no reason to leave the party as did Northerners who, despite their early partisanship, found themselves politically isolated after their communities shifted to new parties. The southeastern Indiana counties that sent him to Congress sixteen of the twenty times he ran were as loyal to him as he was to the Democracy. Only once was he denied renomination, and only once from 1832 to 1892 did his home county of Dearborn not vote Democratic in a presidential election. Nor did his religion—he was a Baptist of a moderately pietistic congregation—provide a conflict with his party ideals. Finally, the unchanging conditions of his rural grain-growing community, where the nineteenth century's alterations seemed those of scale, not of kind, fostered partisan persistence.[20]

Moreover, there were impelling personal reasons to stay. For William Holman's Democracy was an imperative learned in his youth from his father, Jesse. The latter was one of those restless early nineteenth-century pioneers who arrive at the take-off point of their community and remain to organize its affairs. Newly married into the politically active Butler family,[21] Jesse left Kentucky for Indiana in 1811, built a log cabin along the Ohio, farmed, served as a Monroe and then an Adams presidential elector, and in 1836 became a federal district judge. Active in local affairs, he organized the Aurora town library, sat on the school board, developed the curriculum for the Baptist college in nearby Franklin, and somehow found time to serve as pastor of the Baptist church. William was his oldest son, neglected by the busy Jesse for a preferred sister and a sickly younger brother. But it was William who

[19]Logan Essarey, "Pioneer Politics in Indiana," *Indiana Magazine of History* 13 (June 1916): 124; Blake, *The Holmans,* p. 215; quotation from *Congressional Record,* 53d Cong., 1st sess., 1759.

[20]For an examination of this persistence, see V. O. Key and Frank Munger, "Social Determinism and Electoral Decision: The Case of Indiana," in *Political Parties and Pressure Groups,* ed. Frank Munger and Douglas Price (New York: Thomas Crowell, 1964).

[21]His wife, Elizabeth Masterson Holman, was a cousin of William O. Butler, the Democratic vice-presidential candidate in 1848.

absorbed Jesse's political lessons, because he was the right age and sex to do so.

William was fourteen when his father nearly lost his nomination to the federal bench. President Jackson had signed the commission but delayed sending it to the Senate, recalling Jesse's heresy as an Adams elector in 1824 and his rumored abolitionism. Although the former charge was correct, the latter was not. Jesse had indeed freed his wife's slaves, but only because Indiana was free territory, and later as a territorial judge he used the same argument to emancipate an Indiana Negro. When Jesse heard of his delayed nomination, ever the man of action, he left immediately for Washington, traveling in winter over the mountains to confront President Jackson. By summer Jesse had his seat on the bench as well as a leg injury from his dangerous journey, and his family enjoyed a frequently told tale of political efficacy.[22]

Six years later Jesse was dead, at a crucial time in his son's political development. William had finished the district school in Aurora, had graduated from the Baptist Manual Labor School his father had started, and was reading law with Jesse. At twenty-one he faced his first act of citizenship—voting in the fall congressional and local elections. Thus his coming of political age coincided with his father's death, and this conjunction meant that Jesse's public commitments—his tradition of civic participation as well as his intense partisanship—became legacies as important for the oldest son of a large family to preserve as any property or estate. Within the year William had joined the Democratic party and had been elected to his first office, that of probate judge. He continued to cultivate this family patrimony, and there were some who believed that by the end of his life he had increased old Jesse's Democratic inheritance.

What William Holman learned from his father, surrogate parents taught Marcus M. Pomeroy, the Wisconsin journalist.[23] The results,

[22]Blake, *The Holmans,* p. 28; "Documents: Seeking a Federal Judgeship under Jackson," *Indiana Magazine of History* 35 (September 1939): 311–25.

[23]The following biography is based on Pomeroy's autobiography, *Marcus Mills Pomeroy: Journey of a Life: Reminiscences and Recollections of "Brick" Pomeroy* (New York: Advance Thought, 1890); Mary Eliza Tucker, *Life of Mark M. Pomeroy* (New York: Arno Press and the New York Times, 1970); Frank L. Klement, "Brick Pomeroy: Copperhead and Curmudgeon," *Wisconsin Magazine of History* 35 (Winter 1951): 106–13, 156–57; [Marcus M. Pomeroy], *Pomeroy's American Finance* (Chicago: J. J. Spalding, 1877); idem, *Condensed History of the War, Its Causes and Results. Plain Home-told Facts for Young Men and Working Men of the U.S.* (n.p., 1868); idem, *Brick Dust: A Remedy for the Blues and Something for People to Talk About* (New York: G. W. Carleton, 1871); Ruth A. Tucker, "M. M. Brick Pomeroy: Forgotten Man of the Nineteenth Century" (Ph.D. dissertation, Northern Illinois University, 1979).

however, were the same, for like Holman Pomeroy became a lifetime Democrat whose loyalty is best understood in biographical terms. Deserted by his father, an itinerant peddler-merchant and sometime watchmaker, young Pomeroy was raised by his aunt and uncle after his mother's death. By all accounts the latter's deathbed request that a brother bring up her son testified to her husband's irresponsibility, and in fact Pomeroy's father kept infrequent account of his son, delivering bad advice (he wanted "Brick" to be a merchant) and little affection. Later Pomeroy recalled his early years on a New York farm as unpleasant, full of the incessant, tedious labor that drove many young men into cities, others to the West. Pomeroy left at fifteen, walking alone and penniless to a neighboring village, where he apprenticed himself to the printer of a Democratic newspaper. Like Ben Franklin, whom he admired as another self-made man, Pomeroy got his formal education, along with his political training, in the small, overcrowded county newspapers where as an apprentice he set type, read copy, doubled as a janitor, all the while absorbing the Democratic persuasion. He learned these lessons quickly and well, for within fifteen years he operated his own press in Wisconsin.

Once installed, Pomeroy's partisanship never lapsed, although in the 1870s he dallied with the Greenback Labor party. Having appropriated the Democracy of his early sponsors—the county newspapermen who had fed, sheltered, and trained a homeless boy—Pomeroy remained loyal, and first by chance, then by selection, his patrons were Democrats. Like a respectful son who displays affection by adopting his father's party, Pomeroy repaid his benefactors by aligning his party membership with theirs. His were the politics of gratitude.

Pomeroy's services to the party were those of a journalist, for his highest elective office came in 1860 as a delegate to the Charleston convention, and he held only one patronage position. But Pomeroy touted the party through his pen and, unlike editors who traded their editorial pages for financial support, refused to bargain his partisanship. He used the name Democrat in the masthead of all his papers, even the unsuccessful *New York Democrat* he started in the late 1860s, and he meant by that term a party, not a political theory based on the people's sovereignty. Only a zealot would have chiseled into the marble cornerstone of the *La Crosse Democrat:* "Democrat—M. M. Pomeroy. *Nemo me impune lacessit / Principia non homines.*"[24] Some Democrats, es-

[24]Tucker, *Pomeroy,* p. 107; Pomeroy, *Journey,* p. 223.

pecially during the Civil War, were embarrassed by Pomeroy's vehemence, but others hired him to write their campaign newspapers.

From all accounts Pomeroy's industry and talent offset his belligerence, for he was an angry man, unappealing in looks and behavior. Although it is impossible to separate youthful pranks from neurotic cruelty, Pomeroy verged on the latter. He put mustard on cats' tails, humiliated Jewish merchants, placed his chalked fingers on the faces of Negro classmates, and, utterly insouciant about his viciousness, proudly recalled these incivilities for his biographer. Just as his journalism was later marked by cruel hyperbole (it was Pomeroy who first called Lincoln a "widow-maker"), so his practical jokes furnished acceptable occasions to manifest his anger. Throughout his life Pomeroy considered human existence a struggle against unjust foes; he once described his life as "a plain history of a poor boy—a laborer—a hard working man who has won success by battling for it determined to win."[25] In later life, when he took to writing sentimental fiction for the Saturday night reading of working-class Americans, his characters were always at war with capitalists, speculators, and unfaithful wives. "What a battle life is," sighed one; "How few of us realize the warfare! We hardly know who our friends are. . . . Life is a school—most of us study on hard benches."[26]

Literature reflected life, for Pomeroy had his share of personal battles, beginning in his youth with his stern Presbyterian aunt and uncle, his schoolteachers, Negroes, classmates, and, on one occasion, a girlfriend who snubbed him because she thought him "a poor dirty-fingered type-stocker."[27] As he grew older, new foes emerged—creditors who threatened his sometimes faltering newspapers; a partner who did not support his choice of Stephen A. Douglas in 1860; the greedy, pro-Negro editors of competitive newspapers; the rich who displayed their furs and gold (hence the title of Pomeroy's popular story *Better than Gold*); and, finally, the three wives whom he divorced.[28]

Eventually his invective settled upon the Republicans, and the childhood sticks and stones he had hurled at neighborhood boys became the barbs of his editorials. His nickname, "Brick," was appropriate, for it

[25]Tucker, *Pomeroy,* pp. v, 7, 13, 14, 16; Klement, "Brick Pomeroy," p. 106.

[26]Marcus M. "Brick" Pomeroy, *Better Than Gold* (New York: Advance Thought, 1889), pp. 4, 63.

[27]Tucker, *Pomeroy,* p. 61.

[28]L. H. Pammel, *Reminiscences of Early La Crosse, Wisconsin* (La Crosse: Liesenfeld Press, 1928); Marcus M. Pomeroy, *Our Saturday Nights* (New York: G. W. Carleton, 1879), p. 26.

acknowledged one especially satiric attack on a Republican. Without politics as a release for his spleen, it is easy to imagine Pomeroy as a revolutionary, intent on throwing out the government, not just its incumbents. In his case party rivalry was social conflict, carried out by mostly nonviolent means. Today's psychologists might suspect that the Republicans stood as surrogate targets for the suppressed rage of an abandoned child, but whatever its source, the effect was to create a lifelong Democrat whose loyalty was embedded in childhood experience and whose partisanship was based on the psychological necessity of combat.[29]

Pomeroy's tendency to hate the Republicans at least as much as he loved the Democrats was at no time more apparent than during the Civil War, when he attacked Lincoln as "a military dictator," "a clown," "a buffoon," and, in his vicious 1864 image, "a widow- and orphan-maker."[30] Unlike other journalists, who discovered heroism and self-sacrifice in military camps, Pomeroy encountered only prostitutes, drunken soldiers, and coffins—"these rough brown cheap wormeaten coffins piled up there like oyster cans silently waiting to fold their wooden arms about our sons, brothers and fathers.[31] In 1864 his attacks on the Republicans sharpened. "The man who votes for Lincoln now," he threatened, "is a traitor because Lincoln is a traitor and murderer. And if he is elected to misgovern for another four years, we trust some bold hand will pierce his heart with a dagger point for the public good." Later in the campaign, Pomeroy provided a bitter rendition of "When Johnny Comes Marching Home":

> The widow-maker soon must cave,
> Hurrah, Hurrah,
> We'll plant him in some nigger's grave,
> Hurrah, Hurrah,
> Torn from your farm, your ship, your raft,
> Conscript. How do you like the draft,
> And we'll stop that too,
> When little Mac takes the helm.[32]

[29]David Lynn and William L. Saurey, "The Effects of Father Absence on Norwegian Boys and Girls," *Journal of Abnormal and Social Psychology* 59 (September 1959): 258–62.

[30]*LaCrosse Democrat,* 17 February 1863; 2, 23, and 29 August 1864.

[31]Quotation from ibid., 16 December 1862; Pomeroy, *Journey,* pp. 182–86.

[32]Quotations from *La Crosse Democrat* 23, 24, and 29 August 1864; Frank Klement, "Brick Pomeroy," p. 106, idem, "A Small-Town Editor Criticizes Lincoln: A Study in Editorial Abuse," *Lincoln Herald* 54 (Summer 1952): 27–40.

Using the same type of inflammatory appeals at public rallies, Pomeroy relished his appearances as an audacious Democrat surrounded by the enemy. Wisconsin was, after all, Republican territory, and La Crosse County, with its consistent Republican majorities of over 60 percent, no less so. But Pomeroy did not hesitate to single out Republicans and ridicule them on their home ground as "itching for wool." Nor did he consider the opposition's rallies off limits. On one occasion he interrupted the invited speaker at a county fair; at another he threatened to fight anyone who harassed him.[33]

The notoriety earned from pen and tongue improved his paper's circulation, and what had been a little-noticed county paper became, by 1864, the nationally known, internationally quoted *La Crosse Democrat* with more than ninety thousand readers. A more timid editor might have feared for life and property; lesser insults had led northern mobs to destroy presses and assault Democratic editors. But, well versed in aggression, Pomeroy announced that he would "ruin the business of anyone who attacks my home or newspapers with my own hands. I will set fire to every Republican house, store, or place of business in La Crosse that I can reach." Ready for an attack that never came, Pomeroy hid stones in flowerboxes, bought ammunition for his rifles, and somehow persuaded La Crosse's Republican mayor to stand outside his press.[34]

After the war, politics was for Pomeroy "a milk and water affair," although he did his best to provide controversy by attending Republican meetings, where on occasion he took the podium from invited speakers. Even his controversy with Benjamin Butler seemed contrived. (Pomeroy had given the Republican Butler the nickname "Spoons," for his alleged thievery while military commander of New Orleans.) In turn, Butler, no mean opponent, represented Pomeroy's wife in divorce proceedings, and in his autobiography the Massachusetts general implied that the grounds were syphilis—"the terrible disease with which [Pomeroy] afflicted his wife."[35] Flashes of the old party man appeared in Pomeroy's crusade against Republican bondholders, whose income from high interest rates went untaxed, and in 1868 Pomeroy's campaign rhetoric contained an inflammatory threat of action reminiscent of his style during the war: "We will by pen, voice, and ballot work for [equal

[33]Pammel, *Reminiscences,* p. 64; Tucker, *Pomeroy,* pp. 90–102, 123–25, 129.

[34]Quotation from Tucker, *Pomeroy,* p. 94; Pomeroy, *Journey,* pp. 170–74, 195.

[35]Benjamin F. Butler, *Autobiography and Personal Reminiscences of Major General Benjamin F. Butler. Butler's Book* (Boston: A. M. Thayer, 1892), p. 43.

taxation] in 1868. If the right be denied us, we will inaugurate another revolution in which labor will fight aristocrats to kill, that our children shall not be slaves to bondholders."[36] Replacing abolitionists with Republican financiers, Pomeroy also exchanged heroes. New objects of affection, northern white workingmen and their wives, replaced the southern whites whose interests he had earlier defended. To be sure, he did not offer any precise programs but instead relied on the amorphous concept of laborers as producers whose opportunity for advancement must not be clogged by institutions and practices favoring the rich. Clearly, his understanding of workers as individual entrepreneurs blinded him to any class-derived solutions. But in this he was faithful to the ruling ideology of his party, and Pomeroy's final contribution to the Democracy came in his popular sentimental tales written "about the fallen for the wives and workmen of the world."[37]

## *The Old Jackson School*

William Allen, Ohio governor, United States congressman, and two-term senator, rarely mentioned his childhood. Like Brick Pomeroy he was orphaned early and, following nineteenth-century custom, apprenticed, in his case to a saddler. When Allen finally regained a semblance of family life in his half sister's household in Chillicothe, Ohio, he clashed with her minister husband. Nor did Allen like to remember the loss of his inheritance—the 75,000 acres in North Carolina claimed by his father but after a series of court decisions surrendered to squatters and relatives.[38]

One memory, however, Allen cherished, and in many ways this recollection defined not only his own Democratic origins but also those of his generation. Allen recalled a special day in his youth, with flags, music, and a parade of the local militia. The purpose of this celebration was to welcome two dignitaries: one was on his way to Washington as a military hero; the other had ridden over from his nearby estate. After the mayor's speech the two men retired to the Byrd Tavern in Lynchburg where Allen, the saddler's apprentice, tended their horses. Drawn to these heroes as ordinary men are to giants of their kind, Allen, in his

[36]Tucker, *Pomeroy,* p. 189.

[37]Pomeroy, *Our Saturday Nights,* pp. 1, 2, 3.

[38]The following biographical sketch is based on the William Allen Papers, Library of Congress (hereafter cited as Allen Papers); Reginald Charles McGrane, *William Allen: A Study in Western Democracy* (Columbus, O.: F. J. Heer, 1925). For evidence of family tension, see Mary Thurman to "my very dear brother," 31 December 1834, Allen Papers.

account, "peeped into the parlor reserved for their discussion," only to find himself face to face with Thomas Jefferson and Andrew Jackson. "Ah," said the latter, placing his hand benevolently on the young orphan's head. "And what is your name, my brave little Democrat?"[39]

By every reasonable reconstruction this political baptism in 1815 did not occur in the way that Allen remembered it. Among other discrepancies, Jackson would not have used the word *Democrat*—at least not in the party sense that Allen received it. Yet legends are not significant for their accuracy; instead they are remembered for the ways in which beholders color historical circumstances and impose meaning on events. Allen's was a parable of political socialization—the process whereby, like all children, he personalized the government, coming to understand the abstract notion of authority through a person.[40] In the twentieth century these individuals are customarily policemen and presidents; in a time of fewer officials, George Washington often served. Although Allen's experience was unusual because he actually met a president, his story embodies typical features of socialization. Not only was Jackson perceived by this twelve-year-old orphan as a benevolent heroic figure, but the reference to "brave little Democrat" fused the partisanship of the organization that Allen faithfully served throughout his life with the national ideal of popular sovereignty.

William Allen's generation, born in the first two decades of the new century, came of political age during a period of American history dominated by Andrew Jackson, "the symbol of an age," as John Ward has called him. Every generation makes fresh contact with a different world, and this one moved from political adolescence to maturity during the years when Jackson was the epicenter of American life. Their vision of government was embodied in him, and, acquiring an attachment before they voted, they developed affiliations before they understood the nature of political parties or what they stood for. According to one Jacksonian, "I found myself a Democrat without being able to explain why I was of that party. I began as a follower of Jackson and knew nothing of the Force bill. . . ." A eulogist made the same point after Old Hickory's death in 1845: "The spirit of an age sometimes

[39]Clipping from *Ohio Democrat* (New Philadelphia, Ohio), 24 July 1879, Notebooks, Allen Papers.

[40]Lewis Fromen and James K. Skipper, "An Approach to the Learning of Party Identification," *Public Opinion Quarterly* 27 (Fall 1963): 472–85; Fred Greenstein, "The Benevolent Leader," *American Political Science Review* 54 (December 1960): 934–43; Roberta Sigel, "The Image of the American Presidency," *Midwestern Journal of Political Science* 10 (February 1966): 123.

descends to future generations in the form of a man in proportion as an individual concentrates within himself the spirit which works through masses of men and which moves and should move them through the greatest cycles of time."[41] Of course, Jackson was also detested, and Whigs, or, as they often called themselves, anti-Jacksonians, negatively referenced their politics to him. But for the fatherless Allen, Old Hickory crystallized both a political movement and an emotional attachment. Thus a chance encounter became a charged episode. Later Allen designated himself a member of the "Old Jackson School"[42]—an expression used in American politics until the last alumni died at the end of the century. Throughout his life Allen was a loyal graduate; his identification was so complete that he dated even events in his private life from a Jacksonian calendar.

As a young man the ophaned Allen had few political mentors, and when he joined his half sister's household she tutored his deficient English, not his political awareness, while her husband neglected both for his own children. Lacking any partisan direction from adults, Allen was susceptible to hero-worship, and it happened that he cast his first ballot the very year Jackson won a plurality of the electoral vote but lost the presidency in the House of Representatives to Adams. Eight years later, at twenty-nine, Allen won the congressional seat for Ohio's seventh district in a crowded field of National Republicans, anti-Masons, and Jacksonians, who agreed on only one thing—that the issue of the campaign was Jackson. The youthful Allen won by one vote, but just as Jackson had been challenged after his presidential victory in 1824, so Allen's election was assailed by opponents who charged that "the overgrown schoolboy had left school too soon and had brought his underage chums to vote illegally."[43] Allen also faced a formal challenge in the House but refused to appear before local reviewing boards and survived the inquiry. Two years later he lost his seat, but he returned to Washington during the depression of 1837, when Jacksonian Democracy was on trial for its fiscal policies. For the next twelve years Allen represented Ohio in the U.S. Senate.

Unlike some of his colleagues, Allen never surrendered his early identification; wearing what he described as a "Jacksonian collar," he

[41]Michael Holt, *The Political Crisis of the 1850's* (New York: Wiley, 1978), p. 23; John William Ward, *Andrew Jackson, Symbol for an Age* (New York: Oxford University Press, 1962), p. 1.

[42]F. Blair to William Allen, 10 February 1854, Allen Papers.

[43]McGrane, *Allen,* p. 32; "Report of the Committee of Elections, Dec. 31, 1833," 23d Cong., 1st sess., House Report, Serial No. 260.

retained partisan vocabularies and behaviors learned in the 1830s. Invariably Allen's speeches included references to banks, specie, and "the moneyed specialists." Fittingly, the longest memorandum in his papers was a "defense of Jackson." Moreover, he worked as hard to make a national holiday of 8 January—the date of Jackson's victory at New Orleans—as at anything else in his public life. Although Jackson was too much the sponsor of a political party for this, Allen could always be counted on for a rousing Jackson Day speech. When, in the 1850s, Salmon P. Chase wrote that the Democrats had fulfilled their mission with the independent treasury and that it was time to reorganize parties, Allen replied that he would remain a Democrat until his death.[44] And so he did, retiring to Fruit Hill—his Ohio replica of the Hermitage—where in the 1860s he thought of secession as nullification and wished Old Hickory could replace "Honest Abe." In 1864 Allen was among the first to support the nomination of General McClellan, on the grounds that it was "in keeping with Democratic principles of the party of General Jackson to select a general such as McClellan for its standard bearer."[45] In 1873, during his last campaign, the seventy-year-old Allen repeated Jacksonian themes and used the Bank War and Specie Circular as parables from which he drew political lessons appropriate to the Gilded Age. "It is only by searching back and securing our grasp of those principles on which our sires founded the government that we are enabled to counteract that inclination to degeneracy and decay inherent in all political institutions." Ohioans responded, and "Rise Up William" (as he was known) completed his long career of continuous Democratic allegiance as the governor of Ohio.[46]

## *A Democratic Community*

Some Northerners grew up in established party centers where the language they heard, the activities they observed, the sentiments they inhaled were Democratic. It can be said of these men that they absorbed their partisanship as much from their surroundings as from their families, although the two reinforced each other. One such community was

[44]McGrane, *Allen*, p. 140; "January 8th Speech," 1845, Notebooks, no. 3; "A Defense of the Jackson Administration," n.d., Notebooks, no. 1; both in Allen Papers. William Allen, *Addresses on the Presentation of the Sword of General Andrew Jackson to the Congress of the United States* (Washington, D.C.: A. G. P. Nicholson, 1855).

[45]McGrane, *Allen*, p. 168; "A Sentiment for a Jackson Day Dinner," Undated Correspondence, vol. 20; R. L. Lloyd et al. to Allen, Undated Correspondence, both in Allen Papers. *Congressional Globe*, 27th Cong., 2d sess., app. p. 214.

[46]Copybook, 1873, Allen Papers; McGrane, *Allen*, pp. 198–209.

Hunterdon, a farming county in northwest New Jersey that began its one-party commitment with the Jeffersonian Republicans and continued this tradition with the nineteenth-century Democracy.[47] Only once in the nineteen presidential elections from 1828 to 1900 did Hunterdon not support the Democratic candidate (the single apostasy occurred in 1840), and on only six occasions during this period did non-Democrats represent the county in the state legislature. Resisting anti-Masons, Whigs, Republicans, Greenback-Laborites, and Populists, the county voted Democratic in forty-five of forty-seven local and state elections and made Flemington—the county seat—and its fourteen townships into party fiefdoms. In Hunterdon even the definition of a landslide needed revising: Democrats routinely received between 60 and 80 percent of the vote, and the usual 4 percent difference between winners and losers routinely ballooned to 25 percent. Typical of this single-mindedness was Hunterdon's record in 1860. Delivered two party candidates by national leaders, Hunterdon's Democrats arranged a fusion ticket, making the point to those who preferred Breckinridge or Douglas that no factional difference should split their party. In November the results were impressive; Democratic electors received nearly 60 percent of the total vote.[48]

No single social, economic, or cultural fact explains Hunterdon's peculiar devotion, and although New Jersey was generally Democratic territory, Hunterdon was first among equals. It was remarkable in nothing else. Neither rich nor poor in terms of value of agricultural production, per capita wealth, size of holdings, cash value of farms, or any other of the statistical benchmarks used to distinguish communities, Hunterdon does not fit the model developed for midwestern counties that voted Democratic because their farms were marginal, their soil infertile, and their origins southern.[49] The median size for farms in Hunterdon was 125 acres, on the small side for New Jersey but not for the rest of the Middle Atlantic states. Most Hunterdon farmers combined market and local crops, and although they were gradually

[47]Scopes Scrapbook, Hunterdon County Historical Society, Flemington, N.J.

[48]Herbert Erskovitz, "New Jersey Politics during the Era of Andrew Jackson, 1820–1837" (Ph.D. dissertation, New York University, 1965), p. 63; Philip Curtis Davis, "The Persistence of Partisan Alignment: Issues, Leaders, and Voters in New Jersey, 1840–1860" (Ph.D. dissertation, Washington University, 1978), p. 58; Kent Allan Peterson, "New Jersey Politics and National Party-Making, 1865–1868" (Ph.D. dissertation, Princeton University, 1970), p. 256; Carl E. Prince, *New Jersey's Jeffersonian Republicans: The Genesis of an Early Party Machine, 1789–1819* (Chapel Hill: University of North Carolina Press, 1964).

[49]Richard O. Curry, "The Union as It Was: A Critique of Recent Interpretations of the Copperheads," *Civil War History* 13 (March 1967): 32, 36.

changing what they raised as well as how they raised and were paid for it, Republican counties were doing the same. Altogether, Hunterdon's efforts at modernization did not differ from those of non-Democratic counties, and social and economic factors are thus slender reeds by which to explain its politics. Although the county grew somewhat more slowly than neighboring communities and attracted little railroad investment until the 1850s, New Jersey's solidly Whig-Republican southeastern counties trailed well behind Hunterdon in terms of economic growth.[50]

Neither a backwater nor a whirlpool, Hunterdon might have called itself (although nineteenth-century communities lacked such boosterism) "America in miniature." During the nineteenth century its farmers had depended on slaves, tenant farmers, and day laborers. By 1860 the two latter groups, added to the county's miners and unskilled workers employed in town manufactories, accounted for 37 percent of the male population—enough to deliver a bloc vote.[51] But Hunterdon's underclasses were neither politically cohesive nor partisanly conscious. In fact, a series of strikes, lockouts, and dismissals in 1860 reduced miners to transients, disenfranchised by New Jersey's residency requirements. Last-minute election appeals to working men (but never to other social, economic, or cultural groups) suggested that workers were not integrated into the county's politics and that a united working class was not the core of Democratic majorities. Nor were residents of the county's towns and villages; they voted no more Democratic than did the farmers, who, according to one resident, "ran things."[52]

Neither markedly deprived nor affluent, working-class nor bourgeois, urban or rural, Hunterdon's four thousand Democrats held no predominant religious affiliation and were not imbued with the sense of right faith that might have encouraged them to embrace the Democracy for its "let do" rather than "make them" public stance. In the nation as a whole, Catholics, Episcopalians, and German Lutherans were most likely to be Democrats for this reason,[53] but Hunterdon, middling in all

[50]Hubert Schmidt, *Rural Hunterdon: An Agricultural History* (New Brunswick, N.J.: Rutgers University Press, 1946); Peter Wacker, *The Musconeticong Valley of New Jersey: A Historical Geography* (New Brunswick, N.J.: Rutgers University Press, 1968); Davis, "Partisan Alignment," pp. 44–48. Lee Benson has argued that transportation fostered Jacksonian Democracy and is an important determinant of voting behavior; *The Concept of Jacksonian Democracy: New York as a Test Case* (New York: Atheneum, 1964), pp. 335–38.

[51]Davis, "Partisan Alignment," p. 44; *Hunterdon County Democrat,* January–November 1860.

[52]*The Home* I (1873): 213. Hunterdon County Historical Society.

[53]In an achievement of extraordinary scope, Paul Kleppner has estimated the effect of ethnic and religious associations on voting patterns. It must be noted, however, that his

things, included as many pietists—German Dunkers, Baptists, and Methodist Episcopalians—who might be expected to vote Whig or Republican. A century earlier a traveler had recognized that "no county in the state has so mixed a population, composed as it is of Huguenots, Hollanders, German, Scotch-Irish, English, and native Americans.[54] Even the townships of Raritan, Delaware, and Alexandria, where eight or nine of every ten voters were Democrats, do not unlock the mystery of the community's extravagant devotion. Hunterdon was exceptional only in its politics.

Whatever its origins, the county came to be a Democratic school for its young. Generation after generation of New Jersey boys unconsciously absorbed their partisanship from their surroundings, and, given Hunterdon's static population figures (persistence as measured by the ratio between a sample living in Hunterdon in 1850 and 1860 was approximately 80 percent), family and community reinforced each other. What Democratic fathers introduced to their sons at home, partisan machinery reaffirmed. There was nothing unique about these agencies, but especially well developed in one-party Hunterdon, they had no competitors.[55]

First in importance were newspapers. By 1860 eight of the county's fourteen townships boasted a Democratic press. The *Lambertville Beacon* and *White House Station News* were fugitive operations with no more than a few hundred subscribers and a few months' life. But at least one party newspaper, the *Hunterdon County Democrat,* survives today. Tightly controlled and partially financed by the Democratic county committee, this durable and engaging party organ played a determined role in keeping its readers Democratic. Publishers and owners changed—there were three during the 1860s and 1870s—but editorial outlook did not. When new owners took over in 1867, they established their credentials by announcing that a Democratic committee had "approved and sanctioned" the sale and that they would continue the paper's policies.[56]

---

approximations exaggerate the homogeneity of ethnic and religious communities. Moreover, his work has not adequately controlled for class or status. See James Wright, "The Ethnocultural Model of Voting: A Behavioral and Historical Critique," *American Behavioral Scientist* 16 (June 1973): 653–73. See also Paul Kleppner, *The Cross of Culture: A Social Analysis of Midwestern Politics, 1850–1900* (New York: Free Press, 1970), p. 70.

[54]Wacker, *The Musconeticong Valley,* p. 37.

[55]Persistence as measured here is based on a sample (every tenth head of household) from the seventh and eighth Manuscript Census, 1850, 1860, National Archives, Washington, D.C. A sample of 252 was used from the seventh census and checked again in the eighth. While persistence ratios were usually less than 50 percent in mid-nineteenth-century cities, in Hunterdon eight of ten names were located in the subsequent census.

[56]*Hunterdon County Democrat,* 5 and 12 June 1867.

These included accepting cords of hickory as payment of the two-dollar annual subscription in election years; encouraging advertisements that used political invectives, such as the Albaugh's Dry Goods' announcements in 1866: "The Veto Sustained: Popular Prices for Clothing" and "White Mark for November: Cotton Sales"; placing notices of Democratic meetings in news columns; and enlivening the paper with sketches of the Democratic symbols of rooster and eagle—the only such graphic work to appear. Not every Hunterdon boy grew up in a home subscribing to the *Democrat,* but most knew of the paper and, in this mostly literate community, could read it. An earlier editor's complaint that only half of the county's residents subscribed suggests a saturation well beyond that of most city papers.[57]

Strategically located on Flemington's Main Street, the *Democrat* shared its premises with another unofficial party agency, A. W. Fleet's "saloon and oyster dining room." Both were across the street from the courthouse and A. V. Wurt's law office, and this concentration of buildings—a partisan press, a popular tavern and meeting place for Democrats, the courthouse, and the offices of a Democratic legislator-lawyer—transformed Main Street into a party commons. Young boys who came to town with their fathers absorbed an atmosphere that made the county seat a Democratic place.

A similar blending of the partisan and the public marked Hunterdon's festivals; what other parts of the country treated as national events, Hunterdon celebrated in distinctly political ways. For years A. V. Bonnell, a Democratic freeholder (New Jersey's term for a county commissioner), organized the annual Fourth of July celebration; on this national holiday Bonnell not only invited Democratic speakers but also decorated Flemington's town square with Democratic emblems and paraphernalia. The Liberty Car—an enormous thirty-six-foot wagon pulled by thirteen white horses and owned by the county Democratic committee—appeared in nonpartisan parades, such as the salute to Vice President George Dallas in 1845. Young Hunterdonians thus discovered public affairs through concrete imagery identified with the Democratic party.[58]

Much the same process occurred when Democrats built a stage in front of the courthouse during campaigns. The first of these, in 1828, extended almost into the street and caused complaints. But in time Hunterdon's tolerance for things Democratic dissolved even the objec-

[57]Ibid., 18 July 1866, 15 July 1868, and 28 October 1870.

[58]John C. Honeyman, "History of the Zion Lutheran Church" (typescript, Hunterdon County Historical Society), p. 575; *Hunterdon County Democrat,* 9 November 1861.

tions that this party appurtenance obstructed transportation. Soon the stage became an expected feature of every election. From this platform, sanctified by its proximity to a public building, speakers delivered the Democratic message, and functions that Americans generally separated—government and regime, laws and men, public and partisan—were spatially linked. They were fused again in an informal way when the local literary association invited only Democrats to its lecture series, and thus another popular forum was transformed into a party organ. Following established custom, the society's invited speakers in 1866—Ohio's Samuel Cox, New Jersey's Chauncey Burr, and Pennsylvania's George Woodward—attacked the Republicans in openly polemical speeches.[59]

A group of influential families also fortified the Democratic atmosphere. In nearly every township a network of related partisans stood at the hub of public affairs, passing their zeal onto their descendants. Three generations of Hunterdon Pickels, Clarks, Bellises, Rockafellers, Albaughs, and Trimmers served as sheriffs, delegates to conventions, freeholders, tax collectors, and coroners. Such offices were not the golden apples of politics, nor were these families among Hunterdon's wealthy patricians, although most were well off. The state legislature was the highest elective office for which they competed and few achieved this. Influential Democratic families depended on other things for their livelihood: the Trimmers ran a flour mill, the Rockafellers a grist mill, the Albaughs owned a dry-goods store in Flemington—occupations that, like the Bellises' printing, placed them in close contact with their neighbors.[60] In modern language such men were opinion-makers who, like old-time apostles, spread the Democratic word in the informal setting of village life. Because they were too well known and respected to fit the antiparty image of "wire pullers" grasping after "the loaves and fishes" of office, their influence was secure and lasting. When the patriarch of the Bellis clan, Adam Bokesfelt (soon anglicized to Bellis), emigrated from Prussia to Flemington in 1738, his political effect was that of one citizen. A century later, five generations of his offspring lived in the county and, linked by marriage to seven other multi-stemmed Hunterdon families, wielded political influence well beyond their numbers. Notable for their persistence in residency and politics, the Bellises, Trimmers, Pickels, and several other families whose Demo-

[59]*Hunterdon County Democrat,* 6 March and 12 December 1866.

[60]The following is based on the unpublished Deats genealogies and biographies in the Hunterdon County Historical Society; John W. Barker, *Historical Collections of New Jersey Past* (New Haven: n.p., 1868).

cratic affiliation had become a part of their lineage resembled southern clans whose influence and surnames pervade a neighborhood. Adam Bokesfelt's grandson Adam Bellis understood this connection and, using domestic arrangements as the source of his partisan imagery, in 1860 encouraged his fellow Hunterdonians to redeem their inheritance: "Join the great American family and support our brothers."[61] In Hunterdon that meant being a Democrat.

Finally, the structure of state and county politics supported a Democratic culture. By the 1840s Hunterdon had refined the party-nurturing procedures common to the second American political system—frequent elections, vote by printed ballots, pyramidal delegate conventions, increased patronage, and close articulation between state and local leaders on its dispensation. To these arrangements Hunterdon Democrats added the township committee system—their partisan version of town meetings, where Democrats in good standing caucused and as a body made nominations for local offices from sheriff to postmaster. Earlier, New Jersey Democrats had installed a proportional system of delegate representation in their county and state conventions and rewarded strongly partisan counties by basing representation on the size of the Democratic vote. Hunterdon Democrats had every reason to remain loyal to a state organization that accorded them influence and prestige. To ensure discipline, nominations were never made until October, when a man's loyalty could be measured by his campaign performance. Those who were not active party men had little chance.[62]

To young boys growing up in nineteenth-century Hunterdon, this Democratic atmosphere was irrefragable. Not only did the party always win elections; it also controlled newspapers, dispensed patronage, organized community celebrations, and, through a handful of interrelated families, dominated several occupations. A son of Hunterdon might expect to marry or have a close friend in the Democratic clans; he might clerk at the Albaughs' and have his flour ground at the Trimmers'—activities that placed him in intimate contact with Democrats. In desperation, opposition papers sometimes dismissed the popularity of the

[61]*Hunterdon County Democrat,* 6 October 1860; William Cook Wright, "Secession and Copperheadism in New Jersey during the Civil War" (master's thesis, University of Delaware, 1965).

[62]Richard McCormick, "Party Formation in New Jersey in the Jacksonian Era," *Proceedings of the New Jersey Historical Society* 83 (July 1965): 161–73; Peter Levine, "The Rise of Mass Parties and the Problem of Organization: New Jersey, 1829–1844," *New Jersey History* 91 (Summer 1973): 91–103: Prince, *New Jersey's Jeffersonian Republicans;* "Rules of the Democratic Caucus" (n.p., n.d.); *Hunterdon County Democrat,* 1 and 22 August, 10 October 1867.

Democrats by referring to the number of young boys at rallies and parades. Such criticism missed the mark, for it was by virtue of their attendance at such rallies that Hunterdon's adolescent citizens began to absorb the community's self-perpetuating partisan culture. Like Brick Pomeroy, these young Hunterdonians would be Democrats "in all places and in every circumstance."

## *The Switchers*

Not every Northern Democrat was as loyal as William Allen, Brick Pomeroy, and William Holman, nor was every community as faithful as Hunterdon. Times changed, surroundings altered, interests shifted, perspectives dimmed, and personalities varied. As a result political attachments faded and were temporarily laid aside or permanently replaced by a new commitment. Some Northerners, including Maryland's former Whig Reverdy Johnson, became Democrats during the 1850s, Unionist Republicans during the Civil War ("I never was a Democrat," announced the forgetful Johnson in 1866), only to return to the party in the 1870s.[63] Others, like Connecticut's Gideon Welles, Missouri's Frank Blair, and Michigan's James Doolittle, reversed the process and, deserting the Democrats in the 1850s, served in high Republican offices during the war, rejoining the Democracy during Reconstruction. A third group of switchers became Republicans on the battlefield (eight of every ten soldiers voted Republican) and stayed on after the war to wave the bloody shirt. Still others followed a more tortuous partisan course, such as the German-born immigrant Charles Reemlin, who was an active Whig during the 1840s in Philadelphia, switched to the Democrats in Ohio during the 1850s, became a Republican in 1860, and finally in the late 1870s dropped out of politics altogether. Finally, there were a few party vagabonds like Salmon P. Chase who were available for any organization.[64]

The largest group of switchers before the 1880s was composed of Northern Democrats who left the party during the 1850s to join the Know-Nothings and Republicans. Sufficiently numerous to produce a massive shift in voting allegiances, most did not return to the Demo-

[63]Quotation from Bernard Steiner, *The Life of Reverdy Johnson* (Baltimore: Norman Remington, 1914), pp. 143, 169; Hannibal Hamlin to William P. Haines, 11 January 1850, Hannibal Hamlin Papers, Columbia University Library.

[64]Reemlin, *Life*. For the soldier vote, see William F. Zornow, *Lincoln and the Party Divided* (Norman: University of Oklahoma Press, 1954), p. 20; Donnel V. Smith, *Chase and Civil War Politics* (Freeport, N.Y.: Library Press, 1972).

crats.[65] As is generally the case with apostates, they explained their behavior in terms of principle, describing their former party as one of slavery, Southernism, and office while transforming the Republicans into a virtuous association based on freedom and Union. In their explanations, these former Democrats dealt with public affairs not necessarily as they were, but as they must be made to seem if apostasy was to be justified.

No one did this more successfully than the former Ohio Democrat Timothy Day, who in his 1856 remarks to the House of Representatives voiced a refrain common among Republican converts. "It has been the pride of my life to rank myself as a Democrat," declared Day in a farewell-to-party speech.

> We frequently hear allusions on this floor to the ancestry of the Cavaliers and Huguenots of the Old World and though I have but little of that description of veneration, I too, can point to a Democratic ancestry which may be equalled but not excelled . . . where from grandfather to grandson no vote has been cast other than for Democrats for Presidents from Thomas Jefferson down—down to Franklin Pierce. Now I find myself in antagonism to what is *called* the Democratic party, for when it inherited its legacy of conservatism, it did not change its name although it did its principles, and like those of old went into the wilderness. . . . [Now] the lion of Democracy has become a jackal of slavery.

The joke at Pierce's expense brought laughter but also had the serious purpose of symbolizing, by comparing presidents, the Democracy's decay. Day then linked the "new" Democracy and the South, insisting that what had earlier been a national organization had degenerated into a slaveholder's tool.[66] Other switchers used Congress as evidence of the party's sectionalism, for after three decades of regionally balanced delegations, in 1856 over three-quarters of the Democracy's congressional delegation came from slave states.

Two months after Day's speech, another Northern Democrat repudiated his party when Maine's senator Hannibal Hamlin (who owed his unusual first name to a grandfather's penchant for ancient history) spoke on the travesty of the Kansas-Nebraska Act, the Southern conspiracy to control the nation, and the Burkean necessity of loving coun-

[65]Walter Dean Burnham, *Critical Elections and the Mainsprings of American Politics* (New York: W. W. Norton, 1970), p. 37.

[66]*The Democratic Party as It Was and as It Is: Speech of Hon. Timothy C. Day of Ohio* (Washington, D.C.: Buell and Blanchard, 1856); Sarah Day, *The Man on a Hill Top* (Philadelphia: Ware Brothers, 1931).

try over party. Refusing to accept his party's position that Congress had no authority over slavery in the territories, Hamlin made this resolution by the national Convention a test of loyalty that, if failed, dealt recusants out of the Democracy. Over the years most Democrats had remained members despite personal disagreement with parts of the platform. Hamlin's insistence that this plank become a measure of faith led to his self-imposed action of "sundering my party ties, as flax is sundered at the touch of fire. I do it now."[67]

On two counts, the image was inappropriate: first, the Maine senator's ties had been of stronger stuff than flax; and second, if the party test was slavery in the territories, then Hamlin had years earlier departed. A Free-Soiler in the 1840s, Hamlin considered himself then a loyal Democrat who had never "scratched a ticket in twenty years." A party man, he was willing to campaign against his Whig brother, and he even tolerated what he considered mistreatment by Democratic leaders. As he explained in 1852, "The President has not used me right but no matter. It is our Administration. I say give it a generous support."[68]

But by the mid-1850s Hamlin had changed his mind and was ready to leave the Democrats. Earlier he had established the philosophic grounds to do so. Asked by President Pierce during the crisis over Kansas whether he could stand up against his party, Hamlin replied that he would serve his constituents to the best of his ability, irrespective of party.[69] But in order to become a Republican, he needed a sign of his new obligation, for he could not simply appear at the Maine Republican state convention, one day a ranking Democratic senator and chairman of an important committee, the next a candidate for the Republican nomination for governor. By creating a fictive loyalty issue—a test of partisan fidelity acceptable to Southern Democrats who encouraged his departure—Hamlin lessened his own impropriety and punctuated his passage into the Republicans. By summer's end he was

[67]The Hamlin biography is based on H. Draper Hunt, *Hannibal Hamlin of Maine: Lincoln's First Vice-President* (Syracuse: Syracuse University Press, 1969); Charles Eugene Hamlin, *The Life and Times of Hannibal Hamlin,* 2 vols. (1899; rpt. Port Washington, N.Y.: Kennikat Press, 1970); Hannibal Hamlin Papers, University of Maine, Oronoco, Maine, and Columbia University Library, New York; Henry L. Dawes, "Two Vice-Presidents: John C. Breckinridge and Hannibal Hamlin," *Century Magazine* 50 (July 1895): 463. The speech quoted is transcribed in *Remarks of Mr. Hamlin of Maine Defining His Position as Chairman of the Committee on Commerce, and the Test of the Cincinnati Convention in the Senate of the United States, June 12, 1856* (Washington, D.C.: 1856).

[68]Hunt, *Hamlin,* pp. 70, 79, 84.

[69]Michael Fosburg, "The Formation of the Republican Party in Maine: A Study of Hannibal Hamlin's Change in Party Affiliation" (master's thesis, Columbia University, 1967), p. 19.

the Republicans' successful candidate for governor. While governor, he was reelected to the Senate and in a spiral that some predicted would end in the White House, as senator he was elected vice-president. Only in 1864, when he was passed over for another former Democrat—Andrew Johnson—did his fortunes reverse, although he returned to the Senate during Reconstruction and ended his long public life as ambassador to Spain. After the Civil War, Hamlin accurately described his career as that of "a political partisan. . . . I have been one my life long. I have little respect for any man who is not."[70] Less important, from this perspective, was party constancy.

Hamlin's party-switching may have reflected an ambitious politician's need to stay in step with, if not in front of, the voters. As Maine went, so went Hannibal Hamlin. Both had been staunchly Democratic in the 1830s and 1840s, supporting an unbroken succession of local and national Democrats from Jackson to Pierce. Hamlin had been one of these and had served in Democratic delegations to Washington and Augusta. But in the early 1850s a massive voter shift, accompanied by new public concerns such as temperance and antislavery, eroded traditional Whig and Democrat support. The Whigs disappeared, and the Democrats split into factions sufficiently institutionalized in Maine to receive quasi-formal names. Within four years normal Democratic majorities of 55 to 65 percent disappeared, and Republicans gained the state's vote by similar margins because some Democrats no longer voted and others, along with new voters, joined the Republicans. This turnover was apparent in Oxford, the county in which Hamlin was born, and Penobscot, the county in which he lived. In the latter, nine hundred Democrats (of the party's usual voting population of forty-five hundred) either stayed home or shifted to the Republicans in the mid-1850s.[71]

Well aware of these developments, Hamlin's Democratic allegiance wavered and, five months before the presidential elections of 1856, was renounced. Hamlin now declared that he and his Maine constituents were part of a changing tide—an apt expression for a down-easter—and his New York friend Preston King described the tangled nature of Hamlin's relationship to his constituents "as holding the position most

[70]Hunt, *Hamlin,* pp. 70–79, 84.

[71]Walter Dean Burnham, *Presidential Ballots, 1836–1892* (Baltimore: Johns Hopkins University Press, 1955), p. 502. I am using a tie-vote model for my calculations, although elections in the 1850s more properly belong to the defection category. Albert C. E. Parker, "Beating the Spread: Analyzing American Election Outcomes," *Journal of American History* 67 (June 1980): 61–87.

serviceable to your principles which the people of Maine imposed upon you."[72]

The mutally imposed position to which King referred was free-soilism; hence Hamlin's shift may be viewed as an ideological resolve that rendered his former party unpalatable. Certainly he saw matters this way, in part because he was viewed with suspicion in the Maine legislature after he organized an anti-gag movement to prevent the tabling of abolitionist petitions. As early as the mid-1830s Democratic newspapers complained of "his treachery," called him an abolitionist, and sometimes, because he was of dark complexion, added "nigger" to their epithets. Once, in the House, Kentucky's Garret Davis referred to him as "that black Penobscot Indian," and in Maine he was frequently called the "Negro turncoat."[73] As a first-term congressman and later as senator, he consistently voted Free-Soil; opposed the annexation of Texas ("a great national question has been dragged down from its towering heights to the grovelling position of a slavery question"); and voted for the Wilmot Proviso and against the 1850 Compromise, earning within the Democratic hierarchy a reputation for, in Polk's words, "following a mischievous course."[74]

The other component of his free-soilism was a growing antisouthernism, and although Hamlin did not give many speeches ("I am a working not a talking Senator"), his opposition to the South emerges as more crucial to his Republican conversion than his antislaveryism. At least he talked more about it. As early as the 1840s Hamlin had responded to southern jibes with a regional paean:

> I protest against the reproaches that have been heaped upon the North. I glory in New England and New England's institutions. There she stands with her free schools and her free labor, her fearless enterprise, her indomitable energy. With her rocky hills, her torrent-streams, her green valleys, her heavenward-pointed spires, there she stands a moral monument around which the graphite of her country binds the wreath of fame.[75]

Five years later and still a Democrat, Hamlin ridiculed southern "scare" talk of nullification, excoriated southern heroes and habits (including

[72]Preston King to Hamlin, 6 January 1855, Hamlin Papers, University of Maine.

[73]Fosburg, "Formation of Republican Party," pp. 1–8; Dawes, "Two Vice-Presidents," p. 466; Hamlin, *Life and Times,* 1:171.

[74]Hunt, *Hamlin,* p. 23; *The Diary of James K. Polk During his Presidency, 1845–1849,* ed. Milton Quaife, 2 vols. (Chicago: A. McClung, 1910), 2: 304–05.

[75]Hunt, *Hamlin,* p. 40; quotation from Fosburg, "Formation of the Republican Party," p. 38.

John C. Calhoun and dueling codes), and convicted the South of trying to take over his party and government. In his view he had not changed as much as the Democratic party, which had been captured by the Southern slavocracy. In 1858, the now-Republican Hamlin answered South Carolina senator James Hammond's attack on the North, repeating his charges of southern "political complicity and collusion to seize the executive."[76] What appears as the victory of principle over party becomes, on second look, a convenient sectionalism accommodating a partisan conversion. In Hamlin's case antisouthernism (and its corollary pronorthernism) linked national controversy to local pride as Maine's Republicans came to view federal issues through the lens of community patriotism.

But Hannibal Hamlin also left the Democracy because he was a Hamlin, surrounded from his childhood by men who hated the Democrats. Other Maine Democrats lacked such a strong partisan tradition and, like Hamlin's early colleague Nathan Clifford and thirty-six hundred other Penobscot Democrats, had no personal reason to oppose what he and they had formerly proposed.[77] Born the third son of Cyrus and Anna Livermore Hamlin, Hannibal grew up in an intensely public atmosphere, encircled by sisters, brothers, cousins, his father's patients, local residents, and travelers. Not only was his birthplace of Paris Hill a cosmopolitan crossroads and the county seat, but his gregarious father collected people. In his roles as clerk of the court, sheriff, and physician of Oxford County, Cyrus Hamlin made his vast three-story house the center of the community. Here Governor Enoch Lincoln boarded for seven years, and the Whig governor was only one of a series of family guests.

Despite their county's attachment to the Democrats, Hamlin family politics were first Federalist, then Whig. At some point in his early life, Hannibal, a third son, rebelled against his father's and brothers' Whiggism to become a Democrat. His iconoclasm gained attention (in a large household this may have been its unconscious purpose), and he became well known for his partisanship. At an early age he argued for Jackson and the United States Bank, and during one such discussion, his father tried to dampen his renegade son with the age-old nostrum, "Live a little longer, live a little longer."[78] Despite such disagreements, Hannibal sensed parental approval of a political career—albeit as a

[76]Hamlin, *Life and Times* 1 232–64; Hunt, *Hamlin,* pp. 48, 77–78, 107; *Congressional Globe,* 35th Cong., 1st sess., 1002–06.

[77]Philip Greeley Clifford, *Nathan Clifford, Democrat* (New York: Putnam, 1922).

[78]Hamlin, *Life and Times* 1:19, 22–23.

Whig. Certainly there existed a family tradition of public involvement: Hamlins had served in William the Conqueror's army, and, more recently, Hannibal's grandfather and two uncles had fought with General Washington at Long Island.

Years later Hamlin explained that he became a Democrat because in such a large family he was always the last one to get the Whig paper, and so was left with Democratic journals. But there was more to his aberration than the need for recognition and the Democratic *Argus*. At a critical time in his youth an attachment that might have been dropped was reinforced by anger. Raised in a prosperous though not wealthy family, Hamlin expected to go to college, following in family footsteps to Harvard, Brown, Bowdoin, or nearby Waterford College. He did well at Hebron Academy, and his father had promised to support him during college. But circumstances changed overnight. An older brother fell ill, and Hannibal was called home to run the farm. Two years later his father was dead, and instead of the wonders of Boston or Providence, Hamlin now considered the prospects of Paris Hill, living as his father had requested in his will, "till he arrives at the age of twenty-one and I further hope and desire that he may live with his mother as long as she lives."[79] Such disappointment reinforced Hamlin's attachments to the Democratic party, for, however inadvertently, his family had disrupted his life. At the very time that he reached political maturity, the grounds for partisan reconciliation disappeared; to give up the Democracy in such circumstances would signal respect for a father who had kept him from college and for a family that had treated him differently from his brothers. At this point Hamlin's partisanship became a symbolic protest. In time, his resentment faded, perhaps because he did not stay long in Paris Hill. Having become first a surveyor, then a schoolteacher, and finally a lawyer, Hamlin began his career as a Democratic politician in Penobscot County.

Yet from the beginning Hamlin's partisanship was tainted, first because he had grown up in a Whig family and had been greatly influenced by his favorite brother Elijah, a Whig legislator and gubernatorial candidate with whom Hannibal lived while teaching school. Later his contacts with the Fessenden family (Hannibal and future Senator William Pitt Fessenden apprenticed with Samuel Fessenden) shaped his feelings about slavery and the South. In the process of learning the law, he absorbed the perspectives of a Democrat-hater. His marginality was further revealed in his personal associations, for Hamlin instinctively chose Whig friends in the Maine legislature as well as in his Wash-

[79]Hunt, *Hamlin,* p. 10.

ington mess and boardinghouse.[80] No longer a neglected third son, his prospects improved in the 1850s, and he had little reason to remain a rebel. What was surprising about his partisan career was not that he switched to the Republicans, but that he had ever been a Democrat.

Thus the partisan upheavals of the 1850s provided an opportunity to join the Republicans, whom Hamlin considered the successors to the Federalists and Whigs. The family dimensions of this conversion were apparent at a ratification meeting held in Bangor in the summer of 1856, just before Hamlin's nomination as the Republican gubernatorial candidate. Facing his brother, who was presiding, Hannibal spoke in personal terms: "For the first time You and I, Sir, stand upon the same political platform, and battle for the same great cause. . . . When you were the candidate of the great Whig party for governor of our native State, you did not receive my suffrage, and when I was the humble candidate of the late Democratic party, I did not receive your vote. Now, thank God we stand firmly together upon a platform as broad as the Union. . . ." So saying, Hannibal extended his hand and the brothers embraced—Republicans both.[81]

Four years after Hannibal Hamlin, Henry Scholte of Pella, Iowa, also left the Democratic party. Like most defecters, Scholte placed his conversion on the high ideological ground of choosing freedom over slavery and did not mention any mundane concerns—an ethnic grudge, local grievance, or private advantage—that might have influenced him.[82] In his first years in Iowa, Scholte had briefly supported the Whigs, having as a young man in the Netherlands admired Henry Clay.

[80]Richard Wescott, "History of Maine Politics, 1840–1860: The Formation of the Republican Party" (Ph.D. dissertation, University of Maine, 1966); Hamlin, *Life and Times,* 1:171. For the importance of Washington boardinghouses, see James Sterling Young, *The Washington Community, 1800–1828* (New York: Columbia University Press, 1966).

[81]Hamlin, *Life and Times* 2:301–02.

[82]The following sketch is based on Lubbertis Oostendorp, *H. P. Scholte, Leader of the Secession of 1834 and Founder of Pella* (Franeker (Holland): T. Wever, 1964); *The History of Marion County, Iowa* (Des Moines: United Historical Company, 1881); Morton M. Rosenberg, *Iowa on the Eve of the Civil War: A Decade of Frontier Politics* (Norman: University of Oklahoma Press, 1952); Leonore L. Scholte, "A Strange Land: Romance in Pella History," *Iowa Journal of History and Politics* 37 (April 1939): 115–203; Jacob Van der Zee, *The Hollanders in Iowa* (Iowa City: State Historical Society of Iowa, 1912); Robert Swieringa, "The Ethnic Voter and the First Lincoln Election," in Swieringa, ed., *Beyond the Civil War Synthesis: Political Essays of the Civil War Era* (Westport, Conn.: Greenwood Press, 1975), pp. 99–115; Jacob Van der Zee, "The Coming of Hollanders to Iowa," *Iowa Journal of History and Politics* 9 (October 1911): 528–74; Henry Lucas, *The Netherlanders in America: Dutch Immigration to the United States and Canada* (Ann Arbor: University of Michigan Press, 1955). For a quantitative study of state politics, see Melvyn Hammarberg, *The Indiana Voter: The Historical Dynamics of Party Allegiance during the 1870s* (Chicago: University of Chicago Press, 1977).

But in the 1850s he became a fervent Democrat, responsible not only for his own partisanship but also, by virtue of his standing in the community, that of the Hollanders in Pella and surrounding Lake Prairie Township. As the dominie of a sect of Dutch Reformed communicants, Scholte had organized the migration of nearly a thousand secessionists from the National Dutch Church, and after considering Java and Michigan, he used the pooled resources of his followers to buy up the claims of native-born Americans in the lush prairie land between the Skunk and Des Moines rivers. To Marion County—the region Willa Cather later described as "the flat land / Rich and somber and ever silent"—the Hollanders came in 1847, their bonds with Scholte reinforced by the bittersweet experience of uprooting.

Once settled, the community continued to depend on the English-speaking dominie, who served as pastor, justice of the peace, school commissioner, postmaster, banker, lawyer, and editor of the bilingual *Pella Gazette*. In this last capacity Scholte instructed the Hollanders in American politics; like many Europeans, they were impressed by the intense interest in public affairs. When their five-year naturalization period ended, Lake Prairie residents followed Scholte's lead and voted 75 percent Democratic in the state elections of 1856, 82 percent in 1857, and 72 percent in 1858.[83]

The explanation of the community's early politics can be referred to its leader (Pellans even voted in Scholte's house), but the origin of Scholte's own attachment to the Democrats is more problematic. Certainly he received no partisan training in Amsterdam. Nor did his politics reflect his pietistic religion, for Scholte was the Dutch version of an English Puritan. Focused on correcting the moral errors of another church, this brand of stewardship ended in the right-behavior politics of Know-Nothings and Republicans.[84]

Inexplicable on religious and family grounds, Scholte's partisan history is best explained by his political environment, to which, given the circumstances, he was especially responsive. In 1853 Iowa's Whigs campaigned to add a prohibition amendment to the state constitution. Scholte and his Hollanders opposed such an amendment with impressive unanimity (the township vote was 90 percent nay), on the grounds that it was an intrusion by the government and just the sort of inter-

[83]Swieringa, "Ethnic Voter," p. 103.

[84]For an analysis of doctrinal differences between Scholte's seceders and the established church, see Oostendorp, *Scholte,* pp. 44–110. Oostendorp neglects the other motive of migration—the economic hardships that accompanied the failure of the Dutch potato. Lucas, *Netherlanders,* p. 55; Van der Zee, *Hollanders,* pp. 213, 219.

ference that had necessitated their emigration. This did not mean that Hollanders were wet, but that, cross-pressured, they chose intemperance over statism. In 1854 the anti-Catholic, anti-immigrant Know-Nothings posed an even more serious threat, and when word of nativist secret societies in the nearby county seat of Knoxville reached Pella, Scholte and the community swung to the Democrats. So apprehensive were some that they built double cellars in which to hide from nativists.[85] In switching to the Democrats, Scholte suspended his anti-Catholicism, but, as he explained from the pulpit, the dangers of a longer naturalization period and delayed voting rights took priority over an ancient prejudice. When the Republicans replaced the Know-Nothings in Marion County, Scholte remained a Democrat, linking the new party to nativism, temperance, and the government interference implied if such policies were to be more than rhetoric. Throughout the 1850s, Lake Prairie continued its impressive support—72 percent Democratic in the county elections in 1858, 71 percent in the state elections in 1859.[86]

Suddenly in the summer of 1859 Scholte deserted the Democrats, appearing at the Republican state convention in Des Moines, where he unabashedly denounced what he had just been—and some said still was. Only weeks before, the dominie had been elected a delegate to the Democratic state convention and was expected to represent Iowa at the national convention in Charleston. Instead, in a remarkable partisan switch, he served as a member of Iowa's Republican delegation, supporting first Seward and then Lincoln. Returning to Pella, he campaigned for the Republican ticket and reassured the inquisitive that it was "no dishonor for any man to change his political principles if he becomes convinced they are wrong. Rather it is dishonorable to remain for parties' sake."[87]

His Hollanders were not listening, and they remained loyal to the Democracy not just in 1860 but well into the twentieth century. A few, perhaps 24 of the usual 370 Democratic voters, followed Scholte into the Republican party, but most, having learned to act as Democrats before they spoke English and became naturalized (thereby reversing the process of the native-born) did not switch parties. Nor did their children, and the process of Democratic transmission from father to son

[85]Scholte, "A Strange Land," p. 177; F. I. Herriott, "The Republican State Convention," *Annals of Iowa,* 3d ser. 9 (January 1910): 442.

[86]Swieringa, "Ethnic Voter," p. 103.

[87]Quotation from Van der Zee, *Hollanders,* pp. 227, 228; F. I. Herriott, "Iowa and the First Nomination of Abraham Lincoln," *Annals of Iowa.* 3d ser. 8 (October 1907): 204.

was not shaken by depression, world wars, or grain prices. Scholte's proselytizing had convinced these Dutch-Americans that the Republican party was controlled by nativists; and this conviction, along with fears of extended naturalization periods, of delayed voting for aliens after citizenship, and of a new registration system for Iowa, dismayed immigrants who had participated in public affairs from the time of their arrival in the United States.[88] Furthermore, ethnic hostility reinforced party regularity; even in Pella, with its high concentration of Dutch, 28 percent of the township was American-born by 1860, and there was occasional conflict between the Yankees and Dutch. Hollanders did not like to be called Germans or "wooden-shoes," and Americans resented the presence of an ethnic majority that allotted them only token positions in local affairs. By making Republicans into a party of Yankees, Hollanders furnished a negative reference group that cemented their Democratic bonds.[89]

There were other reasons for remaining Democratic, some associated with the internal politics of the Hollander community. By the 1850s a group of church elders wished to affiliate with the National Dutch Reformed Church, but Scholte refused, holding firm to the independence that had inspired his migration. This unpopular decision isolated the Hollanders of Iowa and accounted, according to one, for the remarkable number of Dutch-language newspapers mailed to Pella from Holland, Michigan.[90] Eventually a dissenting consistory took over the church, and the dominie was forced to build another for the twenty or thirty followers he called "true believers." There were also secular points of conflict between the dominie and the community. In the 1840s, Scholte had promised that the land across from his home and along Pella's Garden Square would be used for public purposes. In time, however, he sold these valuable lots to business firms, whereupon the elders sued, and the man to whom Hollanders had entrusted their future found himself referred to in court as a greedy entrepreneur.[91] Having challenged Scholte's spiritual and economic leadership, it was easy enough to reject his politics.

Scholte, of course, saw things differently, and the very characteristics

[88]F. I. Herriott, "Republican Presidential Preliminaries," *Annals of Iowa,* 3d ser. 9 (January 1910): 253; *Pella Gazette,* 25 January 1860, 18 February 1858; Hubert H. Wubben, *Civil War Iowa and the Copperhead Movement* (Ames: Iowa State University Press, 1980), p. 19.

[89]Swieringa, "Ethnic Voter," p. 103.

[90]Van der Zee, *Hollanders,* pp. 247, 408.

[91]Ibid., p. 292; Oostendorp, *Scholte,* pp. 166–67; Lucas, pp. 170–91, 499–500.

that made him a successful settlement leader increasingly separated him from his followers. Aggressive, independent, stubborn, and "of fiery and active temperament,"[92] Scholte envisaged his community as an ecumenical Christian refuge (hence its name; Pella recalled the ancient city in east Palestine to which Jerusalem's Christians removed in the first century), not a separatist "Dutch city upon the plain" like that in Holland, Michigan. Unlike the dominie there, Scholte encouraged bilingual schools, published an English newspaper before most Hollanders could read it, helped American businessmen locate in Pella, and promoted the efforts of Baptists to start a church and college. Today he would be called an assimilationist, for he supported religious (though not racial) intermarriage and believed that "intermarriages between white nationalists indicate that distinctions on account of birth are unknown to us."[93] His wife, who never forgave him the exchange of cosmopolitan Amsterdam for parochial Pella, encouraged his associations with Yankees, and in time the Americanized Scholte (his was the only home in Pella that subscribed to *Godey's Lady's Book* and *Harper's*) spent more time with native-born Americans than with the Dutch farmers of his congregation.[94] For such a man the shift from the Democratic party of the foreign-born to the Republican party of New England natives represented one more step in the process of becoming an American. But Scholte was not permitted his reward. Offered the Austrian ministry by Lincoln in 1864, he accepted, only to find that Congress had restricted such appointments to the native-born.[95]

## *The Dropouts*

A third group of Northern Democrats active at some point in their lives later withdrew from politics. Some abstained involuntarily, the victims of residency requirements and military service; others were intimidated by loyalty oaths instituted during the war or by the prospects of army intervention at the polls. Greatly exaggerated, these threats were nevertheless a reason for not participating, especially among border state Democrats.[96] But for the most part this was temporary,

[92]Oostendorp, *Scholte,* p. 108.

[93]Van der Zee, *Hollanders,* p. 227; Lucas, *Netherlanders,* p. 193.

[94]Scholte, "A Strange Land" pp. 162–89.

[95]Henri Scholte to Abraham Lincoln, 8 January 1861, Robert Todd Lincoln Papers, microfilm edition; Scholte, "A Strange Land," p. 179.

[96]Harold Hyman, *To Try Men's Souls: Loyalty Tests in American History* (Berkeley: University of California Press, 1959), pp. 139–66, 251–67. For the effects in Maryland, see Jean H. Baker, *The Politics of Continuity: Maryland Political Parties, 1858–1870* (Baltimore: Johns Hopkins University Press, 1973), pp. 87–88, 90, 95, 104, 108, 131, 133.

war-affected behavior. More permanent were the voluntary dropouts—those once-active Northern Democrats who abandoned politics entirely.

Charles Mason of Burlington, Iowa, was one. He dropped out because being a Democrat no longer eased his lifelong episodes of depression. As a young man, Mason had discerned the therapeutic uses of activity, and over the years he established an exhausting regimen that combined daily five-mile walks with an assortment of demanding professional activities. As Mason frankly admitted, "I need some regular and constant business to keep me from going insane."[97] Political action was part of that business. More than once he found that intensive involvement in party affairs improved his physical and mental well-being. Not only did he gain weight (at the worst of his depressions the six-foot Mason dropped to 130 pounds), but somehow, through the rigors of campaigning, he recovered his interest in what was all too often for this morose Iowan "the desolate waste of existence." But Mason's feeling that he was passing his life "without much purpose" always recurred, accompanied by "sadness when I think of past and future."[98] Because campaigns were passionate mission-filled affairs, they transfused him with much-needed animation. But as he grew older, they no longer helped. Perhaps, although Mason did not say so, habitual practice had emptied electioneering of the drama and excitement he required. At any rate, substituting civic affairs, spiritualism, and economic pamphleteering for being a Democrat, Mason remained active until his death in the 1880s. Clearly, his abstention was not caused by the declining energy of a septuagenarian.

On the surface, this transplanted New Yorker had few reasons for either his melancholy or the puzzling list of physical ailments he suffered. Indeed, save for his health, his life read like a tale of Horatio Alger. Born the second son of poor parents, he had grown up on a hard-rock farm in Onondaga County, New York. His father had little time for politics and few ambitions for his son except that he become a weaver or skilled artisan. Although the senior Mason passed along to

[97]The following sketch is based on the extensive Charles Mason Papers in the Library of Congress (hereafter cited as Mason Papers) and on Charles Remey, ed., "The Life and Letters of Charles Mason," 12 vols. Typescript, Library of Congress. For the quotation, see "Life and Letters," 4: 379; William Toussaint, "Biography of an Iowa Businessman, Charles Mason, 1804–1882" (Ph.D. dissertation, University of Iowa, 1963); George H. Yewell, "Reminiscences of Charles Mason," *Annals of Iowa* 5 (October 1901): 161–76, 251–71; Hubert H. Wubben, "Copperhead Charles Mason: A Question of Loyalty," *Civil War History* 24 (March 1978): 46–65.

[98]Diary of Charles Mason, entry for 4 May 1862, Mason Papers.

his seven children the traditions of righteous hardworking Puritans and revolutionary heroes, he did not transmit either a high level of partisan activity or any special party allegiance as did, for example, the family of Mason's childhood friend and neighbor, Horatio Seymour. Nor did Mason acquire his Democracy at West Point, where he received an appointment in 1825. During his tenure there the idea that army officers must serve country, not party, prevailed. Like his father, but for different reasons, Mason did not have time for politics. He stood first in a class that included Robert E. Lee and Joseph E. Johnston, and he graduated without a demerit. Then, in dizzying succession, he taught engineering at West Point, studied law, worked on the *New York Evening Post,* moved west, became head of a railroad and a land company, served as chief justice of Iowa's territorial court, ran the Patent Office, started a law firm in Washington, D.C., and farmed. Money and fame accumulated, but little pleasure or serenity; Mason continued to suffer periods of depression along with physical ailments that included a self-diagnosed terminal heart ailment in 1857, jaundice in 1859, shingles in 1869, chronic dyspepsia, bowel troubles, and a crick in the neck.

Only Mason's politics remained constant, and in this he was an unremitting Democrat. In the 1860s he emerged as a party leader of national stature although, now in his fifties, he gave some indication of his declining interest. Twice during the Civil War he was nominated for state office in Iowa—once for governor and once for judge—and although he lost both times, Mason enthusiastically accepted the honor, only to regret his decision. After a few weeks he dropped out of the gubernatorial contest, offering several political reasons he later disavowed. In his buoyant periods he announced his intention of "never again mingling in public affairs,"[99] but he remained active as long as he regained his mental equilibrium from electioneering. So, despite his hesitations, he ran again in 1863. In 1864 Mason worked for McClellan's election, organizing a national committee, raising money, sending out documents, and establishing campaign themes in his much-circulated pamphlets "Election in Iowa" and "An Appeal to the People." Given his own preoccupation with illness, he turned to medicine for his partisan images, comparing Republican tyranny to a "festering sore," "a cancer," and "a depleting bloodletting."[100]

After the war, Mason's interest in politics dwindled. As a delegate to

[99]Ibid., entry for 6 June 1861.

[100]"Papers of the Society for the Diffusion of Political Knowledge," microfilm, Library of Congress; Diary of Charles Mason, entries for 4 November 1868 and 10 January 1869, Mason Papers.

the Democratic national conventions in 1868 and 1872, he was more spectator than participant and left early. More and more often during the 1870s he did not vote, and in 1873 he "nearly" decided that he would never do so again. Instead he spent election days on trains between Iowa, Washington, and his birthplace, Pompey, New York, where he made an annual pilgrimage to the Baptist graveyard, lamenting for weeks afterward the passage of time and friends, as well as the death of two of his three daughters. Much to the chagrin of Iowa Democrats, Mason did not even illuminate his Burlington home during party parades. Meanwhile civic affairs—especially his campaign for municipal sewers and his writings on fiscal matters—replaced his former concern for politics. Gradually Charles Mason had become a Democratic dropout.[101]

At the same time that Charles Mason withdrew from the party, so too did Pennsylvanian William H. Sylvis.[102] Although Sylvis's reasons for dropping out differed from Mason's (as did the length and character of his service), in both cases personal history determined partisan course.

An active Democrat during the 1850s, Sylvis not only voted for Pierce in 1852, Buchanan in 1856, and Douglas in 1860; he also found time for parades and rallies. In off years he campaigned for local officials, including candidates for Philadelphia's mayor and aldermen; before moving to Philadelphia he worked for the Democracy in Pennsylvania's Union and Centre Counties. Such partisan activities were unusual because Sylvis was an ironmolder, and, given the ten-hour, six-day work week, few foundry workers had the time or taste for politics. Sylvis often complained that except for Sunday, workingmen did not see their children during daylight for the six months of fall and winter, and more than once he described the exhaustion that made party affairs irrelevant. "The working man," wrote Sylvis in 1868, "who after a hard day's work returns to an impoverished home, shut in from pure air, and packed in a

[101]Diary of Charles Mason, entry for 31 August 1869, Mason Papers. Mason's economic theories were as varied as his occupations. One of his schemes was based on increasing by 1 percent each year the gold content of each greenback dollar.

[102]The Sylvis sketch is based on Charlotte Todes, *William H. Sylvis and the National Labor Union* (New York: International Publishers, 1942); Jonathan Grossman, *William Sylvis, Pioneer of American Labor,* (New York: Columbia University Press, 1945); Reed Richardson, "Labor Leaders, 1860s" (Ithaca: New York State School of Labor Relations, Cornell University, Bulletin no. 31, 1961); James Sylvis, *The Life, Speeches, Labors, and Essays of William H. Sylvis* (Philadelphia: Claxton, Remsen, and Haffelfinger, 1872). For analysis of the more familiar aspects of Sylvis's life as a union organizer, see Daniel J. Walkowitz, *Worker City, Company Town* (Urbana: University of Illinois Press, 1978).

contracted alley or street feels what a mere theorist surrounded by wealth and luxury can never comprehend."[103]

Despite such impediments, Sylvis became an active Democrat in his twenties because, as he explained to his fellow workers, the party might solve the problems engendered by "capitalist greed." These were, according to Sylvis, low pay, unstable currency, and long hours. Like many mid-nineteenth-century labor leaders, he expected the Democracy to become a workingmen's organization that, when supported by mechanics and laborers, would elect its candidates and install its programs. Although he anticipated that all workingmen would become Democrats, he never believed the reverse—that all Democrats would be from the "industrial and laboring classes."[104] Instead Sylvis accepted the national tradition of majoritarianism and, like most Democrats, appealed to all Americans.

In time this youthful vision faded, and in the 1860s the disillusioned Sylvis adopted a nonpartisan, interest-group approach to public life. Convinced that Democratic candidates cynically promised support for workers' issues only to gain votes, Sylvis argued for a "power balance": "It is the duty of every man who earns his bread by the sweat of his brow to vote against any man of any party who is now or ever has been an enemy to working men and to vote for every man of every party who is more favorable to the cause than his opponent."[105] Following his own advice, Sylvis surrendered his reflexive loyalty to the Democracy. In 1864 he worked harder against the Republican candidate for mayor, Morton McMichael, than he did for the Democrat. A year later he reached the final stage of his political activity—the organization of a Labor party:

> If we resort to political action at all, we must keep clear of entangling alliances, with a distinct workmen's party in the field. There can be no distrust, no want of confidence when it becomes a fixed fact that workingmen can vote for men *of them* and *for them*. The incentive will be great to unite the masses in one great struggle for victory. We should then know for whom and for what we voted. Every toiler would feel that he held his destiny in his own hands and the road to reform would be so direct and open that none but the corrupt and false hearted would desert the banner of labor [Sylvis's italics].[106]

[103]Sylvis, *Life, Speeches,* pp. 183–84, 208.

[104]Richard T. Ely, *The Labor Movement in America* (New York: Thomas Crowell, 1886), pp. 3, 43, 46; Todes, *Sylvis,* pp. 11–12.

[105]Quotation from Sylvis, *Life, Speeches,* pp. 49, 54, 101.

[106]Ibid., p. 72; *Ironmoulders Journal,* 7 April 1868.

Rejecting both the Republican and Democratic parties (their leaders were "Iagoes" controlled by capital), Sylvis did not deny the legitimacy of the political system or the importance of party organization. On the contrary, he wanted workingmen to use "their ark of safety, the vote" more effectively, and despite his intermittent questioning of political involvement, his trade-union philosophy was predicated on the differences between enfranchised American workers and their politically deprived European counterparts. He called for improved schooling so that citizens might be better informed about public issues, and he argued for shorter hours on the grounds that workers must have more time for politics. "We possess," he told ironworkers in 1867, "the power to annul any oppressive act. We can compel our rulers to be just." But to harness such power required "cutting loose from party ties and creating a labor-based organization. . . . We are slaves not because we must be, but because we will be." In Sylvis's two-dimensional world of rich and poor, capitalist and worker, nonproducer and producer, "idle-drone and busy-bee," labor so outnumbered capital as to ensure electoral power. Shortly before his death in 1869, Sylvis wrote the National Labor Union resolution that began, "Inasmuch as both the present parties are dominated by nonproducing classes who depend on public plunder for subsistence and wealth and have no sympathy with the working millions." By this time he considered capital and labor natural enemies, but he also believed that the resolution of conflict between them did not require violence, only the adjudication of the ballot box. Even as he worked for a national convention of union men, his solutions remained legislative, for he expected relief from Congress. "Let us adopt," he said in 1867, "the motto of Andrew Jackson. Put your shoulder to the wheel, trust in God and push along the column."[107]

In becoming a Democratic dropout, Sylvis followed cues absorbed as a child. He had learned his sense of civic participation not from his father, but from the wealthy neighbor to whom he was "let out" for seven years. While his father, an underemployed wagonmaker, tramped the countryside looking for work in order to feed a family of eleven, ten-year-old William cleaned, cooked, farmed, and did odd jobs for the Pawling family in exchange for room and board. During this period, Pawling represented Pennsylvania's Lycoming County Whigs in the state legislature, and this exposure to politics influenced the young boy, who later named his first son Henry Clay Sylvis. In an interview after Sylvis was a prominent trade-union organizer, Pawling recalled tutor-

[107]Quotation from Sylvis, *Life, Speeches,* pp. 77, 80, 181, 224–25, 239, 241, 249, 282; Grossman, *William Sylvis,* p. 235.

ing his young servant (for he can hardly be called an apprentice) in politics and allowing him the use of his library. Such memories distorted reality, for Sylvis was illiterate until his twenties, when he taught himself to read and write.[108] What he had absorbed in his adopted family was a sense of political efficacy.

From his father, a self-avowed "talking Jacksonian," Sylvis learned his partisanship. But the elder Sylvis's itinerant circumstances made voting difficult; depending on his feet for transportation, he was often far away from the polls on election day. As his economic prospects deteriorated in the 1830s, the senior Sylvis increasingly blamed the Democrats, at first for the loss of his wagon shop and then for the end of any chance at economic independence. By the 1840s the elder Sylvis no longer voted, and his party history transmitted to his son an exaggerated sense of Democratic power over the economy, along with a negative assessment of its policies.

In many ways William Sylvis duplicated his father's career. He too learned a difficult trade that required a long apprenticeship and he too was briefly a self-employed proprietor. When his business failed, the younger Sylvis, like his father, tramped the Lycoming valley looking for work. By the 1850s Sylvis had undergone travails that most laborers accumulate only in a lifetime: he had worked for a year in a foundry that went bankrupt and never paid him six months' wages; he had permanently injured his foot in an accident with molten iron; and he had forfeited any hope of becoming an independent proprietor. Still a young man, he looked forward to a lifetime as an itinerant ironmolder, although in fact he became a full-time labor organizer.[109]

In moving from a traditional party commitment to interest-group politics and finally to a labor party, Sylvis's course was prompted by the experiences of his childhood. With Pawling he had observed the importance of partisan activism; from his father he had learned of the Democracy's indifference toward workers. At no time did he surrender something inculcated at home and in his jobs—respect for mass organization. Many of his friends in the National Labor Union disagreed with Sylvis, and some, like Patrick Collins of Massachusetts, remained Democrats throughout their lives. Such men, some of whom were elected to office, were sufficiently numerous to transmit to other workers the need to stay within the established party system.[110] Sylvis disagreed, in part because the already weak signals of his Democratic

[108]Grossman, *William Sylvis,* p. 19.

[109]Walkowitz, *Worker City,* pp. 32, 34.

[110]David Montgomery, *Beyond Equality: Labor and the Radical Republicans* (New York: A. A. Knopf, 1967), p. 203.

heritage were gradually dispelled by the camaraderie of his contact with his fellow ironmolders.

Like the other case studies in this chapter Sylvis's party profile was unique. Being a Democrat was for him, as for the others, an individual affair—a disposition personally acquired and practiced and explicable in those terms. Certainly his relationship to the Democracy was affected by that organization's neglect of American workers, just as Hannibal Hamlin's was by its neutrality on slavery, and the Hunterdonians' by its power in their community. But it was also influenced by Sylvis's early life. Every Northern Democrat had such a psychopartisan life history, and as often as not, personal matters affected Northern Democrats' responses to their party. Some men stayed with the Democracy for a lifetime; others were partisan vagabonds; a third group dropped out entirely. Within these styles there were variations in intensity and commitment, and a man's course was influenced not only by outside events—such as the Civil War—but also by his age and circumstances when he confronted these events. And, of course, the family was not the only institution inculcating political habits and behavior.

CHAPTER 2

# *Learning to Be Americans: Schooling and Political Culture*

> The easiest way of becoming acquainted with the modes of thinking, the rules of conduct, and the prevailing manners of any people is to examine what sort of education they give their children.
>
> —Hector St. John Crèvecoeur

While nineteenth-century families shaped their sons' partisan course, schools trained young white males in their public roles of delegating power, rotating leadership, limiting power, and supporting the government. In time, these behaviors were also enacted within the nation's political parties, which, while imitating the general political culture, came to constitute and construct the very thing they imitated. Contemporary studies of political culture suggest that the family has never been the prime agency in this process of inculcating national values; thus, although sons usually took their party choice from their fathers, their attitudes toward authority, understandings of participation and efficacy, and evaluations of government were defined by schools.[1] The reason for this was simple: families were not public environments; Americans learned at home how to be mothers and fathers, and at school how to behave as jurors, magistrates, and voters. Sensing this, the nation's early leaders linked formal schooling and political culture, and the schoolroom became the essential mechanism for training Americans. The challenge was to produce an active citizenry who attended public affairs (thereby preventing tyranny), who accepted a new system of government (thereby installing federalism), and who exchanged positions of leadership without violence (thereby assuring a

[1]M. Kent Jennings and Richard G. Niemi, "The Transmission of Political Values from Parent to Child," *American Political Science Review* 62 (March 1968): 169–83; David Easton and Jack Dennis, *Children in the Political System* (New York: McGraw-Hill, 1969); Robert D. Hess and Judith Torney, *The Development of Political Attitudes in Children* (Chicago: Aldine, 1967), p. 217.

representative government). Convinced that schools should do more than convey moral and academic instruction, early opinionmakers offered extensive plans for a national system of education.

## *Schooling as Civic Training: Theory*

Even before the revolution, Benjamin Franklin and James Otis had cited schooling as the taproot of public culture. In their view, not only did elected officials require training, but the people—at least those possessing citizenship—must vote, run for office, serve as sheriffs, and participate in local affairs. By the late eighteenth century the colonists had become adept in these roles. They operated a political system that required participation, and from this experience many future Americans learned how to behave in a democracy. Even before their own opposition to England had crystallized, Otis and Franklin connected schooling and politics in recognition of the need for colonists to have specific information that formerly only king and court had required.[2]

The revolution reinforced this felt need for formal agencies of political learning. The process of building a nation, even in its comparatively placid American version, had alerted a generation of venturesome conservatives to centrifugal tendencies within their society. Having overthrown king and parliament, political notables worried that disorder and confusion would continue to afflict their communities. Intellectuals as well as politicians expressed these fears; Noah Webster was concerned that "these states will always be exposed to anarchy and faction because these evils approach under the delusive but specious guise of patriotism." Because his nation had none of the institutional mucilage of other societies—no standing army, no national past, no state religion, not even a nearby foreign enemy—Webster considered schooling an essential glue and called for an association of patriots to develop a uniform national character.[3] Benjamin Rush agreed and hoped education would install a stable political culture: "We have changed our forms of government, but it remains yet to effect a revolution in principles, opinions, and manners so as to accommodate them to the forms of government we have adopted."[4] Jefferson might preach the need for

[2]John Hardin Best, ed., *Benjamin Franklin on Education* (New York: Lippincott, 1962), pp. 162–71; Abraham Blinderman, *American Writers on Education before 1865* (Boston: Twayne, 1975), p. 21; Sol Cohen, ed., *Education in the United States: A Documentary History,* 5 vols. (New York: Random House, 1974), 1:476–509.

[3]Henry Warfel, ed., *Letters of Noah Webster* (New York: Library Publisher, 1953), p. 140, 378–79; Jonathan Messerli, "The Columbian Complex: The Impulse to National Consolidation," *History of Education Quarterly* 7 (Winter 1967):420.

[4]Quoted in Messerli, "Columbian Complex," pp. 417–18.

revolution every generation, but by the last decade of the eighteenth century Americans believed theirs complete. Now they must preserve a fledgling political culture and create, through formal agencies of learning, a homogeneous public mind.

In a representative version of such prescriptions, George Washington argued that schooling alone could free youth from "those prejudices" and "unreasonable fallacies which would end in diversity" and destroy the newly established union. Local institutions, however respectable and useful, could never develop American values, and, like most of the founding fathers, Washington sought to neutralize variations. "The more homogeneous our citizens can be made," he concluded in his final message to Congress, "the greater our prospects of permanent union."[5] Washington's fear of diversity included the economic sphere. For it was not only the republic's regional, racial, and ethnic heterogeneity that alarmed this generation; its variations in wealth did, too. Schooling emerged as a potential solvent, responsible for mixing the able poor in with the middle ranks while simultaneously dispelling any dangerous social ideas of the radical and dispossessed. As Ralph Waldo Emerson later explained: "The cause of education is urged in this country . . . on what ground?—Why on this, that the people have the power, and if they are not instructed to sympathize with the intelligent, reading, trading, and governing class; inspired with a taste for the same competitions and prizes, they will upset the fair pageant of Judicature and perhaps lay a hand on the sacred muniments of wealth itself and new distribute the land." The English traveler George Combe agreed: "The ignorance of the masses," he wrote in 1840, "is filling the wealthy with terror for their own safety so that they are ardently anxious to educate the people." From this perspective schooling served the ultimate political function—it preserved the system and kept, as Emerson acknowledged, "The people from our throats."[6]

From the beginning of their national existence, Americans believed their society could not depend on haphazard socialization by family, church or apprenticeship, and this widely held attitude sparked a dura-

[5]John C. Fitzpatrick, ed., *The Writings of George Washington,* 38 vols. (Washington, D.C.: U.S. Government Printing Office, 1940–1944), 35:198–201; James Richardson, ed., *Messages and Papers of the Presidents,* 20 vols. (Washington, D.C.: Bureau of National Literature and Art, 1908–1917), 1:202; David Tyack, "Forming the National Character: Paradox in the Educational Thought of the Revolutionary Generation," *Harvard Educational Review* 36 (Fall 1966): 29–41.

[6]Ralph Waldo Emerson, "Nature, Addresses and Lectures," *The Complete Works* 14 vols. (Boston: Houghton Mifflin, 1855–1876), 1:302; George Combe, *Notes on The United States of North America during a Phrenological Visit in 1838–1840* (Edinburgh: MacLachland, Stewart, 1841), p. 31.

ble commitment to education as an adjunct of politics. First, American schools were expected to cement the young to the regime and instill national values amid the temptations of provincialism; second, by supplying large doses of republicanism and patriotism, they were expected to inoculate citizens from subversive beliefs, whether those of Roman Catholic, monarchist, socialist, demagogue, or Native American. For people with this viewpoint, formal education emerged as more than a cognitive process involving skills in reading, writing, and numbers; and although the development of good moral habits among the young was a continuing expectation, there was little sense of schooling for scholarship, for personal satisfaction, and for intellectual liberation. Instead, the children of the republic must become Americans and never know themselves as anything else.

Once established, schools would serve, along with the republic's other institutions, as models for imitation. Because Americans could not be free and ignorant at the same time, they would be the best informed and therefore the freest. According to Madison, "a well-instructed people alone can be permanently free," and a national school system constructed to protect liberty would "adorn our free and happy system of government."[7] To Joel Barlow, who besides his well-known epic "The "Columbiad" wrote *A Prospectus for a National Institution,* this meant that "mankind have a right to expect this example [of superior schools] from us." Linking patriotism and professionalism, Barlow believed a national system of education would furnish experts—engineers, roadbuilders, and surveyors—whose superior technology would further unite citizens in a collective pride of achievement.[8] To William Manning, a Massachusetts farmer, education was necessary for an understanding of government, laws, and constitution. "Learning and Knowledge," wrote Manning, "is essential to the preservation of Libberty and unless we have more of it amongue us we cannot seporte our Libbertyes long."[9] State charters made the connection explicit. The Massachusetts constitution of 1780, for example, enjoined its elected officials "to cherish the interests of literature and the sciences and all seminaries of them," and in 1789 the state legislature continued the prerevolutionary practice of requiring towns of a certain size to maintain schools. Four years earlier, the Northwest Land Ordinance had

[7]Richardson, *Messages and Papers,* 1:485, 568.

[8]William Bottorff and Arthur Ford, *The Works of Joel Barlow* (Gainesville, Fla.: Scholars' Facsimiles and Reprints, 1970), p. 486.

[9]William Manning, "The Key of Libberty," *William and Mary Quarterly,* 3d ser. 13 (April 1956): 211, 247.

introduced the principle of reserving land in the territories for "public schools," and even the crowded agenda of the constitutional Convention included hot debate on James Madison's proposal for a national university. What was surprising about the latter was not that the proposal lost, but that supporters appeared at all and that Madison—usually so apprehensive of any concentration of power—contended that Congress had the authority to organize a federal university.[10]

By 1820, presidential comments on education had become a staple both in inaugural addresses and in annual messages to Congress. Every president from Washington to Jackson encouraged the formation of a national university, the public funding of local schools, and the necessity of "diffusing knowledge" throughout the republic. The parsimonious Washington felt so strongly that he willed fifty shares of stock to establish what he invariably capitalized as a NATIONAL UNIVERSITY.[11] Even Jefferson and Madison, who flinched at the creation of a United States Bank, lobbied for a publicly financed and administered educational system. Jefferson's usually felicitous prose departed in his tortured pleas for public schools. "Education," he said in his 1806 message to Congress,

> is here placed among the articles of public care, not that it would be proposed to take its ordinary branches out of the hands of private enterprise, which manages so much better all the concerns to which it is equal, but a public institution can alone supply those sciences which though rarely called for are yet necessary to complete the circle, all the parts of which contribute to the improvement of the country and some of them to its preservation.[12]

Armed with his protean constitutionalism, Jefferson transformed schooling into an internal improvement and was thereby able to dissociate it from the great watchword of the time—a specific constitutional provision giving Congress jurisdiction. Meanwhile his colleague

[10]The story of these early efforts is best told in David Madsden, *The National University, Enduring Dream of the U.S.A.* (Detroit: Wayne State University Press, 1966), and Cohen, *Education in the United States,* 2:781–97. For the debate in the Constitutional Convention, see Max Farrand, ed., *The Records of the Federal Convention of 1787,* vol. 2 (New Haven: Yale University Press, 1966), pp. 325, 616.

[11] Richardson, *Messages and Papers,* 1:66, 215, 231, 347, 373, 381, 409, 568; 2:19, 295, 311–12, 437; Albert Castel, "The Founding Fathers and the Vision of a National University," *History of Education Quarterly* 4 (December 1964): 234, 288.

[12]Quotation from Richardson, *Messages and Papers,* 1:409; See also James B. Conant, *Thomas Jefferson and the Development of American Public Education* (Berkeley: University of California Press, 1962), pp. 4, 5, 106.

Madison supported an amendment giving Congress special power over education. Encouraged by pleas to deliberate on educational matters, Congress organized ad hoc committees, and in 1796 one recommended that "a national university be established to help preserve the morals and principles of youth, reduce local prejudices, attract the youth of other countries to the United States, and save American youth the expense of going abroad for higher education."[13]

Despite such widely held convictions, a national university was never organized, and as the republic aged, the importance of political indoctrination lessened. Presidents after Jackson were less concerned with a national school system or university, and by the 1830s the standard presidential paragraph on diffusing public knowledge was omitted from executive messages.[14]

Disregarding the topic's disappearance from national politics, intellectuals continued to provide explicit plans to place schools in the federal service. Benjamin Rush, anxious to lay "the foundations for nurseries of good Americans," proposed the early inculcation of "republican duties." The Philadelphian wished to adopt "our modes of teaching to our peculiar form of government." In 1786 Rush wrote:

> The principle of patriotism stands in need of the reinforcement of prejudice, and it is well known that our strongest prejudices in favour of our country are formed in the first one and twenty years of our lives. . . . Our schools of learning, by producing one general and uniform system of education, will render the mass of people more homogeneous and thereby fit them more easily for uniform and peaceable government.

In Rush's view, only formal schooling could teach Americans that they "do not belong to themselves" but rather are "public property," and he insisted that the purpose of schooling was to make "republican machines." (The pervasiveness of this idea was evident years later, when, in nearly the same language, an Illinois law passed in 1825 held that "the mind of every citizen of a republic is the common property of society."[15]) At the top of Rush's educational hierarchy stood a federal

[13]Madsden, *National University,* p. 35.

[14]Richardson, *Messages and Papers,* vol. 3 passim.

[15]Benjamin Rush, "Of the Mode of Education Proper in a Republic" and "Education Agreeable to a Republican Form of Government," in *The Selected Writings of Benjamin Rush,* ed. Dagobert Runes (New York: Philosophical Library, 1947), pp. 87, 90, 91, 92, 388–89; Cohen, *Education in the United States,* 2: 758–60; Allen O. Hansen, *Liberalism and American Education in the Nineteenth Century* (New York: Macmillan, 1926), pp. 44–63; John Pulham, "Changing Attitudes toward Free Schools in Illinois, 1825–1860," *History of Education Quarterly* 7 (Summer 1967): 191, 192.

university where the youth of all states would be joined "into one mass of citizens after they have acquired the first principles of knowledge in the colleges of their respective states." Here they would learn "the law of nature and nations, the common law of our country, the different systems of government, history and everything else connected with the advancement of knowledge and principles." Only graduates of such a national university would be eligible for power and office. Depending on schooling to ensure similar perspectives and public behaviors, Rush proposed to incorporate his plan into the Constitution by an amendment.[16]

Like Rush, Noah Webster linked political culture and schooling, and the author of the popular blue-backed spellers spun a series of elegant phrases to bolster his points. Not only must schools create a "political bigotry out of which real allegiance springs"; they must also teach the young to "rehearse the history of their country," even to the point of speaking Washington's name as their first "public word." To accomplish this was the "first article in the code of political regulations."[17] Webster grounded his pedagogical system in John Locke's state of nature—a concept well known to Americans of this generation—in which man's ungovernable instincts had necessitated the institution of government. Like Locke, who compared young minds to "water, easily turned this way or that," Webster likened children to "tender shrubs or seedlings in fertile soil," whose political growth required formal pedagogical attention. Without such instruction young republicans would retain their unruly behavior and would lack the personal self-control that sustained their community's self-government.[18]

That children learned political habits at an early age seemed obvious to these nineteenth-century Americans, who frequently referred to the "season of youth" as the time best suited to such learning. Samuel Knox, a Presbyterian minister and principal of Baltimore College, based his prizewinning plan for a national educational system on the need for early political training. His structure of publicly financed parish schools, county academies, and state colleges began with compulsory

[16]L. H. Butterfield, ed., *Letters of Benjamin Rush,* vol. 1 (Princeton: Princeton University Press, 1951), p. 494.

[17]Hansen, *Liberalism and American Education,* pp. 232–56; David Tyack, ed., *Turning Points in American Educational History* (Waltham, Mass.: Blaidsell, 1967), p. 97.

[18]John Locke, *Some Thoughts Concerning Education,* ed. Peter Gay (New York: Bureau of Publications, Teachers College, Columbia University, 1964), pp. 19–20; Harry Warfel, *Noah Webster: Schoolmaster to America* (New York: Macmillan, 1936), pp. 177–80; James Cutbush, *An Oration on Education Delivered before the Society for the Promotion of a Rational System of Education* (Philadelphia: G. F. Goodman, 1812), pp. 1–8.

attendance for all children and ended with a national university attended by the best students, who, in a process Jefferson once described as "raking a few geniuses from the rubbish," would continue their education at public expense.[19] Fearful of his nation's "diversity," Knox intended to "harmonize" schooling by placing it under a federal board of control; such centralization appealed to the American Philosophical Society, which awarded him $100. He shared his prize with Harrison Smith, whose educational system also aimed at homogeneity. Smith argued in his award-winning prospectus that children "belonged" to the state, and that it was the duty of the nation to superintend and even coerce the public attitudes of the young. In both plans, only a few children needed advanced study. It was enough to give the exceptional students access to a federal university, where, in Knox's system as in Jefferson's and Rush's, they learned "the science of government."[20]

In theory, then, many nineteenth-century Americans agreed that young white males must go to school—there to be political as much as grammatical abecedarians. Although statements to that effect often glossed over the issue of who should pay, the decline in deferential politics and the expansion of voting and officeholding provided further impetus to the notion that the republic depended on education. By the 1830s new interest groups espoused the common school cause: businessmen, as Michael Katz has demonstrated, saw it as a capitalist adjuvant delivering properly disciplined workers to the factory. Workingmen's groups viewed education as a passport to the middle class—or at least a protection from any downward slide in social and economic status.[21] Like all prescriptions, such appeals should not be confused with actual conditions. Nevertheless the persistent commitment to education reveals the widespread expectation that schools (more so than any other institution) would provide training in political deportment.

## *Schooling as Civic Training: Practice*

Amid such conscious efforts to link school and society, American history emerged as essential subject matter. "Not teaching U.S. histo-

[19]For an excerpted version of Knox's plan, see Cohen, *Education in the United States,* 2: 776–80; Tyack, *Turning Points,* p. 89; Frederick Rudolph, ed., *Essays on Education in the Early Republic* (Cambridge, Mass: Harvard University Press, Belknap, 1965), pp. 271–372; Samuel Knox, *Discourse on the Present State of Education in Maryland Delivered before the Honorable General Assembly* (Baltimore, 1808); Hansen, *Liberalism and American Education,* pp. 110–36, 139–60. For the quotation from Jefferson, Richardson, *Messages and Papers,* 1: 202.

[20]Messerli, "Columbian Complex," p. 424.

[21]Michael Katz, *The Irony of Early School Reform* (Cambridge, Mass.: Harvard Univer-

ry," explained the editor of the *American Annals of Education and Instruction* in 1832, "is a little like going into a foreign market with a curious collection of ancient coins, but without any circulating currency of the country."[22] Although educators increasingly complained about the amount of attention given the classics—such studies supposedly squandered time better spent on the United States—they nonetheless found in ancient Rome a society that appreciated the didactic importance of history.[23]

Early views of pedagogy reinforced the importance of history to the nation's political culture. Most nineteenth-century Americans believed that children's cognitive development depended on the exercise of memory, which, like a muscle, strengthened with use. Later the influence of object teaching challenged this conception of learning as a mnemonic process. Certainly Jean Piaget did so in the twentieth century. But in the first part of the nineteenth century most Americans held the recall of data to be the proper way to teach children, and with only a few exceptions such as Joseph Neef's Philadelphia school, this approach was universally applied. No better subject existed for such purposes than history, which, by furnishing a never-ending source of facts to be remembered, provided material for recitations. "History," a disgruntled American follower of the Swiss educator Pestalozzi complained, "is a mere thread to string dates and events on"—a judgment with which nineteenth-century children would probably have agreed.[24] A typical catechism on the American Revolution proceeded with the following questions and answers:

> Q. What victory soon followed that at Trenton?
> A. The battle of Princeton [3 January].
> Q. Who commanded the Americans at Princeton?
> A. Washington.
> Q. Where did Washington pass the winter, in the beginning of 1777?
> A. At Morristown, New Jersey.
> Q. Where was the Battle of Brandywine fought?
> A. At Chad's Ford on Brandywine Creek in the southeastern part of Pennsylvania.[25]

---

sity Press, 1968); Rush Welter, *Popular Education and Democratic Thought in America* (New York: Columbia University Press, 1962), pp. 45–72.

[22] *American Annals of Education and Instruction* 2 (January 1832): 2.

[23] Ibid.

[24] *Academican*, 10 July 1819, p. 322; Gideon Hawley, *Instructions for the Better Government and Organization of Common Schools* (Albany: Websters and Skinners, 1819); quotation from *New York Teacher* 7 (April 1858). p. 293.

[25] James Monteith, *Youth's History of the United States Designed for Intermediate Classes in Public and Private Schools* (New York: A. S. Barnes, 1858), p. 35.

History was also admired for its didactic qualities: its heroic homiletics could inspire the young with examples of duty and service to country; it could present for emulation the lives of national leaders—particularly that of George Washington—and with proper handling its chronologies could display the progress of the nation. Most important, it could teach future citizens "the price of liberty"—the cost in personal suffering and sacrifice necessary to create—and, by implication, maintain—the republic.[26] Typically, notions of national uniqueness pervaded such thinking. Not only did early Americans believe they had created a new era whose origins needed telling, but because they knew their beginnings (unlike other societies, in which, according to Madison, "the infant periods are buried in silence and veiled in fable"), they must explain their past for the edification of others. As an example of their exceptionality, "the origin and outset of the American Republic contains lessons of which posterity ought not to be deprived."[27]

Throughout these educational prescriptions ran the theme that American history must be made interesting. Although it did not matter how pupils felt about geometric theorems or the rivers of India, it was essential that they love their country and that its study inspire affection. To accomplish this, most authors of early history books included anecdotal, biographical, and local materials chosen to foster such sentiments. In 1856, John Jay wrote to Horatio Seymour: "There is nothing like commencing with the foundation. The school is the place for implanting correct knowledge and true principles and our children will take kindly to a volume [of New York history] containing so much to kindle their patriotic pride and affection for our noble state and by association to strengthen their attachment to the soil." Seymour responded with *A Lecture on the Topography and History of New York;* similarly dedicated authors wrote "vivacious" histories full of biography and local color.[28] Samuel Goodrich was especially adroit at this; his 170 separate titles—which included the Peter Parley Series—sold 22 million

[26]For typical views on the importance of history in early education, see *American Journal of Education* 3 (January 1828): 148; *North American Review* vols. 8 (March 1818): 420 and 22 (January 1826): 220; *American Annals of Education and Instruction* 2 (January 1832): 2; Gerald Danzer, "America's Roots in the Past: Historical Publication in America," (Ph.D. dissertation, Northwestern University, 1967).

[27][James Madison], *Letters and Other Writings of James Madison,* 4 vols. (New York: R. Worthington, 1884), 3: 140.

[28]John Jay to Horatio Seymour, 25 April 1856, Horatio Seymour Papers, New York Historical Society, New York City. For exhortations to write interesting history, see *American Journal of Education* 3 (November 1828): 672; Noah Webster, "On the Education of Youth in America" in Tyack, *Turning Points,* pp. 97–98; Lambert Lilly, *The History of the Middle States* (Boston: William Ticknor, 1844), ii.

copies, and an admiring President Fillmore concluded that Goodrich had done more than any other American "to infuse information."[29]

Gradually schools included American history in their curriculums. By 1813 Phillips Academy offered American history in its literature department, as did the famous Boston Latin School. But generally the acceptance of a new subject—unfamiliar to teachers, unknown in English schools, and unaccompanied by the texts necessary for recitation—was slow. In 1810 most schoolboys in prestigious northern academies still read Hume and Goldsmith, and even after the War of 1812 American history was taught from English texts. In the nation's few colleges, American history remained an afterthought, relegated, as at Harvard, to Saturday afternoons.

Not until the 1830s did the increased school population, an expansive nationalism, and the installation of history in state systems inspire a profitable enterprise—the writing, publishing, and selling of textbooks,[30] accompanied by that uniquely American feature, the teacher's manual. Popularizers who lacked Richard Hildreth's grasp of events or George Bancroft's ability to procure documents from European archives rewrote these secondary sources into their own versions of the past. Plagiarism was common, and because this generation lacked any sense of historical relativity, it anticipated a uniform version of the past. Hence to copy from another author was not stealing, but was considered "parallelism" and "imitation." John Marshall cribbed from William Gordon; Marcius Willson (who pleaded similar sources and "stereotyped instances") plagiarized Emma Williard; and everyone appropriated Bancroft—who was himself dependent on Edmund Burke's *Annual Register*.[31]

[29]Samuel G. Goodrich, *The Tales of Peter Parley about America* (1827; reprint, New York: Garland, 1977); idem, *The First Book of History for Children and Youth* (Boston: Jenks, Palmer, 1849); Daniel Roselli, *Samuel Griswold Goodrich, Creator of Peter Parley: A Study of his Life and Work* (Albany: State University of New York Press, 1968); S. R. Hall, *The Child's Assistant to a Knowledge of the Geography and History of Vermont* (Montpelier: E. P. Walton, 1829).

[30] Gerald Danzer has described the development of publishing houses and distribution outlets which accompanied the writing of textbooks; "America's Roots," p. 188. See also George Callcott, *History in the United States: Its Practice and Purpose* (Baltimore: Johns Hopkins University Press, 1970), pp. 55–65.

[31]Marcius Willson, *A Reply to Mrs. Willard's Appeal* (New York: Mark H. Newman, 1847); Callcott, *History in the United States,* pp. 134–38; Orin G. Libby, "Ramsay as a Plagiarist," *American Historical Review* 7 (July 1902): 697–703; William Foran, "John Marshall as a Historian," *American Historical Review* 43 (October 1937): 51–64; Alfred Goldberg, "School Histories of the Middle Period," in *Historiography and Urbanization: Essays in American History in Honor of W. Stull Holt,* ed. Eric Goldman (Baltimore: Johns Hopkins University Press, 1941), p. 176.

As a result a standard version of national history emerged by the 1840s, and the different books that children brought from home were interchangeable. Influenced in a narrow sense by Bancroft's *History of the United States from the Discovery of the Continent* but more generally by the political environment of which they were a part, authors focused on the revolution. It became the centerpiece of a story taught thousands of northern school children.[32] Even when authors charted American chronology, they routinely gave disproportionate emphasis to the years 1770–1783. Emma Willard used 124 of 364 pages to cover the revolution, and most of these were devoted to battles. Like Bancroft, who acknowledged that his preoccupation with "the struggle for liberty had destroyed the proper symmetry of his volumes," Marcius Willson and S. R. Hall also concentrated on the revolution. They included in their catechisms the hardships of the Americans, hoping thereby "to enhance the affection"of future generations for the government that warranted such suffering.[33] On the assumption that tales of easy victory would never inspire lives of hard devotion, most textbooks gloried in the "suffering and death of our martyred spirited forefathers—the blood and treasure they sacrificed."[34] To the question what was the climate of 1776, children recited from William Grimshaw's *History of the United States,* "a gloomy season of adversity."[35] In such accounts, the English were so often cast as villains that British visitors complained about their mistreatment in American history. Wrote James Burn:

> Many of our worst Kings and nobles are exhibited in the darkest phases of their characters, and held up as types of their class. If the American instructors of youth in their desire to furnish useful historical lessons had used the

[32]Chauncey D. Jacobs, "The Development of School Textbooks in United States History from 1795 to 1885" (Ph.D. dissertation, University of Pittsburgh, 1939), pp. 58–170; Reverend Enoch Pond, *The Autobiography of the Rev. Enoch Pond* (Boston: Copperhead Sunday School and Publishing Society, 1883), p. 7; O. E. Klingaman, "Textbook Legislation in Iowa," *Iowa History and Politics* 13 (January 1915): 63; Emma Willard, *History of the United States, or, Republic of America Continued to the Close of the Mexican War* (New York: A. S. Barnes, 1849).

[33]Alice Winifred Spreseke, *The First Textbooks in American History* (New York: Bureau of Publications, Teachers College, Columbia University, 1938); Willard, *History;* Marcius Willson, *American History* (New York: Ivison, Phinney, Blakeman, 1856); Samuel R. Hall and A. R. Baker, *School History of the United States* (Andover, Mass.: W.Pierce, 1839); George Bancroft, *History of the United States from the Discovery of the Continent,* vol. 9 (Boston: Little, Brown, 1866), p. 4.

[34]E. C. Wines, *Hints on a System of Popular Education* (Philadelphia: Hogan and Thompson, 1838), p. 88.

[35]William Grimshaw, *History of the United States from First Settlement as Colonies to the Period of the Sixth Census in 1840* (Philadelphia: Grigg and Elliot, 1847), p. 132.

same freedom with Bible history as they have done with that of Great Britain, I think they would have found very few whose lives could be held up as examples for young Americans to follow.[36]

The reason for such criticism went beyond anglophobia or even the unity achieved by hating a common enemy. Intent on producing a serviceable past, writers created polarized images in which free religion in the United States was contrasted with state churches in Europe; republican vigor in the New World with autocratic decay in the Old; monarchy in England with democracy in America. Given the public reasons for learning history, objectivity only cluttered themes best transmitted to the young in sharp, pictorial terms, as occurred in the period's most frequently reproduced line drawing, that of a noble George Washington and a treacherous Benedict Arnold. Without official direction a homogeneous version of national history spontaneously emerged, and this one-sided treatment of past events furnished pre–Civil War schoolboys with a model of proper civic conduct.[37]

George Washington was the central figure in this national history, and both anthologies of oratory and readers included his Farewell Address. Many also provided a biographical section in which the first president emerged as dutiful son, loyal husband, lovable father to his country, and reluctant but effective commander of its revolutionary forces. Thus nineteenth-century children first encountered their government through a personable leader who exemplified correct civic behavior. Parson Weems's legend of the cherry tree was only one of several anecdotes conveying the importance of integrity and self-discipline. As portrayed by textbook writers, Washington displayed the restraint required in a self-governing society, and the emphasis on his sacrifice of private interest, his perseverance amid hardship at Valley Forge, and his lifelong ability to subdue his own passions and "hold them in subjection to reason" provided a forceful model of the ideal American citizen.[38]

Preoccupied with military history and the life of Washington, schoolbooks avoided other periods and topics. Some of this neglect reflected a fear of distorting events by being too close to them. In 1826 the *North*

[36]James Burn, *Three Years among the Working Classes* (London: Smith, Elder, 1856), p. 171.

[37]J. Merton England, "The Democratic Faith in American Schoolbooks," *American Quarterly* 15 (Summer 1963): 191–99; Ruth Elson, *Guardians of Tradition: American Schoolbooks of the Nineteenth Century* (Lincoln: University of Nebraska Press, 1964).

[38]For examples, see Goodrich, *Tales of Peter Parley*. The quotation from Grimshaw, *History of the United States*, p. 107.

*American Review* speculated whether "enough time had passed" to write modern history, "to bring facts to light and to soften down the rough aspects of events and divest them of passion and partiality."[39] As late as the 1850s, schoolbooks shunned the postrevolutionary period; James Monteith's catechism, for example, devoted over a hundred questions to the revolution but dispatched the administrations of Madison, Monroe, Jackson, and Van Buren with four. Abridged versions of William Grimshaw's popular history never mentioned Monroe, Adams, and Van Buren.[40] Such historical astigmatism served two ends: it permitted more attention to be given to the military events considered inspirational for young children, and it solved a difficult interpretative problem. If U.S. history was a providentially directed progression toward liberty and freedom, and if the revolution had already instilled these ideals through its model government, then later events were superfluous. Accordingly, disputes among nineteenth-century Americans might signal a decline in republican virtue, but such pessimism was hardly appropriate for schoolboys, who needed to be instructed in public excellence—what Willard called "the mental sublime of the character of their fathers."[41] Hence the typical pre–Civil War history concentrated on the nation's progress from discovery to the writing of the Constitution.

Those writers who did extend their histories into the nineteenth century replaced domestic history with accounts of the nation's wars, when, united against an enemy, Americans retrieved their patriotism. Careful studies of early textbooks disclose the extent of this preoccupation with military history. According to Chauncey Jacobs, nearly half of the texts published from 1795 to 1860 were devoted to war, with the most bellicose author, the Reverend T. F. Gordon, lavishing 6 of every 10 pages on battles.[42] For the postrevolutionary years, the percentages are higher. Emma Willard allotted 77 of 124 pages covering the period 1800–1848 to American military adventures with the Indians, the English, the deys of North Africa, and the Mexicans. John Frost devoted 3 pages to the internal affairs of Madison's administration and 40 to the War of 1812.[43] Nor was war portrayed as hell; in these early textbooks,

[39]*North American Review* 22 (January 1826): 220.

[40]Monteith, *Youth's History of the United States;* Grimshaw, *History of the United States,* idem, *An Exposition of the Situation, Character, and Interests of the American Republic Absolute and Relative* (Philadelphia, 1847).

[41]Willard, *History,* p. iv.

[42]Jacobs, "Development of School Textbooks," p. 88; Elson, *Guardians of Tradition,* pp. 327–32.

[43]Willard, *History;* John Frost, *A History of the United States for Use of the Common Schools* (Philadelphia: Edward C. Biddle, 1837).

its hardship and sacrifice were redeemed through glory and service to the nation.

Skewed as to time and subject, textbooks neglected domestic controversies. Less harmonious moments from the nation's past—such as the Whisky and Shay's rebellions—were included by some authors as examples of bad conduct. Like the Hessian troops whom Bancroft's God punished for fighting against the Americans during the revolution, these "mobs of insurgents and malcontents" were benevolently dealt with by a just government. Such incidents, according to Willard, must be brought to the attention of "youthful hearts," but unlike good deeds, which "kindled into desires of imitation," they should be only briefly mentioned—the result given, not the details.[44]

Political parties, if mentioned at all in early schoolbooks, were described as vehicles of passion and intemperance; with only their results discussed, presidential elections emerged as a spontaneous expression of the people's will—a republican parthenogenesis unattended by contentious parties. It was the peaceful transfer of power that textbooks emphasized. "The people," explained John Frost of Jefferson's and Jackson's victories, "regarded the change in their executive with very little solicitude." Some authors specifically condemned political parties, thus transmitting antipartyism. According to Emma Willard, "Congress showed how little party spirit cares for the public good." But William Grimshaw was more typical; he avoided party politics by arranging his text around the decadal census rather than presidential administrations, explaining his omission as a "willing exclusion."[45]

In time, authors included information about federal and state governments as well as catechisms based on the U.S. Constitution. Marcius Willson sought to introduce young boys "to the principles and practical operation of our republican institutions," but, like William Sullivan, the author of *The Political Class Book,* he spent more time proclaiming "the moral dignity of our federal representative system" than explaining it.[46] As with American history, imitation—in this case of Francis Wayland's 1837 *Elements of Political Economy*—expedited the

[44]Emma Willard, *History of the United States, or, Republic of America* (New York: A. S. Barnes, 1844), pp. v–vi.

[45]Frost, *History for Common Schools,* p. 304; Willard, *History,* (1844 ed.) p. 269; Grimshaw, *History of United States,* p. 138.

[46]Marcius Willson, *A Treatise on Civil Polity and Political Economy* (New York: J. O. Taylor, 1838); William Sullivan, *The Political Class Book Intended to Instruct the Higher Classes in Schools in the Origin, Nature, and Use of Political Power* (Boston: Richardson, Lord, and Holbrook, 1830); Robert Patton, *A Lecture, On Classical and National Education* (Princeton: D. A. Berrenstein, 1826), p. 6; E. D. Mansfield, *The Political Grammar of the United States* (New York: Harper Brothers, 1834).

creation of a standard interpretation of "the science of politics." And because they were traversing uncertain territory, authors self-consciously claimed impartiality. "On the subjects of party controversy," wrote Andrew Young, "[I] have withheld the expression of [my] opinions, deeming it best to leave the unconfirmed politician to the exercise of his own unbiased judgment in forming his conclusions."[47] Such an approach guaranteed that children would learn the virtues of America, but it also assured little understanding of its weaknesses or of the ways in which public differences were resolved.

Typical of the readings for younger children were Noah Webster's widely used spellers and geographies. They contained a "federal catechism," in which teacher queried student on the principles of government. Thousands of young Americans were indoctrinated in the merits of their political system by chanting Webster's litany:

> Question: What are the peculiar advantages of representative governments?
>
> Answer: . . . the great security of such a government is that the men who make laws are to be governed by them; so that they are not apt to do wrong wilfully. When men make laws for themselves, as well as for their neighbors, they are led by their own interest to make good laws.[48]

By the 1860s, generations of northern schoolboys had absorbed a standard view of American history and government, and their cognitive perceptions in turn framed public values, attitudes, and behavior. There were variations in this information. Not only did Americans differ in their levels of training, but also in regional, religious, and ethnic emphases. A few had read Joseph Story's *Commentaries on the Constitution* and Bancroft's *History;* others had not gone beyond the first Peter Parley readers. Naturalized citizens often did not attend American schools at all, and in some frontier communities only one of every three school-age boys in the 1850s was enrolled in school. In any case the amount of factual material retained from memorized recitations is unknown, and if school reformers of the 1840s were correct, little endured from a process in which imagination and inquiry were discouraged. But regardless of the depth and length of students' exposure or the deficiencies of pedagogical technique, American images, values, and symbols

[47]Andrew Young, *The American Statesman: A Political History* (New York: J. C. Derby, 1855), p. iv.

[48]Noah Webster, *The American Spelling Book* (Boston: Isaiah Thomas and Ebenezer Andrews, 1790), pp. 154–55.

were uniform. A homogeneous message—simultaneously the product and fabricator of nineteenth-century political culture—conveyed the sense of a martial nation susceptible to military engagements fought by citizens, not by professionals. America's most heroic times had occurred on the battlefield, although the personalized image of Washington linked the young to a benign government. Finally, because liberty, union, and Constitution had been accomplished at great sacrifice, the "world's best government" merited keeping.

## *Hidden Agendas*

Schoolbooks and recitation were not the only ways in which young boys learned how to be Americans. Also imbedded in classroom activities—in a student's expected conduct toward a teacher, in the community's attitude toward schools, in the relation of students to one another, and even in the spatial details of the classroom—were various arrangements that conveyed political culture; and, just as didactic literature gave formal expression to the requisite values of democratic citizens, so this hidden curriculum transmitted public habits. Recently historians have focused on the ways in which schooling trained nineteenth-century Americans to become industrial workers, but this influence was not restricted to economic behavior. Latent school agendas also taught young Northerners how to be Americans.[49]

Some schoolmasters were aware of this hidden curriculum and went beyond the formal substance of political learning to explore its effects on their students. The most perceptive was Enoch C. Wines, whose numerous pamphlets on education were the pedagogical counterparts of William Alcott's behavior manuals. Convinced that learning was more than the transmission of facts or the memorization of details, Wines defined education as everything from marble games and ballroom dancing to the internal dynamics of the schoolroom. "I under-

[49]Recently there has been a shift in educational history from the study of formal pedagogy and institutional arrangements to an analysis of education as the transmission of values and attitudes. See, for example, Samuel Bowles and Herbert Gintis, *Schooling in Capitalist America: Educational Reform and the Contradictions of Economic Life* (New York: Basic Books, 1976); Carl Kaestle, *The Evolution of an Urban School System, New York, 1750–1850* (Cambridge, Mass.: Harvard University Press, 1973); Michael Katz, *Class, Bureaucracy, and Schools: The Illusion of Educational Change in America* (New York: Praeger, 1971); Philip W. Jackson, *Life in the Classrooms* (New York:Holt, Rinehart and Winston, 1968); Robert Dreeben, *On What Is Learned in School* (Reading, Mass.: Addison-Wesley, 1968); Kenneth Langton and M. Kent Jennings, "Political Socialization and the High School Civics Curriculum in the United States," *American Political Science Review* 62 (September 1968): 852–67.

stand by education," wrote the New Jersey schoolmaster in 1838, "contact with each other, by business, by newspapers, and circulating libraries, lyceums, public meetings, and conventions, speeches in Congress, in state legislatures—in churches, halls of education, popular assemblies, theatres, race courses, barrooms, the very streets of our cities." Later, Wines linked schooling, culture, and national character: "The mysticism of Egypt, the courage of Sparta, the disputatious subtlety of Attica, the high honour and commanding influence of the early Persians and the military spirit of the Romans may be traced to the schools of these several nations, as of controlling influence in producing the predominant traits of their respective national characters."[50]

The point was clear: the United States must replicate its government within its schools, for, sufficiently developed, the latter would define its political culture. According to Wines, teachers, like political leaders, must establish an authority based on a combination of moral influence and physical force, to which schoolchildren would submit in exactly the same way and for the same reasons that citizens of the republic did. In a directive that might have served constitutional conventions, Wines advised teachers to "avoid the multiplication of trifling rules, seize upon principles as comprehensive as possible. Establish your authority upon a firm basis and require invariable obedience." Pupils, like adult Americans, would "freely submit to a government founded in reason and administered with firmness, consistency and perfect impartiality." In his own classroom, Wines introduced such "reasonability" by means of contracts, negotiation, and even student petitions.[51] But the prerogatives of self-government did not extend to unrestricted majority rule any more than the Constitution did. Unlike Joseph Neef, the Alsatian-born follower of Pestalozzi, Wines did not permit students to have a veto power, and although he did not hesitate to flog "rebellious" students who had committed "treason," he nevertheless delegated considerable responsibility.[52]

Using political images, Wines concluded that the power of the teacher must be absolute, like a sovereign's, and he compared his authority to that of the federal government with its muskets at Springfield and Harper's Ferry:

[50]E. C. Wines, *How Shall I Govern My School? Addressed to Young Teachers* (Philadelphia: W. Marshall, 1838), p. 14; idem, *Hints on a System*, pp. 102, 158. See also idem, *Letters to Schoolchildren* (Boston: Marsh, Capen and Lea, 1839).

[51]Wines, *How Shall I Govern?* p. 41.

[52] Gerald Gutek, *Joseph Neef and the Americanization of Pestalozzianism* (University, Ala.: University of Alabama Press, 1978), p. 125.

> The United States employs its hundred of workmen at Springfield and at Harper's Ferry in the manufacture of muskets. A hundred thousand of these deadly instruments form a violence of slumbering power which has never been awakened. The government never makes use of them. One of its agents, a Custom House officer, waits upon a merchant for the payment of a bond. He brings no musket. He keeps no troops. He comes with the gentleness and civility of a social visit. But the merchant knows that if compliance with the just demand of his government is refused and resistance to it is sustained, force after force would be brought to bear upon him till the whole hundred thousand muskets should speak with their united and tremendous energy. The government of these United States is thus a tremendous engine, working with immense momentum; but the parts which bear upon the citizens conceal their power by the elegance of their workmanship and by the slowness and apparent gentleness of their motion. If you yield to it, it glides smoothly and pleasantly by; if you resist it, it crushes you to atoms.[53]

Other nineteenth-century educators linked the political behavior of the adult world and the hidden curriculum of classrooms, though few as fulsomely as the schoolmaster of Edgehill. Like Wines, most recognized that the internal environment of the nation's schools inculcated public behaviors along with supplying factual information about the political system. Their metaphorical language was suggestive: schools were governments, with teachers granted authority. But power must be reasonably applied in the classroom, and, as with government, the fewer the rules and the less capricious their application, the happier the classroom. To apply sanctions in a tyrannical fashion was to risk a subservient class, unable to made independent judgments and therefore unfit for the administration of government. America was not Turkey or Prussia, where the young might be subjected to brute force without political effect; to coerce unreasonably in a free society was no way to raise citizens. As a midwestern journal suggested, "If you will have republican men, you must have republican education."[54] But the other extreme was equally dangerous; a permissive classroom with no respect for authority encouraged tumult, anarchy, and a rebellious citizenry. Teachers who were too permissive often lost their pupils; in fact some of Joseph Neef's students were uncomfortable with his egalitarian notions of teachers as "playfellows and messmates." Wrote one: "There existed between Neef and his pupils a freedom so great as to be some-

[53]Wines, *How Shall I Govern?* p. 50.
[54]*Transactions of the Ohio College of Teachers* 1(1835): 5.

times, I fear, slightly inconsistent with good breeding or the deference due from pupil to teacher."[55] As in government, ideal management involved using moral influence to inspire a sense of spontaneous allegiance. "The schoolroom," wrote a New York teacher, "is a peculiarly appropriate place to teach respect for the rights of others. The little community here assembled contains all of the great community without."[56]

Throughout these earnest prescriptions ran a common theme: misused authority was a failure of self-government by the schoolmaster and a dangerous example for schoolboys learning to subdue their passions and instincts. Ideal behavior for politician, teacher, citizen, and schoolboy required mastery over self—a control based on individual restraint and a denial of selfish passion. "Those whose feelings are properly trained," explained a New York educator, "are always good citizens. We have enough of laws; now let us train some men for the laws." "Passions are to be regulated into proper discipline for self-command, social order, and regular subjection," wrote William Woodridge of the educational ideals that inspired his prizewinning schoolhouse design.[57] The best schools, agreed Hiram Orcutt, were those in which power was "not visible" and in which teachers could leave the room without the class's lapsing into disorder. In such schools pupils had learned the self-government necessary for "miniature men soon to control the affairs of state." They had gone beyond the "commands and prohibitions regarding what they may or may not do . . . and had been taught that, as ere long as it is theirs to determine in reference to their conduct in life with no parents' and teacher's watchful eye or warning voice to approve or encourage them in the right or deter them from the wrong, then they

[55]The quotation from Gutek, *Joseph Neef,* p. 25. The literature on this point is extensive and repetitious, and this paragraph summarizes a number of prescriptive writings from manuals and educational periodicals before the Civil War. See, for example, *American Journal of Education,* vols. 3 (June 1828): 380 and 4 (January 1829): 75–77; *American Annals of Education and Instruction,* vols. 2 (January 1832): 90 and 4 (April 1834): 167; *New York Teacher,* vols. 8 (November 1858): 68, 156; 12 (May 1863): 285; 13 (May 1864): 295; and 13 (October 1864): 331; Arthur D. Wright and George Gardner, eds., *Samuel Read Hall's Lectures on School Keeping* (Hanover, N. H.: Dartmouth Press, 1929); Wines, *Letters to Schoolchildren,* pp. 23, 147; Frederick Jewell, *School Government: A Practical Treatise* (New York: A. S. Barnes, 1866); John Griscom, *Monitorial Instruction: An Address Pronounced at the Opening of the New York High School* (New York: M. Day, 1825); Alfred Holbrook, *Lecture on School Management* (Lebanon, O: Josiah Holbrook, 1871).

[56]*New York Teacher* 8 (November 1858): 64.

[57]Ibid., vols 15 (October 1865): 35; 16 (February 1867): 155; and 12 (June 1863): 291; William Woodridge, *On the Construction of Schoolrooms* (Boston: Hilliard, Gray, Little and Wilkes, 1832), p. 6.

should accustom themselves to consider what is right and proper under the circumstances."[58]

Teachers who had not conquered their own impulses were the ones who hurled ferules and precipitated either disorder or, at the other extreme, the silent classroom in which brute tyranny had won the day. But government by moral persuasion was not always easy. "I feared," wrote one anguished young teacher, "that if I conquered [a rebellious student] I would be the conquered party."[59]

## *Inside the Classroom*

It was a long way from this advice literature to the northern classrooms of the early nineteenth century. Although many observers acknowledged schools as an entity shaping public life, the institutions themselves were neither universal nor homogeneous. They ranged, by the 1840s, from the nearly extinct dame schools organized by impecunious widows and unmarried women to the prestigious Latin schools where sons of wealthy city merchants studied the classical curriculum necessary for admission to America's handful of colleges. Over the years community-funded systems had superseded informal arrangements, and by the Civil War the private schoolmaster who recruited students had disappeared, replaced by a trustee-approved instructor. Moreover, there were substantial differences between district schools of fifty pupils and Lancastrian schools of nearly a thousand. Some Northern institutions were coeducational; others were single-sex; some were supported by local property taxes, others by private fees, and a few by rates based on parents' income. In the newer states of the West, many children went to a neighbor's home, others to a log house. Some states had constitutional provisions establishing public systems. Others depended on county and township laws to which, in many cases, officials paid little attention. Schools themselves often varied according to the season. What might be in summer a relaxed custodial center supervised by a kindly young woman often became, in winter, a formal institution presided over by a punctilious male disciplinarian.[60] Nor did all Ameri-

[58]Hiram Orcutt, *Reminiscences of School Life* (Cambridge, Mass.: The University Press, 1898), pp. 51, 58, 172.

[59]A Gentleman, *Remarks upon the Art of Teaching and Learning* (Boston: Thomas Badger, 1822); Frederick Adolphus Packard, *The Daily Public School in the United States* (New York: Arno Press, 1969), p. 17.

[60]Warren Burton, *The District School as It Was,* (Boston:Phillips, Sampson, 1850), pp. 17–35; Peter Soderbergh "Mary Payne Beard's Letters," *History of Education Quarterly* 7 (Winter 1968): 497–503; Winifred McGuinn Howard, "The Census of 1840," *Palimpsest* 21 (June 1940): 177.

cans attend school; some, like Ohioan Alfred Holbrook, studied at home; a greater number spent their days in apprenticeships, their evenings in night schools, and their Saturdays in so-called half-schools.

Gradually, however, a standard version of Northern schooling developed until, according to one optimistic education manual, every Northern state had a creditable school system based on the district school. In 1840 a majority of Northern children from ages five to nineteen were enrolled in either private or public schools, and in many communities the figures ran as high as 75 percent, with males—the essential group in supervising the nation's political culture—outnumbering females in the early grades. Not only did the length of the school year increase (by mid-century rural schools were open five months of the year, urban schools eight); the average student's daily attendance also improved. By the time of the Civil War, primary schools had thus become the essential institution in teaching children to be Americans.[61]

Whether Lancastrian or Pestalozzian, common or secondary, district or academy, English or Latin, Presbyterian or Methodist, rate, free, or charity, Northern schools had similar internal arrangements for instructing young boys in American values. In their preoccupation with external variations, historians have sometimes neglected these internal similarities, such as the use of student assistants and monitors, the lack of age-grading, the inconsistent postures toward authority, and the physical environment of the classroom. Such mechanisms inducted young Americans into their national political culture, and although the expectations of educational theorists like Rush, Knox, and Washington for a uniform system were not achieved, their aim was served by this universally applied hidden curriculum. Like moons, American schools reflected community goals, but like the sun, they diffused political culture by educating future citizens in their civic roles. And if uniformity within the classroom was any test, there was broad agreement on the matter of training future citizens.

For the observer of political culture, the most significant mechanism was the use of students in positions of authority. Primarily associated with Lancastrian schools, monitors—students who served in an official

[61]John Folger and Charles B. Nam, *Education of the American Population,* (Washington, D.C.: U.S. Bureau of the Census, 1967), pp. 3–5: Carl Kaestle and Maris A. Vinovskis, *Education and Social Change in Nineteenth-Century Massachusetts,* (New York: Oxford University Press, 1980); Alfred Holbrook, *Reminiscences of the Happy Life of a Teacher* (Cincinnati: Elm Street Printing, 1871); Barbara Finkelstein, "Governing the Young: Teacher Behavior in American Primary Schools, 1820–1880: A Documentary History" (Ph.D. Dissertation, Columbia University, 1970), p. 134.

capacity—were to be found in nearly all northern schools. Joseph Lancaster gave the most explicit statement of their duties:

> To promote emulation, and facilitate learning, the whole school is arranged into classes, and a monitor appointed to each class. A class consists of any number of boys whose proficiency is on a par. These may all be classed and taught together. If the class is small, one monitor may teach it; if large it may still continue the same class, but with more or less assistant monitors, who under the direction of the principal monitor are to teach subdivisions of the class. . . . In teaching the boys to print the alphabet, the monitor first makes a letter on the sand, before any who knows nothing about it; the boy is then required to retrace over the same letter which the monitor has made for him with his fingers.[62]

Armed with an extensive patronage system of money, toys, and food, monitors not only heard recitations but also gave out rewards, assisted in discipline, helped younger children with their handwriting, stoked the fire, made and repaired quill pens, supervised from prominently arranged desks, and conveyed student problems to the teacher. Their term of office was at the pleasure of the schoolmaster who had picked them; sometimes an automatic rotation took place within a specific group. As Lancaster explained, "Though he [a monitor] may be one minute a commander, yet he feels no hesitation in yielding the most prompt and decided obedience to another. When he retires to his seat as a private member of his class, he is succeeded by another."[63] Despite the transience of power, boys (girls were never monitors in coeducational schools) aspired to such prestigious posts, where they were distinguished by the special badges, chains, and stars they wore as well as by the power they wielded.

Most teachers in a system lacking sufficient personnel found the mechanism useful. In one Boston school during the 1830s three schoolmasters presided over 1,547 students, and in the 1850s the city's 164 primary school teachers supervised 11,000 pupils. Even in rural schools with smaller numbers of students, the diversity of tasks and range of ages made monitors a welcomed addition. Because teachers "kept" schools before 1840, neither interpreting nor explaining material, proficient young males filled roles of authority and prestige with ease.[64]

[62]Joseph Lancaster, *The Lancastrian System of Education with Improvements* (Baltimore: privately published, 1821), p. 6.

[63]Ibid.

[64]Michael B. Katz, *Education in American History: Readings on the Social Issues* (New York: Praeger, 1973), p. 18; idem, *Class, Bureaucracy, and Schools*, p. 60; Josiah Quincy, *An*

One reason for Lancaster's instant success in the early nineteenth century was that many American schools already used his techniques. His appeals for cheap mass education on a nonsectarian basis meshed with the needs of a growing nation, and an early poll of Massachusetts schoolteachers revealed that most were familiar with his system in practice, if not theory. In some schools, monitors were called preceptors, in others tutors or assistants. But as Edward Everett reported, even in rural schools "special" boys held official responsibilities such as procuring wood, tending the all-important fire, making pens, as well as teaching. The pervasiveness of mutual instruction was illustrated in one. Sent "to spell" another student who was cutting firewood, a New Hampshire boy promptly took on a monitor's role and, instead of replacing his toiling classmate, heard his spelling lesson.[65]

For the student of political culture, the significance of monitors rests with the delegation of powers to pupils who performed official functions, who wielded authority based on coercion as well as persuasion, and who competed for their position. Chosen from the student body because of their achievement and obedience as well as their skill at ingratiation, monitors served as models for their fellows, who could simultaneously aspire to such honorific posts and observe authority exerted by an equal. Even the rewards monitors dispensed were reminiscent of political patronage; certainly the system acquainted young Americans with the repertoire of roles they would meet as citizens, including shared officeholding, rotation in office, and representation by untrained officials. After 1860, reformers, intent on training teachers who could interpret and explain subject matter, sought to replace monitors with professionals. But the use of student assistants survived beyond the Civil War, and this unique arrangement introduced thousands

---

*Address to the Board of Alderman and Members of the Common Council on the Organization of City Government* (Boston, 1828), p. 10. For figures on class size, see *Report of the Social Committee of the City of Boston on the State of the Schools, May 1826* (Boston, 1826); and "Monitorial System," *American Annals of Education and Instruction* 1 (February 1831): 135–40. For a perceptive description of the process by a well-known nineteenth-century educator, see Francis Wayland, *A Memoir of the Life and Labors of Francis Wayland* (New York: Sheldon, 1867), pp. 23–24.

[65]Burton, *District School,* pp. 89–91. For other applications of the monitorial system in non-Lancastrian schools, see William Alcott, *Confessions of a Schoolmaster* (Andover, Mass.: Gould, Newman and Saxton, 1839), p. 58; Walter Herbert Small, *Early New England Schools* (Boston: Ginn, 1914), p. 263; Lawrence Cremin, *The American Common School, an Historic Conception* (New York: Bureau of Publications, Teachers College, Columbia University, 1951), pp. 187–88; *Report of a Sub-Committee, Recommending Various Improvements in the System of Instruction in the Grammar and Writing Schools of this City* (Boston, 1828), p. 10.

of Northerners to the structure of leadership in a republican society.[66]

Northern schools also had similar internal environments. Externally there was wide variation: an "unpainted drab leaky edifice" in New Hampshire; a substantial brick building with a "commodious garden" in Massachusetts; a basement in a New York church; and a log cabin with an earth floor and no windows in Franklin County, Indiana. But whatever the exterior of their building, children learned their lessons in one large common room that varied in size from the typical 15-by-20-foot district school to the huge 150-by-75-foot schoolrooms in larger towns and cities.[67] Only in the 1840s did the idea of separate places for recitation develop, and even then children still spent most of their time in the same room. As late as 1830 William Alcott, anxious to improve schools by providing better air circulation, retained the traditional common room in his prizewinning design. Typically, this was one rectangular space with two doors, a chimney at one end, and small raised windows—usually shuttered or covered with broken glass or paper. In any case it was against the rules to look outside. Schoolchildren, arranged on long hickory, walnut, and pine benches or seated at separate (though connected) desks, turned inward. What they saw, heard, touched—and doubtless smelled—in their allotted five or six square feet of space was their neighbor.[68] There was little privacy amid the constant activity of such surroundings. But these serried ranks were often broken, when groups of children took their places in semicircles for recitation where they read, spelled, and summed aloud; as a result of proficiency in such exercises, pupils either gained or lost rank before the entire student body.

Although Lancastrian schools were renowned for the activity of their students, all schools fostered busyness, with a daily program based on

[66]Joseph Lancaster, *Improvements in Education as it Respects the Industrious Classes of the Community* (New York: Collins, 1804), pp. 18–19. See also idem, *The Practical Parts of Lancaster's Improvements and Bell's Experiment,* ed. David Salmon (Cambridge: Cambridge University Press, 1932); Carl Kaestle, ed., *Joseph Lancaster and the Monitorial School Movement: A Documentary History* (New York: Teachers College Press, 1973); James Carter, *Letters to William Prescott on the Free Schools of New England* (Boston: Cummings, Hill, Land, 1824).

[67]Burton, *District School,* pp. 12–13; Finkelstein, "Governing the Young," p. 242; Vera M. Butler, *Education as Revealed by New England Newspapers* (New York: Arno Press, 1969), p. 181: Michael Bossert, "Early Days of Franklin County," *Indiana Magazine of History* 26 (September 1930): 223. Evidently the little red schoolhouse was a fiction. Comtemporary descriptions make it clear that most schoolhouses were not painted at all. An early fictional reference occurs in Artemus Ward's "The Showman's Courtship": "blushin as red as the Baldinsville skool house when it was fust painted."

[68]William Alcott, *Essay on the Construction of School-House* (Boston: Hilliard, Gray, Little, and Wilkins, 1832); Holbrook, *Reminiscences;* Orcutt, *Reminiscences of School-Life,* pp. 14–15; Small, *Early New England Schools.*

participation. Punishments were community affairs, with work suspended for a public viewing of some fellow pupil's humiliation. In Stratham, New Hampshire, the names of those who had broken rules were entered in a "Black List or Book of Disgrace" and reported not only to parents but also to the school committee and selectmen.[69] Even when individual recitation in a separate room was possible, schooling was an open process, and the so-called loud schools, where collective recitations could be heard for miles, though not typical were symbolic of this collective arrangement. Many pupils recognized the communal aspect of their education and spoke, as did one New York boy, of a "common purpose and unity" in the classroom. Another felt as if he were part of a sea.[70] Given the communal atmosphere, it was natural to invite parents and local officials to recitations—a practice also employed in colleges. As the organizer of his local district school, Henry Van der Luyn soon found that his appearances at recitations took most of his free time, and after listening to endless school exercises, he reported that he knew the names of New York's sixty counties.[71]

Within this community there was no age-grading, and although students were arranged according to their individual proficiencies, such groups varied widely. In one Vermont school, a seventeen-year-old teacher instructed pupils from ages four to twenty-five. Even when classified according to ability, a reading group often included, as did John Badger's third class in a Vermont school, one five-, three six-, two seven-, one eleven-, and one twelve-, and one fourteen-year-old.[72] Respecting such diversity, early American textbooks made no effort to classify their materials into age grades.[73]

Later, Americans would separate pupils spatially and chronologically, but before they did, the pedagogical universe was a little community, its inhabitants what David Tyack has called "a tribe," and what a contemporary described as a "moral community with conforming sentiments."[74] This is not to say that all classes, races, or even sexes attended

[69]Burton, *District School,* p. 122; Finkelstein, "Governing the Young," p. 254; Holbrook, *Reminiscences,* p. 32; "Abstract of the Massachusetts School Returns," 1837, 1841–1842; Stratham, New Hampshire, Box of Miscellaneous Papers, Sturbridge Village Library, Sturbridge, Mass.

[70]Holbrook, *Reminiscences,* p. 249; Barbara Finkelstein, "Pedagogy as Intrusion; Teaching Values in Popular Primary Schools in Nineteenth-Century America," *History of Childhood Quarterly* 2 (Winter 1975): 361.

[71]Diary of Henry Van der Luyn, entry for 28 August 1831, Van der Luyn Papers, New York Historical Society (hereafter cited as Van der Luyn Papers).

[72]Finkelstein, "Governing the Young," p. 235.

[73]John Nietz, *Old Textbooks* (Pittsburgh: University of Pittsburgh Press, 1961), p. 150.

[74]David Tyack, "The Tribe and the Common School," *American Quarterly* 24 (March

the same schools. Neither equality of opportunity nor of condition characterized early classrooms. Girls, blacks, the very rich, and the very poor rarely sat side by side on the hardwood benches learning about each other. Nor were students encouraged to work together in groups. Instead, cheating—from the beginning of formal schooling the most heinous of academic sins—restricted collective learning and compelled individual attention to lessons.[75] Moreover, as the diaries of nineteenth-century schoolchildren indicate, there was considerable individual competition to be the best speller.

But the one-room environment did promote a sense of community, for, as Benjamin Rush explained, "young men who have trodden the paths of science together or have joined in the same sports . . . generally feel, thro' life, such ties to each other as add greatly to the obligations of mutual benevolence."[76] Even private academies were neighborhood ventures dependent upon the involvement of leading citizens and officials. Moreover, the competition between towns for pupils transformed these academies into something more than isolated private institutions. In the case of district schools, elected committees hired and fired teachers, set rules, and supervised financial affairs in a manner that linked public and private worlds. Later, a man's town, district, or county would become a larger likeness of the neighborhood he first experienced in the one-room schoolhouse.

Like all institutions, schools developed rituals that by the 1840s were so universal as to demonstrate the homogeneity of American education. At the end of each year parents and the district committee visited the classroom for a day of patriotic oratory. In most districts these celebrations extended beyond the schoolhouse. In Seneca Falls, New York, for instance, children annually paraded on "School Day," carrying banners emblazoned, in the 1850s, with "We believe in Progress"and "Russia depends on her bayonets, America on her common schools."[77] Encouraged by officials seeking community support, such festivals linked pupils to their neighborhoods and began the process of layered affections whereby primary groups connect citizen to nation in a spiral that, according to Morton Grodzins, "energizes and expresses" national loy-

---

1972):3–19. Tyack's "tribe" includes the community of parents and local officials as well as students. The contemporary source is quoted in Charles Bidwell, "The Moral Significance of the Common School," *History of Education Quarterly* 6 (Fall 1966): 50.

[75]Finkelstein, "Governing the Young," pp. 158, 161.

[76]Benjamin Rush, "On the Mode of Education," in Cohen, *Education in the United States,* 2: 758.

[77]*New York Teacher* 3 (October 1854): 33.

alty. A nineteenth-century teacher expressed this idea in stronger language. "Schools," he wrote, "grind children into the vortex of human society, for our government depends on such sentiment."[78]

Even the ritualized spelling bee in which schools as well as individuals competed had public overtones; it began with the singing of "America," "Columbia," and "I Love My Native Land Best." In such affairs a series of national values was enacted: the sense of competition, or, as nineteenth-century Americans preferred to call it, "emulation"; the spirit of differential achievement based on individual merit (there was no group consultation for a correct spelling); and the merging of individual success with that of the school.[79]

Within their educational communities, however, schoolchildren faced inconsistent patterns of authority. On the one hand, teachers held absolute power, like old-fashioned despots. In theory, few disputed the control of the male schoolmasters who presided over most pre–Civil War classrooms, although by the 1840s some reformers spoke out for disciplinary practices based on moral persuasion rather than on physical coercion. Most Northerners accepted the convention that the internal government of schools must be complete and arbitrary, for only in this way could future citizens learn submission to distasteful laws. "Order in school," concluded the Boxford, Massachusetts, school commissioners, "is of the first and of the greatest importance. Here are the materials that will soon form an active and influential part of the community. . . . If the members of the schools are well trained, they will likely to be in after life, the promoters, supporters and defenders of good order in the community and in the country."[80] Just as society required subordination to legitimate authority, so pupils must not dispute the teacher's word. Certainly few parents did, and the rare suits brought against teachers for physically abusing children and their summary dismissal by judges who nearly always ruled in the teacher's favor reflected the general acceptance of the schoolmaster's jurisdiction. Of ten cases whose

[78]Morton Godzins, *The Loyal and the Disloyal: Social Boundaries of Patriotism and Treason* (Chicago: University of Chicago Press, 1956), pp. 51, 60; *American Journal of Education* 2 (November 1827): 683.

[79]Marcius Willson, *A Fourth Reader of School and Family Readers* (New York: Harper Brothers 1860), p. 73; John Dean Caton, "Memoirs and Observations," John Dean Caton Papers, Library of Congress (hereafter cited as Caton Papers); Lawrence Larson, *The Log Book of a Young Immigrant* (Northfield, Minn.: North American Historical Association, 1939), pp. 103–108.

[80]John Preston, *Every Man His Own Teacher; or, Lancaster's Theory of Education* (Albany: E. E. Hosford, 1817); Carter, *Letters to William Prescott;* "Account of a Visit to an Elementary School," *American Journal of Education* 4 (January 1829): 75; quotation from Kaestle and Vinovskis, *Education and Social Change,* p. 148.

verdicts have been studied, only one teacher was found guilty and fined. The case of Jonah Parker, a twelve-year-old Connecticut student, was typical. His parents swore out an assault warrant against his teacher, Nancy Morgan, but despite his broken arm and lacerations, she was acquitted on the grounds that her efforts to keep order did not constitute criminal force.[81] The raised podium and elevated schoolmaster's desk symbolized the prescribed relation of pupil to teacher, as did regulations requiring boys to bow and girls to curtsy to their teachers. A schoolmaster who could not keep order with such prerogatives usually found himself out of a job.

Most teachers used a variety of coercive techniques to prevent such humiliation. Punishment in a New Hampshire school was typical. According to Warren Burton: "Some were feruled on the hand; some were whipped with a rod on the back. Some were compelled to hold out, at arms length, the largest book which could be found on a great leaden inkstand, till muscle and nerve, bone and marrow, were tortured with the continued exertion."[82] Other teachers used shaming techniques, publicly humiliating students with dunce caps and lazy-boy stools, and forcing disobedient pupils to stand with noses wedged into circles drawn on walls.[83]

Teachers gained added power from the didactic practices of the day. Serving as drill sergeants and overseers, schoolmasters before the Civil War neither interpreted nor discussed materials. Instead they relied on recitation and rarely engaged students in the more egalitarian process of discussion. Barbara Finkelstein has found only three instances of the latter in a sample of a thousand cases, and even at an innovative school like that in Round Hill, Massachusetts, there was little self-directed study or debate.[84] Nor was there any sense of pedagogy as a means of increasing creativity. Instead the schoolbook (properly called the text) provided a litany and became the final word—an educator's Constitution and Bible—with pupils memorizing the catechism according to Webster, Bingham, and Parley. "Why do we bring down that number?"

[81]Butler, *Education as Revealed,* p. 454; *New York Teacher* 2 (October 1853): 190.

[82]Burton, *District School,* p. 64.

[83]"My School Boy Days in New York City Forty Years Ago," *New York Teacher and American Educational Monthly* 6 (March 1869): 91; Donald Raichle, "The Abolition of Corporal Punishment in New Jersey," *History of Childhood Quarterly* 2 (Summer 1974): 53–75.

[84]Finkelstein, "Governing the Young," p. 81; Frederick Brune's School Exercise Book, Round Hill School Papers, Maryland Historical Society, Baltimore; *Outline of the System of Education at Round Hill School* (Boston: N. Hale Steam Power Press, 1831); Round Hill School Papers and Brune-Randall Papers, Maryland Historical Society.

inquired one student perplexed by an addition problem. "Because," snapped the teacher, "the book tells us to."[85]

By the 1850s, critics complained that such techniques made pupils into "passive receptacles" burdened, according to one New England reformer, "like Roman maids crushed under the weight of golden bracelets."[86] It was possible, as visiting committees discovered, for students to know the name of every Turkish city but not know where Turkey was, and it was possible to memorize Webster's *Speller* but not know how to read. Whatever its pedagogical deficiencies, this catechistic process increased the authority of schoolmasters, who asked the questions and controlled the responses. According to Finkelstein, "teachers sought to exercise near-total control over the intellectual progress of their students. . . . [They organized] classroom activities in such a way as to force each student systematically to practice skills and acquire knowledge from carefully defined, skillfully blocked-out, predetermined courses of instruction."[87] Imagination was actively discouraged, for it might result in spontaneous, unprescribed answers. That such procedures made students intellectually submissive was clear to one New Yorker who described his classroom experience of the 1840s: "The dictator paces to the next class and continues. Second of the class: May: M-a-y- first enunciating the word, then spelling it and turning the wooden block. Hands instantly unlock themselves from behind, grasp pencils and write down the word quickly on ruled slates. At the next word of command hands again revert to their places and the dictation thus proceeds from class to class. . . ."[88]

District schools replicated these arrangements, with pupils using slates for their dictation. Writing classes repetitively traced copy such as "Our nation rules the best" and "Education forms the common mind" from a model set in the teacher's elegant hand. Compositions based on independent thought were unknown in early nineteenth-century schools. "Frequent repetition of the same subject," explained the trustee of a private academy in New York, "is necessary to fix it indelibly on a young man's mind and unless this is done, it passes through their memories."[89] Even advanced classes memorized history and geography

[85]Holbrook, *Reminiscences,* p. 99.

[86]Convers Francis, *Errors in Education: A Discourse Delivered at the Anniversary of the Derby Academy* (n.p., 1828), p. 2.

[87]Carter, *Letters to William Prescott,* p. 81; Finkelstein, "Governing the Young," pp. 15–16.

[88]Finkelstein, "Governing the Young," p. 252.

[89]Diary of Henry Van der Luyn, entry for 28 August 1831, Van der Luyn Papers.

texts, giving rote replies to the teacher's questions or writing countless imitations of set letters. Such instructional methods added intellectual weight to the physical force already granted the schoolmaster.

Rarely encouraged to challenge or investigate the givens of their texts, students parroted the "right" answer under threat of a tweaking on the nose, rapping on the knuckle, or wearing of the dunce's cap. Because most nineteenth-century Northerners believed the failure to learn to be an aberration of will—and therefore a form of misbehavior—the schoolmaster's physical and intellectual authority converged. As New York's Governor De Witt Clinton explained: "The beauty of the system is that nothing is trusted to the boy. He does not only repeat the lesson before a superior but he learns before a superior.[90] This repetition without understanding, challenge, or choice conditioned future citizens to accept givens—whether of geography or government—and in this way the hidden curriculum of the mid-nineteenth century taught Americans the basic lessons of political compliance.

Yet, despite the teacher's supremacy in this repressive mode of pedagogy, schoolboys dissented, protested, and disobeyed. Just as America's revolutionary traditions, heterogeneous population, and frontier settlements guaranteed ambivalent attitudes toward established sources of authority and inspired continual fears among traditionalists that the nation's political center might fall apart, so schools sanctioned equally inconsistent behavior. Early nineteenth-century education taught obedience to the government at the same time that it developed three other characteristics—an instinct of participation, a sensitivity to tyranny, and an understanding of the difference between an office and its holder. Occasionally (although this became more common in the late nineteenth century) self-government was consciously encouraged. At Enoch Wines's Edgehill, according to one observer, "the boys have a lot of power over each other."[91] Some district schoolteachers even permitted voting for special offices, although they limited the areas of decision and reserved final authority for themselves.

But even in schools without self-government there was student resistance. Certainly some mischief was to be expected—boys will be boys—but young Americans went beyond personal rebelliousness to organize collective acts of disobedience. Contemporary accounts distinguished between rowdies who misbehaved as individuals and class-

[90]De Witt Clinton, *An Address to the Benefactors and Friends of the Free School of New York* (New York, 1810), p. 9.

[91]Wines, *How Shall I Govern?* pp. 303–08; *New York Teacher* 10 (April 1861): 214.

room-supported challenges to a teacher's domination. According to one Nebraska schoolgirl, when "the teacher went beyond his authority the whole school community seized his arm, wrested his ruler," and throwing this symbol of command into the stove, "rolled him down the hill and admonished him." In Manchester, New Hampshire, according to one pupil, "After due deliberation, the larger boys all agreed in not liking the Master and then one of them climbed on top of the house and stopped up the chimney and smoked him out." Alfred Holbrook remembered an incident from his schooldays in which "bad governance" in the form of capricious punishment produced "indignation beyond control" and led eventually to the closing of the school."[92] This unified resistance was quite different from an Indiana schoolboy's personal battle with his teacher. John Caton resolved "not to quietly submit to her government," and later as a teacher himself he distinguished between personal rebelliousness and classroom mutiny. Confronted with challenges to his public power, not to his private self-restraint, Caton felt that his class must submit to his authority or he must "abdicate."[93]

Nineteenth-century schools provide numerous examples of ungovernable classrooms driving out schoolmasters and committing what teachers called treason. Each term the contest was renewed, and according to Geraldine Clifford, "The teacher who lost the battle lost community support." Most districts dismissed those who could not control these rebellions, making clear their disapproval by hiring a replacement or in some instances refusing to supply wood to heat the school.[94] Apparently parents, trustees, and district commissioners approved the punishment of fractious individuals, but communities withheld support from inept teachers who could not control their classrooms. The well-known aphorism "Cuff 'em, thrash 'em, Anyway to learn 'em / But whatever you do / Don't let 'em thrash you" was fair warning.[95]

One practice that occurred so frequently as to become a ritual by the 1830s was that of "barring out" the schoolmaster, who then negotiated with student leaders before being readmitted to the classroom. One

[92]Louise Beall, "Early School Experiences in Nebraska," *Nebraska History* 23 (July 1942): 200; "Memorandum of Susan Blunt," 15 May 1843, New Hampshire Historical Society, Concord, N.H.; Holbrook, *Reminiscences*, p. 45.

[93]John Caton, "Memoirs and Observations," Caton Papers.

[94]Geraldine Clifford, "Home and School in 19th Century America: Some Personal-History Reports from the United States," *History of Education Quarterly* 18 (Spring 1978): 23; School Committee Rules, 1833, Stratham, New Hampshire, Box of Miscellaneous Papers, Sturbridge Village Library; *Greenfield (Mass.) Gazette*, 4 December 1832.

[95]James Mickel Williams, *Our Rural Heritage: The Social Psychology of Rural Development* (New York: A. A. Knopf, 1925), p. 155.

New Hampshire district school reversed the process by carrying its teacher, kicking and swearing, out of doors. "To the side-hill, to the side-hill, cried Mark. . . . To this pitch, then, [the teacher] was borne, and in all the haste that his violent struggles would permit. Over he was thrust, as if he were a log; and down he went. . . ." Later, student leaders agreed to the return of this particular schoolmaster but warned, "The ship is no longer yours so look out, for we are our own men now." The teacher refused their conditions, muttering in the political language typical of these encounters: "But there is another law besides club law, and that you have to take."[96] In Ohio, future congressman Alexander Long and his classmates triumphantly locked out the teacher and before entering into negotiations renamed their log-cabin schoolhouse Fort Defiance.[97] The best-known description of barring out occurred in Edward Eggleston's fictional account of an inexperienced Indiana schoolmaster who was warned that "the boys in Flat Crick deestrict have driv' off the last two [schoolmasters] and licked the one before them like blazes. . . . They'd pitch you out of doors, sonny, neck, and heels, afore Christmas."[98]

European travelers were continually surprised by the extent of organized dissent within American classrooms. Austrian-born Francis Grund described northern schools as "a congregation of young republicans" who would not give obedience "to the uncontrolled will of their masters" any more than their fathers "would submit to the mandates of kings.[99] The Swedish educator Per Adam Siljestrom detected a similar ambivalence toward authority in the northern classrooms of the 1840s. According to Siljestrom, in theory Americans accepted the supremacy of the schoolmaster, but in practice they challenged his power. Siljestrom's travels introduced him to a few peaceful, "well-regulated" American schools, but more often he encountered collective insubordination "unheard of in our country," including the barring out ritual practiced in district schools.[100]

[96]Alcott, *Confessions of a Schoolmaster,* pp. 43, 75–77; I. L. Kephart, "Barring-Out One Teacher," in *Pennsylvania History as Told by Contemporaries,* ed. Asa Earl Martin and Hiram Herr Shenk (New York: Macmillan, 1925), pp. 392–96; Burton, *District School,* pp. 158–61.

[97]Alexander Long, "Autobiography," Alexander Long Papers, Cincinnati Historical Society.

[98]Edward Eggleston, *The Hoosier Schoolmaster: A Story of Backwoods Indiana* (New York: Orange, Judd, 1871), p. 37.

[99]Francis J. Grund, *The Americans in Their Moral, Social, and Political Relations* (New York: Johnson Reprint, 1968), pp. 133–34.

[100]Per Adam Siljestrom, *The Educational Institutions of the United States,* cited in Finkelstein, "Governing the Young," p. 339.

It is clear that the youth and inexperience of schoolteachers undermined authority and encouraged efforts to impeach officials. A recent study of schoolteachers in pre–Civil War Massachusetts reveals that 70 percent of those hired in a typical rural district taught only one term, and the longest tenure was four consecutive terms. The same rate of turnover existed in Baltimore, and in Illinois fourteen-year-old Esther Hornaker was surprised when "the directors thought I might have trouble with my former schoolmates," many of whom were older than she.[101] Most teachers boarded with local families, and it was hard to be an effective disciplinarian after carrying out the slops or receiving a tonguelashing from parents. Hiram Orcutt, a well-known nineteenth-century schoolmaster, attempted to separate his position in the classroom from his offduty associations with pupils but finally admitted that the boarding-out system lacked propriety and threatened his discipline. Alfred Holbrook agreed and concluded that, besides disrupting his family life, the informal contact with pupils diminished his authority.[102] Women constantly discovered that their presumptive power was eroded by sexual politics. A teacher at New York's Oxford Academy found it more difficult to control her classroom after rumors spread about her boarding with a "dissolute" local family, and Frances Meritt, a young Massachusetts schoolteacher, nervously declined a party. "I feel," she wrote in her diary, "that I ought to go on account of my being teacher in the district. Yet I have doubts whether it is right for me to give countenance by my attendance to anything of that kind."[103]

No more than king to valet could schoolteacher be hero to local schoolboy. In sociological terms there was little distance between nineteenth-century pupil and teacher, and the necessity of reappointment by a committee that often included the fathers of rebellious pupils further limited power. Nor was schoolteaching an admired occupation. The contempt that led one Baltimore merchant to discourage his daughter's romance with a schoolteacher by singing "ABC. ABC. . . . That's a hell of a way to make a living" was widely shared.[104] Moreover, by in-

[101]For comments on the youth of teachers and their brief tenure at various schools, see Willard Elsbree, *The American Teacher: Evolution of a Profession in a Democracy* (New York: American Book Co., 1939), pp. 127–77; Carter, *Letters to William Prescott;* Kaestle and Vinovskis, *Education and Social Change,* p. 153; Helen Buss, "Esther Hornaker: A Pioneer Teacher," *Journal of Illinois State Historical Society* 16 (April 1923): 76; Papers on Education, Maryland Historical Society.

[102]Orcutt, *Reminiscences of School Life,* p. 49; Holbrook, *Reminiscences,* pp. 30–34, 94.

[103]Quotation from Clifford, "Home and School," p. 20; Diary of Henry Van der Luyn, entry for n.d., and 30 July 1832, Van der Luyn Papers.

[104]Quoted from Robert P. Adams, "James Alfred Gary" (master's thesis, Catholic University, 1967), p. 15.

creasingly accepting women—the very symbols of public powerlessness—as schoolteachers, nineteenth-century Americans muted classroom authority and demonstrated that whereas they expected obedience to the law, the dispensers of that law were not the source of its sanction. Finally, by delegating both community and family control to others, district committees and parents modeled the shared decision-making and derived authority of their government. The resulting prerogatives were limited, not overwhelming; episodic, not continuous; subject to contest, not irresistible.

For a few Northerners—about six thousand in the 1840s—the influence of the hidden curriculum did not end in primary school or an academy but continued during college. Despite differences in curriculum and living arrangements, the classrooms of northern colleges were remarkably similar to those of schools. This was partly because so many academies had been upgraded to colleges. Yet even at older institutions like Harvard, Yale, and Brown, college men found that their classrooms duplicated those of their school years. The process of transmitting information was the same—endless recitation, memorization, and public examination. Nor had the trappings of authority changed. At Brown, for example, students had to stand when officers of the college entered a room.[105] But in college the barrings out of schooldays became organized student "rebellions," so large and frequent that they merited special names. Graduates of Harvard remembered the Great Rebellion of 1832 (to distinguish it from the earlier Uprising of the Rotten Cabbage); those at Yale spoke of the Bread and Butter Riot and the Conic Revolt—the latter one of the rare confrontations involving an intellectual issue, in this case the interpretation of a geometric theorem.[106] Few colleges managed to avoid collective disobedience, which usually erupted over public issues—food, a change in the rules or an alleged misuse of power.

Recently Burton Bledstein has interpreted these nineteenth-century challenges to college administrations as efforts by students to achieve more systematic professional training—and thereby to assure themselves the benefits of a career in an established discipline.[107] Another explanation is possible. Nineteenth-century students were protesting the insufficient self-government that left them, as one recognized, "dis-

[105]Walter Bronson, *The History of Brown University, 1764–1914* (Providence: By the University, 1914), p. 517.

[106]Frederick Rudolph, *The American College and University: A History* (New York: A. A. Knopf, 1962), p. 98.

[107]Barton J. Bledstein, *The Culture of Professionalism: The Middle Class and the Development of Higher Education* (New York: W. W. Norton, 1976), p. 229.

enfranchised." Ready for public life, men cloistered in college residence halls resented treatment that made them political children without rights and privileges. In this sense episodic rebellions acted out the republican instincts of future citizens shut off from politics by institutions that disdained partisan issues and social involvement. "We have no political parties here," wrote Yale's president Timothy Dwight in a representative judgment. "We ask what kind of a scholar is he—not to what party does he belong." But Dwight's students, restless in their apolitical setting, sought, through their protests against college authorities, "to stand with the Founders." Their arson, shuffling in chapel, boycotts, and destruction of property were aspects of learning in a political culture created by revolutionary dissent and maintained by participatory democracy. Both administrators and students recognized the parapolitical nature of the student revolt. Brown's president Jonathan Maxcy was typical. After a long confrontation with students, he negotiated what both sides called a "Treaty of Amity and Intercourse between the President of Rhode Island College and the Party of the Rebellious." According to its terms, if students returned to the commons, the faculty would grant amnesty and review the boarding charges likened by undergraduates to England's oppressive taxation of the colonies.[108]

Similar student needs fostered the vibrant extracurricular life on pre–Civil War college campuses. Life outside the classroom was often the most memorable of the college years for the very reason that it focused on politics. Students organized their own literary societies, wrote constitutions for their debating clubs, elected officers of their associations, and held debates. Only in such associations did they act as public men; accordingly, these were the activities alumni recalled with satisfaction when they reviewed their college years.[109]

Learning to be Americans through the formal and informal curricula of antebellum schools and colleges was not restricted to future Democrats, but it was limited to Northerners once Southerners developed a qualitatively different educational system.[110] One way of assuring na-

[108]Stephen Novak, *The Rights of Youth: American Colleges and Student Revolt, 1798–1815* (Cambridge, Mass.: Harvard University Press, 1977), pp. 18, 73.

[109]David F. Allmendinger, *Paupers and Scholars: The Transformation of Student Life in Nineteenth-Century New England* (New York: St. Martin's Press, 1975), pp. 107–111. For examples, see George R. Cutting, *Student Life at Amherst College* (Amherst, Mass.: Hatch and William, 1871); Novak, *Rights of Youth,* p. 35.

[110]I have omitted the South from this analysis, on the grounds that schooling in the region was qualitatively different from that in the North. Indeed, this difference partly accounts for the South's success in establishing a different political culture before the

tional consensus within a competitive party system was to provide standard training inside the classroom. Thus, as a means of conveying the nation's political culture, northern schoolrooms became miniature theaters where those who might later disagree over tactical matters of partisan policy learned to agree about public strategies of authority, decisionmaking, allegiance, and leadership. Inside the disparate exteriors of northern schools, the national system of education envisaged by the founding generation emerged, for it was here that future citizens first became members of a community at the same time that they maintained their individuality as competitors. Through the classroom's environment as much as through its transmission of subject matter, schoolboys from Maine to Oregon learned how to delegate and then rotate authority among equals, how to separate the powers of the office from its holder, how to impeach those in power, and, finally, how to participate in public events. This form of political schooling provided important instruction in maintaining a system sufficiently new to be considered an experiment for its first century. Schools did not introduce their students to public issues or political parties, as twentieth-century civics courses would. Instead, they taught future Democrats and Republicans to conform to the American way—in Noah Webster's provocative image, "to lisp the praise of liberty and become political bigots for their nation."[111] Having absorbed the lessons of compliance, collective support, and individual participation, young Northerners whose fathers had already shaped their selection of the Democracy brought these lessons to their party.

---

Civil War. One of the few statistical measures available for the period demonstrates this difference. In 1850, 18 percent of the school-age population went to school in the South Central states, 17 percent the the South Atlantic, 65 percent in the North Atlantic, and 50 percent in the North Central states; Folger and Nam, *Education of the American Population,* p. 5. For a further exploration of the differences, see William R. Taylor, "Toward a Definition of Orthodoxy: The Patrician South and the Common School," *Harvard Educational Review* 36 (Fall 1966): 412–26; John S. Ezell, "A Southern Education for Southerners," *Journal of Southern History* 17 (August 1951): 302–27; Cohen, *Education in the United States,* 2: 1001–16; Cremin, *American Common School,* pp. 24–27; David Madsden, *Early National Education,* (Detroit: Wayne State University Press, 1966) pp. 91–92, 115–16. As to chronology, there are significant changes in the internal climate of American schools after 1840. Such changes include the development of the high school, the use of trained female teachers, age-graded classrooms, the introduction of Pestalozzian methods, and the decline of corporeal punishment. But the legacy of this new hidden curriculum was not apparent until well after Reconstruction, when its graduates came of political age. For a broad discussion of the general issue, see Edward Pessen, "How Different from Each Other Were the Antebellum North and South?" *American Historical Review* 85 (December 1980): 1119–63.

[111]Hansen, *Liberalism and American Education,* pp. 239–40.

## Chapter 3

# *A Sense of Party: George Bancroft, Martin Van Buren, and Samuel Cox*

Whereas schools instilled general civic behavior and families established specific partisan attachments, the Democratic party exposed its following to a particular version of national values. In this sense the organization performed as a socializing agent through which members learned not only how to think about particular issues, but also how to lead their public lives. As such, the Democracy became an arena where the activities of delegating authority, choosing leaders, and formulating policies were practiced. Unlike the established institutions of school and family, however, the party did not perform this function from the outset; only after a period of self-identification could the Democracy transmit its version of how to be an American.

Nowhere was this hesitancy more apparent than in the party's relationship to white males under age twenty-one who represented potential members but who were never recruited. Before 1850, party organization was too tentative to do so; in fact, some historians contend that there were no national parties until the end of the nineteenth century.[1] Also, the notion of formal indoctrination was unknown in a society that believed free will essential for all republican citizens, and especially for those entering political life. Moreover, Democrats lacked any understanding of youth as a stage of life deserving special attention; hence they did not follow the example of those northern churches that organized Sunday schools. Nor did they enlist their followers' sons in age-specific groups, as did the Know-Nothings, who recruited future members through the Junior Order of Americans and the Sons of America.[2] The closest the Democrats came to such organizations were their Asso-

[1]James Mohr, ed., *Radical Republicans in the North: State Politics during Reconstruction* (Baltimore: Johns Hopkins University Press, 1976), p. xii.

[2]Jean Gould Hales, "Co-Laborers in the Cause: Women in the Ante-bellum Nativist Movement," *Civil War History* 25 (June 1979): 120–21, 123; idem, "The Shaping of Nati-

ciations of Young Men, which provided lectures, and sometimes picnics, for youthful urban supporters.

Moreover, the party lacked the trappings of legitimacy that in the late nineteenth century would render partisan organizations such effective agencies of political learning. The first of these was inclusion in the national past, and, like all political associations, the Democracy received no mention in the history books. By the 1840s there was no lack of material, for the Democrats had all the stuff of which history is made—public influence, rituals, an inventory of symbols, dramatic electoral battles, a persistent fellowship, and a basic creed. Its leaders had run state and national governments, its principles and platforms had inspired generations of Americans, and its programs had defined public policy. Yet the party was not yet acknowledged as a part of the national past, and would not be until after the Civil War.

Once a believer, however, partisans could always find their roots in campaign literature. By the 1830s congressmen franked speeches to constituents describing the Democracy's past achievements, and paperbound pamphlets such as Nahum Capen's *The History of Democracy* used party history as propaganda. A few periodicals—notably John O'Sullivan's *United States Magazine and Democratic Review*—furnished one-sided interpretations of Democratic contributions to American freedom, as did hundreds of county newspapers loosely affiliated with the party. From the official Washington press of Democratic presidents—Andrew Jackson's *United States Telegraph and Globe,* James Polk's and Franklin Pierce's *Union,* and James Buchanan's *Constitution*—came a standard view of Democratic history to accompany elections. Through such sources emerged two basic images of the party's past: Democrats were freedom fighters protecting the people from the power-hungry Federalists and Whigs, and they were carriers of the flag expanding the republic across the continent. In the mimetic fashion of party politics, Federalists, Whigs, and Republicans fashioned negative images of Democrats as corrupt patronage seekers and prosouthern lackeys. Exposés such as *The Ruin of the Democratic Party,* published by the Republican Congressional Committee in 1860, and William Jones's *History of the Democratic Party* turned official Democratic history on its head. Like the efforts of local antiquarians, both interpretations were particularistic and parochial. They merely placed one organization on the side

---

vist Sentiment, 1848–1860 (Ph.D. dissertation, Stanford University, 1979); Jean H. Baker, *Ambivalent Americans: The Know-Nothing Party in Maryland* (Baltimore: Johns Hopkins University Press, 1978), pp. 111–12.

of the angels while identifying opponents with the devil. This one-dimensional approach was incapable of producing a historical view of the nation's oldest political party.

The Democracy also lacked public buildings to give physical expression to its institutional existence. In quite a literal sense, the party remained homeless and thereby denied its following the sense of durability that a physical presence would have engendered. This was surprising, for Northerners of this period energetically constructed public buildings to house their organizations. The results of what Tocqueville called the Americans' self-described "march across these wilds draining swamps, turning the course of rivers, peopling solitudes and subduing nature," appear in today's historic registries of antebellum courthouses, churches, Masonic temples, and nativist lodges.[3] Yet while voluntary associations of limited resources produced permanent homes for their organizations, the Democrats (and to a lesser extent the Whigs and Republicans) continued to meet in rented halls, fraternal lodges, and taverns. Private houses and, in good weather, public squares, picnic grounds, and clearings became party headquarters, and the correspondence of early nineteenth-century Democrats was filled as much with details about where to go as with discussion about what to do.[4] So frequently were taverns used as meeting places that their names became appropriate nicknames, and party watchers could distinguish among political factions such as the Tontine Coffeehouse, the Pewter Mugs, and the Lewis Tavern Martling Men.

In Massachusetts the arrangements that George Bancroft made were typical. After founding Boston's *Bay State Democrat* in the 1840s, he set aside an upstairs room in the newspaper's building as a meeting place where Democrats from all over the state could talk politics and read party literature. But like most such reading rooms this was temporary, and when a new owner took over the paper the faithful had to go elsewhere. Only in New York did Democrats have a permanent home, but even the substantial brick Tammany Hall on Nassau Street had originally belonged to a fraternal association. The rival city organization met in more typical quarters, and gained its name—Mozart Hall Democrats—from its rented music hall.[5]

[3]Alexis de Tocqueville, *Democracy in America* (New York: Vintage Books, 1957), 2: 78.

[4]For recent examples of how buildings reflect social attitudes, see Richard Sennett, *The Fall of Public Man* (New York: A. A. Knopf, 1977); Clifford Clark, "Domestic Architecture as an Index to Social History: The Romantic Revival and the Cult of Domesticity in America, 1840–1870," *Journal of Interdisciplinary History* 7 (Summer 1976): 33–56; Richard Pare, ed., *Court House: A Photographic Document* (New York: Horizon Press, 1978).

[5]Russel B. Nye, *George Bancroft, Brahmin Rebel* (New York: A. A. Knopf, 1944), pp.

In fact Democrats did not have an official name until well into the nineteenth century; at the same time that, like foster children, they had too many. Having no title, they lacked any sense of themselves as a group transmitting a version of national values. Party leaders sometimes traced their partisan roots to those who had opposed the Constitution in the 1780s. But these anti-Federalists were inappropriately named, for their title suggested opposition to the separation of powers and support of a strong central government—the very opposite of the Democracy's commitment to local government and diffused authority. Furthermore, the anti-Federalists had not supported the Constitution, and to accept such a heritage was heretical. Recognizing the danger, Martin Van Buren called "this caprice of names a signal perversion of the true relationship between party names and party objects."[6]

In the 1790s the party of Jefferson had called itself the Republicans, thereby claiming America's revolutionary heritage and the principles that had inspired the founding of the nation. Federalists, on the other hand, labeled their opponents "democratical," hoping to associate them with the civil disorder evoked by that epithet.[7] By conviction, of course, all Americans were republicans and, as Jefferson pointed out, federalists as well. Later, in the 1820s, when parties devolved into individual factions and local cliques, the supporters of William Crawford, John Quincy Adams, and Andrew Jackson used their favorites' names as labels. This process of identification lay at the heart of the second American party system. According to Richard McCormick, national structures formed in the 1830s not over divisions in Congress or explicit doctrinal issues, but as a result of presidential contests in which support or opposition to Andrew Jackson determined political affiliation. Accordingly, Democratic iconography began with Jackson, whose craggy features soon decorated election tickets throughout the country.[8] After Jackson,

116–18, 136; see also W. Harrison Bayles, *Old Taverns of New York* (New York: Frank Allahan Genealogical, 1915); M. R. Werner, *Tammany Hall* (New York: Greenwood Press, 1968), p. 15; Jerome Mushkat, *Tammany: The Evolution of a Political Machine* (Syracuse: Syracuse University Press, 1971).

[6]Martin Van Buren, *Inquiry into the Origin and Course of Political Parties in the United States* (New York: Augustus M. Kelley, 1967), pp. 36, 223.

[7]Joseph Charles, *The Origins of the American Party System* (New York: Harper Torchbooks, 1956), pp. 54–56; Adrienne Koch and William Peden, *The Selected Writings of John and John Quincy Adams* (New York: A. A. Knopf, 1946), p. 326; Roy N. Lokken, "The Concept of Democracy in Colonial Political Thought," *William and Mary Quarterly* 16 (October 1959); 568–80.

[8]Richard McCormick, *The Second American Party System: Party Formation in the Jacksonian Era* (Chapel Hill: University of North Carolina Press, 1966), p. 14; Jarboe Election Ticket Collection, Maryland Historical Society, Baltimore.

however, the practice of identifying parties with a leader's name disappeared, a casualty of structured nominating conventions, official platforms, and statewide organizations less dependent on a central figure. Even the most devoted could not make of Polk, Pierce, or Buchanan, and later Cleveland, Wilson, or even FDR, a synonym for the Democratic party.

Various elements of political culture were reflected in this process of taking a name. In the early days of the republic, identification with Jefferson and Hamilton forced provincial Americans to look beyond local affairs, and because national leaders embodied collective opinion and intended programs on a variety of public issues, the use of their names as party labels served as a shorthand method of understanding national policy. Today's students of political learning have found that children first apprehend government by reference to an individual.[9] The same was true of this first generation of Americans, political children in a new nation. They might not know the specifics of Hamilton's assumption plan, but they held pictures in their minds of what Hamilton and Jefferson represented. Associations with notables thus expanded local loyalties, channeling parochial allegiances into a larger framework—the process described by Morton Grodzins as transposing loyalty to one's pinochle club into support for the state.[10]

When Jackson called his followers republicans and Van Buren referred to "old-time republicans," they linked their party to the patriots who first fought the English and then opposed the Federalists. Later, as self-designated Democratic-Republicans, they associated themselves with newer traditions and laid claim to two central themes of American political thought: independence and popular sovereignty. By the 1840s, however, the desire for a tightly structured organization required greater discrimination, and a term as catholic as Democratic-Republican could not be adapted to the reductive imagery of mass politics. It was both too cumbersome in a literary sense and too inclusive in a political sense. Party managers, led by the New York Regency, sought a disciplined band of loyal workers who were willing to stump for candidates in competitive elections, not an amorphous collection of believers. Hence the party discarded the second half of its name, which soon would serve its opponents, and knew itself as the Democracy. The christening had been a slow, unconscious process, and only in the 1840s

[9]David Easton and Jack Dennis, *Children in the Political System: Origins of Political Legitimacy* (New York: McGraw-Hill, 1969), pp. 114–18.

[10]Morton Grodzins, *The Loyal and the Disloyal: Social Boundaries of Patriotism and Treason* (Chicago: University of Chicago Press, 1956), p. 29.

did the name Democracy correspond to an enduring set of principles and practices available for transmission to its following.

Throughout this naming process, opponents denied the claims of Democrats to national ideals and instead provided contemptuous nicknames that, like those of children, stuck. Thus Democrats were called Loco-Focos after a New York faction used this brand of matches to light up an assembly hall. The name soon conjured up images of party machinations, dirty tricks, and radical ideas. Like members of other parties, Democrats occasionally accepted their nicknames and wore them as badges in an effort to display their opponents' lack of judgment. This was the case during the Civil War, when Northern Democrats called themselves Copperheads, hoping to demonstrate the fanaticism of Republicans who had so labeled them. Sometimes nicknames were unavoidable, and answering to the epithet was simply good politics. The American party did this in the 1850s when it called itself, as did everyone else, the Know-Nothings. Sometimes namecalling backfired; for example, it was the Federalists who had first tarred the pro-French Jeffersonians with the radical and revolutionary term *democrat*. But by 1813 even John Adams admitted that Jefferson's "steady defence of democratical principles and invariable favorable opinion of the French Revolution laid the foundations of his popularity."[11]

Names, of course, provide identity, but, unlike individuals, political parties choose theirs. That the early Democrats had at once no name and too many revealed two things about the nation's early political culture: Americans were ambivalent about parties, and the partisan structures they produced before the 1830s were too local and too tentative to have a national presence. It was this same uncertainty that prevented partisans from building permanent headquarters, and historians from mentioning the party as a part of the national past. That the Democrats had a name by the late 1830s reflected new conditions that encouraged members to think of themselves as a single entity, not as a series of tribelike local units. That the party called itself by a term earlier associated with social disorder indicated a shift in attitude toward a doctrine that had frightened earlier Americans. But by the mid-nineteenth century, *democracy* had become a word that evoked warm sentiment and high emotion. The Democratic party both affected and reflected this process.

[11]Charles Francis Adams, ed., *Life and Works of John Adams* (Boston: Little, Brown, 1852), 10: 54. See also John Quincy Adams, *The Jubilee of the Constitution* (New York: Samuel Colman, 1839), pp. 56, 57, 87–88, 94–95, 98, 112.

This organization was to be the world's first and most enduring Democratic party, and although the name has become a common enough label throughout the world, its early use in the United States established its influence. Other titles might have been used, such as Unionist, Constitutionalist (a name that John Quincy Adams sought for his followers), Confederate, American, Washingtonian, Republican, and States' Rights. By referring to themselves as the Democracy rather than as the Democratic party, supporters figuratively established a people's movement rather than an organization, and by omitting the word *party* they avoided a still-dangerous label. Finally, by assuming the cognomen *democrat,* they identified themselves with a future based on popular government, leaving to their opponents the tyrannical past.

Christened by the late 1830s, the Democrats still had neither history nor respectability, and although they continued to transmit information about public issues, their role as an agent of political socialization was restricted by the general climate of antipartyism. Many Americans continued to regard their partisan contacts as an embarrassment, necessary for public life but nothing to celebrate. Sometimes this distaste reflected the sensibilities of a gentry required to participate, on fairly equal terms, with artisans and clerks in ward assemblies and delegate conventions. But such tensions originated in public thought as much as in class structure, for the country had absorbed, along with the radical Whig theory of revolution, a dose of English antipartyism. Making no distinction between faction and party, some Americans viewed both as self-seeking cliques temporarily clustered around a season's political star.[12] In Lord Bolingbroke's oft-cited comparisons, party men were "like sheep who will stand sullen and be run over till they hear the bell wether, and they follow without knowing very well where." In similar vein, they resembled "hounds who grow fond of the man who shows them game and by whose hello they are used to be encouraged."[13] English views of party contained no sense of a persistent brotherhood unified by principles, and, given their history, Americans had little reason to think differently. No association of what Edmund Burke called "good men" had combined against George III or the parliamentary factions of his time, and Burke himself, although he saw a place for

[12]Such a distinction came later when Americans accepted the label *party,* reserving the term *faction* for their opponents. "We are a party, but you are a faction" was fairly common political rhetoric by the 1850s. See Franklyn George Bonn, "The Idea of Political Party in the Thought of Thomas Jefferson and James Madison" (Ph.D. dissertation, University of Minnesota, 1946), p. 55.

[13]Archibald S. Ford, *His Majesty's Opposition* (Oxford: Clarendon Press, 1964), p. 116.

party as "a noble and necessary instrument," had eventually left the Whigs.[14] Instead, factions entered American thought as examples of the degeneracy that had corrupted England and forced free men to rebel. Even after the revolution, when the new republic retrieved some of its traditions and installed constitutional arrangements based on English practice, parties remained outside the accepted framework of government.

In part, this was because Americans celebrated what they considered uniquely theirs—the Constitution, the Union, and the War of Independence. Actually their political originality consisted in a reconstruction of old concepts modestly infused with novelty, but because parties were never considered truly American, they could not become sources of nationalistic pride. For a long time, according to Fred Somkin, "The notion of unprecedentedness, of utterly new beginnings remained . . . a primitive assumption of the American mind."[15] Accordingly party appeared as an unwanted English procedure, as outmoded as the monarchy. Even George Washington, who acknowledged factions as a legitimate check on the king's rule, considered them unnecessary as a balance to the people's will.

Appropriately, Washington, whose life so preoccupied pre–Civil War Americans, provided the basic text for antipartyism. In his Farewell Address of 1796, Washington indicted political parties for their "disorder and miseries" and "tendencies to distract public councils and enfeeble the public administration." Party strife, he said, "agitates the community with ill-founded jealousies and false alarms; kindles the animosity of one part against another; foments occasionally riot and insurrection. It opens the door to foreign influence and corruption which find a facilitated access to government itself through the channels of party passion."[16] Here Washington spoke to the fear that parties reduced free citizens to servile followers of ambitious power-seekers. By making some men depend on others and by requiring an exclusive rather than a universal allegiance, parties destroyed civic virtue and thus posed an especially dangerous threat in a new political society.

As Washington's successors recognized, there were compelling reasons to remain apprehensive about political divisions in a country that

[14]Edmund Burke, "Thoughts on the Cause of our Present Discontent," in *Edmund Burke: Selected Writings and Speeches*, ed. Peter J. Stanlis, (New York: Doubleday, Anchor Books, 1963), p. 141.

[15]Fred Somkin, *Unquiet Eagle: Memory and Desire, the Idea of Freedom, 1815–1860* (Ithaca: Cornell University Press, 1967), p. 57.

[16]James Richardson, ed., *Messages and Papers of the Presidents*, 20 vols. (Washington, D.C.: Bureau of National Literature and Art, 1908–1917), 1: 219.

lacked common traditions, a homogeneous population, and a national past. The United States could not afford the special-interest groups that might destroy unity. Strict allegiance to a partisan organization contradicted the idea of America as an organic commonwealth. "Party," wrote Charles Davies in 1825, "may be regarded as a simple expedient for mutilating the state of a measure of its force, paralyzing one side of its power, depriving the country of a portion of its effective strength for the promotion of its great objects. There were always . . . two parties in Carthage, one for peace and the other for war. The consequence was that Carthage never enjoyed the full advantages of either peace or war."[17] Such views reflected a continuing concern that the union of states might shatter into economic, religious, regional, and partisan groups.

When Americans described the evil effects of party, they often employed slavery as a metaphor to express the thralldom they feared would undermine republican virtue. Political enslavement, as Washington and his colleagues saw it, was a twofold process: First, citizens relinquished their intellectual independence to a demagogue; then, the resulting faction sought selfish, particularistic ends rather than the welfare of the whole. Jefferson explained it thus: "I am not a Federalist, because I never submitted the whole system of my opinions to the creed of any party of men whatever in religion, in philosophy, in politics or anything else where I was capable of thinking for myself." Paraphrasing Bolingbroke, Jefferson saw such associationalism as "the last degradation of a free and moral agent. If I could not go to heaven but with a party, I would not go there at all."[18]

To Washington, Jefferson, and most of their generation, subservience to party was corruption, a word they used in its original sense of breaking apart. For those familiar with the writings of classical antiquity, the word held special meaning: corruption was a lethal and contagious civic disease that sapped the people's moral health, thereby undermining the virtue of their society. This is why, adopting a spiritual idiom, Americans referred to "the greed" of patronage seekers, "the lies" of party newspapers, "the passion" of election competition, and "the lust" of partisans. Parties, in the frequently used metaphor, were "fires" that, like worldly passions, destroyed virtue and civic humanism. What is more, a new nation based on self-rule was especially

[17]Charles Davies, *An Address Delivered on the Commemoration at Fryburg, May 15, 1825* (Portland, Me., 1825), p. 4.

[18]Julian Boyd, ed., *The Papers of Thomas Jefferson*, vol. 14 (Princeton: Princeton University Press, 1958), 14: 650.

susceptible to such corruption. Although Machiavelli had established this point, Americans were also fond of citing the seventeenth-century English martyr Algernon Sidney:

> Men have a strange propensity to run into all manner of excesses, when plenty of means invite, and there is no power to deter. . . . Again, all things have their continuance from a principle in nature suitable to their original: all tyrannies have had their beginnings from corruption. . . . [Popular and well-mixed governments] are ever established by wise and good men and can never be upheld otherwise than by virtue.[19]

Much of the political drama of the late eighteenth century was concerned with this problem of withholding the means of corruption, and although Americans dealt with this issue by separating powers between coordinate branches of the government, by dividing authority between state and federal governments, and by forbidding trespass on individual liberties, they also placed great emphasis on preventing the growth of parties.

For all their theoretical antipartyism, Jefferson and Washington, along with Americans before and since, behaved as partisans in spite of themselves. Hardly had the new government begun when organized disagreement erupted over Hamilton's economic programs and Jay's Treaty; and, as Joseph Charles and Richard Hofstadter have noted, the more partisan George Washington became, the more he condemned political parties.[20] Jefferson, who denied such organizations any place in government, nevertheless spent much of his life creating one. Even James Monroe, who viewed parties as defects in government because they created distinct orders and increased the public's "passion and excitement," invested his considerable energies in establishing a one-party system. Of all the nation's early leaders, only Madison appreciated the inevitability of political divisions; viewing parties as an unavoidable

[19]H. Trever Colbourn, *The Lamp of Experience: Whig History and the Intellectual Origins of the American Revolution* (Chapel Hill: University of North Carolina Press, 1965); J. G. A. Pocock, "Machiavelli, Harrington, and Political Ideologies in the Eighteenth Century," in Pocock, ed., *Politics, Language, and Time: Essays on Political Thought and History* (New York: Atheneum, 1971), pp. 104–47; Algernon Sidney, *Political Classics: Life, Memoirs,* (London: Dill Eaten, 1794), 1: 542.

[20]Rudolph Bell, *Party and Faction in American Politics: The House of Representatives, 1789–1801* (Westport, Conn.: Greenwood Press, 1973); Richard Buel, *Securing the Revolution: Ideology in American Politics, 1789–1815* (Ithaca: Cornell University Press, 1972); Charles, *Origins of Party System,* p. 44; Richard Hofstadter, *The Idea of a Party System: The Rise of Legitimate Opposition in the United States, 1789–1840* (Berkeley: University of California Press, 1969).

evil, he moved beyond reflexive opposition to offer a means of controlling faction through a federal government, a large republic, and a separation of powers. Fittingly, Madison superintended one of the nation's first political organizations—the cadre of congressmen who voted together in opposition to Hamilton's economic program.[21]

As the nation prospered along with its parties, a few Americans turned the doctrine of antipartyism on its head and held parties to be one of the reasons for the republic's stability. For example, along with their failings the Maryland Democrat Philip Friese discovered seven benefits the nation had already derived from its parties, including instruction in public affairs. In his inaugural address John Quincy Adams applauded "the splendid talents, spotless integrity, ardent patriotism, and disinterested sacrifices" that American parties had made to the "formation and administration of this Government." Frederick Grimké, brother of Sarah and Angelina, went even farther to argue that parties were necessary to uphold and preserve government. "It is most certain," wrote Grimké in 1848, "that the distinguishing excellence of free institutions consists in their giving birth to popular parties. . . ."[22]

Yet such propartyism was rare before the Civil War. More typical and more important to the Democracy's ability to acquaint its northern members with expected public roles was the organization's internal sense of itself. By mid-century three images had developed which, while neither mutually exclusive nor chronologically sequenced, were nonetheless necessary antecedents to its emerging role as an agency transmitting information, values, and feelings. More than any lever of recruitment or form of indoctrination, these senses of party bound the Northern Democracy into a loose fraternity of believers whose views of the world were molded by their partisan organization. Rarely mentioned in official platforms or resolutions, such attitudes are best studied through the lives and writings of three Northern Democrats: George Bancroft, Martin Van Buren, and Samuel Cox.

[21]James Monroe, *The People the Sovereigns* (Philadelphia: Lippincott, 1867), pp. 16, 76, 160. Begun in 1825, this manuscript was unfinished at his death and was finally published in 1867. See also Monroe to L. W. Tazewell, 20 October 1808; Monroe to Colonel John Taylor, 9 November 1810, both in Stanislaus Murray Hamilton, ed., *The Writings of James Monroe,* (New York: Putnam, 1902); Jacob Cooke, ed., *The Federalist Papers* (Middletown, Conn.: Wesleyan University Press, 1961), pp. 56–65, 395–99; J. G. A. Pocock, "The Classical Theory of Deference," *American Historical Review* 81 (June 1976): 517; Charles S. Sydnor, *Gentlemen Freeholders: Political Practices in Washington's Virginia* (Chapel Hill: University of North Carolina Press, 1952).

[22]Philip Friese, *An Essay on Party Showing Its Uses, Its Abuses, and Its Natural Dissolution* (New York: Fowler and Wells, 1856); quotations from Hofstadter, *Idea of a Party System,* pp. 234, 265.

In 1860, when George Bancroft—historian, diplomat, and Democrat—completed the eighth volume of *The History of the United States from the Discovery of the Continent,* no one noticed that his recounting of the nation's beginnings did not mention political parties. Given the persistence of antipartyism, Americans did not expect him to. Instead reviewers praised a "historical classic of great spirit and dramatic effect."[23] Nor did Bancroft's postwar works mention political parties; when they appeared at all in his immense production of nearly two million words, parties were offhand insertions that served as identification tags rather than as historical forces. Although Bancroft praised other nascent institutions such as newspapers and schools, even in his later volumes American democracy had little to do with partisan organizations. Instead it represented "the triumph of the mind of humanity displaying its energies in visible movement of its intelligence." In short, democracy was God's will, not man's politics.[24]

Bancroft's omissions can be explained in part by his choice of subject matter. Preoccupied with the moment of national creation, he directed his energy to the revolutionary period and devoted two leisurely volumes to the years 1774–1776. Political parties, as organized mass movements with stable constituencies, popular appeals, and national leaders, simply did not exist in this period, and only with difficulty have modern historians located the roots of the Democratic party in the anti-Federalism of the 1780s.[25] Writing for a new nation with (according to Tocqueville) "no roots, no memories, no prejudices, no routine, no common ideas, and no national character," Bancroft wished to create a national past, "bedaubed," as his colleague Richard Hildreth explained, "with patriotic rouge."[26] There was little room for sallow factions in

[23]George H. Callcott, *History in the United States, 1800–1860: Its Practice and Purpose* (Baltimore: Johns Hopkins University Press, 1970), p. 23.

[24]Russel B. Nye, *George Bancroft* (New York: Washington Square Press, 1964); idem, *Bancroft, Brahmin Rebel;* Robert H. Canary, *George Bancroft* (New York: Twayne, 1974). On the reaction to Bancroft's writing, see Nye, *Bancroft, Brahmin Rebel,* p. 200, and for his number of words, p. 283; on his popularity, J. Franklin Jameson, *The History of Historical Writing in America* (Boston: Houghton Mifflin, 1891), p. 103; Bert James Loewenberg, *American History in American Thought* (New York: Simon and Schuster, 1972), pp. 241–49. The quotation is from George Bancroft, *Address at Hartford before Delegates to the Democratic Convention* (Boston: Bay State Democrat, 1840).

[25]For a review of the literature, see Ronald P. Formisano, "Differential Participant Politics in the Early Republic's Political Culture, 1789–1840," *American Political Science Review* 68 (June 1974): 473–87.

[26]Quoted in Yehoshua Arieli, *Individualism and Nationalism in American Ideology* (Baltimore: Penguin Books, 1964), p. 17; Harvey Wish, *The American Historian: A Social-Intellectual History of the Writing of the American Past* (New York: Oxford University Press, 1960), p. 62.

such a makeup. Given his intentions of instilling patriotism and inspiring nationalism, it is not surprising that Bancroft celebrated only one party—that of patriots—and one national leader—George Washington.

Despite his preoccupation with a time when parties were only shadows and his indifference to them even after they had developed, Bancroft inhabited a partisan present. Like many Americans he tolerated a wide gap between his antiparty theories and his public practices. Early in life he had become a Democrat, but his politics were not the reflexive sort of most Americans, who simply followed their father's choice. Instead Bancroft denied his political lineage, rejecting his father's Federalism as well as the fervent Whiggism of his Dwight in-laws and his brother-in-law John Davis, a Whig governor of Massachusetts. In the 1840s Bancroft brought the Massachusetts Democrats the much-needed intellectual prestige of a doctor of philosophy, and his stature helped dispel the identification of the party with radical unschooled workingmen's groups.[27] (This same notion of the Democrats as not quite respectable inspired Varina Howell's comment in 1843 about her future husband, Jefferson Davis: "Would you believe it, he is refined and cultivated, and yet he is a Democrat.")[28]

By the 1840s Bancroft's politics delayed his writing, and the long hiatus between the third volume of the *History,* which appeared in 1839, and the fourth, in 1852, had nothing to do with the difficulty of locating sources and doing research. Party service had intruded on his scholarship. Unsuccessful campaigns for governor and congressman as well as service in a number of appointive posts, including collector of the Port of Boston and secretary of the Navy, left little time for writing. Never self-conscious about the simultaneous process of writing and making history (only in the twentieth century did Americans become so), the nation's most influential historian ordered Zachary Taylor's troops to the banks of the Rio Grande in 1846, organized the Naval Academy, and negotiated a postal treaty with Great Britain. Throughout, he lived on intimate terms with politicians, providing campaign oratory that some called "gilded, ornate, and on stilts,"[29] and arranging coalitions between workingmen's and anti-Masonic groups in the byzantine world of Massachusetts politics. Nor was Bancroft ignorant of the ways of patronage; he ingratiated himself with Martin Van Buren through gifts of iced salmon and a copy of his *History* and with James Polk

[27]Nye, *George Bancroft,* pp. 6–7.

[28]James T. McIntosh, ed., *The Papers of Jefferson Davis,* vol. 2 (Baton Rouge: Louisiana University Press, 1975), p. 53.

[29]Samuel S. Green, *George Bancroft* (Worcester: Charles Hamilton, 1891), p. 9.

through a gift even more gratefully received—his support at the 1844 Democratic national convention.[30] A great historian, Bancroft was also a shrewd party operator.

Even after the Civil War, Bancroft's *History* continued to be delayed by his public service, first as a presidential speechwriter and then as minister to Berlin. It was Bancroft who wrote Andrew Johnson's 1865 message to Congress, a state paper of such erudition that unsuspecting editorial writers applauded the new president's intellectual talents along with the educational system that had produced him.[31] Retirement in the 1870s assured uninterrupted time for research and writing. Leaving historiographers to wonder why he had not undertaken a partisan narrative of Jefferson's triumph in 1800 or the rise of Jacksonian Democracy, Bancroft revised his *History,* wrote the story of the Constitution, and answered the complaints of angry readers who believed their ancestors had been maligned in earlier versions of the *History*. Even his last book, a revised 1844 campaign biography of Martin Van Buren, slighted that president's considerable political talents for a panegyric of American values. A fervent partisan and accomplished historian who believed that corrupt Whigs could not rest at night for their "guilty consciences" but who granted Democrats "a quiet heart and tranquil sleep," Bancroft inhabited two worlds. Other nineteenth-century writers neglected parties because they were unaware of their significance or believed them to be ephemeral, single-issue lobbyists; not so Bancroft.[32]

Neither the climate of antipartyism nor a desire for deferential politics explains Bancroft's ambivalence toward parties. He was born too late to indulge in the reflexive opposition of a generation whose public lives, for the most part, preceded the development of organized political associations. In the 1790s it was possible to see factions as a potential threat to a fragile republic, but by 1840 the nation seemed more like tensile steel. It had not broken apart during the War of 1812 or even during the tumultuous years of Jackson's administration, and as it grew,

[30]George Bancroft to Martin Van Buren, 17 November 1834 and 12 June 1843, both in "Van Buren–Bancroft Correspondence" *Proceedings of the Massachusetts Historical Society* 42 (1908–09), 382, 408.

[31]Nye, *Bancroft, Brahmin Rebel,* p. 230.

[32]M. A. DeWolfe Howe, ed., *The Life and Letters of George Bancroft,* 2 vols. (New York: Scribner's, 1908), 1: 258. John Stuart Mill, *Considerations on Representative Government* (Indianapolis: Liberal Arts Press, 1958). Mill wrote of majorities and minorities, but gave little attention to parties in a work devoted to the theory and structure of representative government. See also *Personal Representation: Speech of John Stuart Mill Delivered in the House of Commons, May 29, 1867* (London, 1867).

so did political organizations. A few Americans tentatively connected the two and called parties, in the common metaphor of the time, "engines of progress."[33] A fading elite might translate its loss of authority into a distrust for parties, but Bancroft had benefited from the politics of deference. He had never won an election except within his party, and the public service he considered a national duty depended on patronage favors from Democratic officials. Nor could his two worlds be explained by any brooding concern that parties would lead to national perdition. An unshakable optimist and believer in America's destiny, Bancroft never limned the dark side of the national mind, where self-doubt and the sense of the United States as a precarious experiment lingered. Instead he envisaged progress in all things American. The Civil War briefly shook that faith, but by 1865 even the war had become another national challenge successfully surmounted.[34]

A better interpretation of Bancroft is to see him as representing the transition in American attitudes toward political parties. Unlike Washington, Jefferson, and Madison, Bancroft did not condemn parties so much as deny them a place in history. In his early speeches he even acknowledged a natural tripartite division among mankind:

> The tory idolizes power; the whig worships his interests; democracy struggles for equal rights. The tory pleads for absolute monarchy; the whig for the wealthy aristocracy; democracy for the power of the people. The tory regards liberty as a boon, the whig regards it as a fortunate privilege, democracy claims freedom as an inalienable right. . . . The tory adheres to the party of Moloch; the whig still worships at the shrine of Mammon; Democracy is practical Christianity.[35]

In the same speech Bancroft argued that parties served to educate the people in public affairs and hence to resolve the tension between anarchy—a condition of diverse individualistic opinions—and tyranny—a condition of one fixed principle. But this was theory, delivered in an oration full of metaphysical concepts. The practice of partisanship could not enter Bancroft's history, for he had no sense of a party system in

[33]Nahum Capen, *The History of Democracy in the United States* (Hartford: Case, Tiffany, 1852), p. 2.

[34]George Bancroft to Sandy Bliss, 21 January 1863, Bancroft-Bliss Papers, Library of Congress (hereafter cited as Bancroft-Bliss Papers); Howe, *Life and Letters of Bancroft*, 2: 141–42.

[35]Quoted in George Bancroft, *An Oration Delivered before the Democracy of Springfield, Mass. and Neighboring Towns, July 4, 1836* (Boston: Merriam, 1836), pp. 2–3; see also "The Necessity, the Reality, and the Promise of the Progress of the Human Race", in George Bancroft, *Literary and Historical Miscellanies* (New York: Harper Brothers, 1855), p. 486.

which competing organizations exchanged power. Instead he gazed beyond the controversies of the present into a harmonious future in which the party of both Whig and Tory would have been replaced by the people's Democracy. Already American history demonstrated his expectations, for in Bancroft's rendering, the division of the colonies into Tory traitors and Whig patriots had given way in the postrevolutionary period to one nation of democrats.

Armed with his providential view of history, Bancroft saw the United States as the ultimate triumph of God's will expressed in the people's voice—"the spirit of God breathing through the combined intelligence of the people."[36] Eventually there must be one voice, just as there was one God. In political terms Bancroft's inability to distinguish between the Democracy of his politics and the democracy of his nation underwrote a capacious one-party arrangement wherein the public mind was undivided and public affairs established a homogeneous "spirit of the age."[37] Thus politics and history intersected in a kind of democratic functionalism: whatever was should be, and whatever would be was shaped by the irrevocable progress toward Democracy—the law of God in the soul of man.

Such views led later historians to complain that the *History* voted for Andrew Jackson. J. Franklin Jameson found the work "redolent of the ideas of the new Democracy." Bancroft was not alive to respond, but he had been perplexed when the German historian Ranke pronounced the *History* the best ever written from the Democratic point of view, and his friend, the French statesman and historian François Guizot, also proclaimed it "very Democratic." Two generations removed from historical relativism, Bancroft felt he wrote, in accordance with Ranke's own axiom, history as it actually was, namely, a progression of triumphs leading toward freedom and democracy. As he explained in speeches and letters, "Truth is one. . . . One truth cannot contradict another truth." Bancroft never believed that he took sides, for there were no sides to take. "I deny the charge; if there is democracy in the *History* it is not subjective, but objective . . . and so has necessarily its place in history and gives its colour as it should. . . ."[38]

[36]Bancroft, *Literary and Historical Miscellanies,* p. 425. For examples of Bancroft's treatment of the revolution's traitors and patriots, see Bancroft, *The History of the United States from the Discovery of the Continent,* 10 vols. (Boston: Little and Brown, 1844–1874), 8: 176, 285, 297, 304–07, 407; 9: 31–32, 171, 215, 257, 282, 357.

[37]The term *capacious party* is used in John Zvesper, *Political Philosophy and Rhetoric* (Cambridge: At the University Press, 1977), p. 6.

[38]Jameson, *History of Historical Writing,* pp. 104, 107; Howe, *Life and Letters of Bancroft,* 2: 183; Wish, *American Historian,* p. 120; Bancroft, *Literary and Historical Miscellanies,* p. 415.

From this perspective, there was no need to consider the opposition—whether Federalist, Whig, or Know-Nothing—and in both his life and his writing Bancroft became the ultimate partisan, refusing even to acknowledge the existence of opponents. Based on the inevitability of the Democracy, Bancroft's teleological sense of party left no room for a minority. He was a majoritarian who had moved beyond antipartyism but who could not accept the possibility that party conflict contributed to republican society. His friend and fellow Massachusetts Democrat Frederick Robinson expressed this position directly: "It is impossible for a true democrat to be a party man. . . . For how can he be a partisan who looks upon all men as equal and contends that there is no power, no advantage, and no privilege which can be enjoyed by any one man or class of men. . . . How indeed can that be called a party which embraces and equalizes all citizens?"[39] Like other Democrats of his generation, Bancroft acknowledged the consensus of the Era of Good Feelings as an ideal, and he worked for a similar expansiveness in his own party.

Predisposed toward a permanent one-party system, Bancroft promptly joined what he considered its wartime version—the Union party—and, unlike most Northern Democrats, served the administration throughout the war. Despite initial hesitation about Lincoln (Bancroft wrote in 1860 that the president "had no brains" and was fit only "for summer wear"), he volunteered his talents and was soon at work researching historical precedents for Lincoln's suspension of the writ of habeas corpus. In return, he sought his stepson's promotion to quartermaster of an army corps, but the practices of deferential politics did not hold—at least not for a prominent Democrat during wartime—and Colonel Bliss remained in the infantry. Meanwhile Bancroft enjoyed his trips to Washington and at one reception was identified by a forgetful president as "History, History of the United States."[40] Bancroft could forgive such oversights, for in his view Lincoln, whom he quietly supported in 1864, had come to represent "the national voice of the people." Only when Republicans approached him to run for Congress in New York—not Massachusetts as his principal biographer states—did Bancroft refuse, inhibited by his Democratic attachments, which he

[39]Quoted in Joseph Blau, *Social Theories of Jacksonian Democracy* (Indianapolis: Bobbs-Merrill, 1959), p. 323.

[40]Howe, *Life and Letters of Bancroft,* 2: 132–34, 155–56; Nye, *Bancroft, Brahmin Rebel,* p. 209; George Bancroft to Elizabeth Bancroft, 14 September 1861, George Bancroft Papers, Cornell University; Montgomery Meigs to Samuel Hooper, 11 February 1863, Bancroft-Bliss Papers; Library of Congress.

resumed after the war.[41] In 1866 he provided Congress with a grandiloquent eulogy of Lincoln. Faithful to his providential vision of American history, he explained the war as an instrument of God to which his fellow citizens had responded as patriots—none more heroically than the martyred president: "As the sum of all, the hand of Lincoln raised the flag, the American people was the hero of the war; and therefore, the result is a new era of republicanism. The party for slavery and the party against slavery are no more and are merged in the party of Union and freedom."[42]

Whatever his importance as an American historian and Lincoln eulogist, Bancroft's definition of party was crucial during the war years, when some Northerners saw their choice as one between the patriotism of the Union movement and the disloyalty of the Southern-dominated Democratic party. Stephen Douglas's statement typified the dilemma of party supporters: "There are only two sides to the question. Every man must be either for the United States or against it." The Democratic *Daily City Fact* of Columbus, Ohio, offered a similar choice in 1861: "Those who are not for the stars and stripes are against them. There is no middle ground."[43] Knowing themselves to be patriots, some Northern Democrats retrieved Bancroft's historical casting of a unified patriotic front struggling formerly against English, now against Southern tyrants. They replaced their previous Democratic attachments with what they considered the crisis-spawned successor of Unionism. Because these Northern Democrats understood party as a consensual instrument of Americanism, they easily joined their former enemies and were called for the duration Unionists.

Whereas Bancroft made the Democracy into an instrument of American unanimity (not, as antipartyism had it, a divisive destroyer of the commonwealth), Martin Van Buren's sense of party reflected the reality of partisan life in the 1830s and 1840s. Not only did the New Yorker respect the opposition; he also acknowledged the significance of party activities—whether voting, electioneering, or choosing a candidate—as training exercises. Perhaps no one was better equipped to understand the Democratic party in this way than was this son of a New York tavernkeeper who learned his politics in the most natural of settings—

[41]Nye, *Bancroft, Brahmin Rebel*, p. 217.

[42]George Bancroft, *Memorial Address on the Life and Character of Abraham Lincoln* (Washington, D.C.: Government Printing Office, 1866), p. 50.

[43]*Illinois State Register*, 3 May 1861; *Chicago Tribune*, 26 April and 2 May 1861; quotations from *Speech of Senator Douglas, before the Legislature of Illinois*, April 25, 1861 (n.p., 1861); and Howard Perkins, ed., *Northern Editorials on Secession*, vol. 2 (New York: D. Appleton, 1942), p. 728.

the local bar—and who rose from Columbia County surrogate to the White House. No nineteenth-century Northerner was more conscious of or grateful to political parties. "There are few men in the state more indebted to the favor of the Jeffersonian Republican Party than myself and none more willing to acknowledge it," Van Buren admitted in 1826.[44] More important for Northern Democrats, Van Buren helped to mold an organization of loyal supporters united by belief, work, and shared experience. Among the first to appreciate the benefits of competition, he spent his early life "resuscitating the old democratic party."[45] He did not undertake or accomplish this task alone, but as much as anyone else—including his fellow members of the New York Regency and his patron, Andrew Jackson—Van Buren recognized the role that parties would play in a democratic society.[46] Instinctively he sensed that politics followed the nation, and his struggles for a party of ritualized behavior and internal democracy acknowledged the extension of voting and officeholding rights in nineteenth-century America. And because parties reflected as well as influenced society, Martin Van Buren expected a few leaders to run the organization, just as they did the nation, and he believed that the objectives of liberty and democracy were best achieved through well-established machinery. Accordingly, nominations for office depended on the selection, at the ward and precinct level, of delegates who usually held some sort of partisan credentials and whose nominations were often engineered by insiders.

The nation's first professional politician, Martin Van Buren reserved his sharpest denunciations for heretics, and of these James Monroe and New York's governor De Witt Clinton were the worst.[47] Van Buren was outraged when Clinton promiscuously attached himself to various coalitions, and throughout his life he condemned those who, in his friend Jabez Hammond's words, "tried their chance in a caucus and then because [their] wishes weren't gratified . . . attempt to defeat the result of the deliberations of [their] friends." It was always, as Ham-

[44]Draft of a speech to be read at the Herkimer Convention, 3 October 1826, Martin Van Buren Papers (Microfilm edition; hereafter cited as Van Buren Papers).

[45]Martin Van Buren to Thomas Ritchie, 13 January 1827; Van Buren to Charles E. Dudley, 10 January 1822, both in Van Buren Papers; Charles R. King, ed., *The Life and Correspondence of Rufus King* (New York: Putnam, 1878), p. 438.

[46]Jackson's contributions were symbolic, not organizational. For one study of his minor role in reconstituting the Democracy, see Thomas Abernathy, "Andrew Jackson and the Rise of Southwestern Democracy," *American Historical Review* 33 (October 1927): 64–77.

[47]John C. Fitzpatrick, ed., "The Autobiography of Martin Van Buren," *Report of the American Historical Association* (Washington: Government Printing Office, 1920), pp. 87, 124–26, 197; Van Buren to Dr. Worth, 22 April 1819, Van Buren Papers.

mond explained, "Van Buren's intention to substitute party principle for personal preference," and it is clear that the New Yorker expected the Democracy to serve as an antidote to sectionalism.[48] Monroe's errors were equally egregious, for, in Van Buren's words, he practiced "the amalgamationist heresy" of trying to absorb everyone into a one-party movement.[49]

Van Buren's sense of party was different; he hoped for a band of Democrats—"a political brotherhood" loyal to an organization rather than to a leader or an issue.[50] From such a base, he expected the Democracy to become a disciplined majority, not a transitory coalition, a legislative caucus, or an amorphous fraternity of all Americans. Thus in 1820, when Monroe, in a demonstration of capacious one-partyism, was reelected to the presidency with no opposition and only one dissenting electoral vote, Van Buren was busy organizing newspapers, encouraging local conventions to get out the Democratic vote, and complaining about the "cant against parties" that hindered his efforts. As a U.S. Senator in the 1820s, Van Buren was well known for his interest in political machinery, and his bill to assign electoral votes on a district basis was written to induce party competition for the presidency.[51]

Unlike his campaign biographer, George Bancroft, Van Buren inhabited one world—that of politics, in which men inherited their allegiances from their fathers, fought to instill the faith during their life, and passed their party on to their sons, as treasured a legacy as any family heirloom.[52] In such a world parties were animate entities worthy of passionate, enduring allegiance, not just collections of ideas, associations of national leaders, or impersonal bureaucracies. With Martin Van Buren's encouragement men sang to parties, cursed them, gambled on them (Van Buren and his son bet everything from champagne to a thousand dollars on elections), and sometimes even fought for them at

[48]Jabez Hammond, *The History of Political Parties in the State of New York from the Ratification of the Federal Constitution to December, 1840*, 2 vols. (Cooperstown, N.Y.: H. and E. Phinney, 1844), 1: 192–93; Van Buren to Thomas Ritchie, 13 January 1827, Van Buren Papers.

[49]"Autobiography of Martin Van Buren," p. 194.

[50]Ibid., p. 163.

[51]Van Buren to Jesse Hoyt, 31 January 1823, Van Buren Papers; Van Buren to Flagg, 22 December 1826, Flagg Papers, Columbia University Library; "Autobiography of Martin Van Buren," p. 125; Robert Remini, *Martin Van Buren and the Making of the Democratic Party* (New York: Columbia University Press, 1959), p. 15; Van Buren to Thomas Ritchie, 13 January 1827; both in Van Buren Papers.

[52]"Autobiography of Martin Van Buren," p. 123.

the polls.[53] Americans who shared this understanding might not praise parties, but they seemed ready to die for them. Viewed from such a perspective, competition was natural, beneficial, and purposeful.Not only did the election battles inspire loyalty to the organization, but the existence of an enemy also provided the best of institutional glues. A zero-sum game, two-party politics could not be played, in Martin Van Buren's league, without an opponent.

Before Van Buren, there had been only fleeting recognition of the importance of an opponent for self-determination, but by the 1830s the New York Regency understood that parties were most in jeopardy when their opposition was not sufficiently defined. So, too, did an Alabama Democrat who also reversed Bancroft's political ideals: "I think the only danger to the Democratic party is that it will become an omnibus in this state. We have nothing to fear from either the Union, or Whig party or both combined. From their friendship and adherence much."[54] Such statements implied limits to partisan capaciousness, but they did not suggest that rivalry benefited nation as well as party.

In many ways, Van Buren typified a new managerial class. Service to his organization precluded any private life, although, no colorless bureaucrat, he was remembered by New Yorkers for his white duck trousers, snuff-colored broadcloth coat, orange tie, and yellow vest, as well as for his good humor and diverting anecdotes. In 1831 on a voyage to Europe the middle-aged Van Buren reflected on his master passion:

> For more than a quarter of a century, there was scarcely one day during which I had been wholly exempted from the disturbing effects of partisan agitation . . . whether as a subordinate and doubtless at times over-zealous member of the political party in which I had almost literally been reared from childhood or as its leader for many years. . . . Politics had always absorbed my time and faculties.[55]

Even at seventy-one, enjoying the splendor of Italy's coastline near Amalfi, he saw himself as a party man, not as a farmer, lawyer, businessman, father, or husband. The public had absorbed the private: his personal history became the chronicle of an early visit to the legislature, his first election to the state senate, and his electioneering for the Democracy. Today only devoted students of New York politics take pleasure in such tales, and not even the *ex officio* significance accorded most

[53]George Bancroft, *Martin Van Buren to the End of His Career* (New York: Harper Brothers, 1889), p. 386; Remini, *Martin Van Buren,* p. 123.

[54]Quoted in Michael Holt, *The Political Crisis of the 1850s* (New York: Wiley, 1978), p. 13.

[55]"Autobiography of Martin Van Buren," p. 445.

presidential writings has saved these memoirs of a partisan from oblivion.

Not only did Van Buren see himself as a professional; he also accepted his defeats with the equanimity of a technician who knew the rules. In the bittersweet world of electoral politics, he acknowledged the possibility of losing. When George Bancroft wrote that the cause of humanity was at stake and liberty and freedom were endangered because Van Buren had lost to the Whig Harrison in 1840, the defeated candidate explained his personal failure in less apocalyptic terms and pointed out that his loss would have little lasting effect on the Democratic party.[56] In 1832, when the Senate refused to confirm him as ambassador to the Court of St. James (although he was already in London and heard the news at a reception), and in 1844 when his own party replaced him with the relatively unknown James Polk, he accepted the outcome as the fate of practicing politicans. Conscious of politics as a career and remembering the personal snubs he had suffered as a young boy from Federalists, Van Buren accepted his political opponents as personal friends and, like a lawyer who defends the guilty as well as the innocent, avoided moral judgments. It was typical of Van Buren that after Jackson's famous toast to Union and John Calhoun's to Liberty, he raised his glass, at Jefferson's birthday celebration, to "mutual concessions and forbearance." Rivals were never enemies; even Alexander Hamilton, the Democracy's bête noire, emerged in Van Buren's writings as a well-intentioned, if misled, opponent.[57] Such partisan tolerance was not remarkable, for most Americans came to behave the same way and never cared, in the ultimate test, whether their daughters married out of party. But Van Buren was among the first to value what the English call "dining with the opposition."[58] In other political cultures, party differences divided neighborhoods, destroyed romances, and broke up families. If the mutual forbearance of Americans is explained by widespread acceptance of the governmental system—as distinguished from agreement over the allocation of its resources—Martin Van Buren deserves credit for fostering an interparty comity that came to mark the nation's public habits.[59]

[56]George Bancroft to Martin Van Buren, 2 November 1840; Van Buren to Bancroft, 20 November 1840; both in "Van Buren–Bancroft Correspondence," pp. 386–88, Remini, *Martin Van Buren,* p. 190.

[57]Van Buren, *Inquiry,* pp. 73–74; James Curtis, *The Fox at Bay: Martin Van Buren and the Presidency, 1837–1841* (Lexington: University of Kentucky Press, 1970), p. 32.

[58]Rodney Barker, ed., *Studies in Opposition* (London: MacMillan, 1971), p. 32.

[59]Van Buren, *Inquiry,* pp. 166, 180, 220. For studies of other party cultures, see Lucien W. Pye and Sidney Verba, *Political Culture and Political Development* (Princeton: Princeton University Press, 1965), p. 548.

Such tolerance did not mean that Van Buren's parties lacked principles, for the Democracy was grounded in a set of beliefs. Like his friend Nahum Capen, Van Buren expected progress from the clash he believed had always divided Americans into Hamiltonian Federalists, who distrusted the people, and Jeffersonian Democrats, who believed in popular government. According to Van Buren, Democrats protected the people by diffusing power and preventing its centralization, whether in the form of high tariffs, a public debt, or a United States bank. In this role, they were "lions in the path" of those who distrusted popular sovereignty. Numbers, in such a political calculus, were on the Democratic side, but this advantage was offset by the resources of power-hungry money-grabbers who, in their various guises of Federalist, Whig, and Republican, lusted after authority. Government, according to Van Buren, must never serve such special interests, for favoritism tipped the scales against the libertarian universe he and his followers hoped to establish. In the Democracy's ideal world, a system of natural liberty prevailed in which men were free to use their talents, privilege was outlawed, and the invisible hand of market forces and local custom regulated society. "All communities are apt to look to government for too much," he wrote in 1837. "The real duty [of government] is to enact and enforce a system of general laws commensurate with, but not exceeding, the objects of its establishment, and to leave every citizen and every interest to reap under its benign protection the rewards of virtue, industry, and prudence."[60] That such a system favored white male property owners reflected Van Buren's definition of the Democracy in terms of an ancient enemy—moneyed aristocrats—and not future protagonists—the working class, women, and blacks.

As fervently as Bancroft or any other believer in a capacious one-party system, Van Buren expected his party to be victorious. It usually was in the years before the Civil War when the Democrats won six of the nine presidential elections held from 1828 through 1860, controlled the House of Representatives for twenty-four of those thirty-two years, and the Senate for twenty-eight. With an enduring majority on the Supreme Court, Democratic convictions clearly informed what Stephen Douglas called "the great measures of the day,"[61] and this national power was replicated at the local level.

[60]Richardson, *Messages and Papers,* 3: 344. For the development of these ideas, see Robert Kelley, *The Transatlantic Persuasion: The Liberal-Democratic Mind in the Age of Gladstone* (New York: A. A. Knopf, 1969); for Van Buren's version, see *Inquiry*.

[61]Stephen A. Douglas to Sidney Breese, 20 October 1840, Sidney Breese Papers, Illinois State Historical Society, Springfield.

But winners required losers, and because Van Buren's sense of party included an opposition, he was able to do what Bancroft could not—write American history with the parties left in. "No free country," he concluded in 1856, "can exist without political parties,"[62] and his posthumously published works—the *Inquiry* and the "Autobiography"—established party competition as the centerpiece of the national past. Initiating what became a commonplace interpretation, Van Buren offered the history of parties as the history of the United States. But despite the persistent and sometimes violent conflict during his lifetime among Federalists, Whigs, and Democrats, he never encouraged the bitter revanchism that made partisans, in other nations and times, yearn to replace each other by any tactic. Instead Van Buren acknowledged the possibility of error: the anti-Federalists, for example, had wrongly opposed the Constitution, while the Federalists had correctly understood its merits. He remembered an early mistake of his own when he voted federal monies for an interstate road. Like Edmund Burke, he believed that parties combined men of like principle, and when party erred—for humans did follow false trails—true men departed. "Perfection does not appertain to men or associations of men,"[63] and it was in such terms that Van Buren explained his own apostasy. When Democrats refused to support an antislavery pledge in the territories, he reluctantly became the presidential candidate of the third-party Free Soilers in 1848. Despite his return to the Democracy in the 1850s, he was ever after, according to one regular, "a fallen angel."[64]

There was irony in such a fate, for Van Buren had become the victim of his success. Democrats who had benefited from his sense of party as an organization based on specific habits and activities condemned him for his failure to abide by his own rules. Those who remembered the Panic of 1837 and his opposition to Texas annexation forgot his devotion to the organization; even Davy Crockett, not known for his own probity, accused the former president of worshiping office and money. A master of equivocation, Van Buren became famous for speeches that avoided specific commitments, and he soon symbolized the partisan trimmer. Even George Bancroft, who had been commissioned in 1844 to write "a full statement of his cause and character . . . a textbook for orators,"[65] withheld his work after Polk's nomination, and only years

[62]*Letter of President Van Buren, June 28, 1856* (n.p., n.d.).

[63]Ibid.

[64]*Speech of Fernando Wood, February 7, 1860* (New York: Office of the Daily News, 1860), p. 4.

[65]"Autobiography of Martin Van Buren," pp. 169–71; Alvin Kass, *Politics in New York*

later published a biography that celebrated Van Buren's brief apostasy, not his activism.

Van Buren died before the Civil War ended, but he left an important legacy for his party. Having moved beyond the reflexive antipartyism of Washington's generation and the one-partyism of Bancroft, he intended parties to be the durable associations that a twentieth-century observer once described "as something simpler and more permanent, something which can be loved and trusted and which can be recognized at successive elections as being the same thing that was loved before."[66] Many Northern Democrats could not give up their affection even during the Civil War; partisan habits such as selecting delegates, meeting in conventions. listening to speeches, talking about party affairs, and casting ballots had become a part of their lives. The behavior of the Marshall family in Indiana typified this sense of party. According to Thomas Marshall, "My father and grandfather were notified during the Civil War that their Methodist preacher would have to strike their names off the role if they continued to vote Democratic. My grandfather announced he was willing to take his chance in Hell but never on the Republicans." And in Carlock, Illinois, Democrats felt this partisan kinship so strongly that they buried their dead in a Democratic graveyard.[67]

A few Northern Democrats moved beyond Van Buren's "party of practice" to a new understanding of parties as being essential to republican government because they offered choices and reviewed policies. No one developed this sense of party more effectively than Ohio's Samuel Sullivan Cox. The son and grandson of active partisans, Cox was born

---

*State, 1800–1830* (Syracuse: Syracuse University Press, 1965), p. 7; Remini, *Martin Van Buren*, pp. 1, 31; Quotation from Van Buren to Bancroft, 25 February 1844, in "Van Buren–Bancroft Correspondence," p. 417: See also George Bancroft, *Martin Van Buren to the End of his Public Career* (New York: Harpers, 1889), p. 371.

[66]Graham Wallas, *Human Nature in Politics* (New York: F. S. Crofts, 1921), p. 103.

[67]Thomas R. Marshall, *Thomas R. Marshall* (Indianapolis: Bobbs-Merrill, 1925), pp. 70–71, 89; for other examples of party habits, *New York Times*, 2 November 1980; Michael W. Cluskey, *The Political Textbook* (Washington: C. Wendell, 1857), p. 22. For the persistence of parties, see Joel Silbey, *A Respectable Minority: The Democratic Party in the Civil War Era 1860–1868* (New York: W. W. Norton, 1977), pp. 1–15; Walter Dean Burnham, *Critical Elections and the Mainsprings of American Politics* (New York: W. W. Norton, 1970); Angus Campbell et al., *Elections and the Political Order* (New York: John Wiley, 1966); Ray Myles Shortridge, "Voting Patterns in the American Midwest, 1840–1872" (Ph.D. dissertation, University of Michigan, 1974); Peyton McCrary, "The Civil War Party System, 1854–1876: Toward a New Behavioral Synthesis" (Paper presented at the Meeting of the Southern Historical Association, 1976).

to be a Democratic politician. Whereas many American families embellished their traditions with tales of noble lineage or natural phenomena attending a birth, the Cox apocrypha included the appearance of a scroll of fire inscribing the words "Salus populi suprema lex" on the bedposts when young Samuel Sullivan was born in 1824. There was no fantasy about Grandfather Sullivan's will, which charged his grandson to remember that "his inheritance was the result of democratic institutions" and directed his namesake to "sustain those institutions in their democratic form and tenor with ballot and bullet." Such traditions encouraged Cox's political precocity. By fourteen he was a clerk in his county's court of common pleas; by seventeen, as a college student at Brown University, he asked for a subscription to Duff Green's *Telegraph* ("oh! but he is a scorcher," wrote Cox approvingly); by twenty-two he had already apprenticed in the most serviceable of political careers, law and journalism. At thirty-two he was the head of the Ohio Democratic State Central Committee and had managed a successful gubernatorial campaign. Ten years later he began the first of thirteen terms as a Democratic congressman.[68]

Successful in winner-take-all elections, Cox also understood minority politics. During his youth, Ohio had shifted from close competition between Whigs and Democrats to Republican hegemony. By 1861 Democrats had lost the governorship as well as control of the state's congressional and legislative delegations, and after the Kansas-Nebraska Act they suffered the defection of leaders such as Salmon P. Chase and Jacob Brinkerhoff to the newly formed Republicans. In his study of the Democratic party during the war years, Joel Silbey has classified Ohio as Republican controlled and only moderately competitive,[69] and although Cox managed to keep his seat until 1864, reelection was always perilous in the normally Republican district around Columbus. A member of the minority in his state, Cox also represented a

[68]David Lindsey, *Sunset Cox: Irrepressible Democrat* (Detroit: Wayne State University Press, 1969); William Van Zandt Cox and Milton Harlow Northrup, *Life of Samuel Sullivan Cox* (Syracuse: M. H. Northrup, 1899); Edward Stemple Wells, "The Political Career of Samuel Sullivan Cox during the Ohio Phase" (master's thesis, Ohio State University, 1935); Samuel S. Cox, *Eight Years in Congress, 1857–1865: Memoir and Speeches* (New York: D. Appleton, 1865); idem, *Three Decades of Federal Legislation* (Providence: J. A. and R. A. Reid, 1885); "Memorial Address of the Life and Character of S. S. Cox," in *Miscellaneous House Documents,* 51st Cong., 1st sess., p. 743. Cox's father was a state treasurer, his grandfather Sullivan a county judge and state senator, his grandfather Cox a congressman and friend of Jefferson's. My interpretation of a loyal opposition has been influenced by George Dennison, "The Idea of a Party System: A Critique," *Rocky Mountain Social Science Journal* 9 (April 1972): 31–52.

[69]Silbey, *Respectable Minority,* pp. 21–22.

minority within his party after he supported popular sovereignty in the territories and opposed the LeCompton Constitution. President Buchanan, who supported LeCompton, promptly rebuked the errant Ohioan by removing a Cox postmaster, and the young congressman later switched positions, voting for the administration's compromise bill.[70]

Able to hold conflicting positions simultaneously, Cox took a number of seemingly contradictory stances during the war. He opposed slavery but was against its abolition by Congress, the president, or the military. Ready in January 1865 to vote for the Thirteenth Amendment, he left his boardinghouse with a prepared speech favoring the amendment, only to vote no on the grounds that passage would interfere with peace negotiations and encourage the South to continue to war.[71] An imperialist and fervent nationalist who wanted to annex Cuba, Cox nonetheless supported states' rights. An enthusiastic expansionist, he displayed sensitivity to foreign cultures in his book *A Buckeye Abroad.* An Ohioan who reversed Horace Greeley's directive and moved to New York during the war, Cox was a faithful Democratic supporter of Republican war policies. At the same time, he encouraged a peace convention and approvingly quoted John Crittenden's paradox—"I do not fight the South because I hate her but because I love her." Some complained that this was political trimming, similar, as the nineteenth-century image had it, to fitting one's sails to catch any wind. Cox preferred the expression "saddle-bagging," and he defended his own tergiversations as examples of weighing priorities.[72] For this Democrat, like his mentor Edmund Burke, politics was not a pure science based on rigid abstractions, but a muddy terrain of uncertain causes, insoluble issues, proximate solutions, and reversed positions.

Such a mind understood the benefits of alternating power between parties, and Cox ransacked the past for the contributions of opposition parties:

> The time of war being the time of danger, the unreflecting and unphilosophical may wonder how such an opposition at such a period could consist with patriotism. Do they forget how England was saved from disgrace in the Crimean War by the onslaughts of the opposition led by the

[70]Cox, *Eight Years in Congress,* pp. 15–16; *Congressional Globe,* 35th Cong., 1st sess., 1880.

[71]Cox, *Three Decades,* pp. 322–28; *Congressional Globe,* 37th Cong., 1st sess., p. 331.

[72]*Congressional Globe,* 37th Cong., 1st sess., 331.; Cox, *Three Decades,* pp. 62–79, 314; Cox, *Eight Years in Congress,* pp. 109–19, 209; Cox, *Why We Laugh* (New York: Harper Brothers, 1876), p. 355.

*London Times?* May not the government be magnified by exposing the weakness of its administration?

Eventually Cox found so many examples in international sources that he concluded: "In all free countries an opposition is an element of the government. It is as indispensable to the safety of the realm as a free press or a free pulpit. To dispense with it is to endanger, if not to dispense with liberty."[73]

Cox did not rest his case with history, although he depended on historical evidence to buttress his argument. Nor did he limit opposition to that between political parties. Employing arguments from the American Revolution and axioms from Burke, he grounded the need for institutionalized antagonism in the power-seeking urges of human nature. Insatiable instincts propelled men, Cox believed, to acquire authority for their own advantage, and, like Jefferson, Cox considered the persistent criticism engendered by free speech, press, and elections an essential restraint on power's ineluctably "gliding to the few." Such views were part of his nation's antiauthoritarian tradition, but unlike Jefferson, Cox promoted parties to a position as a necessary check on majorities. "There is always a party out of power to watch the party in power," concluded Cox; he viewed Jefferson's "elective despotism" as demonstrating the consolidated authority of a one-party system. Like most Democrats, Cox thought his party less likely to corrupt power because it supported state and local rights, but unlike many of his fellow partisans, he did not believe the separation of powers a sufficient "clog" on the majority.[74] In his judgment, the expected equipoise of executive, legislature, and judiciary had not survived the growth of political organizations, which sometimes dominated, as did the Republicans by 1865, all three branches of government. What check on Lincoln, wondered Cox, was exercised by the Republican majorities in both House and Senate?

The only corrective was to establish a party opposition that publicly scrutinized administrative personnel and offered alternative policies. Cox's sense of opposition was twofold: first, to rectify, repeal, and, at the very least, challenge mistaken policy (that is, "to canvas the policy of the existing Administration"); and second, to replace the majority's

[73]Cox, *Three Decades,* p. 28; Cox, *Eight Years in Congress,* pp. 5–6, 235. Evidently Cox had read one of the few analyses of the concept in the *Edinburgh Review* 101 (January 1855); 2–22.

[74]Cox, *Eight Years in Congress;* p. 309; Cox, *Three Decades,* p. 28; *Congressional Globe,* 37th Cong., 3d sess., 1267.

errors with different programs and leaders. "The noblest use of free speech in this or any free county," Cox announced, "is to criticize closely the political agents. . . . A healthy state of the politic requires a party at all times standing up on the fundamental law as the basis of its existence and fearlessly vigilant against the encroachment of power." He repeated the point often: "We have our parties of Administration and opposition. These differences of opinion are privileges of constitutional sanction and individual conscience."[75]

But as a member of the opposition party, Cox never challenged the system of government, only its administration. Nor did he oppose the Civil War; to do so would have turned opposition into obstruction, disagreement into conflict. Instead he collaborated with the Republicans in voting men, money, and materials and thereby left unanswered the extent of a "disloyal" opposition's rights. Cox's intolerance of the extreme peace Democrats suggested narrow boundaries for even verbal dissent, and because the intention of Cox and his party was to restore America's past, not to remake the present, the Northern Democrats hardly tested the limits of opposition in a democracy.

To be sure, the crowded agenda of wartime politics furnished numerous examples of Republican encroachments on civil liberties, and Cox's sense of oppression was not entirely phantasmagorical. Republicans did interfere with elections, did install a vast patronage system, did award contracts to party followers, and did jail Democrats only to release them without explanation after an election. On one occasion they arrested nearly all the Democratic members of the Maryland legislature. To protect himself from any such violation of his civil rights, Cox devised an elaborate bell system with which to alert his Columbus neighbors, should he be taken off to a military prison.[76] The Ohioan remained a free man, but incidents like the arrest of his colleague Clement L. Vallandigham provided the specific indictments in his case for Republican tyranny. Though he did not oppose the war, he outspokenly challenged these usurpations of authority.

Cox's Democratic heritage encouraged him to find in "these frowns of power" a corruption long associated with Federalists, Whigs, and now Republicans.[77] In his view, the successors of Biddle's bank directors and Hamilton's speculators had reappeared during the Civil War as

[75]*Congressional Globe,* 37th Cong., 3d sess., 1267; Cox, *Three Decades,* p. 28; Cox, *Eight Years in Congress,* pp. 5–6.

[76]Cox to Manton Marble, 14 June, 16 and 17 August, 24 September, and 21 October 1863, Manton Marble Papers, Library of Congress.

[77]Cox, *Three Decades,* pp. 237, 589.

tax collectors, provost marshals, and "shoddy" contractors. Because his party had always protested the intrusions of those who tampered with free choice concerning schools, drinking habits, and, increasingly in the 1850s, slavery, Cox saw the Republicans as a reincarnation of the detested Puritan conformity he associated with New England. In his opinion, Republicans intended not to achieve peace, but rather to meddle with the South and the prerogatives of its state governments. Only an opposition party could restrain the "falsehood of such extremes."[78]

To make these points, Cox played the traditional role of a partisan, and his rhetorical means were familiar to Americans who had listened to party dialogue over the years. As Jabez Hammond pointed out in the 1840s, Americans frequently exaggerated the threat to the republic and charged each other with subversion.[79] Such political habits allowed wartime Democrats to call Republicans "fanatics." But Cox never crossed the boundary separating permissible criticism from threatening intention, which when trespassed by Ohio's Vallandigham and Long led to charges of Democratic disloyalty. Cox usually cloaked his complaints in the most protective of all guises, humor, and even Republicans laughed at his description of ermine-attired Republican judges singing the "Marseillaise." Although he later came to disapprove of the English political system—believing it too "consolidated"—he would have made the best of backbenchers.[80] But behind the laughter rested a serious purpose: Cox could make the case for a loyal opposition only if Americans understood that rhetoric did not require action. His words as a critic must not be misperceived as a call to arms, any more than his opposition to Lincoln should be taken as a desire to overthrow the United States government by any means other than a free election. Even before the war he had unsuccessfully cautioned Southerners to separate Republican language from actual intent, and during the war he tried to explain the way men and parties work. The Republican senator Henry Wilson, he told Congress, "did not literally mean he would grind the slave power into powder. He never intends to use the powder, only the power." Repeating the point, Cox cautioned that "Lincoln in the White House may not be the rail splitter out of it. Abraham,

[78]Cox, "Puritanism in Politics," *Eight Years in Congress,* pp. 281–303.

[79]Hammond, *History,* 2: 533. For similar political rhetoric, see John Howe, "Republican Thought and Political Violence in the 1790s," *American Quarterly* 29 (Summer 1967): 147–65.

[80]*Speech of S. S. Cox on Legislation to Admit the Cabinet to the House for Debate and to Answer Questions,* House of Representatives, January 26, 1865. For a sample of Cox rhetoric, see "The Meaning of the Elections of 1862," in *Eight Years in Congress,* pp. 258–81.

in faith, may offer up his irrepressible offspring. He will be a conservative, with a total oblivion of the radical."[81] Behind such spoofing lay an intention of putting politics in perspective and of demonstrating the virtues of an opposition, not just to the members of the Democracy but to all Americans.

Having little reason to become so, Republicans were unpersuaded of the virtues of partisan conflict and sometimes made the Democrats into what they never were—opponents of the Union. On the occasions when Republicans saw themselves as the government, not as a party in power, they silenced opposition newspapers and arrested Democratic leaders in the name of wartime necessity. Occasionally Republican efforts to make Democrats appear disloyal were necessary to justify their own partisan excesses. Such was the case in the great Copperhead scare of 1863, when midwestern Republicans manufactured a vast Democratic network of pro-Confederate secret societies.[82] On balance, however, Republicans never tried to destroy their opponents and did not act on their own exaggerated claims that Democrats were traitors. Such reciprocity provided the essential other half of a loyal opposition, and Republicans showed that they too were beginning to understand the merits of party systems. Republican Edgar Cowan provided an apt image; "A party is like a ladder. It is useless unless it has something to lean on and it gets support from its opposite. Take away its wall of opposition and it will fall to the ground."[83]

Cox was one of the Democrats responsible for maintaining this wall of opposition, and although some of his colleagues never believed their party could survive the war, it did. Cox himself returned to Congress in 1868, and four years later his party gained a majority in the House for the first time since 1859, an event the now–New York congressman celebrated "in measureless content . . . that the old party of our love is in the ascendant."[84] With typical bravado, Cox had expected to replace the Republicans, and as early as 1862 had likened his political enemies to "ghosts" and "corpses." But Cox's contribution to his party did not come from his sharp attacks on the Republicans or even from his membership in the Democratic majority that controlled the House for most of the remaining nineteenth-century Congresses. It rested instead in his popularizing of the national benefits of partisan rivalries. Nurtured in

[81]Cox, *Eight Years in Congress,* p. 205; *Congressional Globe,* 36th Cong., 1st sess., 376.

[82]Frank L. Klement, "Civil War Politics, Nationalism, and Postwar Myths," *Historian* 38 (May 1976): 419–38.

[83]*Congressional Globe,* 37th Cong., 3d sess., 1469.

[84]Cox and Northrup, *Life of Cox,* p. 127.

the lean years of war and Reconstruction, his sense of party systematized the antiauthoritarian spirit of American politics.

After the war, acceptance of Cox's theory of a loyal opposition as beneficial came quickly. Historians who had previously considered parties as disreputable, though necessary, now acknowledged their contributions and built American history around political competition. James Ford Rhodes, as representative of historians after the war as Bancroft had been of those before it, explained in his introduction that "under a constitutional government the history of political parties is the civil history of the country. I shall have to relate the downfall of the Whig party, the formation of the Republican, and the disruption of the Democratic party, that, with brief intermissions, had conducted the affairs of government from the election of Jefferson."[85] This does not mean that historians always praised parties. Reformers often held them up as examples of corruption and urged the adoption of better disciplined, more-cohesive organizations, based on the English system.[86]

Americans' acceptance of a healthy antagonism between organized parties was soon symbolized in physical expressions of partyism. Unlike their prewar predecessors, Democrats no longer believed their organization would disappear when its ideals became public policy. They housed their party in permanent buildings, provided a firmer national basis for its organization, and created a specialized iconography that included symbols, songs, and holidays. All of this was possible because members now recognized the legitimacy of their organization—in and out of power—and could anticipate its durability.[87]

It is ironic that Democrats who during the Civil War had demonstrated the beneficence of an oppositional two-party system became victims of twentieth-century efforts at political unity. During both world wars, Cox and his loyal opposition served as historical examples of a fifth column that had supported the intolerable principle of peace without victory. "All things considered," concludes historian Wood Gray, "it is hard to find much good in the [Democratic] leaders of the peace movement. In their opinionated views many of them were willing to sacrifice the Union rather than permit the carrying out of a policy

[85]James Ford Rhodes, *History of the United States from the Compromise of 1850*, vol. 1 (New York: Macmillan, 1910), p. 2.

[86]The most famous modern statement of this viewpoint was the declaration of the Committee on Political Parties of the American Political Science Association, "Toward a More Responsible Two-Party System: A Report of the Committee on Political Parties," supplement to *American Political Science Review* 44 (September 1950).

[87]Ronald Stinnett, *Democrats, Dinners, and Dollars: A History of the Democratic Party, Its Dinners, Its Rituals* (Ames: Iowa State University Press, 1967).

that had been adopted against their wishes. . . . Some were willing to connive with agents of the Confederacy."[88] By this time, however, the notion of a loyal opposition was too firmly embedded in American theory and practice to permit a return to the one-party system now associated with totalitarian regimes. Historians might provide examples of the unpatriotic by turning Civil War Democrats into a disloyal faction, but twentieth-century Americans expected bipartisan agreement in foreign policy and loyal opposition in domestic affairs. Speaking to Republicans after his defeat in 1940, Wendell Willkie repeated Cox's now-familiar message: "[We must] stand ready to serve our country behind our commander-in-chief but retain the right and I will say duty to debate the course of our government. Should we ever permit one party to dominate our lives completely, democracy would collapse and we would have dictatorship."[89]

Underlying this principle were three nineteenth-century conceptions of the Democratic party: first, George Bancroft's all-American structure, which, because it anticipated consensus, buried fears of parties as threats to the survival of the commonwealth and encouraged the establishment of winner-take-all-electoral rules based on majoritarianism; second, Martin Van Buren's party of habits and behaviors, which bound its supporters into a fellowship of participants, thereby serving the Democracy's emerging role as an agent of political socialization; and, finally, Samuel Cox's sense of the Democracy as a loyal opposition, which, because it made competition a necessity, rendered the party a permanent national institution. All three senses of party overlapped, and few Northern Democrats distinguished among them. These three stages of identification promoted the Democracy's development from an inchoate local association into a powerful agent of American political training. What, then, did the Democracy teach?

[88]Richard O. Curry, "The Union as It Was: A Critique of Recent Interpretations of the Copperheads," *Civil War History* 20 (September 1974): 215–38; Wood Gray, *The Hidden Civil War; The Story of the Copperheads* (New York: Viking Press, 1942), p. 224; George Fort Milton, *Abraham Lincoln and the Fifth Column* (New York: Vanguard, 1942).

[89]*New York Times*, 12 November 1940.

Part II

# THINKING AS DEMOCRATS

CHAPTER 4

# *The Revival of Republicanism*

In the process of becoming Americans and Democrats, prewar Northerners acquired well-defined perspectives that, like stage directions, cued their positions on public issues. Ohio Democrat Samuel Medary simplified these attitudes as "the Sovereignty of the People, the Rights of the States, and a Light and Simple Government."[1] Such values underwrote the Democrats' opposition to protective tariffs, the United States Bank, and federally sponsored internal improvements, as well as the party's support of "weak treasuries" and local autonomy on slavery matters. Believing Americans to be better off left alone, prewar Democrats were generally suspicious of legislation and included in their antistatism everything from controlling drinking to enacting the principle of eminent domain.[2] The party's semiofficial journal, the *United States Magazine and Democratic Review*, held legislation responsible "for nine-tenths of all the evil, moral and physical, by which mankind has been afflicted."[3] Democrats cast themselves as watchmen guarding their republic from such statutory affliction and promoted to heroic legend Jefferson's challenge of Hamilton's economic program, Matthew Lyon's resistance to the Sedition Acts, and Jackson's struggle against the United States Bank. By mid-century, party members believed the essential difference between themselves and their opponents to be, in Horatio Seymour's words, that they were "a let-alone party, the latter were a meddling party."[4]

[1]*Western Hemisphere*, 2 October 1848.

[2]Rush Welter, *The Mind of America, 1820–1860* (New York: Columbia University Press, 1975), p. 80.

[3]*United States Magazine and Democratic Review* 1 (October 1837): 6 (hereafter cited as *Democratic Review*).

[4]"Speech of Horatio Seymour," clipping from *St. Paul* (Minn.) *Weekly Pioneer and Democrat*, 11 August 1859, Horatio Seymour Papers, New York State Library, Albany (hereafter cited as Seymour Papers).

According to Robert Kelley, such views were part of a nineteenth-century "transatlantic persuasion" that English and Canadian shopkeepers, small proprietors, craftsmen, and independent farmers shared with their American counterparts.[5] Anxious for release from economic restraints in a world of expanding opportunities and fearful of the connections between an entrenched gentry and the government, men like Martin Van Buren, Andrew Jackson, and their political equivalents in England, Robert Peel and John Bright, opposed corporate privilege and sought instead a pluralistic society free of state-directed favoritism. During the early nineteenth century this libertarianism showed itself most often in economic controversies, but it also surfaced in social and constitutional issues. No matter what the specific concern, Democrats drew on a well-established vein of Anglo-American thought that compared market forces to nature and held that both worked best when left alone—"untrammelled," in the party's cliché. According to John O'Sullivan, editor of the *Democratic Review,* "The natural laws which will establish themselves and find their own level are the best laws. The same hand was the Author of the moral as of the physical world. . . . We cannot err . . . in trusting to the same fundamental principles of spontaneous action and self-regulation which produce the beautiful order of the latter."[6]

As Joyce Appleby has demonstrated, such thinking lessened the distance between older notions of a virtuous commonwealth dependent on community responsibility and newer ideas of natural rights and individual competition. For most Democrats, the public welfare was not antithetical to personal benefit. "On the contrary," as Thomas Paine earlier explained, "the public good is the good of all because it is the good of every individual collected."[7] What might have been the vice of private materialism became instead the God-approved virtue of entrepreneurial ambition. After gaining the sanction of expected behavior, the acquisitive instincts crucial to nineteenth-century capitalism were construed as part of man's nature. "The wealth and happiness of the citizens," wrote Walt Whitman, "can hardly be touched by the government. . . . Men must be masters under themselves and not look to Presidents and legislative bodies for aid. In this wide and naturally

[5]Robert Kelley, *The Transatlantic Persuasion: The Liberal Democratic Mind in the Age of Gladstone* (New York: A. A. Knopf, 1969).

[6]*Democratic Review* 1 (October 1837): 7.

[7]Quoted in Eric Foner, *Tom Paine and Revolutionary America* (New York: Oxford University Press, 1976), p. 89. See also Joyce Appleby, "The Social Origins of American Revolutionary Ideology," *Journal of American History* 64 (March 1978): 942.

rich country the best government is indeed that which governs the least."[8]

Over the years Democrats established positions that set them apart from other nineteenth-century Americans. Too vague to be an ideological system, too often compromised to serve as official doctrine, and too close to the opposition's to be precise points of partisan dogma, these attitudes served more as movable fences than as solid barriers. Sometimes other political organizations were closer to the national platform than were its own supporters, and frequently the Democracy was, as Mr. Dooley said, "not on speaking terms with itself." In Illinois, Democrats encouraged state-financed canals in the 1840s and complained when President Pierce vetoed river and harbor improvement bills in the 1850s. Pennsylvania Democrats, alert to the special problems of their state's iron industry, usually supported higher tariffs, and, as Richard McCormick has pointed out, Democrats as well as Whigs, Republicans, and Know-Nothings dispensed resources, charters, and licenses in the mid-nineteenth century. Although Democrats did so more reluctantly than their opponents, they accepted general banking bills, and even approved Buchanan's strategy of ending the 1857 depression by selling interest-bearing treasury notes.[9]

Still, by mid-century the Democrats had habits, instincts and traditions; their characteristic commitments included states' rights, federal restraint, and an assertive Unionism based on a white man's government. Although all parties held as their stated objectives the democratizing of American enterprise and the limitation of national power, Democrats, even as they dispensed franchises and charters, stood for scaling down governmental authority, limiting special privilege, and preventing federally sponsored land allocations. Once in power, they did not always effect these principles, and increasingly in the 1850s their leaders participated in the distribution of economic benefits that Richard McCormick has isolated as the major achievement of nineteenth-century party government. Even so, the Democracy's distinctive position was to limit such distribution to the states and to preserve liberty as much as possible by restraining public authority. Reduced to its simplest level, they were for state rather than national government, for

[8]*Brooklyn Daily Eagle,* 26 July 1847, quoted in Cleveland C. Rogers and John Black, *The Gathering of the Forces,* (New York: Putnam, 1920), 2: 52.

[9]Richard McCormick, "The Party Period and Public Policy: An Exploratory Hypothesis," *Journal of American History* 66 (September 1979): 279–98; Paul Randall, "Gubernatorial Platforms for the Political Parties of Michigan, 1834–1864" (master's thesis, Wayne State University, 1937), pp. 6, 64, 130.

white rather than black, and for freedom rather than control. From these general sentiments emerged specific public policies that symbolized their liberal persuasion: opposition to the United States Bank; protection of the Union during the nullification crisis of the 1830s; expansion of American territory in the 1840s; and, in the 1850s, keeping slavery out of national politics. In local matters, the Democrats' commitment to a light and simple government led them to reject public policies directed at changing the private habits of Americans—whether drinking, church-going, schooling, or slaveholding.

No one has paid much attention to what happened to these ideas during the 1860s and 1870s, when a new generation came to define party ideals. Instead of analyzing what Northern Democrats said and how they said it, historians have swallowed the Republican complaint that the Democrats supported slavery and the Confederacy. Like the party itself, Democratic platforms have been dismissed as either the Northern version of the Southern mentality or the disloyal demagogism of a power-hungry minority. For both, the Republicans provided striking images: Democrats were Doughfaces (Northerners with Southerners' views) and Copperheads (traitors to the Union). In time, even Democrats came to accept this malign version of themselves, choosing their heroes from other times and places. Today's revisionists, less severe in their assessments, still avoid the party's doctrines. Joel Silbey's recent "anatomy of the Northern Democrats," for example, neglects ideas for behavior—the mind, as it were, for the body.[10]

The problem is not so much what Northern Democrats said or how to analyze it, but rather what ideology itself is. The principles of political parties fall all too neatly into what Clifford Geertz has defined as "interest theory,"[11] and it is hard to imagine partisan appeals as anything more than self-serving efforts to win votes. Parties seek power and place; by definition, their beliefs have ulterior motives. Certainly, Democratic platforms were never the disembodied reflections of disinterested philosophers: they exhibited the thinking of active office-seekers who hoped to use party doctrine as an electoral weapon. Traditionally, analysis of such appeals seeks to explain the success of these

[10]Joel Silbey, *A Respectable Minority: The Democratic Party in the Civil War Era, 1860–1868* (New York: W. W. Norton, 1977), p. xv.

[11]Clifford Geertz, *The Interpretation of Cultures: Selected Essays* (New York: Basic Books, 1973), pp. 201, 193–223. See also Karl Mannheim, *Essays on Sociology and Social Psychology* (London: Routledge and Kegan Paul, 1953); J. G. A. Pocock, *Politics, Language, and Time: Essays on Political Thought and History* (New York: Atheneum, 1971), pp. 12, 28, 105.

weapons among various voting groups, and from such a perspective the contests of Northern Democrats with Republicans become a competition of interests thinly disguised as a clash of principle.

Such a one-dimensional analysis places too much emphasis on rationality and not enough on context. If party beliefs are seen only as an effort to win elections or, at the other extreme, are not considered to be ideology because they fall short of some all-embracing "ism," they disappear as an expression of political culture. Behind every set of Northern Democratic messages rested an accumulation of symbols and traditions, a kind of switchboard on which languages, themes, and modes of expression connected belief and believer, past and present, perception and reality. Geertz calls this "ideology as a culture system," meaning a layer of culture that fuses sentiments into significant belief systems. It is not just that ideas express, emerge from, or reflect their society, although they do these things, but rather that ideology itself is a part of reality. Accordingly, when Democratic beliefs are seen as a societal phenomenon existing within a particular ideological tradition, and when the language employed is viewed as part of that legacy, the preoccupation with unmasking partisan rhetoric and attaching it to voter self-interest disappears. No longer weapon, mask, symptom, or remedy, partisan beliefs become historical scene and subject.

So viewed, the messages of Northern Democrats reveal the continuing importance of republicanism, that cluster of beliefs defined by a suspicion of power, a fear of human motives, an expectation of conspiracy, and, as Gordon Wood has written of its rhetoric, "an obsession with corruption and disorder, [a] hostile and conspiratiorial outlook and [a] millennial vision of a regenerated society."[12] During the late eighteenth century, Americans had reformulated English oppositionist thought into "a logic of rebellion,"[13] and, confronted nearly a century later with another crisis, Northern Democrats retrieved the never-for-

[12]Gordon Wood, "Rhetoric and Reality in the American Revolution," *William and Mary Quarterly* 23 (January 1966): 26. Throughout this chapter I have used the lowercase *republican* to refer to the revolutionary ideology based on English radical–Whig oppositionist thought. It is best described in Gordon Wood, *The Creation of the American Republic, 1776–1787* (Chapel Hill: University of North Carolina Press, 1969), pp. 3–123. See also Bernard Bailyn, ed., *Pamphlets of the American Revolution, 1750–1776* (Cambridge, Mass.: Harvard University Press, Belknap, 1965), pp. 38–201; Robert Shallhope, "Toward a Republican Synthesis: The Emergence of an Understanding of Republicanism in American Historiography," *William and Mary Quarterly* 29 (January 1972): 48–80; Caroline Robbins, *The Eighteenth-Century Commonwealthmen* (Cambridge, Mass.: Harvard University Press, 1959).

[13]Bernard Bailyn, *The Ideological Origins of the American Revolution* (Cambridge, Mass.: Harvard University Press, 1967), pp. 94–143.

gotten postulates of this republicanism. In so doing, they did not give up their libertarian economics; grafting it onto a compatible political theory, they argued that the common welfare required neither civic nor economic interference by the government. The specific components of their message included basic arguments and themes of seventeenth-century English Whigs as well as eighteenth-century American revolutionaries such as James Otis, John Adams, and Josiah Quincy. Self-conscious about the sources of their thinking (for they hoped Northerners would hold Republicans accountable, as patriots had Tories), Democratic leaders made selective comparisons to events in Western history, concentrating on England's civil war and the French and American Revolutions, when, in their view, those resisting authority had protected liberty and freedom. Northern Democrats not only cited the works of those polemicists whom Caroline Robbins has memorialized as the "commonwealthmen"; they also adopted their images and vocabulary. As cultural symbols, these appeals were efforts to place their party in touch with the dissenting tradition that had created the Republic and that Civil War Democrats insisted was the only way to maintain it.[14]

## *War and Liberty*

Democratic reliance on seventeenth-century English thought and its eighteenth-century American version began before the war and was at first as much a matter of orientation as of formal principle. Years before, Edmund Burke had described the colonists "as auguring misgovernment at a distance and sniffing the approach of tyranny in every tainted breeze." The eighteenth-century pamphleteer John Dickinson agreed: "The crucial question [is] not what evil has actually attended particular measures but what evil is likely to attend them."[15] Such an antiauthoritarian tradition instilled apprehensiveness about liberty and a need to anticipate future encroachments. Seventy-five years after the revolution, it was natural for Northern Democrats to foresee in the approach of war the dangers of what one called "a single government and unrestrained despotism." "We have become sentinels on the ramparts," asserted one congressman, who predicted that war, and most especially civil war, would destroy the moral excellence necessary for a

[14]George Woodruff to Thomas Seymour, 18 July 1861, Thomas Seymour Papers, Connecticut Historical Society, Hartford (hereafter cited as Thomas Seymour Papers).

[15]Edmund Burke, "Speech on Moving His Resolution for Conciliation, March 22, 1775," in *Edmund Burke: Selected Writings and Speeches*, ed. Peter Stanlis (New York: Doubleday, Anchor Books, 1963), p. 161; Wood, *Creation of American Republic*, p. 5.

free society. Holding that republican governments flourished in peace (although they were sometimes spawned in war), Democrats argued that the peacetime possibility of corruption became a wartime probability. According to California's Milton Latham, as with the progressive contamination of gangrene, prevention was worth any cure.[16] Recalling that their ancestors had not waited for the effects of the Stamp Act but had acted immediately, Northern Democrats were sympathetic to, although they did not approve of, Southern secession.

Once the Civil War began, Northern Democrats prophesied the worst, but their message has been incorrectly construed as support for slavery and the Confederacy, when its primary purpose was to warn. "Right succumbs to force," wrote Samuel Cox, who compared liberty's disappearance to an hourglass with the sands of freedom pouring away during war. "The brute rules and reason dies. . . . yokes of wood bind men rather than cords of silk, and yokes of iron instead of yokes of wood."[17] Relying on the founding fathers' pessimistic view of human nature, Democrats argued that war, which they variously termed "the bloody goddess of despotism" and "the Trojan Horse of tyranny," released passions normally restrained by the structure of their government. "Our ancestors did not admit this doctrine of necessity but proceeded under the guise of a wise and just policy to tie up the hands of official power by constitutional limitations, by checks and balances established in the framework of government, and by inculcating among the mass of people in whom was to be lodged the ultimate or sovereign power a profound respect for all private rights and for the laws by which they are secured," explained Delaware's James Bayard.[18] In an effort to instruct Congress on this point, Bayard repeated the republican litany: "Human nature is the same in all ages and in all countries. Power always tends to corruption, and it is that tendency which requires, in all free governments, the division among separate and independent departments for the prevention of its abuse."[19] War, according to Bayard, inevitably broke down these protections, and although the Delaware senator did not rule out all military adventures, he considered liberty and war (not peace and war) antinomies as similar in their contrariety as white and black.

For evidence of war's corrosive effects, Democrats turned to history and had no further to look than their own colonial past. Believing

[16]*Congressional Globe,* 37th Cong., 2d sess., 2505; ibid., app., p. 37.

[17]Samuel S. Cox, *Eight Years in Congress, 1857–1865.* (New York: D. Appleton, 1865), pp. 200, 278.

[18]*Congressional Globe,* 37th Cong., 1st sess., App. 18.

[19]Ibid.

England's eighteenth-century wars had spawned a cycle of debt and taxes, oppression and usurpation, Thomas Kettell, an editor of the *Democratic Review,* explained the American Revolution in terms of the monarchy's military adventurism—an interpretation with which historians later concurred. In a widely circulated pamphlet, Kettell contended that the spiraling burden of eighteenth-century war debt drained off capital, created a depression, and eventually led to revolution in the colonies and political repression in England.[20] Congressman Cox applied the point to current affairs, predicting that Northerners would soon "copy" the English and find themselves "crushed between perpetual debt and standing armies."[21]

Such thinking stopped short of any suggestion that wars might be catalysts for change and that they might generate, as in the American Revolution, a more liberal political order. But if the republic was a product of English militarism, then conflict had once served liberty and might again. On just such grounds Southerners justified their new government, but Northern Democrats did not go so far. Like the English Whigs, who denied the legitimacy of revolution after 1689, Northern Democrats applied their doctrine in piecemeal fashion, denying its relevance to other circumstances.

To Northern Democrats familiar with the concept of natural law, civil war was the worst of all society's disorders. By definition, it lay beyond the sanctioned restraints of civilized warfare. On this point Democrats quoted the Swiss theorist Emmerich Vattel, who had assimilated natural law theory to international affairs, thereby legitimizing wars between nation states. But Vattel took a darker view of internal conflicts, which he believed "broke the bonds of society and government or at least their force and effect." Thus Vattel influenced Democrats to believe two things: first, that the common laws of war—"maxims of humanity, moderation, and honour"—must be observed by both parties during a civil conflict; and second, that this was exceedingly difficult to do, "for the flames of discord in civil war are not favourable to the proceedings of pure and sacred justice."[22] Citing Vattel, Stephen Douglas despaired of "a war of kindred, family, and friends; father

[20]Thomas Kettell, "The History of the War Debt of England; The History of the War Debt of the United States; and The Two Compared," *Papers from the Society for the Diffusion of Political Knowledge,* (hereafter cited as *SDPK*), 17: 2–16. Charles Andrews, *The Colonial Period of American History* (New Haven: Yale University Press, 1938), pp. 422–25.

[21]Cox, *Eight Years in Congress,* p. 200.

[22]Quoted in Joseph Chitly, ed., *The Law of Nations; or, Principles of the Law of Nature* (Philadelphia: P. H. Nicklin and T. Johnson, 1835), pp. 424, 426.

against son," and after ransacking history, the Illinois Democrat could find no examples of a "government strong enough to crush ten million people [Douglas here included blacks] into subjection when they believed their rights and liberties were imperiled without first converting the government into a despotism and destroying the last vestige of freedom."[23] Douglas's colleague Clement Vallandigham predicted the destruction of "property and prosperity and the demoralizing of character." So threatening were internal wars that, in Vallandigham's view, the English had learned the lessons "our fathers taught them" and now compromised rather than risk domestic conflict. Not so the Americans: "We have forgotten."[24] James Bayard described civil war as "the greatest curse which the Providence of God can inflict in a nation" and quoted Burke's letter to the sheriffs of Bristol: that it "struck deepest of all into the manners of the people. . . . [Civil wars] corrupt their morals; they prevent even the natural taste and relish of equity and justice." What Burke had said of the Americans in 1777, Bayard now applied to the South: "To part with them as a limb, I would have parted with more if more had been necessary. Bodies tied together by so unnatural a bond of union as mutual hatred are only connected to their ruin." For Bayard and many other Democrats, restoration by force might be as life-threatening as amputation, for it endangered intrinsic values that were the essence of public life. Accordingly, "Anything is better than a fruitless, hopeless, unnatural civil war."[25]

As the war continued, Democrats did not abate their warnings. Nor did they change their position that civil liberties were the essence of Americanness. As a result, any transgression of what Vallandigham catalogued as "free speech, a free press, public assemblages, political liberty and above all or at least the foundation of all, PERSONAL LIBERTY or freedom from illegal and arbitrary arrests (the latter an Anglo-Saxon right declared in the GREAT CHARTER in the time of King John)," was as threatening as an invading army.[26] "Without [these rights]," wrote Ohio's George Pendleton, "life ceases to be: it is like taking a man's upright form, his living soul, and reducing him to a brute."[27] The image was suggestive, having been used in Paine's *Common Sense* and before that in English oppositionist thought. But unlike

[23]*Congressional Globe,* 36th Cong., 2d sess., 1461.

[24]*The Record of Hon. C. L. Vallandigham* (Columbus: J. Walter, 1863), p. 78.

[25]*Congressional Globe,* 37th Cong., 1st sess., app., pp. 13–14. For the source of Bayard's views, see Stanlis, *Burke,* p. 193.

[26]Vallandigham, *Vallandigham,* p. 137.

[27]"Hon George H. Pendleton's Address," *SDPK,* 7: 10.

earlier pamphleteers, Democrats never were clear on the point at which a citizen's allegiance was annulled and resistance to tyranny justified. Nor, given their belief in local power, could they invoke the constitutional clause guaranteeing republican governments to states as the Republicans did in order to justify military Reconstruction during the 1870s.

Fearing the worst, Democrats accepted the war (they had not "made" it) in order to preserve "the constitution as it is and the Union as it was." This famous slogan confirmed the preservationist instincts of anxious Northerners, who saw themselves fighting for the same ideals as their grandfathers. In July 1861 Democrat Milton Latham defined the war's purpose: "this war is not waged . . . in any spirit of oppression, or for any purpose of conquest or subjugation, or purpose of overthrowing or interfering with the rights or established institutions of those States, but to defend and maintain the supremacy of the Constitution, and to preserve the Union with all the dignity, equality, and rights of the several states unimpaired."[28]

Throughout the war, Democrats clung to these principles; opposing what they termed "innovations," their vocabulary became a thesaurus of maintenance—preserving, restoring, upholding, and keeping. When Republicans tried to include emancipation as a war aim, Pennsylvania's Democratic congressman Charles Biddle protested that the war "is to preserve the old frame of the government, to rally to it to the old affections, to divide the enemy, and to offer always terms that make submission better than resistance." In the same vein, another Democratic congressman encouraged the nation "to watch with extreme jealousy that disposition toward which most governments are prone—to introduce too soon, to extend too far, and to retain too long."[29]

There was more to these wartime messages than reactionary carping. In fact Democrats were using the most militant language available, for in the United States maintaining, protecting, and preserving had once been calls to action. American revolutionaries had believed they were defending established privileges and, as Gordon Wood has shown, considered their adversaries so corrupt as to be unable to "keep" the ancient liberties of Englishmen.[30] By placing their appeals within this antiauthoritarian tradition, Democrats conveyed a threat that is difficult to apprehend today. Historians have correctly set about the task of

[28]*Congressional Globe,* 37th Cong., 1st sess., 222.
[29]Ibid., 2d sess., 2504; ibid., 3d sess., 132.
[30]Wood, *Creation of American Republic,* pp. 43–45.

acquitting the party of disloyalty, but, being closer to the revolution, nineteenth-century Americans read between the lines and remembered how talk of Sidney and Hampden, corruption and usurpation, had led to Bunker Hill. Most discomfiting were the frequent allusions to the fate of Charles I, who to intemperate Democrats had done less to deserve his fate than had Lincoln's cabinet officers.

Central to the Democrats' symbolism was the Constitution, which even before the war had defined the party's, and indeed most Americans', faith. But Democrats had always believed themselves its special protector. During the war they reminded Northerners that the revolution had centered on the meaning of the English constitution. "Never before and surely never since, has any single nation's constitution so dominated Western man's theorizing about politics," Gordon Wood has written. "The colonists stood to the very end of their debate and even after on those natural and scientific principles of the English constitution. And ultimately such a stand was what made their Revolution seem so unusual, for they revolted not against the English constitution but on behalf of it."[31] The American version of constitutionalism inspired great reverence in popular culture, and, from their beginning as a political organization, Democrats upheld the position that the Constitution was a formal set of rules, not, as Republicans would have it, a living document that incorporated laws, customs, and practices. By referring to the Constitution as "a rock," "a sheet-anchor," "a rampart of freedom," "the rubicon of our rights," "the great temple of our liberties," "our shield and protector," and "an ark of safety," Democrats conveyed their inflexible interpretation.[32] Graphically, they expressed this idea by depicting the Constitution as a pillar shaken by Republicans and Negroes.

Northern Democrats also relied on the ancient image of the ship of state to convey the dangers of war to a democratic society. Used by both parties, the figure of speech expressed the American view of leadership as a hierarchy composed of a pilot, officers, crew, and passengers. But whereas Republicans saw the storm as a temporary condition, in Democratic versions the tumultuous war-tossed seas threatened to capsize the ship of state. "We are upon no summer sea. We are in the midst of the storm of war, our country convulsed from one end to another."[33]

[31]Ibid., p. 10.

[32]*Congressional Globe,* 37th Cong., 2d sess., 2196; –40; *Congressional Globe,* 37th Cong., 2d sess., 2896, 373, 1735; ibid. 38th Cong., 1st sess., 114; ibid., 37th Cong., 1st sess., 67; *Democrats: An Appeal for the Constitution* (Baltimore: W. M. Inness, 1862), p. 5.

[33]*Congressional Globe,* 37th Cong., 2d sess., 1934.

As helmsman, Lincoln stood accused of reckless steering, and Republican transgressions of freedom were likened to dangerous rocks capable of wrecking any ship. Peace, in Democratic usage, was the safe port of call, easily reached under new captains. Later, Lincoln would become the beloved "lost captain" of Walt Whitman's poem, but not until after his assassination was this conception possible for Northern Democrats.[34]

Given their republican instincts, Democrats quickly identified military agents as oppressors and thereby produced bogeys identical to those apprehended by England's seventeenth-century commonwealthmen and America's eighteenth-century revolutionaries. In all three cases the most dangerous instrument of tyranny was "a standing army"—a term that held special meaning for Americans versed in the pamphlet literature of the revolution.[35] By using the expression "standing army" instead of referring, as Republicans did, to the Union forces or Northern armies, Democrats conjured up images of mercenary soldiers who, having nothing to do with protecting the nation from its enemies, instead preyed on the people. Ever since the revolution, Americans had associated standing armies with the British troops sent to Boston in the 1770s, and as a result both parties favored a citizen militia that, in times of need, would spring to the nation's defense. The image of Cincinnatus—Rome's ideal citizen, who exchanged plow for sword—was here counterposed to the Hessian mercenaries bought by George III to subvert American liberties. So embedded was this tradition of a civilian army that even West Point suffered periodic harassment from opponents of a professional military force, and in 1860 only sixteen thousand men served in the U.S. Army.

The Civil War quickly changed this, and by 1863 Northerners faced a draft, a presidentially appointed senior officer corps, and a defunct state militia system. Their sensitive republican antennae quivering, Democrats complained that Lincoln sought a standing army that would be used not against the South but to keep his administration in power. "Lincoln," argued one Democrat, "will use this army to install a unitary system and a strong central government." By 1863 Joel Parker, New Jersey's Democratic governor, believed that Lincoln had already inau-

[34]For examples see *Congressional Globe,* 41st Cong., 2d sess., app., p. 138; Vallandigham, *Vallandigham,* p. 96, 163; Franklin Pierce to Caleb C. Cushing, January 1858, Franklin Pierce Papers, Microfilm edition; *Congressional Globe,* 30th Cong., 1st sess., app., p. 227.

[35]Robbins, *Eighteenth-Century Commonwealthmen,* pp. 103, 123–124; Lois Schwoerer, *No Standing Armies: The Antiarmy Ideology in Seventeenth-Century England* (Baltimore: Johns Hopkins University Press, 1974).

gurated an "absolute . . . uncontrollable government, a perfect military despotism." So disturbed was New York Democrat Richard O'Gorman that he not only encouraged citizens to read John Trenchard's seventeenth-century classic—*An Argument Showing That a Standing Army Is Inconsistent with a Free Government*—but, using states' rights as a corrective, he also urged New York to create its own volunteer army, to be subject only to governor and legislature.[36] In the South governors did just this—they organized units, which only reluctantly and in direst emergency were turned over to the Confederate Army.

In the North, however, the concept of home guards never took hold. Like much revived republicanism, it did not fit the circumstances. For even while Democrats complained that the army was an instrument of oppression and executive usurpation, they also claimed to be supplying most of its soldiers. Accusing Republicans of being the skulkers who stayed at home and the deserters who came home, they believed their supporters gave up (in a phrase resurrected from the revolution) "blood and treasure" for the Union. Thus it was difficult for anyone to believe that the Northern army was anything but a band of stouthearted former civilians which included Northern Democrats and Republicans.

Despite the contradiction, Northern Democrats continued to hammer on the point, and, separating the army at home from that in the field, they located in the activities of provost marshals the intrusions Americans must expect from a standing army. Not only were these officers stationed in every Northern community, but their vague lines of authority (among other duties they presided over the enrollment and selection of conscripts) led to countless encounters with civilians whose previous experience with federal officials extended no farther than contact with local postmasters. The brashest of these officers interfered with elections (a few later ran for office), arrested local Democrats, sent troops to destroy opposition presses, monitored church services, released slaves, and conducted military trials. Several congressmen provided vivid personal testimony: according to Maryland's Henry May, a provost marshal "had entered his home in Baltimore, seized his papers, and frightened his wife, all for no apparent cause."[37] David Turpie, a

[36]Quoted in James G. Randall, *Constitutional Problems under Lincoln,* rev. ed. (Urbana: University of Illinois Press, 1964), p. 2; *Congressional Globe,* 37th Cong., 3d sess., 1215; "Ovation at the Academy of Music," *SDPK,* 7: 13–15, 16.

[37]For complaints about provost marshals, see *Congressional Globe,* 37th Cong., 3d sess., 261, 282, 772, 1052, 1102, 1125, 1215, 1219; app., p. 91. May's remarks are on p. 1052. See also S. L. George to Thomas H. Seymour, 23 August 1861, Thomas Seymour Papers; Delaware General Assembly, *Joint Commission on Military Interference with the State Election of November 4, 1862* (Dover, Del.: James Kirk, 1863).

Democrat from Indiana, complained that the function of provost marshals was to institute racial mixing, for the officers were scattered in every village "except Ceredo and Oberlin which being inhabited by white and black Americans need no such guardians of liberty."[38] The common theme in such protests was that provost marshals were the president's men: they practiced favoritism and unequal justice, arresting "freemen" not for any commission of crime but because they were political opponents. According to Vallandigham, army men were not competent to judge loyalty, having neither the authority nor the sensitivity to do so, and the Ohioan was certain that provost marshals would have arrested Chatham and Burke for their denunciation of English policy in the 1770s. "Every Congressional district in the United States is to be governed by this petty satrap—this military eunuch—this Baba—and he even may be black."[39]

Nowhere was the corruption of war more apparent than in the draft laws. Democrats objected to conscription on several grounds: it infringed on individual freedom and was an unconstitutional delegation of war powers from Congress to president. It expanded the powers of the provost marshals, who by 1863 could arrest deserters, confine spies, and report treasonable acts. Finally, by allowing substitutes and commutation, the draft displayed just the kind of indulgence for the rich and powerful that Democrats believed would destroy the republic.

Besides the dangers of military oppression, war offered immense possibilities for civilian corruption, and the fallibility of human nature was apparent to Northern Democrats in the "swollen" civilian service full of patronage holders, "shoddy" contractors, and stockjobbers, who swarmed over the land "like locusts." Some Democrats believed that Lincoln had assured himself a second term by creating a federal bureaucracy composed of tax collectors who lived off the people, brokers who sold mules for quarterhorses and collected for thoroughbreds, and speculators who bought cheap and sold dear to the government. "Your president stands in the place of a King," thundered Vallandigham. "He is the God whose priests are a hundred and fifty thousand and whose worshipers are a whole army of jobbers and contractors." For the same reasons George Pendleton referred to Lincoln as an "imperial power."[40]

[38]"Speech of Mr. Turpie Delivered in the Senate of the United States," 7 February 1863, *SDPK*, 2: 7.

[39]"Speech of Amasa J. Parker at the Cooper Institute,"*SDPK*, 15:5. *Congressional Globe*, 37th Cong., 3d sess., app., pp. 93, 178; Vallandigham, *Vallandigham*, pp. 67, 209; *Congressional Globe*, 37th Cong., 3d sess., 1256.

[40]Vallandigham, *Vallandigham*, p. 75; *Congressional Globe*, 37th Cong., 3d sess., 1256. For the eighteenth-century view of placemen, see Bailyn, *Pamphlets*, p. 359.

Similar imprecations had colored prewar antipartyism, but their tone in the 1860s was different, and it is this difference that locates Democrats within the republican ideology of their grandfathers. Using a term long identified with royal patronage and one that in America specified corrupt officials sent to govern the colonies, Democrats spoke of "placemen," meaning anyone who depended on the administration for money and opportunity. Northern Democrats saw the eighteenth-century process of absentee governance at work in what they called "the prodigious growth of federal patronage" accompanying the wartime "innovations" of draft, confiscation, and income tax. "The people," wrote an Ohio Democrat, "are drunk on blood and greenbacks." Examples were everywhere: in the removal of veterans' pensions from Democrats, in the granting of special leaves to Republican soldiers, and even in the unfair treatment of Democratic generals like George McClellan and Fitz-John Porter. Special interests endangered the community Democrats knew as the Union. "I use the word corruption," explained Vallandigham, "in the sense the British used it," and what alarmed the Ohio congressman was an archetypally republican fear: the replacement of public instincts of virtue and prudence by exclusive interests affiliated with a centralized government.[41]

Complaints about placemen drew on another vein of Democratic thought—the party's economic liberalism. Since the late eighteenth century, speculators had been a special target of Democratic censure, as had a national debt, an expensive government, a national bank, and public power wedded to private influence. The ideal Democratic world was an untrammeled synchrony of free markets and competition, and it was this world of opportunity, unimpeded by monopolies or contrivances, that appealed to shopkeepers, artisans, and small farmers. By assimilating the virtues of entrepreneurial aggressiveness to an older notion of republicanism, Democrats tried to diminish the contradiction between private interest and public welfare.

Wartime economics constantly transgressed this deeply held Democratic faith. From its beginnings, when Lincoln gave treasury money to New York businessmen to buy armaments, until 1865, when the national debt stood at three billion dollars, the war expanded the government's role in economic affairs and blurred the boundaries between public and private matters. Not only did Republicans violate an essential Democratic shibboleth when they created a national banking system

[41]P. Bradstreet to Alexander Long, 12 December 1863, Alexander Long Papers, Cincinnati Historical Society, Cincinnati, Ohio (hereafter cited as Long Papers); Vallandigham, *Vallandigham,* p. 68.

in 1864, but in Iowan Dennis Mahony's prediction, this "Massachusetts school of politics" also intended "imposition of a high protective tariff, the substitution of specie money by paper currency, and the legal and social distinction of classes in community and society by which capital shall become the ruler and poverty the serf."[42] Mahony's swift escalation from specific policy complaints to fear for America proved typical of Northern Democrats, whose republicanism indexed economic matters to freedom and liberty. Thus Lincoln's policies were not only condemned as inflationary, but in the Democratic view they also "abused power" by making a forced loan on the people. "Every dollar more borrowed or collected and every dollar spent is just added to the power and value of the executive office," explained Vallandigham.[43]

## *The Martyrs*

As Northern Democrats had prophesied, the war soon produced martyrs who became, like England's Sidney and Wilkes, passwords for legitimate resistance to tyranny. The first of these was John Merryman. Not only did Merryman's imprisonment occur early in the war, giving his name time to settle into the political idiom, but because the Merryman affair involved the suspension of the writ of habeas corpus as well as the relative powers of the three branches of the government and the relationship of military and civilian authority, it confronted basic issues of American freedom.

Ancient liberties were thus at stake when Merryman, a Baltimore County farmer and member of the county's Democratic executive committee, was arrested in June 1861. In the words of his complaint, he "was compelled to rise from his bed, taken into custody, and conveyed to Fort McHenry where he was imprisoned by the commanding officer without warrant from any lawful author."[44] There he stayed for six weeks while a dramatic confrontation ensued between Roger B. Taney, the Chief Justice of the United States, and George Cadwalader, the military commander of Fort McHenry. Presented with Taney's order (the aging Chief Justice's sense of history did not fail him: he believed he had been "kept alive for just such an occasion"),[45] Cadwalader re-

[42]*Dubuque Herald,* 19 April 1861.

[43]*Congressional Globe,* 37th Cong., 3d sess., 335; Vallandigham, *Vallandigham,* p. 68.

[44]The relevant documents are in Samuel Tyler, *Memoir of Roger Brooke Taney* (Baltimore: John Murphy, 1876), pp. 640–92.

[45]George W. Brown, *Baltimore and the Nineteenth of April* (Baltimore: N. Murray, 1887), p. 90.

fused to honor the writ, noting that his authority came from the president's power to suspend habeas corpus for public safety. The military commander did not say so, but Merryman was being held as a suspected saboteur. In the early days of the war, he had destroyed railroad bridges to prevent troops from marching through "the free state" of Maryland. Taney was unimpressed with this explanation and made clear his objection in the language of the English Whig:

> If the authority which the Constitution has confided to the judiciary department and judicial officers may thus upon any pretext or under any circumstances be usurped by the military power at its discretion, the people of the United States are no longer living under a government of laws, but every citizen holds life, liberty, and property at the will and pleasure of the army officer in whose military district he may happen to be found.[46]

The case promptly became a symbol of what the Democrats had forecast. Using Merryman as their example, Democrats explained how Lincoln, who in their view had no authority to suspend the writ, would seize control of the government. Believing that the power to suspend belonged to Congress because it was listed under the legislative articles of the Constitution, Democrats held Merryman's imprisonment an unwarranted assumption of authority by the military. They contended that civilian courts should try Merryman for treason, if that was the government's charge. To make these points, Democrats revived the language of the 1760s and assailed the president for persecuting a "free born" American, "usurping" constitutional rights, and "subverting" the government. "To believe," thundered James Wall of New Jersey, "that an executive could suspend [the writ] without statutory enactment is a pestilential heresy."[47] Democrats compared Lincoln's arrogance to John's before Runnymede, Charles's before the 1628 Petition of Right, and George III's before the War of Independence. Some concluded that the English better understood the inviolability of a free mind, safe person, and secure property, for in more threatening circumstances they had abided by Magna Carta, "the great charter of mankind," to protect Irish revolutionaries.

Democrats counted only five weeks between the beginning of the war and Lincoln's efforts "to burn through" constitutional safeguards

[46]Quotation from Tyler, *Memoir of Taney,* p. 659; *Ex Parte Merryman,* 17 Fed. Cas 144 (CCD, Md. 1861), No. 9,487; Neal A. Brooks and Eric Rockel, *A History of Baltimore County,* (Towson, Md: Friends of the Towson Library, 1979) pp. 240–41.

[47]*Congressional Globe,* 37th Cong., 3d sess., 1460.

in the Merryman case. Convinced of the delicate nature of republicanism, Vallandigham warned the public that it took only a day to lose liberties accumulated over centuries.[48] James Bayard, the senator from Delaware, agreed. His comparative study of history revealed that Lincoln had suspended the writ more often in a year than five English kings had in two centuries, and the ease with which this had been accomplished concerned the Senator, who converted tampering with the constitution into a blueprint for future oppression. Alert to the same danger, several Democratic editors quoted Lord Shelbourne's prophecy: "Your country will lose habeas corpus. The English know its value, for they have fought for it. It is ingrained in their creed. Your people will attempt to use it but having cost them nothing, at the first internal feud you have, the majority will trample upon it, and the people will permit it to be done."[49] And when Congress exempted military personnel from civilian prosecution and in the 1870s delegated to the president the power to suspend the writ "if in his judgment public safety required it," Democrats saw the fulfillment of their warning that "where the sword reigns, the genius of liberty runs off in terror and in fright."[50]

If the issue to which Merryman gave his name became a legal and political backwater, so too did its principal. Never charged with any crime, after six weeks in Fort McHenry Merryman was released. He returned to his Maryland rye and horses, hayfields and Democratic politics, but his antiauthoritarian instincts were unchastened; in 1863 he was detained by the provost marshal for "disloyal acts."[51] Later he showed his gratitude to his fellow Marylander and Democrat by naming his son Roger Brooke Taney Merryman, and eventually his party and state elected him treasurer. But the cry "Merryman and Habeas Corpus" never took its place beside "Wilkes and Liberty." Crowds did not protest his arrest or march through Baltimore's streets clamoring for his release. Later generations never read his imprisonment as a cautionary tale of trampled liberties.[52]

Another Democrat, Clement L. Vallandigham, had a better under-

[48]Ibid., p. 52; Vallandigham, *Vallandigham,* p. 93.

[49]*Congressional Globe,* 37th Cong., 1st sess., app., pp. 14–15; "Ovation at the Academy of Music," 4 July 1863, *SDPK,* 7: 101.

[50]Quotation from George Woodruff to Thomas Seymour, 18 July 1861, Thomas Seymour Papers; Randall, *Constitutional Problems under Lincoln,* p. 135.

[51]Jean H. Baker, *The Politics of Continuity: Maryland Political Parties, 1858–1870* (Baltimore: Johns Hopkins University Press, 1973), pp. 58–61, 190.

[52]For the reaction in England to Wilkes's arrest, see George Rudé, *Wilkes and Liberty: A Social Study of 1763 to 1774* (New York: Oxford University Press, 1963).

standing of how the blood of martyrs became, in Sidney's phrase, "the blood of the Church." Not only did the Ohio congressman have the self-righteousness that sustains those willing to suffer for the faith (he once wrote that he "learned early to do right"),[53] but Vallandigham wielded the active tongue and agile pen necessary to draw attention to his martyrdom. Unlike Merryman, he enjoyed a national reputation and was well known for his 1862 resolutions accusing Lincoln of dictatorship and for a speech in which he sprinkled over the audience the blood of a Democrat supposedly assassinated by Republicans.[54] In 1863 the army arrested Vallandigham for violating a military regulation "prohibiting the habitual declaration of sympathy with the enemy," an order promulgated by General Burnside to do just what Democrats charged—silence the government's critics. A military commission convicted Vallandigham, and only Lincoln's intervention prevented his imprisonment. Instead Vallandigham was exiled to the South, but not before he provided his followers with the traditional martyr's farewell—a letter smuggled from prison. As a "friend to liberty" (the phrase had been used by Wilkes's supporters and was a popular prerevolutionary toast in America), Vallandigham addressed his fellow Democrats:

> I am here in a military bastile, for no other offense than my political opinions and the defense of them, and the rights of the people and of your constitutional liberties. . . . I am a Democrat, for Constitution, for law, for Union, for liberty. This is my only crime. For no disobedience to the Constitution, for no violation of law, for no word, sign, or gesture of sympathy with the men of the South but in obedience to their demand as well as the demand of Northern Abolition disunionists and traitors I am here today in bonds.[55]

Later Vallandigham was delivered across the lines to a startled Confederate captain, who was reluctant to accept his well-known prisoner. The famous Democrat knew his role better, and proclaiming himself "a citizen of Ohio and the United States," surrendered as a prisoner of war. By summer Vallandigham had escaped to Canada; by fall, Ohio Democrats had nominated him for governor, and he became the only American ever to campaign while in exile.[56] He did not win, but his

[53]Vallandigham, *Vallandigham,* p. 175.

[54]Frank L. Klement, *The Limits of Dissent: Clement L. Vallandigham and the Civil War* (Lexington: University Press of Kentucky, 1970), p. 241.

[55]Vallandigham, *Vallandigham,* p. 253. Vallandigham's letter was reprinted throughout the Midwest. See, for example, *Crisis* (Columbus, O.), 13 May 1863.

[56]Klement, *Limits of Dissent,* pp. 190–228.

case—the illegal arrest, the military trial, the unusual punishment—provided a focus for many a Democrat's republican principles. Vallandigham recognized this and, applying Burke's aphorism that the people "want to draw themselves from abstract principles to personal attachments," offered himself as a victim.[57] Ohio Democrats promptly linked their martyr's persecution to an older revolutionary tradition and to the tune of "Buckeye Boy" sang:

> The great warm heart of Burke is thine,
>     Vallandigham, Vallandigham
> His love of Peace that love divine
>     Vallandigham, Vallandigham
> Illustrious Chatham spoke in thee
> And generous Barre bold and free
> Our first exile for liberty
>     Vallandigham, Vallandigham
> The page of Sidney's Hampden fame,
>     Vallandigham, Vallandigham
> Will give to future years thy name
>     Vallandigham, Vallandigham.[58]

As Vallandigham had expected, many Democrats remained outraged by his treatment. Not only had one of their leaders been silenced; he had also been subjected to the discretionary justice typical of war-created despots. "I have seen," said fellow Ohioan George Pendleton to a crowd of cheering Democrats in 1863, "a citizen torn from his home at the dead hour of night, his house broken into, his family terrified and himself carried to a military prison, sentenced by a drumhead trial, and sent to a punishment unknown to our law."[59]

Democrats placed the Vallandigham affair in the context of English oppositionist thought. According to George Curtis, Ohio was behind the lines; thus because seventeenth-century English precedent established martial law "as warrantable only where the king's scouts or army were in the field," Vallandigham's arrest was "the kind of single palpable violation of liberties which in England not only aroused the public indignation but would endanger the throne itself—for these sacred rights and immunities are designed to be protected and preserved."[60]

[57]Quoted in Rudé, *Wilkes and Liberty,* p. 46.

[58]*The Vallandigham Song Book, Songs for the Times* (Columbus, O.: J. Walter, 1863), p. 11.

[59]"Hon. George H. Pendleton's Address", *SDPK,* 7:10.

[60]Curtis, "True Condition," *SDPK,* 1:6; John L. Pruyn et al., "Reply to President Lincoln's Letter of June 12, 1863," *SDPK,* 10:2–3.

George Pugh, Vallandigham's friend and attorney, challenged Democrats to move beyond talk to action: "Let each man take counsel in his own heart, and then come to the resolution that arbitrary arrests and imprisonments shall be stopped—peaceably if possible, but stopped at all events. The best security to people for their liberty, is the conviction that they will defend it."[61]

In time other Democrats joined Vallandigham and Merryman. The most prominent of these martyrs were the senators and congressmen who faced charges of disloyalty and resolutions of expulsion in the Thirty-seventh and Thirty-eighth Congresses. Most survived; a few did not. Northern Democrats never denied the right of Congress to determine its membership, for they understood this to be an essential safeguard established during Parliament's seventeenth-century struggles with the king. But they objected to the imposition of test oaths affirming past as well as future loyalty. After 1862 such statements were required of government employees, and some Republicans, particularly Charles Sumner, wished them extended to elected officials. Holding his senatorial oath to be sufficient expression of his patriotism, Delaware's Bayard protested what he considered to be a war-inspired interference by the government in matters of conscience. Placing his actions in the tradition of the struggle for a constitutional republic, Bayard reminded his colleagues of the revolution, when Americans knew liberty must be preserved and "their habits of thought and action, their cherished principles, their hopes, their life as a people were all bound up in it. They knew if they suffered it to be lost, there would remain for them nothing but a heritage of shame and ages of confusion, strife and sorrow."[62] After taking the detested oath Bayard resigned his seat, neatly demonstrating the martyr's sacrifice of station for principle.

A few Democrats were expelled by vote of the heavily Republican Senate. One of these was former party leader, Jesse Bright of Indiana, who was ejected in the spring of 1862. Even some colleagues had difficulty accepting Bright's defense that his letter of March 1861 to Jefferson Davis introducing a Northern munitionsmaker was an innocent act of personal friendship. But because Bright had written the letter before the war started, Democrats considered him guilty of poor judgment, not of treason. In their view, Republican efforts to unseat Bright were acts of clumsy partisanship. In his defense of the Indiana senator, Cal-

[61]"Speech of George Pugh," *SDPK,* 9:4.

[62]*Congressional Globe,* 38th Cong., 1st sess., 51–55, 253, 263, 266, 341, 342; app., p. 31; Harold Hyman, *To Try Men's Souls: Loyalty Tests in American History* (Berkeley: University of California Press, 1959) p. 164, 262.

ifornia's Milton Latham compared himself to Cato the Younger—a suggestive image for nineteenth-century Americans familiar with the set of revolutionary pamphlets printed as *Cato's Letters*. Quoting Cato, Latham explained to his colleagues that he spoke only when he had "things to say that deserve to be known", and in this instance he defended the right of Indianans to choose their own representative.[63]

Latham's arguments were unavailing, and hardly had the Republicans expelled Bright when Charles Sumner urged the Senate not to seat Oregon Democrat Benjamin Stark, on the grounds that the newly elected senator had made pro-Southern remarks after the war began. Again party leaders saw in his treatment an example of the way despotic governments "accumulated power by silencing their opponents."[64] In their view, Congress should seat Stark, turn his case over to the proper committee, and act according to long-established procedures. To do otherwise placed an American legislature in the same untenable position that Parliament had adopted in 1768 when it had refused to seat John Wilkes, the elected member from Middlesex. Recalling that instance, Democrats aligned themselves with Wilkes's defenders, who had sustained the right of the people to elect their delegates without intrusion. Delaware's Bayard moved beyond the specifics of the Stark case and admonished his colleagues "to adhere to established forms in times of high excitement when the mind becomes biased and prejudiced. Opinion must be separated from act," a distinction, according to the Delawarean, understood by both seventeenth-century English opponents of the king and the Americans who wrote the treason clause of the Constitution and the Bill of Rights.[65]

Similar controversies inflamed the House, where Northern Democrats also believed themselves to be on trial for their oppositionist opinions, and not for what they held to be the only grounds for such tests—their actions. Alexander Long became another martyr to the Republicans' failure to understand the difference. In April 1864 the young Ohio congressman found himself the subject of an expulsion resolution the day after he proposed an immediate armistice. Within the week the usually languid House had voted his dismissal. Republicans considered his opposition to war and his claims that the "masses are for peace" an arrogant recognition of the Confederacy's independence. More to the point, they held that such sentiments gave

[63]*Congressional Globe,* 37th Cong., 2d sess., app., p. 37
[64]Ibid., pp. 183, 863, 872.
[65]Ibid., p. 184.

aid and comfort to the enemy. Long believed otherwise. His desire to end the war stemmed, he insisted, from his civic duty to protect the commonwealth. "I am not in favor of sacrificing our republican form of government for territorial aggrandizement and the establishment of despotism."[66] Because the war had destroyed liberties inextricably involved with his citizenship, Long insisted on stopping the first in order to retain the second. Maryland congressman Benjamin Harris agreed and, like Long, explained his opposition to military appropriations as "the ancient right of the English commoner to say he will not intrust the money to carry on a War to the King. I do not know that a commoner of the American House of Representatives ever lost that right." Like Long, Harris saw the North contaminated by the "unruly passions of human nature unleashed in war," and the Marylander measured his alienation by an aphorism from Cato: "When vice prevails and impious men bear sway, The post of honor is a private station."[67] Yet Harris did not follow his own advice. He won reelection to Congress in 1864, was censured by this body, and later was convicted by a military court for "harboring" Confederate soldiers.

## *Conspiracy*

Like their colonial ancestors, Northern Democrats went beyond demonstrations of martyrdom to locate the source of their oppression in a conspiracy.[68] Believing they had discovered the plot's origins in the secret meetings of abolitionist fanatics, a few Northern Democrats held misguided English philanthropists and "meddling preachers" responsible for inciting the Republican party to connive against government by "free white men." Most, however, began their tales of intrigue with the organization of New England's abolition societies in the 1830s. Whatever its origins, the conspiracy's machinations were sufficient to threaten the nation. According to Vallandigham, "Fanaticism, and a false, religious zeal, conjoined with that pestilent, but ever-potent spirit, which is so sorely offended at the mote that is in our brother's eye and which makes each man jealous over his neighbor's conscience, could easily be arrayed under the banner of sectional hate and bigotry, and thus a distinct political faction be compounded out of these elements."[69] By the 1860s

[66]Ibid., 38th Cong., 1st sess., 1499–1517, 1631–35. See Alexander Long, "Autobiography," Long Papers.

[67]*Congressional Globe,* 38th Cong., 1st sess., 1515–16.

[68]For a discussion of earlier fears of conspiracy, see Bailyn, *Pamphlets* I: vii, ix.

[69]Vallandigham, *Vallandigham,* p. 25.

Vallandigham's prediction had been fulfilled. Not only had "designing men" organized "wild crusading forces" within the Republican party, but, according to Delaware's Saulsbury, John Brown's "hellish scheme" furnished a sample of how "abolitionist conspirators would undermine free government."[70] Consequently, Democrats held antislavery agitators and their fellow travelers, the Republican party, responsible for secession and the war "forced on us by conspirators hostile to our free institutions North and South."[71] Even during the war, many Northern Democrats continued to distinguish between Southerners, who acted openly and with cause, and abolitionists, who behaved "like miners and sappers, mining and trenching around the temple of liberty, surreptiously working for war and not saying so. . . . a dark enclave of conspirators, freedom-shriekers, and Bible spewkers."[72]

Always strong, the images of conspiracy became even more intense during the war, when Democrats matched in tone, style, and symbolic content the virulence their ancestors had reserved for religious opponents. Grotesque metaphors, reminiscent of Foxe's *Book of Martyrs,* were used to describe clergy from "high steeple" churches and schoolteachers from New England as "plotters," "cabalists," "fanatics," "vipers," "destroyers of home and hearth," and "the worst of the slime."[73] Like most believers in political intrigue, Northern Democrats exaggerated their enemies' influence by supplying in vehemence what was lacking in evidence. As a result, even the innocent meetings of Republican governors in Providence, Rhode Island, and, later, in Altoona, Pennsylvania, became secret enclaves where abolitionist "schemers" connived to raise a black army.[74]

For the most part, Northern Democrats exempted Lincoln from these plots. Having accepted the president as a national symbol (once elected, according to one Democrat, "he ceases to be president of a party and is president of a nation"),[75] Lincoln was ill cast as a conspirator. The president could be a tyrant, a dunce, and, in the negrophobic smear, a baboon, but not a schemer. Instead, according to Democrats

[70]*Congressional Globe,* 37th Cong., 2d sess., 2896.

[71]Ibid., app., p. 53.

[72]Vallandigham, *Vallandigham,* p. 8, 22.

[73]*Congressional Globe,* 37th Cong., 2d sess., 2896; J. Cotton Smith to Thomas Seymour, 28 December 1862; John Danforth to Thomas Seymour, 19 January 1861; both in Thomas Seymour Papers; Vallandigham, *Vallandigham,* pp. 12, 27.

[74]*New York Daily News,* 20 September 1862; *New Hampshire Patriot,* 7 October 1860; William B. Hesseltine, *Lincoln and the War Governors* (New York: A. A. Knopf, 1955), pp. 128, 138, 261; *Congressional Globe,* 37th Cong., 3d sess., 1421.

[75]*Congressional Globe,* 37th Cong., 2d sess., 1738.

who borrowed the term from English oppositionist thought, "his ministry" used the controversy over slaves to intrigue against the rights of white freemen. Focusing on the cabinet, Northern Democrats repeated Secretary of State William Seward's boast that he could arrest anyone in the United States. They accused Secretary of War Edwin Stanton of more desperate crimes. Stanton, in Democratic demonology, read congressional mail; he acted on *ex parte* evidence to discredit political opponents; he intrigued against Democratic generals and organized sinister meetings of the Committee on the Conduct of the War; he furloughed Republicans before elections but sent Democrats to the front; he quartered troops in peaceful communities; and, worst of all, he arrested without cause everyone from the son of a famous revolutionary general to a hunchbacked newsboy who delivered a propeace newspaper in New York. Here indeed was evidence, according to one Northern Democrat, of "a contest between the advocates of constitutional liberty on one hand and base conspirators on the other."[76]

As Americans, Northern Democrats came naturally to these expectations of conspiracy; the notion of a secret cabal that used slavery agitation to mask its intended subversion of liberty was more a reprise of political culture than a partisan manipulation. Northern Democrats had inherited not only the commonwealth tradition that apprehended Jacobite and Tory networks behind every English crisis, but also the colonial perception that the king's ministers schemed to destroy liberty and to install, according to one Bostonian in 1777, "their desperate and deep-laid plan of imperial despotism." Gordon Wood has concluded that "by the 1770's there was hardly a piece of Whig writing that did not dwell on this obsessive fear of a conspiracy."[77] After the revolution Americans retained an apprehensiveness that became the distinguishing characteristic of their republicanism, and at various times they held the Society of the Cincinnati, the Bavarian Illuminati, the Catholic Church, and the Freemasons guilty of what Jefferson once called "a deliberate systematical plan reducing us to slavery."[78]

[76]*Baltimore Clipper*, 19 February 1862; *Congressional Globe*, 37th Cong., 2d sess., 261, 1421, 372, 1570, 1732, 1735–38; Samuel Boyden to Horatio Seymour, n.d., Seymour Papers; *Congressional Globe*, 37th Cong., 3d sess., 1070; Vallandigham, *Vallandigham*, p. 97. For an example of the Seward myth in the South, see C. Vann Woodward, *Mary Chestnut's Civil War Diary* (New Haven: Yale University Press, 1981), pp. 167, 176, 179, 206, 417, 444, 624.

[77]Bailyn, *Pamphlets*, p. 86; idem, *Ideological Origins*, pp. 144–159; Wood, *Creation of American Republic*, p. 39. For nineteenth-century expressions of conspiracy, see David Brion Davis, "Some Themes of Countersubversion: An Analysis of Anti-Masonic, Anti-Catholic and Anti-Mormon Literature," *Mississippi Valley Historical Review* 47 (September 1960): 205–24.

[78]Bailyn, *Pamphlets*, pp. 213, 387.

Primed to see political enemies as schemers who conspired against the republic, Democrats promptly placed themselves in a state they called, without irony, slavery. Given the concurrent existence of black bondage their use of the word seems preposterous, but Northern Democrats believed that only white men had sufficient training and consciousness to understand freedom and its converse. "Now, step by step we are becoming slaves under a government which revels in power," wrote New York Democrat Amasa Parker, and Richard O'Gorman felt that he was being "swept over Niagara" in a "current" of conscription and confiscation policies. Every instance seemed to O'Gorman to follow a mischievous pattern: what started with an illegal call for troops ended in the draft; what began with the army's refusal to return fugitive slaves ended with black soldiers patrolling white polling booths.[79] By 1862, Democrats believed their fall to servility complete. As a result, according to Delaware's Saulsbury, "men converse in whispers; even woman dare not speak above her breath. A deadly tremor seized upon all classes, except those who, themselves being spies and informers, were conscious of reposing under the shadow of executive protection." Appropriately, the senator's warning ended with an admonition from Shakespeare's *Julius Caesar:* "Judgment hath fled to brutish beasts / And men have lost their reason."[80]

From a distance, these Democratic complaints seem the rankest vote-getting demagogery. But within the political culture of mid-nineteenth-century America the expectation of conspiracy transformed them into natural responses. Republicans who shared the national tendency to explain catastrophe by intrigue produced their own version, magnifying the Knights of the Golden Circle into a dangerous Democratic plot against the Union. Having no other way to explain the failure of their political system, Americans of both parties believed that calculated plots determined events. A century before, the wonder-working ways of Providence had served to explain complex, crisis-producing phenomena, but by the 1860s few Americans confused God with history. Instead the acceptance of progress as not just an ideal, but as a characteristic of their society ("our nation cannot retrograde," said George Bancroft), left Northern Democrats without a logical explanation for political deterioration. Accordingly the plots of abolitionists and the intrigues of cabinet ministers became more than description; they also served as explanatory principle.

[79]"Speech of Amasa J. Parker at the Cooper Institute," *SDPK,* 15:5; "Address of Richard O'Gorman Esq," *SDPK,* 7:13.

[80]*Congressional Globe,* 37th Cong., 2d sess., 2896, 2898; ibid., 3d sess., 229, 234.

But what, in Vallandigham's insistently repeated question, "remains to be done?"[81] If a band of conspirators was indeed destroying the vital signs of America, at what point should verbal dissent become physical resistance? To this question Northern Democrats gave varying answers. A few did not consider the point at all, refusing to be drawn into an uncertain schedule of behind-the-lines resistance. Others held that the critical point in the suppression of freemen's liberties had not been reached and, like Ohio's Thomas Lowe, argued that "the circumstances justifying revolution do not exist right now." According to Pennsylvania's Charles Biddle, when events justified action, then an "outraged people," in the spirit of Hampden and the men of the English revolution, would rebel.[82] A still larger group of Northern Democrats expected "to purify the popular mind and turn out the conspirators" through elections. William Allen was one of these. "We will bide our time," wrote the Ohio senator. "When we take possession and assume control of the national government our patriotism and consistent adherence to constitutional rights will shame its enemies." Wrote another Democrat, "Men should remember how mutable is party ascendancy and that the bitter cup which they mix for other lips, the next may be tendered to their own." Even the stormy Vallandigham agreed that the people must check tyranny through peaceful means: "If we are about to pass through the usual stages of revolution, it will not be the leaders of the Democratic party who will hurl your tea into the harbor. We seek no revolution save through the ballot box."[83]

Vallandigham included in his correctives an end to indoctrination "by New England schoolteachers and perverted fanatics who abandoned their proper spheres to pollute the public mind with abolitionism."[84] Turning his attention to education, the Ohioan was typical of a group of Democrats who located the source of conspiracy in Northern classrooms where radical notions of antislavery and higher law had undermined the prudential moderation necessary for a republic. But no one suggested removing wrong-thinking teachers or objectionable books. Instead, according to Democrats, republican principles would spontaneously reenter the classroom. "Political change must begin," argued Horatio Seymour in 1864, "at the bottom not at

[81]Vallandigham, *Vallandigham,* p. 32.

[82]Thomas O. Lowe, manuscript of a letter to the *Dayton Journal,* 6 May 1863, Thomas Lowe Papers, Dayton County Public Library, Dayton, O.; *Congressional Globe,* 37th Cong., 3d sess., 27, 1215.

[83]*Congressional Globe,* 37th Cong., 3d sess., app., pp. 176–77.

[84]Ibid., p. 17, Vallandigham, *Vallandigham,* pp. 195, 202.

the top. . . . To the impatient this seems a slow process, but we must bear in mind that our people must be reformed and educated by the evils brought upon them by their own errors."[85] His New York friend Samuel Tilden was even less specific: "Americans have no comprehension of the political philosophy of our wise ancestors"—in part because "abolitionist conspirators have replaced its principles with their dangerous doctrines of higher law theory," and in part because politicians discussed "small administrative questions" and did not use their platforms as "republican schoolmasters." Lincoln was a typical example of Tilden's mid-century politician who, in his youth, competed so hard for "petty honors and emoluments of office" that he never understood the "inherited wisdom."[86]

To combat such ignorance, party members recalled an earlier political language, and, refurbishing its principal form—the pamphlet—twenty-two Northern Democrats established the Society for the Diffusion of Political Knowledge as a clearinghouse for their publications. As one explained, "This is the time for pamphleteers and essayists, and if we expect to save constitutional liberty, no time should be lost in furnishing food for reflection."[87] Remembered here was the importance of inexpensive eighteenth-century printed sheets as a source of political thought and action, and even the society's awkward name suggested its revolutionary roots. In its two years of existence, members circulated thirty-nine pamphlets "intended to save constitutional liberty" by furnishing committees of correspondence, editorial writers, and stump speakers with the essential arguments of the Democracy's revived republicanism. If Northern Democrats sounded alike during the 1860s and 1870s, it was because their information came from the society. But although the revolutionary metaphors were in evidence, these documents did not ignite public opinion as they had in the eighteenth century. Most contributors relied on stilted language and difficult historical examples rather than on the catalytic invective and ironic ridicule that had transformed belief into action during the eighteenth century. Although the society's slogan, "When the Party in Power Violates the Constitution and disregards States Rights, Plain Men Read Pamphlets—Read—Discuss—Diffuse," recalled Thomas Paine's *Common*

[85]Horatio Seymour to "Dear Sir," 24 November 1864, Seymour-Fairchild Papers, New York Historical Society, New York City.

[86]"Letter from Mr. Tilden," *SDPK,* 1:13.

[87]Winslow S. Pierce to Horatio Seymour, 29 April, 1862, Seymour-Fairchild Papers; Frank Friedel, ed., *Union Pamphlets during the Civil War, 1862–1865* (Cambridge, Mass.: Harvard University Press, Belknap, 1976), pp. 14–16.

*Sense* and the entire process by which prerevolutionary convictions had been converted into antigovernment activities, its texts on Jamaica cotton production and the scriptural basis for Negro slavery were anemic reproductions of eighteenth-century political discourse.

Although most Northern Democrats limited their opposition to words, a few did encourage physical resistance. But even these partisans revealed uncertainty, using questions rather than assertions to make their case. "Is there none of the spirit of 1776 left?" inquired one Democrat. After comparing Lincoln to George III and asking if freemen would submit to Republican tyranny, George Pugh importuned Democrats to prevent his arrest with the innocuous query: "If I am arrested as I may be tomorrow and dragged into the presence of a military commander, will you act?" D. A. Mahony, the Indiana editor who wrote under the pseudonym Sidney Cromwell, was even less forceful: "If citizens do not choose to preserve the government, what right has the government to compel them to do so against their will?"[88]

Even the most notorious sample of Northern Democratic rhetoric—Governor Seymour's Fourth of July 1863 attack on the draft—encouraged debate, not action:

> We only ask freedom of speech—the right to exercise all the franchises conferred by the Constitution upon an American. Can you safely deny us these things? . . . We stand today amid new-made graves. . . . We can, if we will, avert all these disasters and evoke a blessing. If we will do what? Hold that Constitution, and liberties, and laws are suspended? Will that restore them? Or shall we do as our fathers did under circumstances of like trial, when they battled against the powers of a crown? Did they say that liberty was suspended? Did they say that men might be deprived of the right of trial by jury? Did they say that men might be torn from their home by midnight intruders?

The New York governor concluded with the muted subjunctives of a Chautauqua lecturer: "If you would save your country and your liberties, begin at the hearth-stone; begin in your family circle; declare that their rights shall be held sacred; and having once proclaimed your own rights, claim for your own State that jurisdiction and that Government which we better than all others can exercise for ourselves, for we best know our own interests."[89] Such language could not serve as a call to

[88]*Old Guard* 1 (January, 1861): 6; "Speech of Mr. Pugh to 50,000 Voters," *SDPK,* 9:4; *Congressional Globe,* 37th Cong., 3d sess., 533–34; ibid., app., p. 172.

[89]Horatio Seymour, *Public Record* (New York: I. W. England, 1868), pp. 118–24. See

resistance against the government, although some New Yorkers used it as a sanction to protest the draft and to attack Negroes.

Thus, a note of scolding and plaintiveness had replaced the moral certainty of the late eighteenth century. Pugh, for example, offended Ohio listeners by concluding that they were cowards who would never act because they lacked the courage of free men. On various occasions Benjamin Wood, Henry May, and other militants condemned "the people" for not "rising" to protect their rights. Vallandigham added further insult by quoting Sidney's injunction that only a lazy people "gave away their fundamental privileges." "I have seen and heard," wrote New Jersey's Chauncey Burr, "freemen who act like slaves," and New Jersey Democrat Thomas Dunn English repeated the point:

> Our fathers were men in the days that are past
> What a pity it is that our fathers are dead!
> They left us a heritage glorious and vast
> A charter of rights which they fancied would last
> Perhaps it is good that our fathers are dead.[90]

Even the party's rare calls for action appealed for resistance not in the name of moral regeneration, but in terms of restoring the past. Like all other Americans, Democrats were caught in the perfectionist framework of their national history; for if the founders had installed the world's best government, then public life must always be measured by the past. Americans must be reformers, not transformers. The language of the party's revived republicanism displayed the difference: Patrick Henry's ringing denunciation became Lazarus Powell's dogmatism—"If loyalty to the Constitution of my country be treason, then I am a traitor." The eighteenth-century revolutionary had become a self-defined martyr even before the deed. "We will choose our own destiny," asserted Delaware's Saulsbury. "If that be treason, everybody who chooses so to consider it may make the most of it." After an antiwar speech New Jersey's Democratic senator James Wall reiterated as taut-

---

also the Tilden Papers in the New York Public Library and State Archives. Included in the Tilden Papers is a memorandum from William Kidd, who remembered Seymour as answering the crowd's "Governor, we are your friends" with "well: if you are my friends you will go to your homes like peaceable citizens." See William Kidd to Henry S. Miller, 3 January 1893, Tilden Papers, New York Public Library, New York City.

[90]"Speech of Mr. Pugh," *SDPK,* 9:4, 5; P. Bradstreet to Alexander Long, 12 December 1863, Long Papers; *Old Guard* 2 (July 1863): 154. "Poems," Thomas Dunn English Papers, New Jersey Historical Society, Newark.

ology what had earlier stirred Americans: "If this be treason, let it be treason."[91]

Philosophically as well as historically, Democrats were trapped, for even the most selective disobedience placed them in the company of their detested rivals—the "higher law" abolitionists like William Lloyd Garrison and John Brown who decided for themselves which statutes to obey, thereby placing law on the personal basis that Democrats believed destroyed community imperatives. For years, Democrats had inveighed against violations of the fugitive-slave laws, whether by state-approved personal-liberty statutes or by individuals who refused to return slaves. What for some Republicans seemed the highest of humanitarian acts—the Anthony Burns rescue—was mere anarchy for the Democrats. Nor was the party's favored method of protest, nullification, possible, because screening national legislation required the control of local governments which Democrats did not have. To be sure, Democrats often referred to the Virginia and Kentucky resolutions as "their treasured contribution to national theory," but their idea of a state veto over federal legislation had been summarily dealt with by Jackson and was hardly relevant to their circumstances.

Some party members defined legitimate opposition in community terms: "I would counsel my people [of Kentucky] to resist [illegal laws] by every mode of resistance they could devise," proclaimed Garrett Davis, who later denied that "every mode" included force. "Would you revolutionize?" asked Chauncey Burr of his fellow Democrats in Rockland County, New York. And his answer was "No, Sir, I would not, but I would stop others from revolutionizing. I would shake off the shackles applied to the hand of a freeman. I would beat down prison doors that consign men to dungeons." But what did this mean? For Vallandigham, who usually stood in the vanguard of dissent, it did not include avoiding military service, for "whoever shall be drafted is in duty bound, no matter what he thinks of the war to either go, or find a substitute, or pay the fine which the law imposes; he has no right to resist, and none to run away."[92]

Differences in historical circumstances were crucial. In the eighteenth century when it became a felt necessity to break the law in order to keep

[91]*Congressional Globe,* 37th Cong., 2d sess., 2, 110; Charles M. Knapp, *New Jersey Politics during the Period of Civil War and Reconstruction* (Geneva, N.Y.: W. F. Humphrey, 1924) p. 121; *Delawarean,* 16 February 1861.

[92]*Congressional Globe,* 37th Cong., 2d sess., 2062–64; ibid., 38th Cong., 1st sess., 136, 342; "Speech of Chauncey Burr at Rockland, New York, 1864," *Old Guard* 3 (July 1864): 15; Vallandigham, *Vallandigham,* p. 47.

it, republican thought led to physical resistance. But in the nineteenth century when it was believed necessary to end the war in order to restore the law, republicanism pushed toward peace. Considering the war an unnecessary evil inflicted by Northern and Southern fanatics, Democrats denied that the restoration of freedom lay on the battlefield. They believed it would come at the peace table; hence they developed various plans to end the war: an armistice, the mediation of European powers, a negotiated settlement, a national peace convention attended by elected delegates from North and South, and the appointment of Northern peace commissioners. This last proposal originated in Congressman Cox's July 1861 resolution "to appoint a commission of seven who shall request from the so-called Confederate states appointment of a similar commission to meet in Louisville." Six months later, Fernando Wood proposed a similar strategy: "Resolved: that the President appoint three Commissioners to negotiate at Richmond to the end that the bloody destruction and inhuman war shall cease and the Union be restored on terms of equity, fraternity, and equality."[93]

Seen as aspects of political culture, Democratic proposals for a peace convention were neither radical nor traitorous. They emerged from the ingrained notion that the people in consultation could resolve public conflicts. Whereas in England such meetings originally brought together the estates of the realm, in America representative assemblies transformed themselves into bodies that expressed popular sovereignty and legitimate authority. No longer legally deficient, nineteenth-century conventions made fundamental law, and Americans used them to call, write, and ratify their constitutions.

But to convene such an assemblage required support from Republicans, who believed the unconditional surrender of the South was the only way to end the war. Accused of treason for their efforts, Democrats appealed to the people and spoke of the "human thunder" that would force the convoking of such a body. "We will solicit such conventions through state legislatures," insisted one Democrat. "The people want an armistice," wrote a midwestern editor; "let us come together and stop this war.[94]

But the people never did come together in the kind of spontaneous movement Democrats remembered from the War of Independence and expected by 1863. Opposed by Republicans, peace strategies embroiled Democrats in internal squabbles that forced the party's 1864 presidential

[93]*Congressional Globe,* 37th Cong., 3d sess., 725, 1497–98; ibid., 1st sess., 331.
[94]Ibid.,3d sess., 1265; app., p. 135; *Cincinnati Daily Enquirer,* 7 and 8 January 1863.

candidate, George McClellan, to distinguish his position from that of the national platform. Democrats continued to vote the men and munitions to fight while they argued for peace initiatives. Quoting Shakespeare, one Pennsylvania Democrat reminded the House that "a peace is of the nature of a conquest, for then both parties nobly are subdued, and neither party loser."[95] But Republicans paid little attention to such a paradox. "They cry peace, peace. . . . How can there be an honorable peace?" asked Benjamin Wade, to which a Democratic editor, paraphrasing Benjamin Franklin, replied that there was "no such thing as a dishonorable peace among brethren."[96]

Although Republicans suggested otherwise, only a few Northern Democrats wanted to recognize the Confederacy as a precondition to negotiation. Those who did proceeded from the republican premise that allegiance must be freely given and that freedom was worth more than union. From this perspective there could be no reconstruction of a political society by coercion. Yet such sentiments remained unpopular and were not, despite Republican propaganda, the distinguishing feature of the so-called Peace Democracy. War-deafened ears were unable to distinguish among the party's various proposals to end the war. Eventually peace came without conditions, but the Northern Democrats' idea of making peace while fighting a war was much more than an opposition party's weapon to retain Southern supporters. The deeper resolve was to end the circumstances that threatened the republic.

But as Northern Democrats learned, the party in power had the stronger hold on public opinion; the war permitted Republicans the sense of moral regeneration that, a century before, had accompanied the revolution. Given long-established national values and battle-stirred hearts, war purified, exalted, and transformed self-interest into patriotic sacrifice. No organization held exclusive rights to this martial fervor, but because their party was mortgaged to the less intoxicating peace policy, Democrats forfeited the propaganda of the bloody shirt for that of trampled liberties.

As a result, the Democrats' revived republicanism became a miscellaneous excerpting from the antiauthoritarian traditions of a previous era—an unhappy retread of an eighteenth-century philosophy ill suited to a nineteenth-century civil war. The party added nothing and, failing to reinvigorate its inheritance, neglected two essential components—the sense of collective national regeneration and the notion of

[95]*Congressional Globe,* 37th Cong., 3d sess., 1088.
[96]Ibid., 2d sess., 1736; *Cincinnati Daily Enquirer,* 21 January 1865.

virtue within a commonwealth. The latter had served as a check on executive tyranny, but in the nineteenth century it had been submerged by individualism. Hence what Democrats sought to protect during the Civil War were private rights of free speech, free press, and a free ballot. By 1860, according to Democractic doctrine, Americans had to be free to be virtuous, not, as an early generation insisted, virtuous to be free.

For all its failings, it would be a mistake to infer that the Democrats' republicanism was a meaningless phantom. In varying degrees all Americans shared the party's antiauthoritarian legacy, although it was left to Southerners to develop its most dynamic nineteenth-century version. Hardly a deception fostered by demagogic politicians, republicanism was social fact, and in the way of determinative ideologies, its assumptions outlined the political behavior of the United States. Because of the warnings of the past there were some things Republicans could not do. They could not organize a coup d'état or postpone elections; they could not institute any systematic censorship of mail and newspapers; and they could not violate civil liberties too often or extend the doctrine of state necessity too far.

CHAPTER 5

# *Conservative Naturalism: The Racial Views of Stephen Douglas and the Delaware Bayards*

By itself their republican ideology does not explain how Northern Democrats felt about the great social issues of the mid-nineteenth century: slavery, emancipation, and black citizenship. The party's antiauthoritarian instincts might have led to the obvious analogy that slaves stood in the same relation to corrupt Southern masters as prerevolutionary colonists had to English kings. Democrats might have viewed slavery as a discordant institution undermining the harmony of their society. Linked with natural rights theory, such comparisons would have ended at antislaveryism, and to a limited degree Republicans followed this progression. Holding slaves to be a part of God's humanity, they accorded them a conditional equality and grudgingly hammered the necessity of freedom into limited civil and political rights for blacks.[1]

Northern Democrats also believed in natural rights and republicanism, but, reversing priorities, they concentrated on the fragile nature of republics and their tendency toward corruption and tyranny. To this, they added an intense racism based on three currents of nineteenth-century thought: the pseudo-scientific view of Negroes as biologically

[1]Herman Belz, *A New Birth of Freedom: The Republican Party and Freedmen's Rights, 1861–1866* (Westport, Conn.: Greenwood Press, 1976); Michael Les Benedict, *A Compromise of Principle: Congressional Republicans and Reconstruction, 1863–1869* (New York: W. W. Norton, 1976); Glenn Linden, *Politics or Principle: Congressional Voting on the Civil War Amendments and Pro-Negro Measures, 1838–1869* (Seattle: University of Washington Press, 1976). As all three authors make clear, military and political expediency often dictated Republican legislation, a fact recognized by Salmon Chase, who complained, when Lincoln considered colonization in order to deprive the South of manpower, "How much better would be a manly protest against prejudice against color!" Jacques Voegeli, *Free but Not Equal: The Midwest and the Negro during the Civil War* (Chicago: University of Chicago Press, 1967), p. 45.

inferior,[2] the revision of Genesis that denied the single creation, and an Americanized version of Edmund Burke's conservatism that emphasized historical continuity and experience over abstract theory.[3]

By themselves, all three postulates led to conclusions quite different from those reached by Northern Democrats. For example, the belief that there were immutable God-given differences between whites and blacks predisposed its adherents to support slavery; yet Republican charges to the contrary, this was not the position of most Northern Democrats. Without the influence of racism, republicanism confirmed the doctrine that masters were tyrants and that blacks needed civil protection from this oppression. And if undiluted racism was inevitably reducible to slavery and unadulterated republicanism to freedom, unleavened conservatism, with its emphasis on an organic community etched by custom and tradition, would have replaced the federal union with the original units of civic life—the states. But this was not the position held by even the most enthusiastic supporters of states' rights. In fact nearly all Northern Democrats believed secession illegal. Had party members been strict Burkean conservatives, they would have opposed the territorial expansion that instead they applauded as progress. It was the combination of these insights that furnished Northern Democrats with their perspective of conservative naturalism.

Not all Northern Democrats blended the elements of republicanism, racism, and conservatism in the same measure, and this fact accounts for the variations in party opinion. Northern Democrats who concentrated on race came to deny the Christian orthodoxy of a single creation and accepted instead a theory of plural creationism which placed blacks within the lowest order of God's creatures. "It is," wrote John Van Evrie, the New York physician and Democratic pamphleteer, "a palpable and unavoidable fact that Negroes are a different species." Van Evrie relied on physiological evidence provided by the new science of ethnology to buttress his argument that Negroes were inferior to whites. But to classify blacks as a different species required more than science, and Van Evrie transformed the Old Testament account of Adam and Eve into a story of the white man's origins. By suggesting that blacks had their own beginnings, Van Evrie freed himself from the na-

[2]For a discussion of the development of this idea, see George Frederickson, *The Black Image in the White Mind* (New York: Harper & Row, 1971) pp. 71–96; William Stanton, *The Leopard's Spots: Scientific Attitudes toward Race in America, 1815–1859* (Chicago: University of Chicago Press, 1960).

[3]Peter Stanlis, *Edmund Burke and Natural Law* (Chicago: University of Chicago Press, 1963).

ture–nurture conundrum and rendered black inferiority an incorrectable status. This line of thinking denied religious arguments on behalf of the unity of mankind, and in the view of many Northern Democrats by the 1840s, God had created man unequal.[4]

Democrats had not always taken such a position. As late as 1842, the *Democratic Review* had answered yes to the question "Do the various races of man constitute a single species?" But by 1850 the God-given unity of mankind had given way to newer theories of polygeniticism. "Few or none now seriously adhere to the theory of the unity of races" explained the *Democratic Review* in its revised position on the matter. "The whole state of the science at this moment seems to indicate that there are several distinct races of men on the face of the earth, with entirely different capacities, physical and mental." By the 1860s many Northern Democrats believed that Genesis made sense only if one accepted the doctrine that other types of humans existed before Adam and Eve.[5]

But this harsher racism of multiple species left unanswered questions. In the past, sterility had served as a test of species, with only a few exceptions, such as matings of goldfinches and canaries granted to the rule of infertility across species. If blacks were to be considered inferior, adherents of the new theory must explain the mulatto population that contradicted the standard. Following Van Evrie, most Northern Democrats who considered the problem argued that the sterility of racial hybrids occurred in the fourth generation—a position that only a determined genealogist could dispute. This notion of a delayed inter-species sterility, so essential for polygenetic theory, encouraged the popular stereotype of mulattos as "pale, weakly, desiccated yellows."[6] On this tangent the seemingly extraneous issue of interracial sexual contact entered politics, and it is impossible to read the Democratic messages of the 1850s and 1860s without noting their preoccupation with what Van Evrie christened "miscegenation." When Northern Democrats introduced the issue into congressional debates and stump speeches, they were trying to establish a new racial orthodoxy, for their position was

[4]J. H. Van Evrie, *White Supremacy and Negro Subordination; or Negroes a Subordinate Race and (So-called) Slavery Its Normal Condition* (1861; reprint, New York: Negro Universities Press, 1969), pp. 48, 52, 57; Stanton, *Leopard's Spots,* pp. 3–10.

[5]*United States Magazine and Democratic Review* 11 (August 1842): 113–139 (hereafter cited as *Democratic Review*); "The Natural History of Man," *Democratic Review* 26 (April 1850): 328; 27 (August 1850): 133–46; and 28 (September 1850): 209–20. The quotation is from the April issue, 328.

[6]Stanton, *Leopard's Spots,* pp. 66–68, 76; quotation from Van Evrie, *White Supremacy,* p. 191.

heresy. When Northern Democrats discussed "the vileness of amalgamation," they did so not just to awaken racial hysteria and derive electoral benefit from labeling their Republican opponents "miscegenators," but also to rail against the visible contradiction of their racial theory. Even in the busy wartime sessions of Congress, Samuel Cox found time to instruct his colleagues in genetics. "The physiologist," he said in 1864, "will tell the gentlemen that the mulatto does not live. He does not recreate his kind; he is a monster. Such hybrid races by a law of Providence scarcely survive beyond one generation."[7]

Any doctrine that confuted the common ancestry of mankind reinforced the equality of whites. Again Van Evrie provided the basic doctrine. "The subordination of whites to whites," he wrote in his popular paper, the *Caucasian*, "is unjust and artificial. The English are ruled by those who are not naturally superior, while American democracy assures self-government of, by, and for naturally equal whites."[8] Such views appealed to his German- and Irish-born readers, for Van Evrie considered antislavery agitation a delusion inherited from "European aristocrats who by holding up the imaginary wrongs to American slaves diverted attention from their own mistreatment of the white working class."[9] From his perspective, black slavery could not exist, because only whites trained in republican integrity understood freedom, and Van Evrie therefore renamed the South's peculiar institution "subgenation." By adopting such views, Northern Democrats refurbished their party's traditional links to the People, now explicitly defined as white, and by excluding blacks from public affairs they offered political democracy and an inclusive patriotism to white male Americans.[10]

There were other implications to the Democracy's theory of racial hierarchies. If God had made the Negro different from—and inferior to—the white man by virtue of a separate creation, then blacks must be governed differently from whites. On the other hand, if blacks and whites shared a common origin, then both races must inhabit the same

[7]*Congressional Globe*, 38th Cong., 1st sess, 709.

[8]*Caucasian*, 3 October 1863; see also 21 November 1861.

[9]Van Evrie, *White Supremacy*, p. 24.

[10]J. H. Van Evrie, *Subgenation: The Theory of the Normal Relation of the Races: An Answer to Miscegenation* (New York: J. Bradburn, 1864); Ronald Sanders, *Lost Tribes and Promised Lands: Origins of American Racism* (Boston: Little, Brown, 1978). Some historians relate this new American racism to industrial society's need to define a portion of humanity for exploitation. The assumption here is that industrial society destroys traditional class structures and requires a new hierarchy. Racism provides the under-class for modern civilization.

public universe, which in the United States implied equal privileges. A nineteenth-century journal probed the issue:

> If the whole race have but a common origin, then common systems may be applied to all, and the greatest license is given to latter-day theorists who would organize the world upon certain uniform bases and fit the same institutions and laws to every stage and condition of civilization. If on the other hand these mad schemers will at once be refuted [then] the world [will] discover that parliament and Congress are unsuited to the Hottentot and African.

The logical conclusion of such views was apartheid, and possibly, as George Frederickson has described for South Africa, the removal of blacks to territories or reservations. Not every Northern Democrat accepted these ideas but given their popularity, the importance of the Civil War and Reconstruction was not what was accomplished for blacks in terms of emancipation and civil rights, but rather what was avoided.[11]

Not all Northern Democrats took race as the foundation of their political thinking. Many started with Burke's postulates on the importance of community, the sanctity of established institutions, the authority of existing arrangements, and the necessity of public policies that harmonized with local customs. From such a perspective, issues related to slavery and, later, to the freedman's status were improper subjects for national attention, and those who focused on abolitionism, in the words of New York Democrat John Kirke Paulding, "trampled on all the feelings of humanity and immolated the laws of their country . . . on the altar of a wilful misrepresentation of the law of God." Because circumstances realized human theories and not the reverse, "what might be sport to us [in the North] is death to the South."[12] Like Burke, this group of Northern Democrats cited the diversity of human arrangements as a manifestation of natural law (God gave uniform laws but diverse environments to man). Thus Democrats who followed Burke might be for or against slavery (Paulding wished it would "go out like a candle"), emancipation, and black suffrage, but their policies held no categorical imperatives and were tied to local history, tradition, and experience. Believing human nature to be flawed, these Northern

[11]*DeBow's Review* 9 (August 1850): 243–44; George Frederickson, *White Supremacy: A Comparative Study of American and South African History* (New York: Oxford University Press, 1981).

[12]James Kirke Paulding, *Slavery in the United States* (1836; reprint, New York: Negro Universities Press, 1968), pp. 281, 296–98, 53.

Democrats denied the primacy of abstract reason as a guide to social and political matters.

Some Northern Democrats were inadvertent Burkeans; for them the English statesman's pragmatism was simply a congenial philosophy. Others, who had begun their schooldays declaiming Burke's speeches on taxation and conciliation, had absorbed his objections to English policy and had progressed to his *Reflections on the Revolution in France*. A few Americans knew his written works with an intimacy that fostered paraphrasing and quotation-mongering. Only Shakespeare and Milton were quoted more often in the mid-nineteenth-century Congresses, and Burke's influence in the United States, unlike that in England, remained constant and significant. Non-Democrats also found Burke's ideas attractive, and as a result there were four American editions of the complete works by 1866, along with numerous pamphlet editions of the popular *Reflections* and *Speeches on the Revolution*.[13]

Through Burke, Americans learned the concept of natural law, for pervading his writings was the idea that there were axioms existing before human institutions and not subject to manmade assertions, what he called "the great immutable preexisting law paramount to our feelings by which we are connected in the eternal frame of the universe." This concept, as Burke made clear in the *Reflections,* was not an abstraction. Rather, metaphysical rights entered into "common life" in the same way that "rays of light pierce into a dense medium." The notion that natural law was affected by local conditions ("refracted from their straight line") permitted Americans a realistic encounter with a potentially rigid philosophical system. And just as Burke referred the differences in civil liberties accorded eighteenth-century Indians in Bengal and Englishmen in London to custom and practice in those dissimilar settings, so Democrats held no uniform position on slavery. Yet from Burke Northern Democrats derived the conservative charter that what

[13]For examples of schoolbooks with Burke's speeches see David Harsha, *The Most Eminent Orators and Statesmen* (Philadelphia: Porter and Oates, 1854); also Donald Bryant, "Edmund Burke: A Generation of Scholarship Discovery," *Journal of British Studies* 2 (September 1962): 29–114; Naomi Townshend, "Edmund Burke: Reputation and Bibliography, 1850–1954" (Ph.D. dissertation, University of Pittsburgh, 1955): Chauncey Goodrich, *Selected British Eloquence* (New York: Harper Brothers, 1854). For the influence of Burke on another conservative, see Russell Kirk, *Randolph of Roanoake: A Study in Conservative Thought* (Chicago: University of Chicago Press, 1951); Donald Bryant, "Edmund Burke: New Evidence, Broader View," *Quarterly Journal of Speech* 38 (December 1952): 434–45; Shearer Davis Bowman, "Antebellum Planters and Vormärz Junkers," *American Historical Review* 85 (September 1980): 799.

had been wrong to begin with nonetheless became consecrated over time.[14]

Preoccupied with the fragility of republics, a third group of Northern Democrats began their calculations with a fear of tyranny and a sensitivity to corruption. Contending that the war had strengthened these political infections, such self-appointed watchdogs of the republic as Reverdy Johnson and James McDougall focused more on the civil liberties of white Northerners than on the emancipation of black Southerners. Increasingly, however, the status of blacks intersected with their vision of a white man's government, and although they complained of the "Negromania" of their opponents and dismissed Negro issues as irrelevant, the changing circumstances of black men required their attention. Unlike those Democrats who concentrated on race and the biological inferiority of the Negro, these republican-oriented Democrats opposed the Freedmen's Bureau, the Civil Rights Acts, and the suffrage amendment on the basis that the inclusion of the Negro in public matters would incorporate a defective civic population into American politics. And because most Northerners opposed black citizenship, they believed the government would be required to force acceptance of black rights, thereby threatening the harmony of the republic.

Although most Northern Democrats shared these attitudes, a few provided representative statements of the party's racial views. One of these was Stephen Douglas, who felt as he did about slavery and race because he lived in Illinois, because he was a Democrat of national importance, and because he was a white American. Blending racism, republicanism, and Burke's sense of community, Douglas forged a position on slavery (for this was the great issue of his time, as emancipation would be during the war and black citizenship and suffrage after it) which depended on federal neutrality, popular sovereignty, and local choice. Not every Democrat agreed. Some left the party after the Douglas-sponsored Kansas-Nebraska Act opened the way for what they considered the nationalizing of slavery. Others found John Breckinridge's plan for congressional protection of slavery in the territories more congenial. But there were many whose racial attitudes were shaped and articulated by Douglas. Of all the party's leaders, he

[14]Ross Hoffman and Paul Levack, eds., *Burke's Politics: Selected Writings and Speeches of Edmund Burke* (New York: A. A. Knopf, 1949), 1: 284–85, 294; Stanlis, *Burke and Natural Law,* pp. 71, 76; *The Works of Edmund Burke,* 16 vols. (London: C. J. Rivington, 1826–1827), 13: 166.

worked the hardest to spread his views and in turn to listen to what he called, in his cliché-ridden language, "the voice of the People." Even Lincoln acknowledged Douglas's "vast influence, . . . so great that it is enough for many men to believe anything, when they once find that Judge Douglas professes to believe it." The senator's admirers believed that he swayed "the tides of public opinion as vassals to his will."[15]

In fact Douglas did not so much sway public opinion as represent it; his racial views were intimately associated with those in his adopted state. When Douglas came from Vermont to Morgan County in the early 1830s, Illinois was already reconsidering its antislavery constitution. Although this regression from freedom to slavery was defeated, controversies involving fugitive slaves, the rights of free blacks and Negro migration remained a part of his public world. In 1848, after seven out of ten Illinoisans voted to exclude free blacks, the state's new constitution included a provision "prohibiting free persons of color from immigration and settling in the state." (Fifteen years later, in the midst of the Civil War, nearly the same proportion of citizens again voted to keep Illinois white.)[16]

First as a state legislator and then as a state attorney Douglas dealt with racial matters, and as an ambitious new resident he listened closely to the opinions of his adopted community. At twenty-three, as a first-term legislator, Douglas supported resolutions that declared property in slaves "a sacred institution," that denied Congress the right to abolish slavery in the District of Columbia without a referendum, and that denounced abolitionist meddling. (Across the aisle the Whig delegate from Sangamon County, Abraham Lincoln, was one of only six representatives in a legislature of eighty-three to oppose these resolutions.) A few years later, as a state judge, Douglas ruled against an abolitionist who had argued, to a charge of aiding fugitive slaves, that Illinois statute was superseded by federal law. Sustained on appeal, Douglas's

[15]Roy P. Basler, *The Collected Works of Abraham Lincoln,* vol. 2 (New Brunswick, N.J.: Rutgers University Press, 1953), p. 27; *Congressional Globe,* 37th Cong., 1st sess., 36. For the way in which some men become "lenses through which we read our own minds," see Ralph Waldo Emerson, *Representative Men: Seven Lectures* (Boston: Phillips, Simpson, 1850), pp. 9–40.

[16]John Moses, *Illinois, Historical and Statistical* (Chicago: Tergus, 1892), p. 331; Jay William McKim, "State Exclusion Laws: The Conflict between State Laws Prohibiting the Entrance of Free Negroes and the Privileges and Immunities Clause of the Federal Constitution in the Period 1789–1860" (Ph.D. dissertation, Ohio State University, 1934); Tom LeRoy McLaughlin, "Popular Reactions to the Idea of Negro Equality in Twelve Nonslaveholding States, 1846–1869: A Quantitative Analysis" (Ph.D. dissertation, Washington State University, 1969); Norman D. Harris, *The History of Negro Servitude in Illinois and the Slavery Agitation in that State, 1719–1864* (Chicago: A. C. McClurg, 1904).

ruling—that the state fugitive-slave law was necessary for public safety—foreshadowed his later position that slavery was a local matter best handled by each community.[17]

Along with most nineteenth-century Democrats, Douglas's views on slavery were interwoven with his conception of race; having come to accept polygenetic theory, he believed Negroes irredeemably inferior to whites. Neither their individual achievements nor their oppression in the United States shook this idea, and his comments on blacks were invariably harsh in tone, biological in metaphor, and popular in idiom. "Between all contests between negro and white," he said during his famous debates with Lincoln, "I am for the white man. In all questions between negro and crocodile I am for the negro."[18] Eventually Douglas elevated black inferiority and the resulting necessity of a white civic community to the status of natural law. "We here do not believe in the equality of the Negro socially and politically. Our people are white people; our state is a white state, and we mean to preserve the race pure without any mixture with the negro." In the debates with Lincoln he returned often to this theme, linking race with national destiny. "This government was made by our fathers, by white men for the benefit of white men and their posterity forever and is intended to be administered by white men in all time to come."[19]

Republicans, according to Douglas, were unclear on this point and did not understand the natural laws of race. Thus when Lincoln tried to make Douglas into the advocate of slavery that he was not, Douglas countered that Lincoln accepted black equality, which he did not. Comparing himself with Lincoln, Douglas advanced the point that the Negro was not "kin of mine,"[20] thereby implying two things: first, that Lincoln's theories made all men the equals that kinship guaranteed, and second, that Lincoln himself might have Negro blood.

Occasionally Douglas's racism collided with his view of popular sovereignty. In theory the Illinois senator remanded to local communities decisions about the biracial society best suited to their political culture,

[17]Robert Johannsen, *Stephen A. Douglas* (New York: Oxford University Press, 1973), pp. 54–55, 103–04.

[18]This metonymy also appeared in minstrel shows. The quotation of Douglas is from Harry Jaffa, *Crisis of the House Divided* (New York: Doubleday, 1959), p. 312; Basler, *Collected Works of Lincoln,* 2: 35.

[19]*Congressional Globe,* 33d Cong., 1st sess., app., p. 328; Douglas to James M. Scofield, March 1859, in Robert Johannsen, ed., *Letters of Stephen A. Douglas* (Urbana: University of Illinois Press, 1961), p. 440. For other versions see Paul Angle, *Created Equal: The Complete Lincoln-Douglas Debates* (Chicago: University of Chicago Press, 1958), pp. 18–19.

[20]Angle, *Created Equal,* pp. 62, 375.

although he expected whites to control this process. In 1850 he wrote a party platform giving blacks privileges and immunities "congruent" with public safety, and in 1858 he returned to the same theme during the Springfield and Ottawa debates, when he conceded that the Negro "as an inferior race ought to possess every right, every privilege, every immunity which he can safely exercise consistent with the safety of the society in which he lives." But in a frantic effort to save the Union in 1861, he proposed two constitutional amendments as inconsistent with his doctrine as his shift on the Missouri Compromise: one denied Negroes the right to vote; the other, the right to hold office.[21] By sanctioning a national policy, both violated the pluralistic principle of local control over domestic arrangements and at the same time demonstrated the uses of the Negro issue to white nationalism.

To this racism Douglas added the republican's fear of political uniformity installed by a central government. Certainly the strands of his life—his birth in New England, his residence in Illinois and Washington, and his marriages—first to a Southern slaveowner's daughter and then to a Roman Catholic—embodied the diversity he wished to retain in the United States. Even Douglas's version of American history, which he briefly recounted to Illinois schoolchildren, located the cause of the American Revolution in Great Britain's effort to prevent local self-government. According to Douglas, "the preamble to the Stamp Act" served as a symbol of the monolithic policies that transformed a negotiable political dispute into a contest between "uniformity and particularism." Colonial charters, Douglas believed, substantiated his position; these seventeenth- and early eighteenth-century constitutions, he claimed, provided the precedent for states' "managing their own domestic concerns and internal affairs." "No society," he said in various ways throughout his life, "can dictate to another."[22]

Douglas thus found his safeguard to tyranny in self-governing jurisdictions with equal rights to pursue their own ways, protected in and by their diversity. "Uniformity," he once remarked, "is the parent of despotism the world over, not only in politics, but in religion."[23] The

[21]Ibid., pp. 60, 294–95; Johannsen, *Stephen A. Douglas,* p. 817.

[22]Jaffa, *House Divided,* p. 29; *Speech of Senator Douglas at the Democratic Celebration of the Anniversary of American Freedom,* Philadelphia, July 4, 1854, p. 1; Stephen A. Douglas, "The Dividing Line between Federal and Local Authority," *Harpers Monthly* 19 (September 1859): 522–24; *Speeches of S. A. Douglas on the Occasions of his Public Receptions by the Citizens of New Orleans, Philadelphia, and Baltimore* (Washington: Lemuel Towers, 1859), p. 2; *Congressional Globe,* 32d Cong., 1st sess., app., p. 66.

[23]Jaffa, *House Divided,* p. 19; quotation from Douglas, *Speech at Independence Hall, January 4, 1859* (n.d., n.p.), p. 4.

word became a controlling theme of his politics: "It is a fatal heresy," he said in 1858, "to proclaim the doctrine that there ought to be or can be uniformity among the states. Our fathers knew that variety and dissimilarity of local and domestic institutions were an essential element in confederated republics."[24] Douglas elaborated on this point in a speech to Congress in the 1850s:

> Our Government was not formed on the idea that there was to be uniformity of local laws or local institutions. It was founded upon the supposition that there must be diversity and variety in the institutions and laws. Our fathers foresaw that the local institutions which would suit the granite hills of New Hampshire would be ill adapted to the rice plantations of South Carolina. They foresaw that the institutions which would be well adapted to the mountains and valleys of Pennsylvania would not suit the plantation interests of Virginia. They foresaw that the great diversity of climate, of production, of interests, would require a corresponding diversity of local laws and local institutions.[25]

On these grounds he objected to the *Dred Scott* decision, to the Republicans' apocalyptic metaphors of a house divided becoming either slave or free, and to congressional restrictions on local choice in the territories.

Douglas's solution to slavery in the territories was community government, and he provided a Northern counterpart to Calhoun's sectionalism. The uniformity that Calhoun would thwart through a concurrent majority, the Illinois senator would dispel through political fragmentation. To these units Douglas remanded authority, reserving for the general government matters of overlapping jurisdiction but giving local areas power over domestic concerns and habits. Unlike Calhoun, he had neither the time, inclination, nor intellectual depth to refine his views into a systematic theory, and he never answered the question of ultimate provenance except to refer to the sovereign people. A vague pluralism suffused his thought and influenced his public policies.

At times Douglas cited territorial, county, and even municipal government as the taproot of authority, although in practice nonelected officials often presided over these jurisdictions. At times he expressed his party's traditional reverence for state sovereignty. In every case his atttachment to community followed Burke's understanding of political

[24]Angle, *Created Equal,* pp. 18–19; also *Speech of Stephen A. Douglas at the Public Recognition in New Orleans* (Baltimore: Travers, 1860), p. 4.

[25]*Congressional Globe,* 35th Cong., 1st sess., app., p. 200.

systems in "just correspondence and symmetry with the order of the world . . . with the happy effect of following their nature." On those occasions when his localism went lower than the state level, the Illinoisan held that "communities must be perfectly free to form and regulate their domestic institutions in their own way subject only to the constitution." At no time did he extend to these smaller units his republican fears that men might become tyrants, nor did he discuss the possibility of conflict between repressive local government and individual rights. By establishing liberty through the community, he destroyed any dialectic between individual and society. Encouraging popular sovereignty for the territories, Douglas held that the Constitution left the people of the states free to run their domestic affairs, and he agreed with a New York correspondent that if the national government had been meant to regulate slavery, the Constitution would have said so.[26]

Douglas's views on popular sovereignty were often challenged on the grounds of precision, for no one, not even Douglas himself, was certain whether territories could prohibit slavery before their congressional organization (which seemed to give a handful of early settlers too much authority and which after 1857 violated the *Dred Scott* decision) or only after they had begun drafting a constitution prior to admission. This question—so perplexing to mid-century Americans—involved procedure as well as timing. Could the territorial legislature simply pass a statute? Should the matter be referred to referendum—as issues of Negro exclusion and suffrage sometimes were—or, as some argued, should a special convention decide the issue? In 1859 Douglas tried to answer these questions, and his "Dividing Line between Federal and Local Authority," a rebuttal to Attorney General Jeremiah Black's attack on popular sovereignty, remained the most explicit delineation of his views. But after a detailed examination of the somewhat peripheral issue of the powers Congress might exercise but not confer, and, alternatively, those it might confer but not exercise (he had written to George Bancroft for help on precedents), Douglas's principle remained as opaque as ever. Explicit about the revolutionary traditions of local government, the sources of legislative power in the territories (they did not emanate from Congress), and the limitations on Congress, he never

[26]Ibid., p. 194; John Bonadile to Stephen A. Douglas, 8 February 1861, Stephen A. Douglas Papers, University of Chicago Library, Chicago (hereafter cited as Douglas Papers); Quotation from Stephen Douglas, *Kansas, Utah, and the Dred Scott Decision: Remarks of Hon. Stephen A. Douglas Delivered in the State House at Springfield, Illinois* (n.p., n.d.), p. 3; Hoffman and Levack, *Burke's Politics,* p. 295.

sufficiently refined an idea that needed scrupulous formulation. Instead Douglas's article reiterated the themes of his political career: equality must be granted to Westerners, who did not lose "their intelligence and virtue" by migration. "Every distinct political community loyal to Constitution and Union must receive all the rights, privileges, and immunities of self-government in respect to their local concerns and internal polity."[27] Decisions on slavery were no exception. Douglas later explained that too much attention to technical details masked the more important point: the people were the best judge of their domestic institutions.[28]

Leaving questions unanswered seemed a hallmark of the Illinoisan's politics, not because he was morally obtuse or because he was always trying to catch the public's favor by sailing with the wind, but rather because he was a conservative in the Burkean mode who did not accept doctrinaire positions, who believed moral issues improper subjects for legislative consideration, and who insisted that the uniform laws of God's making were differently executed. Unlike lawmakers who were inclined to believe that they could solve problems by their own product, Douglas distrusted legislation. For him, local statutes made and sanctioned by political communities were the only effective rules—hence his commitment to popular sovereignty—and he believed that tyranny began with those who shared neither the circumstances nor the history of those for whom they legislated. When a Democratic friend sent him a coin dating from the American Revolution, Douglas applauded its motto—"Mind Your Own Business." In the same spirit he told cheering Baltimoreans that "it is not my business to inquire whether Maryland's arrangements relative to the position of Negro and white were wise or unwise."[29] As much as any entrepreneurial ambition or partisan tactic, the understanding that habits were more important than laws inspired Douglas's legislation during the 1850s.[30]

Like Burke, whom he often paraphrased, Douglas separated the legal sanction to do something from its necessary exercise. "Statesmen do not always act on the principle that they will do whatever they have a

[27]Douglas, "The Dividing Line," pp. 519–37; Stephen A. Douglas to George Bancroft, 11 April 1859, in Johannsen, *Letters of Douglas,* pp. 442–43.

[28]Stephen A. Douglas to the editors of the San Francisco *Daily National,* 16 August 1859, in Johannsen, *Letters of Douglas,* pp. 453–66.

[29]Philip Tucker to Stephen A. Douglas, 1 August 1860, Douglas Papers; *Speeches of S. A. Douglas on the Occasions,* p. 14.

[30]For a review of an issue belabored by historians for generations, see Roy F. Nichols, "The Kansas–Nebraska Act: A Century of Historiography," *Mississippi Valley Historical Review* 43 (September 1956): 207–54.

right to do. A man has a right to do a great many silly things; a statesman has a right to perpetrate acts of consummate folly, but I do not know that it is a man's duty to do all that he may have a right to do."[31] Douglas made the same point in his stump speeches, and his anecdote about Fridley and the sheriff reaffirmed an important principle of his politics: "If man chooses to make a darnation fool of himself, I suppose there is no law against it."[32]

Douglas derived this idea of "not straining a power" from a public tradition of which Burke was a part. Burke had opposed discriminatory legislation against Irish Catholics on similar grounds; "The question with me is, not whether you have a right to render your people miserable; but whether it is not in your right to make them happy." In his 1775 speech on conciliation, the English Member of Parliament had admitted the completeness of Parliament's legislative authority, but questioned its use: "The question is whether you will choose to abide by profitable experience or a mischievous theory."[33]

Such a political posture fostered inconsistency, and Republicans often reminded Douglas that he had accepted the Missouri Compromise line, only to reject it in the Kansas-Nebraska Act. Douglas made a virtue of his switch, explaining that the congressional intervention embodied in the original Missouri Compromise had then the sanction of time and men of all parties and was embedded in the spirit of the age.[34] Later, when conditions changed, the principle of local sovereignty better served the nation. "I think," explained Douglas, "as circumstances change the action of public men ought to change in a corresponding degree." And here he paraphrased Burke's dictum that "circumstances give in reality to every political principle its distinguishing color and discriminating effect." To a group of Southerners he repeated: "A wise statesman will adopt his laws to the wants, conditions and interests of the people."[35] When Douglas reversed himself to support the extension of the Missouri Compromise in 1861, he explained to Republican sena-

[31]*Congressional Globe,* 36th Cong., 1st sess., p. 2155. See also Madison Cutts, *A Brief Treatise upon Constitutional and Party Questions* (New York: D. Appleton, 1866), p. 16.

[32]Quotation from Angle, *Created Equal,* p. 61; Lionel Crocker, *An Analysis of Lincoln and Douglas as Public Speakers and Debaters* (Springfield O.: Charles Thomas, 1968), p. 126.

[33]*Works of Burke* (Rivington ed.) 9: 351; Stanlis, *Burke and Natural Law,* p. 42.

[34]Jaffa, *House Divided,* p. 123.

[35]*Congressional Globe,* 36th Cong., 2d sess., 1391; quotation from Johannsen, *Stephen A. Douglas,* p. 725; David Barbee and Milledge I. Bonham, "The Montgomery Address of Stephen A. Douglas," *The Journal of Southern History* 5 (November 1939): 542; Hoffman and Levack, *Burke's Politics,* pp. 284–85.

tors whose intransigence he believed had caused the crisis, "The country has no very great interest in my consistency. The preservation of this Union, the interest of the Republic, is of more importance. . . . I would vote as if I had never given a vote or had an opinion."[36] To his opponents this seemed self-serving sophistry or spineless pragmatism. But Douglas's first principle was to insist that no question be removed from its setting, and because he believed that circumstances changed, he thought that specific policies, not basic principles, varied. Douglas thus displayed his party's approach to politics: the casual intermixing of means and ends, the priority given the past (other things being equal), the acceptance of the people's right to decide local policies, and the reliance on the Constitution.

These same political instincts determined Douglas's position on slavery. Although his famous comment—"I don't care whether [the slavery clause] is voted up or down"[37]—is taken out of context, it does not distort his position that abstract propositions should be sidestepped because they lead to uniformity. Douglas did not view slavery as a malevolent institution violating human rights, but as a set of diverse arrangements embedded in the nation's biracial culture. His chosen state of Illinois embodied this diversity: there were pockets of abolitionism in De Kalb and Kendall Counties while in southern Illinois blacks were still sold at auction and placed in apprenticeship arrangements resembling peonage.[38] Thus the *Dred Scott* decision did not shake his argument, for he agreed with Chief Justice Taney that Congress should not control slavery. Lincoln's Freeport question—can the people of a United States territory exclude slavery prior to the formation of a state constitution?—was not, as Harry Jaffa argues, a "sharply drawn spear"; rather, it conveniently gave Douglas another opportunity to reiterate his point that if the people oppose slavery, it is "barren," "worthless," a "useless right." "If they are for it, they will support and encourage it."[39] Thus the senator did care whether slavery was voted up or down—but only in Chicago, where he maintained a residence; in Illinois, where he lived for twenty-six years; and in the District of Columbia, where he spent most of his time after his first election to Congress in 1843. Given his injunction that slavery was "a curse beyond

[36]*Congressional Globe,* 33d Cong., 1st sess., app., pp. 327–28; quotation from ibid., 36th Cong., 2d sess., app., p. 41.

[37]Ibid., 35th Cong., 1st sess., 18.

[38]Harris, *Negro Servitude in Illinois,* pp. 50–67.

[39]Quotation from Angle, *Created Equal,* p. 231; Jaffa, *House Divided,* p. 351.

computation to both white and black"[40] as well as his privately circulated antislavery statements, he presumably would have voted slavery down, if in his view emancipation did not threaten public safety in those communities.

Like many Democrats, Douglas wished to replace moral judgments on good and evil with what he considered effective policy. Southern slavery was no exception; hence he followed Burke's aphorism that government rests not in the "imaginary rights of men but in political convenience and in human nature."[41] "I don't know," Douglas said after the *Dred Scott* decision, "any tribunal on earth or any other institution that can decide the question of the morality of slavery or any institution. I deal with slavery as a political question involving questions of public policy." He returned to the same theme in New Orleans in 1860: "What might be reasonable for one community might not be for another. If you chose to have slaves, it is your business and not ours. If we chose in Illinois to prohibit slavery it is our right."[42] And in Montgomery, Alabama, he said, "If the people of New Mexico want slavery, let them have it. It is their business, not ours." The influence of his own state on his views was obvious. In Quincy, he argued:

> We in Illinois tried slavery when a territory, and found it was not good for us in this climate and with our surroundings, and hence we abolished it. We then adopted a free state constitution as we had a right to do. In this state we have declared that a negro shall not be a citizen and we have also declared that he shall not be a slave. We had a right to adopt that policy. Missouri has just as good a right to adopt the other policy. I am now speaking of rights under the Constitution and not of moral or religious rights. I do not discuss the morals of the people of Missouri, but let them settle that matter for themselves. I hold that the people of the slaveholding states are civilized men as well as ourselves, that they bear consciousness as well as we, and they are accountable to God and their posterity and not to us.[43]

In Douglas's view, Republicans made slaveholders responsible to their own arrogantly imposed benchmarks of higher-law morality; by so doing, a party already indictable for sectional selfishness became

[40]*Congressional Globe,* 33d Cong., 1st sess., 281–82; quotation from Murray McConnell, "Recollections of Douglas," *Transactions of the Illinois State Historical Society,* 1 (1900): 48–49. See also Johannsen, *Stephen A. Douglas,* p. 419.

[41]*Works of Burke,* 6: 257.

[42]Johannsen, *Stephen A. Douglas,* p. 712; *Speeches of S. A. Douglas on the Occasions,* p. 4.

[43]Barbee and Bonham, "The Montgomery Address," p. 547; Angle, *Created Equal,* p. 351.

guilty of separating a human relationship from geography and history and thereby removing it from the people involved, black and white. "They are," he wrote in 1855, "intent on subverting the republic."[44] Just as he believed the Puritans had sought to impose their religious ideas, so now Douglas saw Republican "philanthropists" behaving in similar fashion. Implicit in Douglas's creed was the belief that the people had been given the freedom to make mistakes. "When God created Man, he placed before him good and evil and endowed him with the capacity to decide for himself and held him responsible for the consequences of the choice he might make. This is the divine origin of the great principle of self-government."[45]

Viewed in such terms, Douglas's 1858 debate with Lincoln becomes an American reprise of the disagreements between Paine and Burke about the French Revolution, human rights, and natural law.[46] Like Paine, Lincoln accepted as self-evident the principle that all men were created free and equal. This idea he grudgingly applied to Negroes ("because I do not want a negro for a slave does not mean I do necessarily want her for a wife") and, distinguishing between the rights of man ordained by nature's law and civil privileges granted by society, Lincoln proclaimed black inferiority irrelevant to the issue of natural rights: "It is a question of manhood, not color."[47] Both Lincoln and Paine assimilated human rights into natural law, a common practice in eighteenth- and nineteenth-century thought. In *The Rights of Man* Paine grounded the equality of man in divine authority and argued the classic social-contract position—that man retained certain rights after his contract with society. Those kept became those in which the power to execute was as perfect in the individual as the right itself. Although Lincoln did not always proclaim his racial policies in the name of natural rights—preferring during the war to make the case on the grounds of military expediency—it remained an essential part of his understanding that individuals held rights deposited in "the common stock of society" of which they were a part. Society granted nothing.[48]

[44]Douglas to Parmenas Turnley, 30 November 1855, in Johannsen, *Letters of Douglas*, p. 255.

[45]*Speech of Senator Douglas at the Democratic Celebration in Philadelphia, July 4, 1854*, p. 5.

[46]R. R. Fennessey, *Burke, Paine, and the Rights of Man* (The Hague: Martinus Nijhoff, 1963); Ray P. Browne, *The Burke and Paine Controversy: Texts and Criticism* (New York: Harcourt, Brace and World, 1963).

[47]Angle, *Created Equal*, pp. 39–42, 82–83.

[48]Ibid., p. 41; William Herndon and Jesse Weik, *Life of Lincoln* (New York: Albert and Charles Bon, 1930), pp. 102, 355; Belz, *New Birth of Freedom*, pp. 3, 7; Browne, *Burke and Paine Controversy*, p. 66.

Douglas shared this natural-rights philosophy with Lincoln, as Burke did with Paine. But like Burke, Douglas resisted universal maxims that, untied to any historical circumstance, simply flourished in men's rhetoric. For him, Lincoln's argument that the Declaration of Independence applied to blacks was meaningless, as "specious and sophistical" as, in Burke's view, Paine's argument that natural rights are those which always appertain to man by virtue of his existence had been. Douglas's understanding of equality was based on a different understanding of the sources of natural law. In his prepared remarks at Alton, he said:

> But the abolition party really think that under the Declaration of Independence the negro is equal to the white man, and that negro equality is an inalienable right conferred by the Almighty and hence, that all human laws in violation of it are null and void. With such men it is no use for me to argue. I hold that the signers of the Declaration of Independence had no reference to negroes at all when they declared all men to be created equal. They did not mean the negro nor the savage Indians, nor the Fegee Islanders, nor any barbarous race. They were speaking of white men.[49]

Earlier, Douglas had used his view of natural law to establish not equality, but its reverse. "Now, I do not believe that the Almighty ever intended the negro to be the equal of the white man. If he did, he has been a long time demonstrating the fact."[50] Douglas here made black inferiority a law of nature which, to be sure, might be differently demonstrated in different communities. "The question of slavery is not a question of legislation at all, but of climate, soil, and self-interest. . . . It is a law of humanity, a law of civilization, that whenever a man, or a race of men, show themselves incapable of managing their own affairs, they must consent to be governed by those who are capable of performing the duty."[51] The grounds of Douglas's exception to what he considered the fictive theories of natural rights were historical and empirical. If the rights of black men were part of natural law and sprang from the universal nature of man, he argued, they would appear in history, and men would know them because they had been practiced in human society. But nowhere, he asserted, was this the case. Thus for Douglas as for Burke (but not for Paine and Lincoln), abolitionism

[49]Harry Hayden Clark, ed., *Thomas Paine: Representative Selections* (New York: Hill and Wang, 1961), p. 88; Robert Disham, *Burke and Paine on Revolution and the Rights of Man* (New York: Scribner's, 1971); *Speeches of Douglas on the Occasions,* p. 3; quotation from Angle, *Created Equal,* p. 374.

[50]Angle, *Created Equal,* pp. 374, 112.

[51]*Speeches of Douglas on the Occasions,* pp. 5, 6.

failed not only because it violated human nature but also because it had no historical validity.

Like Burke, Douglas emphasized community rights, and there is more of Burke's organic state than of Locke's social contract in his political thought. For Douglas, rights, privileges, and immunities (he used all three terms interchangeably) proceeded from society where man had his civic existence. Children, blacks, women, and the unpropertied must enjoy only those privileges consistent with community harmony. Not only did this preoccupation with community explain Douglas's interest in organizing territorial governments (he was forever pleading that Western territories needed the protection and aid of organized government); but after the *Dred Scott* decision it allowed him to make slavery into a neighborhood affair. Starting from his bias against uniformity, he readily concluded that individual decisions not congruent with public taste would survive neither local regulations nor a hostile people's will.

The symbol of this communitarianism became the common law—"a rule," he explained to Illinois Governor Joel Matteson in 1854, which "the experience of all men provided to be founded in truth and reason." Later he became more prolix: "The common law is a beautiful system containing the wisdom and experience of ages. Like the people it ruled and protected it was simple and crude in its infancy and became enlarged and improved and polished. It was the common law adopted to our institutions, the habits and customs of the people that formed a basis for the legislature of both territory and state."[52] Here Douglas's conservative naturalism—rooted in Burke and common law, prescription and history—became overwhelmingly functionalist. It presumed that what existed—whether slavery, the Union, or the Constitution—was a prudent arrangement not to be abandoned for some untried theory, however attractive.

But Douglas was too much an American, a Democrat, and a Westerner to foreclose the possibility of change. Like Burke, he separated the innovations imposed on society from reforms established by local progress. He believed, in a paraphrase of Burke, that "as circumstances changed, the actions of public men ought to change in a corresponding degree. A wise statesman will adapt his laws to the wants, conditions, and interests of the people."[53] Perhaps, had he lived through the war,

[52]Quotation from Johannsen, *Letters of Douglas,* p. 272; idem, *Stephen A. Douglas,* p. 601; Douglas, *Kansas, Utah, and Dred Scott.*

[53]*Congressional Globe,* 36th Cong., 1st sess., 915–20; Johannsen, *Stephen A. Douglas,* p. 725.

his understanding of change would have softened his negrophobia, but although he became a hero to Northern Democrats during the war, there is no way of knowing what the Little Giant would have said about emancipation and freedom. His death, which coincided with the rupture of the Union, left to other Northern Democrats the task of formulating the party's position on racial matters.

Douglas represented a prewar version of Northern Democratic views on slavery and race; Delaware's Bayard family expressed those on emancipation and freedom during and after the war. Like most Democrats, James, Jr., and his son Thomas Francis Bayard combined theories of racism, republicanism, and conservatism; but unlike Douglas, who died when emancipation was more an abilitionist's dream than a legislator's reality, the Bayards served in the Congresses that affirmed Lincoln's Emancipation Proclamation and made blacks into soldiers and, to a limited degree, citizens. In the manner of conservatives, the Bayards' ideas responded to changes either sought by Republicans or already accomplished by war. And their rebuttal wove together three specialized understandings of nature: the natural law of race, by which they meant that God had established black inferiority and revealed it to man through its universal practice; the natural rights of man, by which they meant that societal grants of privileges were limited by the requirements of public order; and the physical laws of nature, from which they derived their sense of the fixed patterns of human affairs.

More than time and ideological emphasis separated the Bayards from Douglas, for they were as old, patrician, and firmly rooted in Delaware as the wandering New Englander had been penniless in his adopted Illinois. Bayards had settled in Delaware in the seventeenth century and traced their lineage to French chevaliers and Huguenots, Peter Stuyvesant, and heroes of the American Revolution. Proud of what they called "our traditions," the Bayards established a nineteenth-century political dynasty: the senior James was a Federalist congressman and senator and a peace commissioner at Ghent; his two sons, Richard and James, served in the U.S. Senate, as did his grandson Thomas Francis, who represented the Bayards—and Delaware—as a senator from 1869 to 1885, served as secretary of state and ambassador to the Court of St. James, and in 1880 and 1884 was a Democratic presidential contender. In fact there were few years from 1797—when the elder James entered the House of Representatives—until 1893—when Thomas Francis retired as an ambassador—in which a Bayard was not in the national service. Eventually, in the manner of dynasties, the need to legitimize family behavior claimed one member. During the 1840s Richard retired from public affairs to defend his father, whose decision, as a Federalist, to support Jefferson in the contested election of 1800 had led to charges of bribery—a particularly aggravating stigma for a family so concerned with corruption in others.[54]

The Bayards attributed their political longevity to a congenital sense of service and leadership, properly recognized by their constituents. In fact their tiny state's political culture encouraged it. Other Delaware families—the DuPonts in the twentieth century and the hard-drinking, slaveowning Saulsburys of Sussex County with whom the Bayards feuded—enjoyed similar status. Delaware's size and population, its three counties and forty-five member legislature (nine in the senate, thirty-six in the house) fostered what the political scientist V. O. Key has called a "friends and neighbors political style." Over the years, most nineteenth-century Delawareans had some personal contact with the Bayard family—a favor asked, a patronage appointment secured, a legal matter successfully resolved, or an encounter on Wilmington's streets with a member of this dignified, slightly distant clan. Murat Halstead once described James, Jr., as a "courtly gentleman whose romantic ancestry and name, as well as his long curls and fine features and distinguished air were admirably adopted to concentrate the gaze of the ladies."[55] As favorite sons, Bayards transcended partisan attachments and sometimes earned votes despite, not because of, their affiliation. Only a Bayard could have resigned a Senate seat (as the younger James did over the test oath issue in 1864) and, when his successor died in office, been reelected to succeed himself by the same legislature that elected his son to the state's other Senate seat.[56]

Bayards were never fervent party men; they did not need or want to be. Their status in Delaware fostered an independence that politicians from other states envied. Holding to the Burkean formula, Thomas Bayard believed that "If my party departs from its principles, it is no longer my party but something else. It has gone away from me, not I

[54]Richard Bayard to George L. L. Davis, May 1860, Bayard Papers, Library of Congress (hereafter cited as Bayard Papers); Elizabeth Donnan, ed., "The Papers of James A. Bayard," *American Historical Association Annual Report* (1913): 2, 111–519.

[55]Murat Halstead, *Three against Lincoln: Murat Halstead Reports the Caucuses of 1860* (Baton Rouge: Louisiana State University Press, 1960), p. 116; V. O. Key, *Southern Politics in State and Nation* (New York: A. A. Knopf, 1950), pp. 38–41.

[56]Always a part of the national political culture, family dynasties deserve more systematic study than they have received. For a popular account see Stephen Hess, *America's Political Dynasties* (New York: Doubleday, 1966); Harold Hyman and Morton Borden, "Two Generations of Bayards Debate the Question: Are Congressmen Civil Officers?" *Delaware History* 5 (September 1953):225–36.

from it." Even as a presidential hopeful, the senator from Delaware declared himself "chosen by a party, but not for a party. I may follow it, if I choose. I may join the opposite ranks if I choose, or if I can approve neither, I am still not bound to make any sacrifices of conscience, for I can take my hat and go home."[57] Nor was the family identified with one party, as nineteenth-century Washburnes were with the Republicans and twentieth-century Kennedys with the Democrats. In the case of the Bayards, this was partly because early American parties often exchanged names and positions. Just as their state wavered among the Democrats, Whigs, Republicans, Know-Nothings, Unionists, and People's party (the latter a brief amalgam of the others), so Bayards were variously Federalists, Whigs, and Democrats.

The constant amid such variation was minority status; whether by selection or coincidence, the Bayards were seldom members of the national majority. The elder James served as a Federalist during the Jeffersonian years; James, Jr., and Thomas Francis as Democrats during the long period of Republican hegemony. Earlier, James, Jr., had acquainted his son with the reasons why more of his countrymen did not agree with the family. "Americans do not understand human nature and while more and more of them can read and write, fewer understand human nature, itself the origin of all law. In their ignorance they continue to violate the great principles." This sense of running against the tide marked Bayard politics and sometimes manifested itself in patronizing lectures to colleagues who lacked such reliable supporters. "Minorities may have terrors to some men," proclaimed Thomas Francis, "but I have been in one too long and have found too much comfort in being there myself." From such a perspective, the Bayards saw themselves as sentinels, on guard for the republic.[58]

Certainly the attachment of Delawareans to the Bayards was not based on any populist sense of identification with an elected official, for the Bayards were not "men of the people" in the cigar-smoking, anecdote-swapping style of American partymen. When they smoked cigars, their brands were imported from Cuba, and their tastes ran to madeiras, champagnes, and terrapin. (The Bayard family recipe for the last occasioned a good deal of correspondence, for it required immersing the turtle in madeira sent by private carriage to Washington.) The Bayard library, housed in the substantial family residence on Wilmington's

[57]Edward Spencer, *An Outline of the Public Life and Services of Thomas F. Bayard* (New York: D. Appleton, 1880), p. 57.

[58]*Congressional Globe*, 42d Cong., 2d sess., app., p. 352; ibid., 41st Cong., 3d sess., app., p. 161; James Bayard to Thomas Francis Bayard, 1 August 1862, Bayard Papers.

Clayton Street, included volumes of Burke, Montesquieu, Vattel, and the *London Quarterly* as well as an increasing number of family-authored pamphlets. Hardly typical of their constituents, Bayards were city-dwelling lawyers in a largely rural state. Comfortably fixed (despite periods of financial embarrassment), they held no slaves, although their ancestral home near Bohemia Manor would have been the envy of Southern planters.[59]

Clearly, the ties between Delaware and the Bayards did not rest on mutual identification. Instead they derived their support from the sense of deference that had survived in this conservative border state. Bayards knew themselves to be different from what they called "the masses," and they never hid their distinctiveness. Once when a Senate colleague questioned the younger James on the "common people's" reaction to Bayard's effort to put wine on the free list, the Delawarean announced without hesitation or embarrassment that wine was not a luxury.[60] Like other patrician Democrats, the Bayards maintained a mystical attachment to what they revered, and capitalized, as "the People," by which they meant the source of authority. "The People" did not include everyone, for the Bayards were by no means egalitarian. Like Burke, they would have limited the franchise, and they were always a step behind the political reform of the day—whether the extension of suffrage to white males over twenty-one, the removal of property qualifications for officeholders, or the inclusion of black males as voters. Unlike Douglas, who built his large following on comradely affection with the individuals constituting the abstract "People," the Bayards considered themselves trustees, not delegates, and they expected, according to the younger James, to make their legislative behavior accord with "the common feelings of mankind."[61] It became something of a family tradition to complain about demagogic politicians who knew neither history nor government but were, as the younger James said of Douglas, full of "whiskey ambition." Instead "property must have its influence. This is the natural law of all society." Accordingly, the Bayards favored an independent judiciary over a popularly elected one and civil service over patronage appointments.[62]

[59]Bayard Papers, 1854–1863; Spencer, *Bayard;* Charles C. Tansill, *The Congressional Career of Thomas Francis Bayard, 1869–1885* (Washington, D.C.: Georgetown University Press, 1946). Alert to the ironies of life, James Bayard liked to point out that Benjamin Burton, the largest slaveholder in Delaware, was a Republican during the 1860s; Harold Bell Hancock, "A Divided House," *Delaware History* 7 (September 1957): 361.

[60]*Congressional Globe,* 34th Cong., 2d sess., 249, 296, 355.

[61]Ibid., p. 121.

[62]James Bayard to Thomas F. Bayard, 5 August 1860, 20 March 1862; James A. Bayard

The Bayards, then, accepted leadership (for they did not seek it), and their letters sigh with the sense of duty that forced them to forgo the life of comfortable gentry. To be sure, as self-appointed sentinels they included suffering and tribulation in their definition of leadership, for, remembering Sidney and Hampden, they did not consider their stewardship merely a platform for power and glory. Their understanding of martyrdom in service to liberty encouraged similar actions and led to James's resignation in January 1864 over the Senate's test oath. On that occasion Bayard drew on what he described as "the whole range of English history in all the varied test oaths which political and religious excitement and fanaticism forced upon the people of that country. In past times you will find the great principle of Magna Charta was always adhered to. . . ." And there was a ring of Sidney in his peroration: "If it be disloyal to support the constitution of my country, then I cheerfully accept the imputation of disloyalty, but if made on any other ground, I shall meet it with calm contempt."[63]

The same ideas inspired Thomas Francis's refusal in 1862 to turn over his militia company's arms to federal authorities, although he insisted he would surrender them to the proper local authorities. Unruffled by his son's arrest, James was indignant only that "a dull obscure man who could not threaten the government" had also been arrested by Federal marshals.[64] In the politics of deference, martyrdom was restricted to the well born and intelligent; it was not valid among the rabble.

The self-serving possibilities of such politics are readily indictable from a twentieth-century perspective; some nineteenth-century Delawareans also found them suspect. "Why," inquired one, "if you believe the common people naturally drift into a true and proper course, do you think that the wise only should govern? For you make the People the leaders and the best classes only the administrative machinery."[65] Bayard's response is unknown, although on other occasions he had explained the necessity of restraining the "mere will of a numerical majority" by intelligent leadership and the need to distinguish between the "public sentiment of the People as crystallized in their "representatives' judgment" and "the clamor" of a mob expressed by a delegate who responded to the whims of the moment.[66]

---

to Thomas Francis Bayard, 24 March, 5 August, and 12 December 1860; 17 February 1861; all in the Bayard Papers. Thomas Francis Bayard, *Disinterested Public Service: An Address to Alumnae and Students of the Law School* (Ann Arbor: University of Michigan, 1891).

[63]*Congressional Globe*, 38th Cong., 1st sess., app., pp. 34, 37.

[64]James A. Bayard to Thomas Francis Bayard, 16 and 20 January 1862, Bayard Papers.

[65]W. C. Lodge to James Bayard, 25 April 1864, Bayard Papers.

[66]*Congressional Globe*, 34th Cong., 2d sess., 249; ibid., 36th Cong., 2d sess., 351.

The Bayards were not only politicians (the family preferred the term *statesmen*); they were also lawyers who depended on natural-law theory. Their formal introduction to the ancient notion of a universal human nature and immutable God-given axioms arising from that condition came in college. At Princeton and later at Union College, James, Jr., read and recitated the modern popularizers of natural law—Grotius, Pufendorf, Burlamaqui, and Vattel. These seventeenth- and eighteenth-century writers had applied natural law to international affairs through the concept of the law of nations, and this new understanding modernized a previously church-bound doctrine. As a result, not only did natural law dominate college curriculums, where it appeared as moral philosophy, theology, rhetoric, and natural science, but few personal libraries were without at least one exposition. Moreover, the theory spilled over into life beyond the classroom where early nineteenth-century students debated metaphysical questions such as the relation of *jus gentium* and *jus naturale,* the immanence of God's law, and the relation of natural law and natural rights.[67] These issues were part of the Bayards' political culture. James, Sr., had been at the College of New Jersey when appeals to resist the British in the name of natural law placed colonial opposition on a higher plane than mere fractiousness; James, Jr., debated the importance of natural law in college; and Thomas Francis encountered the doctrine during his legal apprenticeship with his father and William Shippen of Philadelphia.[68]

As lawyers, the Bayards absorbed natural law in its guise as common law, for in statuteless America, attorneys depended on English custom and usage for their precedents. In time, this reliance encouraged Democrats to see the law as reflecting, but not as creating, public behavior.

[67]For a general history of the influence of natural law on American thought see Charles Grove Haines, *The Revival of Natural Law Concepts* (Cambridge, Mass.: Harvard University Press, 1930); Benjamin F. Wright, *American Interpretations of Natural Law: A Study in the History of Political Thought* (Cambridge, Mass.: Harvard University Press, 1931); for extracurricular life, see Thomas Jefferson Wertenbaker, *Princeton, 1746–1896* (Princeton: Princeton University Press, 1946), pp. 93–94, 98, 122, 123, 235, 293–94; Stephen Novak, *The Rights of Youth: American Colleges and Student Revolts* (Cambridge, Mass.: Harvard University Press, 1977), pp. 108–09, 115–23, 157–63. Also Herbert A. Johnson, *Imported Eighteenth-Century Law Treatises in American Libraries* (Knoxville: University of Tennessee Press, 1978).

[68]See Wright, *Interpretations of Natural Law,* pp. 64–70; James Otis, "Rights of the British Colonies," in *Pamphlets of the American Revolution, 1750–1776,* ed. Bernard Bailyn (Cambridge, Mass.: Harvard University Press, Belknap, 1965), p. 454; Otto Gierke, *Natural Law and the Theory of Society* (Cambridge: At the University Press, 1934), pp. xlviii–l; B. F. Wright, "American Interpretations of Natural Law," *American Political Science Review* 20 (August 1926): 524–47; idem, "Natural Law in American Political Theory," *Southwestern Political and Social Science Quarterly* 4 (December 1923); 202–20; Ernest Barker, *Traditions of Civility* (Cambridge: Cambridge University Press, 1948), pp. 263–355.

Nowhere was the notion of common law more explicitly transformed into a manifestation of natural law than in William Blackstone's *Commentaries on the Study of the Law.* From this celebrated document (which Burke acknowledged was more influential in America than in England), attorneys like the Bayards learned that "law was coeval and dictated by God . . . binding over all the globe in all countries and at all times and produced in the common habits of a society."[69] Before the case-study method infiltrated law school curricula at the end of the nineteenth century,[70] apprentice lawyers relied on texts that grounded legal thinking in natural law. Daniel Hoffman's *Legal Outlines,* for example, which was as influential in the Middle Atlantic region as Justice Story's *Commentaries* was in New England, presented natural law as the basis of all jurisprudence because it was "engraven on the hearts and minds by the finger of God." From Henry St. George Tucker's transcription of George Wythe, the Bayards learned of natural law as a "rule prescribed to us by the author of our being and pointed out by our reason which lies at the foundation of all wise and salutary systems of positive law."[71] The implications of such a philosophic system were important, for not only did its adherents deny man the determinative authority over law, but they also challenged Locke's state of nature and its doctrine of intrinsic, natural rights.

To be sure, only Burke's renovation of natural law made the doctrine feasible for nineteenth-century conservatives like the Bayards; for although Americans might distrust manmade statute and discount judicial assertions, their political system celebrated diversity, not the universality of natural law. In racial matters this instinctive pluralism had led some Democrats to revise the Old Testament's tale of man's creation. But because Burke assimilated the universals of God's law—what he called "the immutable law prior to all our devices but which we are connected to in the eternal frame of the universe"—to the specifics of nineteenth-century politics, he became the Bayards' ideological mentor.

[69]Quotation from William Blackstone, *Commentaries on the Study of the Law* (New York: W. Dean, 1844), 1: 2, 27; David Flaherty, ed., *Essays in the History of Early American Law* (Chapel Hill: University of North Carolina Press, 1969), p. 233; Paul Reinsch, "English Common Law in the Early American Colonies," *Bulletin of University of Wisconsin* (October 1899): 397–451; Wright, "Natural Law in American Political Theory," p. 202; John C. H. Wu, "The Natural Law and Our Common Law," *Fordham Law Review* 23 (March 1954): 13–48. For Burke's comment see *Works of Burke,* 3: 55.

[70]William Johnson, *Schooled Lawyers: A Study in the Clash of Professional Cultures* (New York: New York University Press, 1978).

[71]David Hoffman, *Legal Outlines* (Baltimore: Edward Coale, 1829), pp. 11, 12; Henry St. George Tucker, *A Few Lectures on Natural Law* (n.p., 1844), p. 2.

From him these Delaware conservatives appropriated the idea of orderly change accomplished through the prescriptions of time and place, and from him they derived their idea that the racial arrangements of Massachusetts might not be appropriate for Delaware. Such a perspective permitted the Bayards to embrace the completeness and moral inflexibility of natural law at the same time that they acknowledged variations. As Burke had said, "Circumstances give in reality to every political principle its distinguishing color and discriminating effect."[72]

Burke's influence was not a one-dimensional trickling down of ideas from England to faraway Delaware. The Bayards did not need much formal persuasion; they already practiced Burke. Not only did their state serve as an organic society based on custom and habit, but they enjoyed the kind of light and simple government sustained by what Burke described as "nature proceeding in her ordinary course."[73]

By mixing two Burkean concepts of nature—the physical world as an exemplar of universal patterns and natural law as an emanation of God's will—the Bayards transformed nature into the master symbol of their racial doctrines. Not only did James, Jr., and Thomas Francis consider Congress an "unnatural forum" for handling racial matters; they also believed the Civil War's "green soreness" (an expression borrowed from Burke) to be an impossible time for "innovations" (another Burkean term). "The mild voice of reason and wisdom is unheard amid the clash of arms," James cautioned his senatorial colleagues in 1862. Quoting Burke's *Letters to the Sheriffs of Bristol,* Bayard held force to be "an unnatural way to restore the union. Bodies tied together by so unnatural a bond as hatred cannot survive." Abolitionists were "mad." Like "sorcerers playing with nature," they acted "contra naturans." Americans had become animals, "blind beasts," out of step with their normal role as prudent men.[74] And just as twentieth-century Soviets consider political dissidents mentally aberrant, so the Bayards believed that abolitionists demonstrated their derangement by acting against the primary laws of nature. To label such men "mad" was, to the Bayards' way of thinking, no more than description.

From Burke, the Bayards drew their distinction between the En-

[72]Stanlis, *Burke and Natural Law,* p. 71, 231; Hoffman and Levack, *Burke's Politics,* pp. 284–85; Peter Stanlis, "A Preposterous Way of Reasoning," *Studies in Burke and His Time* 15 (Spring 1974): 265–75.

[73]*Works of Burke,* 3: 65.

[74]Ibid., 6: 342; Cong. Globe, 37th Cong., 2d sess., 1477; James Bayard to Thomas Francis Bayard, 22 April and 31 May 1862, 17 August 1863, Bayard Papers; Spencer, *Bayard,* p. 119.

lightenment sense of natural rights and the ancient laws of God's nature. "Sir," explained James Bayard, Jr. in a speech that began and ended with Kansas, but included a definition of the differences between natural rights and the laws of nature: "What is this law of nature? In its modern acceptation the law of nature means nothing more than natural justice and equity—the law of ethics." Distrustful of individual definitions of morality ("the brightest intellects are often perverted and clouded by disease, by the passions, and other causes"), Bayard instead defined the laws of nature as "God's revealed law for the purpose of human law in all Christian communities." To reinforce his point—but make it no more specific—he quoted Blackstone's axiom "that revealed law is of infinitely more authenticity than that moral system which is framed by ethical writers and denominated natural law. Because one is the law expressly declared so to be by God himself; the other is only what by the assistance of human law we *imagine* to be the law."[75]

When James retired from public life in the late 1860s, his ideas survived, barely modified, in his son Thomas Francis. Twenty years after his father's speech on Kansas, Thomas Francis provided Harvard students with a version of natural-law theory differing from his father's only in its separation of common and natural law.

> Having thus stated the impossibility of commanding a course of human action by the instrumentality of written laws, let me now remind you of how infinitely wider is the sphere and more permeating and constant the influence of the unwritten law by which I do not mean Lex non scripta—the common law of custom, acquiescence, and judicial decisions, but the great moral law written as Coke said with the finger of God on the heart of man. Whatever influence written laws obtain they gather from the secret forces of nature which have been considered in their framing and the failure of so many laws passed in disregard of natural laws should instruct us in this great truth.[76]

Throughout the long period of Bayard influence, racial issues varied, but the Bayards' response did not. They continued to base their opposition on three static precepts, which they elevated to axioms derived from God's moral law—the sanctity of private property, the necessity of local authority, and the predetermination of white supremacy. All three were readily observable conditions in mid-century Delaware, but by

[75]*Congressional Globe,* 35th Cong., 1st sess., app., p. 191; ibid., 37th Cong., 471, 1477.
[76]Spencer, *Bayard,* p. 182.

promoting experience to an emanation of God's law, the Bayards transformed unexamined premises into established conclusions.

According to James, Jr., the laws of God long ago created blacks as "more animal than white—indolent but kindly-tempered though when animal passions are aroused they are less within control." According to Thomas, Negroes were "semi-barbarous, thoughtless, easy-going."[77] To interfere with the God-delivered fact of white superiority would upset the harmony of society and transform personal preference into public policy. Holding the superiority of whites and the defectiveness of blacks to be as permanent as the change of seasons, both Bayards cited Lord Kames on racial diversity and used his *Sketches of the History of Man* as evidence that white and black differed as species. James bolstered his types of mankind theory with the popular ethnological argument that "the power of reproduction materially diminishes in hybrids." Thus, efforts at political equality failed because "the two races are so dissonant in their organization that amalgamation is impossible; the options are subjection of the inferior race or its extermination. The Negro must be kept in a state of subjection for his own benefit. Any effort otherwise will end in common destruction of both races."[78]

What appears here as an extraordinary and unnecessary leap—from blacks as free men to blacks as armed liberationists—was more than cheap politics. Had it been the latter, it would have been easier to excise. The Bayards' frequent prophecies of a "servile" war emerged from their conviction that black emancipation and citizenship tinkered with the laws of God—what their fellow Democrat George McHenry condemned as "acts overriding the laws of God and nature which will lead to disorder, confusion, and anarchy."[79] Because Negroes shared with whites (and, for that matter, animals) the God-given impulse of self-preservation, the occasion for conflict in a biracial society existed, as James explained, wherever blacks existed in great concentration and whenever policymakers imposed their private prejudices. Trapped by their understanding of natural law, the Bayards could not acknowledge the contributions of blacks to the Union army, and when in 1866 and 1867 blacks and whites fought in the streets of Memphis and New Orleans, Thomas Francis found his predictions of racial war confirmed.

[77]*Congressional Globe,* 40th Cong., 3d sess., 169; ibid., 36th Cong., 2d sess., 1488.

[78]Ibid., 36th Cong., 2d sess., 1488; ibid., 40th Cong., 3d sess., app., p. 169.

[79]George McHenry, *The African Race in America North and South and the Views of Senator Bayard of Delaware on the Antagonisms of the Caucasian and African Races* (London: 1861), p. 8.

Using the conservative's logic of what James, Jr., called "correcting a priori reasoning" by the "inductive experience of history,"[80] both father and son provided cautionary tales from Jamaica, where racial confusion had, in Bayard mythology, destroyed the stability of society along with the island's sugar production; from Haiti, where interference with nature's law had led to genocide; from Spain, where, centuries before, the African Moors had tried to destroy a "Gothic" nation; and from India, where British disregard for local custom—in this case Indian troops' religious scruples—led to the Sepoy rebellion.[81]

Never did the Bayards hold slavery to be a law of nature. Instead they believed it developed, like all institutions, from local conditions, and thus circumstances, not philanthropy, explained its disappearance in the North. From their perspective, slavery's deep roots in the South gave it a presumptive priority by mid-century. Although in theory the Bayards could have accepted an owner-approved, locally supported, compensated emancipation, in practice even Lincoln's 1862 proposal to reimburse slaveowners in the border states violated their conservatism, because it involved the federal government. In fact no wartime proposals met their standards, for they left the decision to free the slaves with those least likely to do so—the white community, who, according to Thomas Francis, were in touch with the size and temper of the Negro population. The prejudice here favored the status quo; as James, Jr., concluded, "It were better for slaves to remain slaves until the end of time than be broadcast as freemen to disturb the peace of communities."[82]

Along with black inferiority and its corollary, white supremacy, the Bayards elevated local authority to a law of nature. Like many Americans, they believed the voice of the People was a channel through which God revealed the instincts of human nature, and they concluded that societies could apprehend God's will only in local jurisdictions, whether defined as county, municipality, or state. God's primeval contract was with communities, not with nations, and as a result affairs of state that violated nature were immediately apparent in neighborhoods. In this context the voice of the people was not another term for an electoral majority. Instead the Bayards relied on Burke's notion of civil society as an "ancient order into which we are born."[83] For James, the community became the "source of the varying habits, customs, and tones of

[80] *Congressional Globe,* 37th Cong., 2d sess., 1524.
[81] Ibid., 42d Cong., 2d sess., app., p. 354; ibid., 40th Cong., 3d sess., app., p. 165.
[82] Ibid., 37th Cong., 2d sess., 1359.
[83] *Works of Burke,* 13: 165.

thought and the true form of self-rule." For Thomas it was the crystallization of "moral culture."[84] Clearly, the Bayards' surroundings encouraged them to respect tradition and to derive political principle from their personal experience in the unchanging rural atmosphere of Delaware.

For James, Jr., the concrete expression of local government appeared through the common law. Not only did the Delaware senator offer "ancient usages" (by which he meant the procedures and precedents of grand and petty juries, local courts, and county administrations) as a means for decentralizing power and preventing despotism; he also considered the common law a far better expression of the corporate sense of the community than was any political candidate's seasonal pledge to "the will of the people." Less attached than his father to common law—for he inhabited the modern world of contracts and statutes—Thomas Francis used another Burkean precept to render the community a natural emanation of God's law. "Rights," he told the Senate in a paraphrase of Burke, "do not attach to an individual apart from his public existence as a member of an organized community. Local communities are thus authentic expressions of the People's will and should be sovereign in the area of domestic concern."[85] By inverting the Lockean theory of the natural rights of man and locating individual privilege within communities, the Bayards provided the Democrats with a powerful platform from which to oppose Reconstruction. Burke, their mentor, had used the same grounds to oppose eighteenth-century popery laws directed at Ireland, and, just as the English member of Parliament had argued that it was unjust to coerce an entire society, so the Bayards insisted that the Republicans were violating human nature when they passed statutes inimical to the white South. For, according to Thomas Francis, "the influences of the human heart cannot be abrogated by human laws alone."[86]

The Bayards also elevated private property to the status of a natural law; as in the case of localism and white supremacy, a condition of their experience became a God-given norm. With equal enthusiasm James, Jr., and Thomas Francis sanctified private property, which became, for these Delaware conservatives, "the result of the organization of man-

[84]*Congressional Globe,* 33d Cong., 1st sess., 776; ibid., 34th cong., 2d sess., 249.

[85]Ibid., 38th Cong., 2d sess., 1485. For an important study of the legal transformation from common law to more autarchic regulations, see Morton Horwitz, *The Transformation of American Law, 1780–1860* (Cambridge, Mass.: Harvard University Press, 1977) p. 7. *Works of Burke,* 3: 74–75; Stanlis, *Burke and Natural Law,* pp. 53–55.

[86]*Congressional Globe,* 41st Cong., 3d sess., 161.

kind in civilized communities" and "the revealed law for the purpose of human obligation in all Christian communities." Explained Thomas Francis: "The passion for acquisition is indelibly implanted in the heart of man; and if you deprive him of the right of acquisition and transmission to his children you paralyze his energies, and remove the basis of progressive civilization."[87] Applied to slavery, such a doctrine offered additional reason for an emancipation by consent of owners, not by congressional statute.

The inflexibility of the Bayards' racial attitudes is apparent in Thomas Francis's response to Republican policies. Just as his father had opposed emancipation in the District of Columbia in 1862, so Thomas Francis protested, in 1873, the integration of the District schools as unnecessary and unjust because it violated what Burke called the "manners of society." "Who implanted these prejudices?" asked the Delaware senator. "It was the God of nature, and all the human laws that ever were passed or that ever shall be enacted will be futile, indeed." What his father had seen as interference in local affairs by men who did not live in Washington, Thomas Francis also viewed as absentee philanthropism. Twitting the childless Charles Sumner and middle-aged Oliver Morton, he said, "There is not a Senator on this floor who expects his children, his little girls, his little boys, ever to go to these schools and be subjected to this contact. No, sir, no blue-eyed, fair-haired child of any Senator on this floor will ever be permitted to suffer by this proposed contact. They may condemn others who are poorer, but they will be careful to save their own. Is this philanthropy?"[88]

Just as his father had protested Lincoln's wartime suspensions of what the Bayards invariably called the "Great Charter of Mankind," so the Habeas Corpus and Enforcements Acts of the early 1870s evoked Thomas Bayard's denunciations. Republican supporters of this legislation argued that the Ku Klux Klan controlled parts of the South, that blacks were harassed, and that the protection of federal troops and courts must be extended to freedmen. The result was a series of bills, the last of which provided the president with the power, in the case of unlawful combinations against the United States, to suspend the writ of habeas corpus. Bayard was as outraged as his father had been over the Merryman case. As a Democratic member of the Joint Congressional Committee of Investigation, he traveled through the South, and, where Republicans saw violations of Negro rights, he saw only "the

[87]Ibid., 38th Cong., 2d sess., 148; ibid., 37th Cong., 2d sess., 1523–26.
[88]Ibid., 42d Cong., 2d sess., app., p. 355.

general government's" interference with "spontaneous" local arrangements. On this issue his racism combined with his republicanism and Bayard predicted, as had his father during the Civil War, a conspiracy against the nation. Using the whole template of Northern Democratic thought, he made federal judge Hugh Bond, who had conducted the trials of South Carolinians under the Enforcement Acts, into a Lord Jeffrey, and President Grant into Charles II.[89] The Ku Klux Klan survived as "a band of very local character—a protective arm of natural society necessary to offset the influence of blacks whose own pretensions of power were artificially and unnaturally propped up by a standing army." Included in this indictment was the quotation from *Measure for Measure* that his father used so often. The Republicans were the

> . . . proud man
> Drest in a little brief authority
> Most ignorant of what he's most assured,
> His glassy essence like an angry ape
> Plays such fantastic tricks before his heavens
> As make the angels weep.[90]

In Bayard's view, Reconstruction began with a false definition. Allegiance could never be coerced, for, as Burke had said, it was impossible to indict a whole people. Laws like the Civil Rights Acts of 1866 and 1875 violated the experience of nature and therefore would "go forth without authority and return without respect." Seeking instead a "reconciliation" based on mutual understanding, Thomas Francis removed blacks from the process and held the reconstructed governments to be "bald humbugs and wretched shams." To legislate for the freedman not only consecrated favoritism; it also paid the "blacks for defects" implanted by God. From such a perspective, the Fifteenth Amendment was an "especially dangerous claim to power."[91] As an alternative, the Delaware senator offered the parable of the Boston merchant who lent money to a penniless Confederate officer. In Bayard's account the Southerner left for war, carrying all the "civilization" that the inherited wealth and cultivation of generations could provide, only to return after the war to find his relatives dead and his farm destroyed. But aided by

[89]U.S. Congress, *Senate Report,* 42d Cong., 2d sess., Serial No. 1484–98, *Congressional Record,* 43d Cong., 1st sess., 3188–3189; *Congressional Globe,* 42d Cong., 2d sess., app., pp. 452–469.

[90]*Congressional Globe,* 41st Cong., 3d sess., app., p. 161; ibid, 37th Cong., 2d sess., 650.

[91]*Congressional Globe,* 37th Cong., 3d sess., 1495; ibid., 40th Cong., 3d sess., app., p. 165; ibid., 41st Cong., 3d sess., 161, 574; ibid., 2d sess., 535, 1282–83.

the generous Boston merchant, he was able to start again. "Why should not," wondered the Delaware senator, "these two families typify the relations of the northern and southern people?"[92]

Unlike most Northern Democrats, the Bayards did more than talk. For three decades they voted against bills to extend civil rights to blacks, and both father and son were among the most negrophobic senators in the nineteenth century. Although the Bayards were moderates on economic and international matters,[93] their racial extremism was the product of a powerful ideology that wove together three understandings of nature—the black as a naturally inferior human being, the republic as a natural emanation of local communities and private property, and the existence of natural, God-given laws. Such perspectives left little room for change, and as spokesmen of their party's racial beliefs the Bayards bequeathed a pernicious fusion of race and natural law. To be sure, Northerners discriminated against blacks for other reasons: because they were associated with slavery and because they were economic competitors. To this indictment the Democrats (and none more vehemently than the Bayards) added another: blacks were unnatural citizens, by the law of nature and nature's God.

Though rarely articulated as explicitly as by the Bayards, these doctrines permeated the party, and thousands of Northern Democrats who knew nothing of natural law or Edmund Burke absorbed them in the slogan "Keep the Negroes where they are." For decades the party's conservative naturalism—conservative because of its restrictions on racial change, naturalistic because it identified the Negro's status as natural—influenced reactions to public policy. Already committed to a restricted government, Democrats simply extended their earlier libertarianism: a government that should not charter banks and make internal improvements certainly should not interfere with racial arrangements that were, a priori, local matters. Just as the earlier party creed reached beyond the specific agendas of its time to give its adherents a perspective on essential questions such as the meaning of the American Revolution, the resolution of conflict, and the nature of authority, so conservative naturalism was more than a partisan weapon. This doctrine, which seemed a time- and issue-bound response to racial change,

[92]Ibid., 42d Cong., 2d sess., app., 471; Tansill, *Bayard,* p. 66.

[93]Leonard P. Curry, *Blueprint for Modern America: Non-Military Legislation of the First Civil War Congress* (Nashville: Vanderbilt University Press, 1968), pp. 36, 40, 74, 92n.; *Congressional Globe,* 36th Cong., 2d sess., 1015; ibid., 41st Cong., 2d sess., app., p. 138; also Thomas Francis Bayard, *Hard Times and Their Remedy: An Address at McFarlene's Grove* (Wilmington, Del.: James and Webb, 1878); Spencer, *Bayard,* pp. 201–342.

in fact provided Democrats with their antimodern perspectives on larger concerns involving the nature of American society (defined by mid-century as a white man's republic) and the source of its authority (still located in either state or local governments). To be a Northern Democrat included more than reflexive negrophobism, for the doctrine of conservative naturalism shaped attitudes on fundamental concerns of American life. To think like a Democrat was to be trained in national as much as partisan values.

CHAPTER 6

# *The Negro Issue: Popular Culture, Racial Attitudes, and Democratic Policy*

Let me have the making of the songs of a people and I care not who makes their laws.

—Andrew Fletcher

In translating popular opinion into public agendas, leaders like the Bayards and Stephen Douglas articulated party views. More difficult to ascertain are the invisible attitudes of the Democratic fellowship. According to some historians, the magnetism of party politics and the significance of the public crises in the mid-nineteenth century fostered a synchrony between opinionmakers and -holders. What notables like Douglas and the Bayards said about matters of race their supporters accepted, having contributed to it in the first place. But there are problems with such an interpretation. First of all, some partisans may not have been listening, for even within the restricted electorate of mostly white males, one in five did not vote. The presidential election of 1860 seems to have been crucial only in the history books. Measured by actual turnout, it was not exceptional. Letters and diaries reveal the relative importance of politics in the lives of many Northerners. "Piled up manure," wrote a Vermont farmer in 1856; "in P.M. voted for John C. Fremont for president." If this ordering of priorities was widespread, then public attitudes toward race cannot be understood by analyzing the statements of Democratic notables. Most Northerners were not listening.[1]

Second, this view of politics as a consensual phenomenon renders

[1]Robert Lane, *Political Life* (Glencoe, Ill.: Free Press, 1959), pp. 18–20. Between 1840 and 1888 the average quadrennial increase in voter turnouts in presidential elections was 15 percent; between 1856 and 1860, the increase was 16 percent; in 1840 the increase was 54 percent. See Walter Dean Burnham, *Presidential Ballots, 1836–1892* (Baltimore: Johns Hopkins University Press, 1955); Diary of Nathan Parkhill, entry for 4 November 1856, quoted in Lewis O. Saum, "Whig Beliefs and Democratic Ballots" (Paper presented at the American Historical Association meeting, San Francisco, 1978).

irrelevant the attitudes of those who were not party leaders (historically irretrievable, such opinions are conveniently subsumed in expressions of the elite) and thereby neglects popular culture. White Northern Democrats who never gave speeches, framed resolutions, or wrote diaries and letters held attitudes about race expressed in jokes, songs, clichés, tropes, epithets, toasts, cartoons, lithographs, paintings, poems, and fiction. An artistic production free from upper-class correction, popular culture serves as an indicator of public sentiment. This does not mean that there was a unified Northern "taste culture." By the 1840s an antislavery (though never problack) vernacular had developed, reflected in the fiction of Harriet Beecher Stowe, the travel accounts of Frederick Law Olmsted, the children's literature of Peter Parley, and the poetry of Lowell and Longfellow. In this "romantic racialism," as George Frederickson called it, Northerners produced a more sympathetic black, created in God's image and sharing with whites a common humanity.[2]

Yet the belief that blacks were innately inferior, probably of a separate creation, and certainly unfit for freedom, persisted. For every popular expression of the Negro as "God's image carved in ivory,"[3] there was a counterpart. Olmsted's firsthand observations led him to decry the evils of slavery; those of Boston Democrat Nehemiah Adams inspired praise of its virtues and the contentment of blacks in bondage.[4] Abolitionists considered blacks to be men; other Northerners caricatured them as animals. Popular culture, a neglected expression of the historically voiceless, not only defined the nature of the Negro's inferiority but also provided a domain within which Democrats developed specific public policies. By using its language and symbols, party leaders linked popular sentiments to party agenda.

## *Images of Blacks in Minstrelsy and Popular Culture*

The most influential forum for nineteenth-century racial attitudes was minstrelsy. As entertainment it had no rival, and in the manner of

[2]For the concept "taste culture," see Herbert J. Gans, *Popular Culture and High Culture: An Analysis and Evaluation of Taste* (New York: Basic Books, 1974); George Frederickson, *The Black Image in the White Mind* (New York: Harper & Row, 1971), p. 97; John Crandall, "Patriotism and Humanitarian Reform in Children's Literature, 1825–1860," *American Quarterly* 21 (Spring 1969): 3–23.

[3]The expression occurs in Mary Dodge, "Our Contraband," *Harper's Monthly* 27 (August 1863: 403.

[4]Nehemiah Adams, *A South-side View of Slavery; or Three Months at the South in 1854*

public amusements it crossed the historic divide of war and Reconstruction unchanged, remaining an important part of American life well into the twentieth century. Childhood recollections often began with a minstrel show: Mark Twain remembered how in the early 1840s blackfaced theater "burst upon" Hannibal, Missouri, "as a glad and stunning surprise," and Walt Whitman recalled a prewar performance in New York's Old Bowery Theater. Acknowledged as native Americana, minstrel shows were on every international traveler's list and were popular White House fare. After attending a wartime show in Missouri, the English journalist Edward Dicey recalled that homesick Yankees abroad often entertained one another with blackface songs; Mrs. Trollope, ever dismayed by the plebeian ways of the New World, described male audiences in Cincinnati theaters as "without coats . . . shirt sleeves tucked up to the shoulders; the spitting was incessant . . . The noises, too, were perpetual. . . . Every man seemed to think his reputation as a citizen depended on the noise he made."[5]

Inexpensive and available, informal and amusing, minstrel shows were the preferred entertainment of the Northern working class from 1840 to 1880. But it was by no means an urban phenomenon; professional troupes carried the medium far from Broadway to smaller towns and villages, where most nineteenth-century Northerners lived. By taking the show on the road, professionals transformed a big-city entertainment into a national one. So, too, did stagecoach drivers, who dropped off, according to one magazine, a "stove or two at some out of the way tavern" so that local residents could join in singing "blackface." Traveling circuses and showboats also included minstrel routines in their performances.[6] By the 1840s amateur groups offered their version

(1860; reprint, Port Washington, N.Y.: Kennikat Press, 1969); idem, *The Sable Cloud: A Southern Tale, with Northern Comments* (1861; reprint, Westport, Conn.: Negro Universities Press, 1970).

[5]Edward Dicey, *Spectator of America* (Chicago: Quadrangle Books, 1971), p. 168; Mrs. Trollope, *Domestic Manners of the Americans*, 2 vols. (New York: Dodd, Mead, n.d.), 1: 186–87; Robert C. Toll, *Blacking Up: The Minstrel Show in Nineteenth Century America* (New York: Oxford University Press, 1976), p. 30; Bernard de Voto, *Mark Twain's America* (Boston: Little, Brown, 1932), pp. 33–35.

[6]The standard descriptions are Albert McLean, *American Vaudeville as Ritual* (Lexington: University of Kentucky Press, 1965); Frank Davidson, "The Rise, Development, Decline, and Influence of the American Minstrel Show" (Ph.D. dissertation, New York University, 1957); Carl Wittke, *Tambo and Bones; a History of American Minstrel Stage* (Durham, N.C.: Duke University Press, 1930); David Grimsted, *Melodrama Unveiled: American Theater and Culture, 1800–1850* (Chicago: University of Chicago Press, 1968); Hans Nathan, *Dan Emmett and the Rise of Negro Minstrelsy* (Norman: University of Oklahoma Press, 1962); Robert C. Toll, *On with the Show: The First Century of Show Business in America* (New York: Oxford University Press, 1976); idem, *Blacking Up;* Alan

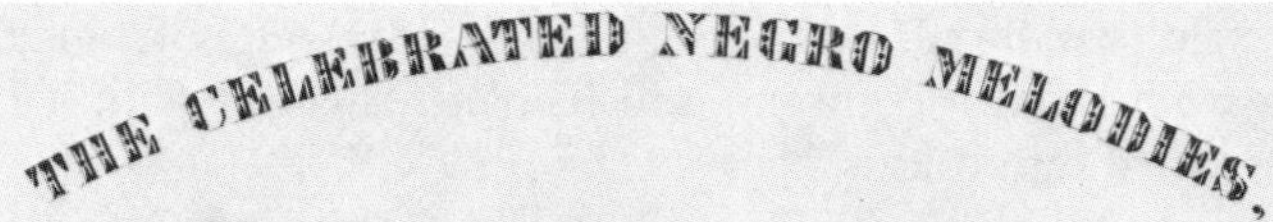

Sheet music cover, 1843. Harvard Theatre Collection.

of "comicalities" to rural audiences, and mass-produced sheet music and colored lithographs helped disseminate the national amusement one paper termed "the genuine syren of our age."[7] Another likened the rapid diffusion of minstrelsy to an "epidemic," but if minstrelsy was a disease, it was endemic. After "taking the national pulse" in 1855, New

Green, "Jim Crow, Zip Coon, and the Northern Origins of Negro Minstrelsy," *Massachusetts Review* 11 (Spring 1970):385–97; Alexander Saxton, "Blackface Minstrelsy and Jacksonian Ideology," *American Quarterly* 27 (March 1975): 3–27; Dailey Paskman, *Gentlemen, Be Seated: A Parade of the American Minstrels* (New York: Charles M. Potter, 1976); Charles Haywood, "Negro Minstrelsy and Shakespearean Burlesque," in *Folklore and Society*, ed. Bruce Jackson (Norwood, Pa.: Norwood Editions, 1974), pp. 77–92; Russell Nye, *The Unembarrassed Muse: The Popular Arts in America* (New York: Dial Press, 1970), pp. 162–67.

[7] *Spirit of the Times* (New York), 21 October 1848; Lester Levy, *Grace Notes in American History: Popular Sheet Music from 1820 to 1900* (Norman: University of Oklahoma Press,

York's staid *Putnam's Monthly* concluded that the songs of minstrels had "flown from mouth to mouth and hamlet to hamlet with a rapidity which seemed miraculous."[8]

Everyone agreed that minstrelsy was the people's entertainment, the common man's culture. According to the *Democratic Review* in 1847:

> Like all things of natural growth [minstrelsy] has taken hold of the public taste almost unperceived. And without any adventions from the press the negro melodists are the only species of national amusement that we can boast of. The lowest orders have in all nations been the source whence the past times or dramas of the people have been derived, and it is in conformity with a universal law that a kind of entertainment which has now become of national importance has sprung up from the very lowest caste of a native population.[9]

Like all popular entertainment, minstrelsy was a synthesis negotiated among audiences, entertainers, and promoters. Present at the creation of minstrelsy, spectators influenced content, a fact that its early organizers acknowledged. When George Christy tried to include Western materials, crowds booed, and, as promoter J. H. Haverly explained, "I've got only one method and that is to find out what the people want and give them that thing. There's no use trying to force the public into a theater."[10] Most students of minstrelsy agree that companies either shaped their shows to suit the needs and desires of audiences or were replaced by those who did. Promoters who tried to alter the format learned that the public would not accept innovations. Like a religious service appreciated for its traditional litanies, performances became mimetic affairs, differing little no matter where, when, or by whom

---

1967); idem, *Picture the Songs: Lithographs from Sheet Music* (Baltimore: Johns Hopkins University Press, 1976); Marian Klamkin, *Old Sheet Music* (New York: Hawthorn Books, 1973).

[8]J. Kennard, Jr., "Who Are Our National Poets?" *Knickerbocker* 26 (October 1845): 331–41; George C. D. O'Dell, *Annals of the New York Stage*, 15 vols. (New York: Columbia University Press, 1927–1949), 4 (1928): 56; *Putnam's Monthly* 5 (January 1855): 73; Gary Nash and Richard Weiss, eds., *The Great Fear: Race in the Mind of America* (New York: Holt, Rinehart and Winston, 1970), p. 172.

[9]"Gossip of the Month," *United States Magazine and Democratic Review* 21 (November 1847): 466; on the same point see Toll, *On with the Show*, p. 7.

[10]Quotation from Toll, *On with the Show*, p. 86. Idem, *Blacking Up*, p. 25. For the interplay of audience and producer, see Herbert Gans, "The Creator-Audience Relationship in the Mass Media: An Analysis of Movie Making," in *Mass Culture: The Popular Arts in America*, ed. Bernard Rosenberg and David Manning White (Glencoe, Ill.: Free Press, 1957), pp. 315–74; O'Dell, *Annals of New York Theater*, 4: 172, 372.

performed, and Americans who never attended a show soon knew minstrelsy from its advance parades, unchanging routines, free concerts, rememberable puns, and hummable tunes.

By the 1840s minstrelsy played throughout the North. Popular enough to support its own houses, the medium straddled classes and entertainment forms. In the nation's largest cities huge, sparsely decorated auditoriums seating several thousand accommodated predominantly white male audiences who were uninhibited by the lavish interiors of the older theaters or the presence of women. Like politics, minstrelsy was all-male territory, with females always barred as performers and usually as spectators. New Yorkers supported five such showplaces, including Henry Wood's Minstrel Palace, a popular emporium on Broadway owned and managed by the younger brother of Democrats Fernando and Benjamin; Brooklyn, three; Indianapolis, two; and Philadelphia, four.[11] In smaller communities amateur troupes performed routines in Masonic halls, lyceums, and musical institutes. During the Civil War the Frederick, Maryland, Mechanics Hall filled, in the best Broadway tradition, even when the Confederate armies threatened the town. In 1864, when New Yorkers could choose among the Christy Minstrels, Charley White's Ethiopian Serenaders, and Frank Dumont's Singers, twenty-five professional companies were on the road, along with uncounted amateur and semiprofessional troupes.[12] Because the gentry often hired companies to perform in their drawing rooms, all classes were exposed to blackface, and, like New Yorker Philip Hone, many a patrician who disliked the camaraderie of a public hall enjoyed afterdinner minstrel shows in a friend's home.[13]

By the 1840s minstrelsy was a formulaic set piece, lasting about an hour and a half and divided into three parts: an introductory series of songs and dances, including an informal walkaround, when performers sat in a semicircle inviting audiences to clap and shout; a longer middle section or olio, consisting of a dialogue between the interlocutor and the end men Bones and Tambo, usually with a short satire on political

[11]Toll, *Blacking Up,* p. 4; O'Dell, *Annals of New York Stage,* 5: 7, 433; Paskman, *Gentlemen, Be Seated,* pp. 129–53. Alexander Saxton has placed minstrelsy's founders in a position of "intimacy with Democratic leaders in New York and San Francisco" and concludes that before 1877 it is difficult to find a professional minstreler who was not a Democrat; "Blackface Minstrelsy," pp. 16, 26.

[12]*Frederick* (Md.) *Examiner,* 15 April 1863; Wittke, *Tambo and Bones,* pp. 58–62; Davidson, "American Minstrel Show," p. 96.

[13]Allan Nevins, ed., *The Diary of Philip Hone, 1828–1851* (New York: Dodd, Mead, 1927), pp. 270, 271, 277; Davidson, "American Minstrel Show," pp. 91, 102–04; Green, "Jim Crow, Zip Coon," pp. 285–97.

affairs; and a concluding section of jokes, songs, and dances.[14] So familiar did this routine become that, according to one performer, audiences knew the material and invariably laughed and shouted in the same places. Essential to minstrelsy (and one of the reasons for its success) was the white entertainer who, after darkening his face with burnt cork, applying camphor-sticking to widen, thicken, and whiten his lips, and fitting himself with a wig of kinky curls, appeared as two stock characters, either Uncle Ned—the contented, docile plantation worker—or Zip Coon—the restless, sexually indulgent, irresponsible free Negro. Each role had its uniform; the ill-fitting tattered rags of Uncle Ned made Zip Coon's satin tails more splendid (and ridiculous), and both costumes invariably included elephantine shoes that suggested and then created, by their enormity, the clumsiness nineteenth-century whites associated with Negroes. Successful minstrels were tireless and versatile, sometimes performing as often as three times a day; they used dialect, played the banjo, tambourine, and fiddle, and danced the jerky, athetoid Jim Crow quickstep—"And eb'ry time I weel about, I jump Jim Crow." In short, they created concrete versions of the abstract notions Northerners held about blacks. White Southerners, who lived in closer contact with blacks, had no need to visualize them in such a manner, but Northerners, who inhabited a largely white world, came to see blacks through minstrelsy's images.

What they saw, of course, was their own imposition. With few exceptions, blacks were not permitted on white stages until after the Civil War, and the popularity of the radio show "Amos 'n' Andy" attests the durability of the blackface convention. Although minstrelsy borrowed African rhythms, dances, and instrumentation, blacks did not contribute specific material; although some of the inspiration was Afro-American, white men wrote both skits and songs.[15] When American groups took their shows overseas, Europeans felt cheated after discovering they were not seeing "real" Negroes. But in minstrel shows whites always impersonated blacks, making it clear through their sheet music, advertisements, and dialogue that they were white, and projecting, by means of this explicit impersonation, the racial hierarchy of the world beyond the stage. Thus, the Christy Minstrels began one of their walkabouts:

[14]Ralph Keeler, "Three Years a Negro Minstrel," *Atlantic Monthly* 24 (July 1869): 80.

[15]Kennard, "Who Are Our National Poets?" pp. 331–41; George Rehin overestimates the black contribution to prewar minstrelsy in his review article, "The Darker Image: American Negro Minstrelsy through the Historian's Lens," *American Studies* 9 (December 1975): 366–67. See Toll, *Blacking Up*, p. 51.

Audience routing a minstrel troupe, White Plains, New York. Harvard Theatre Collection.

> Dose nickers in de South are black,
> Dey live in a house or a hut
> Dem nickers wat is on de stage
> Dey blackface dere face wid smut.[16]

Usually the covers of song collections included the likenesses of white performers in and out of blackface, and a popular conundrum also made the point: "Why am I like a widow?" asked Tambo. "Because," answered Bones, "you're not in black long." For years the only Negroes

[16]Quotation from Cecil Lloyd Patterson, "A Different Drum: The Image of the Negro in Nineteenth-Century Songbooks" (Ph.D. dissertation, University of Pennsylvania, 1961), p. 45; Toll, *Blacking Up,* pp. 38–40; Douglas A. Lorimer, *Colour, Class, and the Victorians: English Attitudes to the Negro in the Mid-Nineteenth Century* (New York: Holmes and Meier, 1978), pp. 86–88; "Nigger Minstrelsy," *Living Age* 11 (February 1862): 398.

associated with minstrelsy were bootblacks assigned to look after costumes and baggage.[17]

As a result, the status inversion that so often accompanies popular entertainment and that clarifies customs and habits by momentarily reversing social roles (the medieval charivari, in which for a day women were in control[18] is an example) never surfaced. Any suggestion concerning white tyranny was avoided. To be sure, there was social commentary on taboo subjects, for minstrel shows were a means by which nineteenth-century Americans came to terms with a strange new world. Often hoodwinked by those who knew their way about the unfamiliar urban terrain, Zip Coon encountered the same difficulties as displaced whites. He was run down by trolleys, shocked by newfangled batteries, and jailed for breaking laws he didn't understand. Minstrelsy also singled out professionals for ridicule. When, in order to save four trips, Brudder Bones simultaneously summoned doctor, lawyer, undertaker, and gravedigger, he lampooned the new experts so offensive to the egalitarian, antiintellectual instincts of some Northerners.[19] But minstrelsy never allowed blacks to reverse roles as it did the working class; in the popular arts, whites remained in control.

Bound together by their color, audiences experienced the collective exaltation of their whiteness (and maleness). The key to minstrelsy rested in the expectations whites held of blacks and the domination this impersonation conveyed. Despite its comic exaggerations, minstrelsy was a double image representing, by means of entertainment, Kenneth Burke's dictum: "And how things are / And how we say things are / Are one." Momentarily suspending what they knew to be the case—that whites defined Negro life on and off the stage—audiences observed a supposedly authentic portrayal of how blacks lived which corroborated how things were in the biracial world beyond the theater.[20]

[17]Keeler, "Three Years a Negro Minstrel, p. 77.

[18]Natalie Zemon Davis, *Society and Culture in Early Modern France* (Stanford: Stanford University Press, 1975), pp. 97, 130–42, 149–51.

[19]Toll, *Blacking Up*, p. 70; Saxton, "Blackface Ministrelsy," p. 3.

[20]Kenneth Burke, *The Philosophy of Literary Form: Studies in Symbolic Action* (Baton Rouge: Louisiana State University Press, 1967), p. 449. Some historians have argued that the so-called Scottish common-sense philosophy made Americans peculiarly receptive to the connection between the presence of objects and their images. Believing that the mind perceives not only images themselves but their external objects, Americans easily fused their empirical world with their mental perceptions. This made the images of minstrelsy even more potent. Alan Green, "The Legacy of Illusion: The Image of the Negro in the Pre–Civil War North, 1787–1857" (Ph.D. dissertation, Claremont Graduate School, 1968); Terence Martin, *The Instructed Vision: Scottish Common Sense Philosophy and the Origins of American Fiction* (Bloomington: Indiana University Press, 1971).

In this way American blacks were linked to a politically primitive but vegetatively lush Africa. (The latter condition was necessary to explain the survival of a race that in white myth worked only under supervision.) Minstrelsy established this African connection in different ways: by the use of non-European instruments such as tambourines, banjos, and bones; by the reiteration of the words *Ethiopian, jungle, congo,* and *hottentot;* and by the use of dialect and lyrics in songs such as "The African Sailors' Hornpipe" and "Nubian Jungle Dance." As unassimilable aliens from another continent, minstrelsy's blacks were further denigrated by their covert associations with demons:

White folk says de debils dead
An buried in a tan vat
De nigger say he raised again
And turned into a ram cat.[21]

This God-given, "natural" link between blacks and Africa provided minstrelsy with another of its pernicious, durable images: Negroes were animalistic—not exactly animals, but close to them in character and mental capacity. In this pre-Darwinian age, racial differences that Southerners understood as God's curse on the sons of Ham,[22] Northerners explained in terms either of a separate creation or of God's assigned positions within the great chain of being. Unconcerned with explanation, minstrelsy simply placed blacks in nonhuman roles: the hair of Negroes was like sheep's wool, their faces and features resembled monkeys, their feet were those of elephants, their eyes like "de coon," their skin tough as animal hide, their arms strong as "the smell of de pole cat," and their hearts bigger than the biggest raccoon. Even their movements as conveyed through the jerky athetoid spasms, body contortions, gaping mouths, and rolling eyes of burnt-cork entertainers

[21]Quoted in Toll, *Blacking Up,* p. 47; also in Charles White, *White's Serenader's Song Book* (New York: 1851), p. 79. Nineteenth-century Americans had little information about Africa, and popular travel accounts invariably emphasized the degraded cannibalistic tendencies of blacks in their native habitat. See, for example, "A Cruise after and among the Cannibals," *Harper's Monthly* 7 (September 1853): 455–74.

[22]For the importance of the religious story of Ham and Japhet as a controlling white racial myth in the South, see Thomas Virgil Peterson, *Ham and Japhet: The Mythic World of Whites in the Antebellum South* (Metuchen, N.J.: Scarecrow Press, 1978). Peterson's argument is dependent on a difference in racial attitudes between Northerners and Southerners, and I agree with his position that Northerners were more likely to accept polygenesis, while religiously purist Southerners kept their literal interpretations of Genesis but used the myth of Ham and Japhet to rationalize slavery.

suggested to white audiences a grotesque, subhuman species unable to control itself.

The offspring of such a race inherited this bestiality, and black children were commonly referred to as "darky cubs," "baby coons," "little monkeys," and "black wools." Whatever the origin of couplets like "My mammy was a wolf, my daddy was a tiger / I'm what you call de ole Virginia nigger,"[23] their effect was not to convey strength and the capacity to survive in the wilderness, as Davy Crockett's half-crocodile origins did; instead, they linked black Americans with the dark continent that white Americans identified as the home of exotic animals, the black no less an example.

Throughout the first half of the nineteenth century, popular songs and cartoons as well as minstrel shows transformed blacks into another of Africa's bipedal beasts. After attending a minstrel show, one Philadelphian concluded that Negroes were "very much like African ourang-outangs," and Frederick Douglass warned Europeans that "American prejudices had begun to creep in with the black minstrels who disfigure and distort the features of the Negro and burlesque his language and manners in a way to make him appear to thousands more akin to apes than men."[24] Indeed, Africa's tailless anthropoid apes with their curiously human appearance (found, as nineteenth-century Americans frequently pointed out, nowhere in the Anglo-Saxon universe) became a model for verbal and visual representations of blacks. The same attitudes that made the riddle "Why should Horace Greeley and Wendell Phillips marry a monkey? Because it is the nearest thing to a nigger"[25] amusing to nineteenth century audiences inspired the wide-nostriled, broad-foreheaded, prognathous, simianlike graphic caricature of blacks. Fearing the impact of such images, Hosea Easton, a Massachusetts Negro, complained that "the cuts and placards descriptive of negroes deformity are everywhere displayed in the North to the observation of the young, with corresponding broken lingo, the very character of which is marked with design."[26]

[23]Toll, *Blacking Up,* p. 41; Saxton, "Blackface Minstrelsy," p. 6; *Christy's Plantation Melodies* (Philadelphia: Fisher, 1854), p. 47.

[24]Edward Corelyou to Dear Sir, April 1857, Corelyou Family Manuscripts, Historical Society of Philadelphia; Lorimer, *Colour, Class, and Attitudes,* p. 63.

[25]Quotation from Toll, *Blacking Up,* p. 114; William Cochrane, "Freedom without Equality: A Study of Northern Opinion and the Negro Issue" (Ph.D. dissertation, University of Minnesota, 1957), p. 76; Patterson, "A Different Drum," p. 45.

[26]Hosea Easton, *A Treatise on the Intellectual Character and Civil and Political Condition of the Colored People of the U.S. and the Prejudice Exercised towards Them* (Boston: Isaac Knapp, 1837), p. 41.

Thus popular culture produced the people's version of the same racial attitudes that led Northern scientists such as Peter Browne, Louis Agassiz, and Samuel Morton to measure skulls, compute facial angles, and even compare the properties of lambswool and Negro hair.[27] Eventually this exaggerated visual bias, which placed blacks closer to animals than to white humans, furnished nineteenth-century Democrats with their most effective trope—Negroes were "wool." Through this form of taxonomic particularizing blacks were identified with the most tractable and useful of barnyard animals.

As a corollary to this subhuman status, minstrelsy attributed to blacks an understanding of beasts that whites could never achieve. Ole Dan Tucker's friendship for his friend Jay Bird exemplified this close relationship, as did Uncle Dan's lament:

As I was playing out on a log,
Out of the pond, dare jumped a frog,
De frog he leaped to hear me sing,
An' began for to cut de pigeon wing.[28]

Less benign sketches suggested that the eating preferences of blacks who supposedly preferred raccoon, squirrel, and possum to more civilized flesh ("Let white folks praise dar finest dishes / Gib us hog and possum so delicious") were dictated by the laws of the jungle, as was the odor of Negroes, which became a continuing source of crude humor in popular culture.[29]

By concentrating on the somatic differences between whites and blacks, minstrelsy imprisoned the latter in their color: they were black as crows, as a Thomas cat, as coal, as a snake, as a black coon, as blackberries, as night—so black in fact that they could not be seen. In one popular song a meeting of one hundred million "darkeys" in the afternoon "blackened up dis planet."[30] When, in a routine used by Harry Wood's Ethiopians, "these sooty Ethiopians" drank black ink to

[27]Green, "Legacy of Illusion," p. 133; John C. Greene, "American Debate on the Negro's Place in Nature, 1780–1815," *Journal of the History of Ideas* 15 (June 1954): 384–96; J. C. Nott and George Gliddon, *Types of Mankind; or, Ethnological Researches* (Philadelphia: Lippincott, Grambo, 1854), pp. 246–71, 298–327, 411–65; Samuel G. Morton, *Catalogue of Skulls of Man and the Inferior Animals* (Philadelphia: Mernhew and Thompson, 1849); Thomas F. Gossett, *Race: The History of an Idea* (Dallas: Southern Methodist University Press, 1963), p. 80.

[28]*Christy's Nigga Songster* (New York: T. W. Strong, n.d.), p. 107.

[29]Patterson, "A Different Drum," p. 326. See also Davidson, "American Minstrel Show," p. 75; Jackson, ed., *Folklore and Society,* pp. 77–93.

[30]*Christy's Plantation Melodies,* p. 15; Green, "Legacy of Illusion," p. 133.

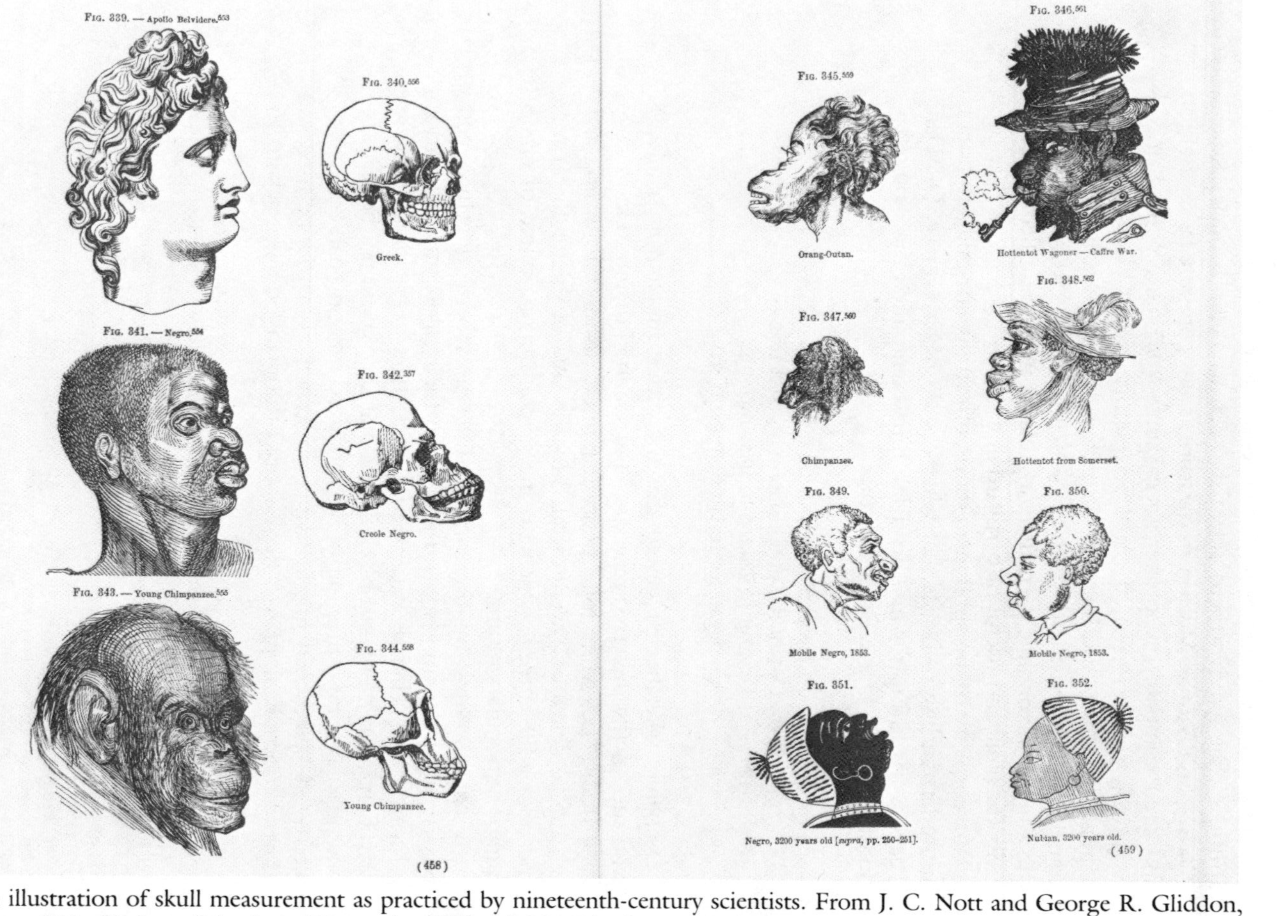


An illustration of skull measurement as practiced by nineteenth-century scientists. From J. C. Nott and George R. Gliddon, *Types of Mankind: or, Ethnological Researches* (Philadelphia: Lippincott, Grambo, 1845).

restore their health, color served the same role as the female womb did for nineteenth-century women: it determined physical well-being. While "spicy yaller gals" appeared in song, fiction, and cartoons (although never on stage in the all-male contrivance of minstrelsy), Negro males came in an unvarying shade of darkest ebony and were thereby incorporated in a single category of race which determined their past, present, and future. Years later, when blacks were finally permitted on the stage, Northern audiences, conditioned to this color bias, were surprised that they came, like whites, in multiple hues.[31] Certainly there was no reason for Northerners to think so; the nineteenth century's arts—graphic, literary, and theatrical—had produced a standard black countenance so different from the newly named Caucasian as to be regarded easily as the visage of a debased species. Nowhere was this better displayed than in the aptly named Democratic journal the *Old Guard,* which in 1868 published a monthly lithograph of each race. The series began with an imposing Caucasian surrounded by the symbols of his political achievements and ended with an indolent Negro resting on the single emblem of his contribution to civilization—a cotton bale.[32]

Physically different from whites, popular culture's blacks spoke not standard English but a childlike gibberish. Full of nouns used as verbs, omitted words, butchered syntax, and transposed articles, this Negro idiom was at times incomprehensible. The effect, in a society that increasingly associated language with nationhood, was to widen the chasm between a responsible white citizenry and a feckless black population unable to pronounce even the words of freedom.[33] In the white man's version of black English, abolition became "bobalition," Union "Onion," and the national anthem "de scar spattered buner." In time, these malicious malapropisms, durative *be*s, and noun derivatives became so fixed in the public mind that white Northerners used their fictive prevalence as further proof of black ignorance. While minstrels perfected this dialect, it was employed in all the popular arts—songs, jokes, poetry, novels, and cartoons. In her best-selling novel about "an ebony idol's" disruption of a New England town, Mrs. G. M. Flanders provided a representative version of the way nineteenth-century North-

[31]Patterson, "A Different Drum," p. 45; Toll, *Blacking Up,* p. 38.

[32]*Old Guard* 6 (January 1868) and (June 1868); p. 62. For the importance of posters, broadsides, and lithographs, see Donald Liedal, "The Puffing of Ida May," *Journal of Popular Culture* 3 (Fall 1969): 292.

[33]Gossett, *Race,* pp. 129–43; J. L. Dillard, *Lexicon of Black English* (New York: Seabury, 1977), pp. x, 8, 45, 62, 103, 109; Deborah Harson and Tom Trabasso, *Black English: A Seminar* (Hillsdale, N.J.: Laurence Erlbaum, 1976).

Racial stereotypes. Lithographs from *Old Guard,* January and June issues, 1868. Collection of the Library of Congress.

erners made Negroes speak: "I'se a poor black debbil, and I'se no consquence to Mass' Stinton no how. I'se nothin but a cuss to all de niggers. I nebber see any 'tickler need of dis child bein' made, enny way—". On the other hand, the white Southerners in Flanders's novel spoke without accent or dialect.[34]

Nowhere was the difference between black and white more apparent than in minstrelsy's stock character, the free Negro Zip Coon, variously known to Northern audiences as Dandy Broadway Swell, Spruce Pink, Jim Dandy, and, in one skit, Caesar Mars Napoleon Sinclair Brown. Self-indulgent, irresponsible, easily misled, and sexually active, Zip Coon was an unleashed licentious id who appeared as thief, lover, and pretentious bombastic but never as worker, citizen, and parent. Zip Coon's theme song was set to an old Irish melody:

> You've heard ob dandy niggers
> But you should see dis coon
> A struttin' down de Broadway
> Some Sunday afternoon.[35]

Lacking any means of support, Zip Coon lived off his girlfriends, and his natural habitat was "the nigga's ball," where, overdressed in pink tails, green vest, and high hat, he unsuccessfully tried to emulate the refinement of whites ("white folks got de manners").[36] As often as not he ended up in jail, strengthening the idea that a black gentleman was a contradiction in terms. Hopelessly self-indulgent, Zip Coon's philanderings held a lesson for white working-class audiences:

> Lubly Rose, Sambo, Mistah Snow and Jeemes
> Danced all night and all day too
> De white trash have nothing to say,
> But to work, work, and de taxes pay.[37]

During the Civil War, Zip Coon danced with whites, and the ballroom setting that had once symbolized the free blacks' immature and imitative nature now conveyed the implicit threat of amalgamation,

[34]Patterson, "A Different Drum," p. 35; Mrs. G. M. Flanders, *The Ebony Idol* (New York: Appleton's, 1860), p. 122.

[35]Quotation from Davidson, "American Minstrel Show," p. 150; see also "The Dandy Broadway Swell," in *Negro Forget-me-Not Songster*, (Philadelphia: Fisher Brothers, n.d.), p. 48.

[36]*Christy's Panorama Songster* (New York: W. Murphy, 1863), p. 85.

[37] *Charley Fox's Sable Songster* (New York: F. A. Brady, 1859), p. 82.

"Zip Coon" in a typical representation. Sheet music cover, Harvard Theatre Collection.

what the English traveler Edward Abdy called "the bugbear of the American mind."[38] The intimacy of Zip Coon with white partners at the "Emancipator Ball" (where Lincoln introduced him to the wives of his cabinet and where he chose Horace Greeley's wife for the Amalgamator's Juba) enacted white fears that any change in the status of blacks would lead in an irreversible regression to a mulatto population.[39]

Off the dance floor, Zip Coon ran from battle; told to "strike" for country and home, deserted; answered his sergeant's command "Eyes right" with "I'se right too"; and insulted abolitionist generals by begging for a dollar. "When the Niggers smell de bullet / Dey yell for Horace Greeley" became a popular statement of the free blacks' cowardice.[40]

Zip Coon had a more congenial Southern relative in popular culture, Uncle Ned—sometimes Uncle Will, Old Uncle Dan, Cato, or Sambo—a contented elderly servant who sang of his happiness under the tutelage of a kind white "massa" and who after the war yearned for the past, not only in Stephen Foster's "Old Folks at Home" but in hundreds of similarly nostalgic songs.

> Under de shade ob de gum tree,
> We happy niggers
> De rooster crow.
> De nigger sing,
> And merrily work.[41]

Just as Zip Coon was limited to strutting on Broadway and dancing at balls, so Uncle Ned was invariably placed in a cotton or watermelon patch or on a levee surrounded by cotton.

Rarely did minstrelsy make a case for or against slavery; more typically blacks were made to proclaim their indifference and at the same time to express yearning for some form of guardianship.

[38]E. S. Abdy, *Journal of a Residence and Tour in the United States of North America from April 1833 to October 1834*, 3 vols. (New York: Negro Universities Press, 1969), 1: 306.

[39]Ibid., 3: 116; *Christy's Panorama Songster*, p. 57; *The Ethiopian Serenaders' Own Book* (New York: Philip D. Coran, n.d.); "De Fancy Ball Colored"; "A Colored Fancy Ball," in Patterson, "A Different Drum," p. 45; David Grimsted, ed., *Notions of the Americans, 1820–1860* (New York: George Braziller, 1970), p. 104.

[40]Toll, *Blacking Up*, pp. 117, 120; Fox's *Sable Songster*.

[41]Patterson, "A Different Drum," p. 153.

Some say de niggers shall be slaves,
Some say dey shall be free.
I'd like to know what difference
Dis trouble makes to me.

Freedom may be well enough, likewise emancipation,
But I guess dat I'se better off daun on de old plantation.[42]

Before the war, shows were full of crude conundrums about the peculiar institution. In a typical exchange the endman asked what a $1,500 candlestick was, and audiences familiar with these riddles shouted back the answer—"A big nigga holding a pine torch."[43] That standard character of prewar fiction—the happy slave of John Pendleton Kennedy's *Swallow Barn* and William Gilmore Simm's *The Foragers*—appeared on Northern stages as a contented worker, suggesting that blacks were better off in the South, "that happy land of Canaan" where they lived under the guidance of whites. Unsupervised, popular culture's blacks deteriorated into clownish, carefree Zip Coons or indolent Sambos, aguefree, in one sketch, because they were too lazy to shake with fever.[44]

Removed from Southern plantations by the mistaken intervention of "cracy preaches and bobalition knaves," Uncle Ned pined for his simple hut and afterhours dancing and strumming—"De sun am set—dis nigger am free."[45] That blacks did not want freedom became a comfortable fiction, conveyed by Uncle Ned's preference: "I'se would rather hob forty stripes from a Southern master than stay among dis-ease Yankees." For, in another skit,

Ole massa to us darkies was good,
Tra la la la
For he fit us our clothes and
Gets us our food
Tra la la la.[46]

[42]*Christy's Panorama Songster; Frank Converse's Old Cremona Songster* (New York: Dick and Fitzgerald, 1864), p. 9.

[43]*Christy's New Songster and Black Joker* (New York: Dick and Fitzgerald, 1863), p. 37.

[44]Alan Henry Simms, "The Image of the Negro in the Pre–Civil War Novels of John Pendleton Kennedy and William Gilmore Simms," *Journal of American Studies* 4 (February 1971): 217–26; Grimsted, *Melodrama Unveiled,* p. 194.

[45]Cochrane, "Freedom without Equality," p. 80.

[46]"Happy Land of Canaan," Sheet Song Collection, Maryland Historical Society, Baltimore; *Christy's Negro Songster* (New York: Richard Marsh, 1855), p. 15.

The "dis-being-free-is worse-den-being-slave" theme reappeared during Reconstruction under a different guise, when minstrelsy portrayed the freedman as unable to care for himself and hence entirely dependent on the Freedmen's Bureau.

> Dont tell me what a blessing,
> 'Tis for Niggers to be here.
> Freedom don't bring bread and bacon,
> Things aren't what they used to be.
> Vittles is the thing
> Without em, liberty ain't worth a cuss.[47]

Stephen Foster, a Pennsylvania-born lifelong Democrat, produced the most durable (and melodic) rendering of Uncle Ned. Not only did his songs imply that blacks must remain where they were geographically and economically; their nostalgia for the past also established the Negro as a symbol of permanence. In a change-tossed world Uncle Ned's yearning was echoed by whites, and his difficulties in the new role of a free man indicated what happened when men tinkered with natural arrangements. In keeping with minstrelsy's traditions, Foster never permitted blacks the right to control their own destiny. Even his emancipated Uncle Neds were to be "carried back to ole Virginny." They could not go by themselves.[48]

Another stock character of the Northern imagination—the black as an ignoble savage—lurked offstage and was only occasionally referred to in song and act. But this character—the modern historian John Blassingame has named him Nat[49]—lived in other forms of popular culture: in proverb, popular saying, and fiction. Like the young everywhere, Northern white children heard about the world before they experienced it, and they heard often of Nat. Many grew up with the parental admonition that misbehavior would bring "the black devil to get them." According to Hosea Easton, most New England parents put their children to bed with the injunction that if they cried "the old nigger would carry them off." The black as evil specter also emerged in popular sayings such as "The old nigger's coming," "I wouldn't do a

[47]Saxton, "Blackface Minstrelsy," p. 18. See also *The Negro Dutch and Irish One Act Sketch Book Especially Adapted to Amateurs* (New York: A. J. Fisher, 1877), pp. 3, 50.

[48]"Stephen Foster and Negro Minstrelsy," *Atlantic Monthly* 20 (November 1867): 608–16; Toll, *Blacking Up,* pp. 36–37. Foster wrote minstrel songs, which he sold to Christy and other promoters.

[49]John Blassingame, *The Slave Community: Plantation Life in the Antebellum South* (New York: Oxford University Press, 1979), pp. 230–35.

"Uncle Ned" in a typical representation. Sheet music cover, Harvard Theatre Collection.

nigger so," "You're uglier than a nigger," "Ya have nigger lips." By the time of the Civil War Northerners spoke a special lexicon that, in Easton's words, "grew up with white schoolboys and strengthened with their strength." Even "the nigger pew" and classroom seat marked not so much a segregated location for blacks as a vile place infected by the spirit of Nat the Brute.[50] Just as minstrelsy provided physical representations of the more benign Zip Coon and Uncle Ned, so cartoons in which blacks appeared as subversives translated a vague presence into a concrete image. Northerners also encountered Nat the Brute in popular novels (Richard Hildreth's *Archie* is one example), in the popular press's "outrage" stories of savage sexual assaults on white women, and in endless graphic images portraying evil, mulish blacks.[51]

Replacing an earlier representation as the trickster of the blue-tail fly, Nat the Brute emerged as a potential insurrectionist during the Civil War.

> Bablyon is fallen
> Massa's donkeys gwine
> Occupy de land.
>
> White man, white man sure as you're born,
> The crows are gwine take your corn.

Warnings of Nat the Brute appeared in:

> When the Negroes shall be free,
> To cut the throats of all they see
> Then this dear land will come to be
> The den of all rascality.
>
> Oh de Sangomingo darkeys
> Had a standard which they bore,
> All dripping in its gore.
> 'Twas a pretty little baby's head

[50] Easton, *Treatise,* p. 41; Grimsted, *Melodrama Unveiled,* p. 194; *The Negro Being: An Inquiry Concerning the Propriety of Distinctions in the House of God, on Account of Color* (Boston: Isaac Knapp, 1837), p. 100. For Nat's eighteenth-century predecessor, see J. Robert Constantine, "The Ignoble Savage: An Eighteenth-Century Literary Stereotype," *Phylon* 27 (Summer 1966): 171–79; Leon F. Litwack, *North of Slavery: The Negro in the Free States, 1790–1860* (Chicago: University of Chicago Press, 1961), pp. 98, 103.

[51] For examples of the outrage story, see *Crisis* (Columbus, O.), 28 May 1862; Cochrane, "Freedom without Equality," pp. 48–50; Jean H. Baker, *The Politics of Continuity: Maryland Political Parties, 1858–1870* (Baltimore: Johns Hopkins University Press, 1965), pp. 127, 128; *Cecil Democrat,* 8 November 1862.

And if we undehstand de President's Proclaim,
He tells de Dixie niggers dey may go and do the same.[52]

Because white Northerners saw racial relationships as a seesaw (when blacks were up, whites were down), a potential enemy in the best of times became a certain one during periods of racial change. As expressed in minstrel shows:

I wish I was a nigger,
I really do indeed,
It seems to me that niggers get
Everything they need.
Congress legislates for them
And white men taxes pay.[53]

Northern audiences enjoyed such songs because they believed that whites and blacks differed as species, not as individuals. Hence racial conflict was as predictable as that in the animal world, and what Northern whites referred to as a servile war awaited those who would tamper with the normal condition of black subservience. The minstrelsy sequence in which Pompey announced that as a free nigger he was "ob more consequence den ten free Scotts" conveyed the widespread white impression that any black's advancement diminished every white's. So, too, did the verses:

A white American was once
Thought equal to a King,
When men the nation founded,
And law did justice bring;
Now, speak against the nigger
In Bastiles you'll repent
For you are not a loyal 'Merican
Of African descent.[54]

A society with a different history might have tried to fulfill prophecies of cooperation; but surrounded by economic, ethnic, and sexual

[52]Broadside, 1864, Broadside Collection, New York Public Library; *Ohio Statesman*, 8 July 1863, 11 August 1864; quotations from *Copperhead Minstrel* (New York: Feek and Banckes, 1863), p. 31; Nash and Weiss, *The Great Fear*, p. 32.

[53]*Ethiopian Serenaders' Own Book*, p. 10.

[54]Verse from "The Negro, the Rising Man," in *Copperhead Minstrel*, p. 54. For other examples, *Ethiopian Serenaders' Own Book; Christy's New Songster and Black Joker*, p. 8.

"Nat the Brute" in a cartoon, *Vanity Fair,* 3 March 1860. Collection of the Library of Congress.

"The Mulatto" in a depiction typical of the Northern Democratic view. Detail from a Currier & Ives print, Stern Broadside Collection, Library of Congress.

superordination and subordination, white Northerners readily believed that Nat the Brute would, in minstrelsy's metonymy for rebellion, "drink Massa's wine and cider." Previously established social, sexual, and economic gradations furnished a ready foundation on which to build a hierarchy of races.

A final character of Northern popular culture, the mulatto, appeared in novels and cartoons but never on stage, where blackfacing depended on monolithic color casting. Invariably, the appearance of the mulatto was the occasion for a didactic message against amalgamation, and the abuse of mixed-blood heroines from the pathetic Frado in Mrs. H. E. Wilson's *Our Nig* to Mary Pike's *Ida May* indicated that there was no room in white America for racial variation. Even the formulaic romance of the abused, near-white female protagonist temporarily rescued by a white lover excluded male quadroons, who instead appeared as effeminate desiccated hybrids, displaying by their sexual impotence the period's scientific axiom that the test of species was fertility. The same point was made in song:

> De white and de black bird sitten in de grass,
> Preachin 'malgamation to de bobolinks dat pass
> To carry out de doctrine dey seem a little loth
> When along cum de pigeon hawk a'leby on dem both.[55]

There was no romance in the inverted utopia described in *Bolokitten,* a savage satire published in 1835. In the city of amalgamation where the directives of abolitionists had been followed and racial mixing was the order of the day, "genteel" white girls had their olfactory nerves removed so they could tolerate their black husbands.[56]

Despite their differences, popular culture's stock black characters shared a common defect: they lacked the self-control of republican citizens. Present-minded and childlike, imitative and irresponsible, these white-imaged blacks required management. Zip Coon's participa-

[55]Mrs. H. E. Wilson, *Our Nig; or, Sketches from the Life of a Free Black in a Two-Story White House, North. Showing That Slavery's Shadows Fall Even There* (Boston: Reid and Avery, 1859); Mary Pike, *Ida May: A Story of Things Actual and Possible* (Boston: Philips, Sampson, 1854); Francis Adams, *Our World; or, the Slaveholder's Daughter* (New York: Miller, Orton, and Mulligan, 1855); Jules Zanger, "The Tragic Quadroon in Pre–Civil War Fiction," *American Quarterly* 18 (Spring 1966): 63–71; quotation from Patterson, "A Different Drum," p. 126; *The Lincoln Catechism* (New York: F. J. Feeks, 1864), p. 29.

[56]For a literary exception that has a male mulatto as its hero, see Richard Hildreth, *Archy Moore, the White Slave; or, Memoirs of a Fugitive* (New York: Orton, and Mulligan, 1856); *Oliver Bolokitten; or, a Sojourn in the City of Amalgamation* (New York: n.p., 1835).

tion in public affairs would be fatal to a self-governing community, and Uncle Ned's ignorance of any matters except fiddling, animals, and nocturnal life made him susceptible to political manipulation. Content in his subordination, Uncle Ned spoke to his race's deficiency:

> We live on excitement, we're bound to hab our fun
> Dars no fun all det pleases 'cept de rising ob de sun
> But politics and humbugs we will throw away
> For to give de white folk a concert.[57]

The comic antics of both Zip Coon and Uncle Ned contrasted with the subversive Nat, whose public imperfection resulted from his ungovernable destructiveness, described by Northern Democrats as the Negro's "uncontrollable will."[58] Even the mulatto diverged from the well-informed, self-directed citizen of democratic theory, and because white Northerners considered schooling the essential precondition for a virtuous citizenry, they deepened the interracial gulf when they withheld it, thereby casting blacks in the roles of the uneducated and uneducable. In the words of Zip Coon:

> Reading, writing and sech doings
> Wasn't meant for folks like us.[59]

In accordance with the racial formulas of minstrelsy, white audiences could identify with the sexual philanderings of Zip Coon or Uncle Ned's love of nature: these were, after all, universal behaviors. But the role of the republican citizen was considered unique, and by holding constant the political defects of blacks across a variety of settings and characters, Northern minstrelsy sharpened the contrast between uncontrollable blacks and self-governing whites. The enduring legacy of this form of demotion was the belief that blacks lacked the republican's virtue and restraint and that they must either copy whites or be ruled by their passions. Both failings made them impossible citizens. When Uncle Ned sang

> Some say de niggers shall be slaves,
> Some say dey shall be free.
> I'd like to know what difference
> Dis trouble makes to me,

[57] *Christy's New Songster and Black Joker,* p. 41.

[58] "Speech of John O'Bryne," 23 January 1868, Broadside Collection, Library of Congress.

[59] "Program for a Play," Christy's Opera House, 2 October 1863, New York Public Library.

he attested a permanent incapacity.[60] In American political thinking, the essential characteristic of a free man was his unremitting struggle for liberty. Thus minstrelsy provided firm ground from which to attack emancipation as well as black citizenship and suffrage. During Reconstruction, when the Freedmen's Bureau Negro emerged as a popular role, minstrelsy produced its final evidence. Blacks could not survive as free men.

Rarely did popular culture's Negroes assume public roles, and those who did were invariably cast as buffoons. A duel between two blacks was not, as it would have been for whites, an affair of honor. Instead, it began over frivolous issues and ended with wounded spectators and forgotten principles.[61] As a stump speaker, Zip Coon usually brought down the house, and so popular were minstrelsy's campaign parodies that they became a high spot of the olios. The interest here was on two levels; on one, first-generation political men enjoyed ridiculing pretentious office-seekers, for the same reasons that they appreciated jokes at the expense of professionals.[62] On another level, minstrelsy offered a somber version of what might happen if blacks were freed and given the vote. Copied by amateur companies, Byron Christy's version of Tobias Elect's stump speech was typical. It began: "Feller citizens—Correspondin' to your unanimous call I shall now hab de pleasure ob ondressin' ebery one of you. . . . When in de course ob human events, it becomes necessary fur de colored portion ob dis pop'lation to look into and enquire into dis inexpressible conflict, . . . it is—it is—it is . . . to return to the subject. . . ." At this point Tobias forgot the Declaration of Independence and what had begun as a grotesque paraphrase deteriorated into an incoherent appeal to "dis glorious Unicorn." Other stump speakers faltered on the names of heroes familiar to every white schoolboy: Patrick Henry became "Henry Patrick" or sometimes just "Heem"; John Hancock was "Boobcock"; committees of arrangement were "committees of derangement."[63] Easily distracted by frivolous temptations, minstrelsy's political Negroes forgot their points in debate, destroyed furniture in convention halls, confused statute and statue in discussions, and lived up to their reputation as plea-

[60]"Sambo's Opinion," in *Christy's Panorama Songster,* p. 34; Patterson, "A Different Drum," p. 126.

[61]*The American Joe Miller; or, Punch for the Millions* (n.p.: T. R. Peterson, 1853), p. 107.

[62]Ronald Formisano, "Political Character, Antipartyism, and the Second Party System," *American Quarterly* 21 (Winter, 1969): 683–709; Davidson, "American Minstrel Show," pp. 110–20.

[63]Quotation from *Christy's New Songster and Black Joker,* pp. 9–11; Nash and Weiss, *The Great Fear,* p. 170; Toll, *Blacking Up,* pp. 67–68; *Christy's Bones and Banjo Melodist* (New York: Dick and Fitzgerald, 1865), p. 14.

sure-seeking incompetents. Sighed one, "If I was de pres. ob des U.S., I'd lick molasses candy and swing on de globe," and the "nigger convention" where incompetents "sulted wid their friends" became standard repertory. Narcotized over the years by such fare, white audiences came to believe that Uncle Ned spoke for all freedmen:

> Oh dars one ting more I'll state,
> Dat is if it ain't too late,
> 'Tis regarding de colored population.
> Oh, let dem all alone in der peaceful quiet homes
> And that the way to save a nation.[64]

Nor did blacks appear as public figures in the graphic arts; their depiction by the few artists who did not use the popeyed, electric-haired caricature was usually that of an indolent, self-indulgent creature. In Richard Woodville's *War News from Mexico,* whites cluster around to learn the news, while blacks are unconcerned. James Goodwyn Clonney's *Sleeping Negro* and *A Negro Asleep in the Cornfield,* David Norslup's *Negro Boys on the Quayside,* and William Sidney Mount's *Farmers Nooning, The Banjo Player, The Bone Player,* and *The Power of Music* portray blacks either asleep or at play, but not in public roles. Evidently, images similar to those in minstrelsy suffused American painting, for it was Uncle Ned who stood in the doorway of Richard Woodville's 1852 Baltimore scene, *The Sailor's Wedding,* who ate watermelon in Alfred Jacob Miller's sketches, and who sold newspapers in Thomas W. Wood's *Moses, the Baltimore News Vendor.*[65]

As myths often do, these racial images helped mediate certain dilemmas in the white mind. The contrast between the restless, unproductive

[64]George Shottle, *Pomp Green's Mistake* (n.p., n.d.); for other examples, "Hughey Daugherty's Oratorical Stump Speaker" in Davidson, "American Minstrel Show," p. 144; Jackson, ed., *Folklore and Society,* p. 80; Paskman, *Gentlemen, Be Seated,* pp. 84, 129; Green, "Legacy of Illusion," p. 125; Bert Richards, *Colored Senators* (n.d., n.p.); *Fox's Ethiopian Comicalities* (New York: Dick and Fitzgerald, 1859), pp. 13, 14, 47; *Christy's New Songster and Black Jokester,* pp. 9–11.

[65]These images of blacks were new and represented the growing racism of the nineteenth century. During the Middle Ages, the Third King at the Adoration was portrayed by Italian and Flemish artists as a dignified eminence, and in several seventeenth-century portraits (among them Jan de Visher's *The Moor*) only color distinguished blacks from whites. See the catalog for the Walters Art Gallery, Winter 1980 show, entitled "The African Image: Representations of Blacks throughout History"; *Walters Art Gallery Bulletin* 32 (March 1980); *The Portrayal of the Negro in American Painting* (Brunswick, Me.: Bowdoin College, 1964); Alfred Frankenstein, *Painter of Rual America: William Sidney Mount* (Washington, D.C.: H. K. Press, 1968); and the superb new three-volume *Image of the Black in Western Art,* ed. Ladislaus Bugler (New York: William Morrow, 1980).

"Old Billy Rice" delivering a stump speech. Harvard Theatre Collection.

Northern Zip Coon and his contented, industrious-by-day Southern cousin Uncle Ned promoted sympathy with the South. The public policies of a region inhabited by Uncle Neds (and his lurking alter ego Nat) would necessarily be different from those of the North, and what some Northerners considered the intransigence of slaveowners became for others a realistic response to the existence of a large politically deficient population. By presenting many more blacks on stage and in song than there were in the Northern population, the popular arts not only conferred status on the Negro as a public issue but also conveyed the impression of a black horde. As a result, the anticipation of a "servile" war—so unlikely given the size and condition of the black population—moved from hysterical fantasy to established fear. On the other hand, and more important, the vision of blacks as contented with their lot in both North and South relieved guilt about their condition and dispelled what other popular sources had created—anxiety about organized interracial conflict. The exceptions reaffirmed the rule: only when blacks took on white roles—by having sexual relations with white women and by trying to practice self-determination—did their happiness disappear into the angry passion of a Nat the Brute and the misery of the mulatto Little Nig. Finally, by considering blacks incapable of self-government, first-generation voters, newly exalted by the award of the ballot, maintained a fictive egalitarianism based on privileges for white males. Just as religion and science depended on a separate creation to explain the nation's terrible inconsistency, so the popular arts provided their own explanation through a complex racial mythology.[66]

If polygenetic theory made for suspect monotheism, its political version made democracy impossible. In holding the public infantilism of blacks constant, Northerners denied what was allowed for in white aliens and male children—the possibility of political maturation—and thereby rejected environment as the source of the black debasement. According to popular culture, the Negro was not the creature of his circumstances, and the wartime slogan "the Negroes where they are" meant more to nineteenth-century Northerners than keeping the blacks in the South. It referred to the Negro's public status, and the phrase advanced the black as an emblem of political continuity. In this way the popular arts, and especially minstrelsy, provided symbolic justifications for keeping the Negro in his place. Clifford Geertz calls such depictions

[66]As with all images, those of blacks held their own contradictions, among them the conflict between the restless hustler Zip Coon and the indolent, ignorant Uncle Ned. Lévi-Strauss calls these "structural polarities" and asserts that they are essential if myths are to mediate contradictions.

"models of reality" that imagically present the relations among nonsymbolic entities by paralleling, imitating, or simulating them.[67] Vernacular expression did not simply mirror public behavior, any more than minstrelsy created racial conditions in the North. Rather, there was an interplay between practice and principle that made antiblack behaviors and attitudes seem obvious and necessary—the only way to think and do.

## *Northern Racial Practice*

The story of the Negro's debasement at the hands of white Northerners has been carefully told, and by now it is clear that further limitations on the blacks' already restricted public activities accompanied the extension of political democracy to white males in the early nineteenth century.[68] Not only did racial prejudice increase as white participation was broadened, but when Northern states placed racial issues on the ballot, the referendum, that celebrated tool of democracy, was turned against blacks. Even local controversies over segregated streetcars were put to referendum,[69] and a term borrowed from minstrelsy—Jim Crow—aptly characterized the white-managed policy of separating the races. One student of statewide referendums in the North for the period 1840–1870 has found that in only two instances out of nineteen did whites accept

[67]Clifford Geertz, *The Interpretation of Cultures: Selected Essays* (New York: Basic Books, 1973), p. 93.

[68]The best of these studies are Litwack, *North of Slavery,* and Nash and Weiss, *The Great Fear;* for the antebellum slave Union states, see Ira Berlin, *Slaves without Masters: The Free Negro in the Antebellum South* (New York: Pantheon, 1974); David Gerber, *Black Ohio and the Color Line, 1860–1915* (Urbana: University of Illinois Press, 1976); Edward Raymond Turner, *The Negro in Pennsylvania: Slavery, Servitude, Freedom, 1639–1861* (Washington, D.C.: American Historical Association, 1911); David Thelen and Leslie H. Fishel, "Reconstruction in the North: *The World* Looks at New York's Negroes, March 16, 1867," *New York History* 49 (October 1968): 405–40; Richard Wade, "The Negro in Cincinnati, 1800–1830," *Journal of Negro History* 39 (January 1954): 43–57; Jay William McKim, "State Exclusion Laws: The Conflict between State Laws Prohibiting the Entrance of Free Negroes and the Privileges and Immunities Clause of the Federal Constitution in the Period 1789–1860" (Ph.D. dissertation, Ohio State University, 1934). Some students of political culture hold that considering behavior to be subsumed in culture merely establishes an inevitable circularity whereby inferences about values proceed from behavior and are then reused to explain behavior. Archie Brown and Jack Gray, eds., *Political Culture and Political Change in Communist States* (New York: Holmes and Meier, 1977); Robert C. Tucker, "Culture, Political Culture, and Communist Society," *Political Science Quarterly* 88 (June 1973): 173–90.

[69]See, for example, a referendum in Philadelphia concerning blacks' riding in separate cars. *Philadelphia Age,* 31 January, 1 and 2 February 1865; *Public Ledger,* 3, 24, 25, 26, and 29 September 1868; William Dusinberre, *Civil War Issues in Philadelphia, 1856–1865* (Philadelphia: University of Pennsylvania Press, 1965), p. 175.

the problack position, and when the votes on Northern referendums are aggregated, eight of ten white males voted to maintain "the white man's government."[70]

There were, of course, regional variations in Northern racial practice; just as Ira Berlin has separated the upper and lower South in their treatment of what he calls "slaves without masters," so it is possible to differentiate among the public privileges of Negroes in New England, the Middle Atlantic, midwestern, and border states. But even in Maine, New Hampshire, Vermont, and Massachusetts, where blacks could vote before the Civil War (New York installed a special property requirement in 1821), the law was an empty letter. Tocqueville found his best example of tyranny by the majority in white efforts to prevent blacks from voting. When the French visitor inquired why Philadelphia's free blacks did not vote when they were entitled to do so, he was told that the people entertained "strong prejudices against the blacks" and that "magistrates were unable to protect them in the exercise of their legal rights." According to one Northerner: "The blacks may have rights and privileges, but it is as much as his life is worth to exercise them. If he entered a jury box, he would be motioned out of it or left alone. If he attempted to vote at an election, he would be hooted or pelted from that pure emblem of uncontrolled liberty, the ballot box."[71]

What was denied by mobs in some places was withheld elsewhere by constitutional provision and judicial lassitude. In Wisconsin a referendum enfranchising the state's two hundred black males passed in 1849, but, challenged in the courts, it was not upheld until 1866.[72] In 1860 only 7 percent of the North's free blacks lived in states that granted

[70]Tom Le Roy McLaughlin, "Popular Reactions to the Idea of Negro Equality in Twelve Non-Slaveholding States, 1846–1869: A Quantitative Analysis" (Ph.D. dissertation, University of Washington, 1969); Phyllis Field, "The Struggle for Black Suffrage in New York State, 1846–1849" (Ph.D. dissertation, Cornell University, 1974). For an analysis of the exception, Iowa's vote in 1865, see Robert Dystra and Harlan Hahn, "Northern Voters and Negro Suffrage: The Case of Iowa," *Public Opinion Quarterly* 37 (Summer, 1968): 202–15.

[71]Berlin, *Slaves without Masters,* pp. 183–216; Charles H. Wesley, "The Participation of Negroes in Anti-Slavery Political Parties," *Journal of Negro History* 29 (January 1944): 36; quotation from Alexis de Tocqueville, *Democracy in America* (New York: Vintage Books, 1960), 1: 271–72. See also George Walker, "Agitation by Blacks for the Suffrage in New York City, 1827–1860," and Edward Price, "Agitation by Blacks of Philadelphia to Regain the Suffrage, 1838–1870" (Papers presented at the American Historical Association meeting in Washington, D.C., December 1980).

[72]Richard Current, "Wisconsin," in *Radical Republicans in the North: State Politics during Reconstruction,* ed. James Mohr (Baltimore: Johns Hopkins University Press, 1976), pp. 147–50.

them the franchise, and of a potential voting population of approximately four thousand, fewer than fifteen hundred actually cast ballots.[73] Nor were there any black officeholders; even during Reconstruction, when blacks were sometimes courted for their votes in the South, they were not considered in the North for officeholding. For the most part, blacks' participation in civic affairs was limited to the celebration of mock "election days," when free Negro communities honored their own notables.[74]

Effectively excluded from politics, Northern blacks were also generally denied attendance in schools, service in the militia, duty as jurors, possession of firearms, and seats in public transportation facilities as well as participation in local lectures or debates. In some places even their right to walk on sidewalks or to wear hats was abridged. Blacks were, according to one observer, "wronged, outraged, scattered, needled, and killed all the day long"—a judgment with which a Northern Negro agreed. According to Hosea Easton, "The mechanical shops, stores, and schoolrooms are all too small for the Negro's entrance as a man."[75] White Northerners encountered blacks as workers, fugitive slaves, competitors for jobs, and even fellow communicants in church, but nowhere as political men.

Instead generations of white Northerners saw blacks in a single public role—as victims of white mobs. So universal were these physical assaults, so habitual a part of community behavior, and so rare the intervention of authorities that Negroes emerged as natural scapegoats, held responsible for whatever was wrong in Northern communities. Given their small numbers and their urban concentration (of the nearly three hundred thousand blacks in the Union States in 1860, 61 percent lived in towns with a population of over twenty-five hundred, 55 percent in cities of over ten thousand), many whites never saw a Negro.[76] But few whites were unaware of the antiblack violence that became public habit. Today we have forgotten the extent of this social fury, because the names of riots obscure their eventual targets, because at-

[73]Litwack, *North of Slavery,* p. 75; U.S. Bureau of Census, 1860, *Negro Population in the United States, 1790–1815,* ed. John Cummings (Washington, D.C., 1918).

[74]Ira Berlin, "Time, Space, and the Evolution of Afro-American Society on British Mainland North America," *American Historical Review* 85 (February 1980): 53–54; Joseph Reidy, "Negro Election Day and Black Community Life in New England 1750–1860," *Marxist Perspectives* 1 (1978): 102–17.

[75]For a careful chronicle of the official and unofficial debasement of Negroes, see the English abolitionist E. S. Abdy, *Journal of a Residence;* Easton, *Treatise,* p. 43.

[76]U.S. Bureau of the Census, *Population of the United States,* cited in Berlin, *Slaves without Masters,* pp. 173–76.

tacks on blacks often occurred at the end, not the beginning, of these affairs, and because the black was so plausible a victim as not to be newsworthy.

As the convicted (though never tried) pollutants of the republic, blacks became available quarry for every community dissatisfaction, no matter what the specific grievance. In Baltimore in 1835 a riot that began against the property of defaulting bank directors turned against blacks; in the same year, whites destroyed the property of the District of Columbia's free Negroes during the Snow Riot. Most of the disturbances that started as demonstrations against whites associated with the antislavery movement—the so-called antiabolitionist riots—ended with destructive assaults on black people and property. Even epidemics of cholera and yellow fever activated antiblack marauders, and, in the manner of the ancient Hebrews, whites living near black neighborhoods sometimes warned off violent crowds by placing candles in their windows.[77] In the best of times, the Northern Negro was not safe. When Philadelphia's blacks gathered in Center Square to hear the annual Fourth of July reading of the Declaration of Independence, whites attacked them for "defiling the government."[78] Such behavior was not limited to Eastern cities. Leonard Richards has located as many rural as urban demonstrations, and after one such occasion outside an Oregon town, a Westerner explained his behavior in terms Easterners understood: "The niggers should never be allowed to mingle with the whites. It will cause a perfect state of pollution. Niggers always retrograde until they get back to that state of barbarity from which they originated."[79]

The most notorious victimization occurred in New York during the draft riot that began in the summer of 1863 with attacks on the offices of conscription officials and ended in a three-day negrophobic orgy. Only a people accustomed to thinking of blacks as the *diaboli ex machina* of public affairs would have held them responsible for the draft; but Democrats had done this from the war's beginning, when they sang to the

[77]David Grimsted, "Rioting in Its Jacksonian Setting," *American Historical Review* 77 (April 1972): 374–77; Leonard Richards, *Gentlemen of Property and Standing Antiabolition Mobs in Jacksonian America* (New York: Oxford University Press, 1970), p. 114; Nash and Weiss, *The Great Fear,* p. 30; Abdy, *Journal of a Residence,* 3: 115; *Baltimore American,* 16–19 August 1835; *Niles' Register,* August, 1835; Arnold Shankman, "Conflict in the Old Keystone State: Anti-War Sentiment in Pennsylvania, 1860–1865" (Ph.D. dissertation, Emory University, 1972), p. 3.

[78]McLaughlin, "Popular Reactions," p. 5.

[79]Quotation from Richards, *Gentlemen and Antiabolition Mobs,* p. 11; McLaughlin, "Popular Reactions," p. 43; Linda Kerber, "Abolitionists and Amalgamators: The New York Race Riots of 1834," *New York History* 48 (January 1867): 28; Abdy, *Journal of a Residence* 3: 319–27.

Whites rioting in a black neighborhood. Woodcut, collection of the Library of Congress.

tune of "Wait for the Wagon," "Fight for the nigger, the sweet-scented nigger." In time, this identification became explicit in party slogans such as "No Draft but War / No War but the Negro"; "This is no time for white folk"; "What is the war for, nigga, nigga"; "God save us from the Nigga"; and "Keep the Nigger where he is."[80] Long accustomed to an antiblack ferocity that had caused riots in the 1830s and 1840s, the city's white mobs in 1863 were simply following accepted practice when they assassinated three thousand Negroes and forced thousands more to flee. Only the extent of their violence was unusual; New York City's black population declined by nearly a third during the 1860s.[81] This misnamed draft riot served as a more extensive version of a familiar activity: the assembling of a white crowd whose enmity was at first concentrated on another target, the redirection of anger toward blacks, and finally assaults on blacks, in this case culminating in the attempted destruction of their physical presence in lower Manhattan.

As a form of public behavior, antiblack rioting simulated attitudes expressed in the popular arts. Considered politically defective, Negroes became convenient villains for community outrage, not by chance but because of their political deficiencies. This belief—that blacks threatened the sacred dream of a virtuous republican society—led whites, no matter what the specific occasion of their social fury, to see themselves as patriots. Mobs called themselves the Sons of Liberty and Minute Men when they destroyed Baltimore's Pigtown, Toledo's Black Quarter, and Cincinnati's Little Africa.

To be sure, rioting was a nonpartisan behavior. But Democrats, as the most vehement public opponents of racial change, were found more often than Republicans in the antiblack mobs that physically and verbally abused Negroes. They were also more likely to organize such affairs and to lead campaigns to exclude blacks from politics.[82] As Lee

[80]*Copperhead Minstrel,* p. 33; Broadside Collection, New York Public Library; James McCague, *The Second Rebellion: The Story of the New York Draft Riots of 1863* (New York: Dial Press, 1968).

[81]*Report of the Merchants' Committee for Relief of the Colored People* (New York: G. A. Whitehorn, 1863); New York *Herald,* July 6, 15 1863; J. T. Headley, *The Great Riots of New York 1712–1873* (New York: E. B. Treat, 1873); Irving Weinstein, *July 1863* (New York: Julian Messner, 1957); McCague, *The Second Rebellion,* p. 178; Albon P. Man, "Labor Competition and the New York Draft Riots," *Journal of Negro History* 36 (October 1951): 375–400; Kerber, "Abolitionists and Amalgamators," p. 28; Leo H. Hirsch, "The Negro and New York," *Journal of Negro History* 16 (October 1931): 450–53. This literature places too much emphasis on interracial economic rivalries as a cause of riots and not enough on historical and cultural factors.

[82]Richards, *Gentlemen and Antiabolition Mobs,* p. 69; Emma Lou Thornborough, *The Negro in Indiana* (Indianapolis: Indiana Historical Bureau, 1937), p. 185.

Benson has shown, New York Democrats in the 1830s were sufficiently identified with antiblack positions to offer a "negative reference point" for anyone sympathetic to blacks, and the most negrophobic whites were Democrats.[83] Just as some nineteenth-century Americans switched to the Republican party because of its antislavery position, so the Democratic party gained adherents because of its negrophobia. William Dusinberre has found the Negro question the dominant issue of the mid-nineteenth-century Democratic party in Philadelphia, and in the Midwest the greatest number of antiblack votes invariably came from heavily Democratic counties.[84] According to humorist Petroleum Nasby, "Ther is an uncompromisin dislike to the nigger in the mind uv a ginooin Dimekrat." Party behavior in Congress confirmed his point, for Northern Democrats in Washington politicized racism through their strict interpretation of the Constitution, adherence to states' rights, and pronounced prosouthernism. According to Glenn Linden, "It is clear that most Democrats were opposed to any measure which would significantly change the status of the Negro," and their opposition remained "clear and constant" during the years 1838–1869.[85]

## *Party Policy and Popular Culture*

These two worlds—the one in which racial intentions were expressed in popular activities from minstrelsy to rioting, the other in which Democratic leaders like the Bayards and Stephen Douglas articulated public policies—were connected. At one level this occurred when party notables used the structure, language, and images of popular entertainment in their campaign literature. For example, Democrats employed minstrelsy's idioms in their songbook the *Copperhead Minstrel,* adapting pidgin English and the stock characters Uncle Ned and Zip Coon to their electioneering. Not only did the national congressional committee underwrite the *Democratic Comicalities,* a political version of minstrelsy

[83]Lee Benson, *The Concept of Jacksonian Democracy: New York as a Test Case* (New York: Atheneum, 1964), pp. 279, 315–20. See also Field, "Struggle for Black Suffrage, 1846–1869"; McKim, "State Exclusion Laws"; Richards, *Gentlemen and Antiabolition Mobs,* p. 103; Litwack, *North of Slavery,* pp. 268–69; McLaughlin, "Popular Reactions," pp. 20, 119.

[84]Eric Foner, *Free Soil, Free Labor, Free Men: The Ideology of the Republican Party before the Civil War* (New York: Oxford University Press, 1970), pp. 115–33; Dusinberre, *Civil War Issues in Philadelphia,* pp. 29, 131; McLaughlin, "Popular Reactions," pp. 78–85.

[85]David R. Locke, *The Struggles (Social, Financial and Political) of Petroleum V. Nasby* (Boston: Lee and Sheppard, 1888), p. 178; Glenn Linden, *Politics or Principle: Congressional Voting on Civil War Amendments and pro-Negro Measures, 1838–1869* (Seattle: University of Washington Press, 1976).

routines based on blackface techniques and adorned with images of Republicans as Jim Crow; state central committees also placed minstrelsy's songs and quicksteps in partisan service.[86] Thus Democrats added a political dimension to the characters Northerners had known for years. Zip Coon became a Freedmen's Bureau "nigger" collecting white tax money; Uncle Ned emerged as the loyal keeper of the plantation, yearning for Massa's return; Jim Crow developed into the irresponsible pawn of the Republicans; and, finally, Lincoln was described as two animals associated with Africa, a baboon and a monkey. Even fiction's stock character—the black mammy—entered partisan affairs when one popular wartime Democratic ballad furnished a lament between a white Southern child and her black nurse:

O Mammy have you heard the news?
Lincoln is going to free you all,
And make you rich and grand,
And you'll be dressed in silk and gold,
Like the proudest in the land.

But this female version of Uncle Ned disdained the Zip Coon ethic and instead played on the physical differences between the races:

Ye sees old mammy's wrinkly face
As black as any coal,
And underneath her handkerchief
Whole heaps of knotty wool.
My darlin's face is red and white
Her skin is soft and fine,
And on her pretty little head
De yeller ringlets shine.
My child whose made 'dis difference
Twixt mammy and twixt you?
De dear Lord.[87]

[86] *Copperhead Minstrel,* passim. There were four editions of this popular anthology, selling for a quarter; all were used by the Democratic political clubs. See also "Black Republican and Officeholders Journal," 1865, Missouri Historical Society, St. Louis.

[87] "A Southern Scene," in Broadside Collection, 1863, Library of Congress. A slightly different version begins: "The Yankee President / Whose ugly picture once we saw / When up to town we went / Well he is going to free you all / And make you rich and grand" and ends: "I tanks mass' Linkum all de same, / But when I wants for free / I'll ask de Lord, oh glory / Not poor buckra men like he."

Political minstrelsy was not always so benign; during Reconstruction especially it drew on sentiments of interracial competition. Far from Washington, Wisconsin Democrats put new words to an Irish melody and sang in their weekly club meetings Fanny Downing's poem "Cuffee in Congress": "I say I'se come here first to sot tonights / To put the black up and fur to put down the whites."[88] Party lessons also conveyed this sense of antagonism, and Democrats used the familiar catechistic form to establish the rectitude of their positions:

Question: What is Congress?
Answer: A body organized for the purpose of taxing people to support Negroes.
Question: What is an army?
Answer: A provost guard to arrest white men and set Negroes free.
Question: Is amalgamation considered the true doctrine of negro equality as taught by Lincoln?
Answer: It is.[89]

The use of these modes of expression was not accidental. When Philadelphia Democrats began a political rally with the walkaround "For it's nigger in de Senate and House / Nigger in de White House, and nigger in de Custom House and nigger on defense," and when, in Dubuque, Iowa, ward clubs outfitted minstrelsy's routines with partisan messages, they fused Democratic politics and popular culture. The cycle was complete when partisan material appeared in minstrel shows. For example, E. P. Christy's 1863 songster included a verse first used in political campaigns:

But now let him be enough emancipate,
Him feel him high him station,
Him get into parliament,
And represent the nigga nation.[90]

[88]"The Negro, the Rising Man," in *Copperhead Minstrel,* p. 54. Also *Ethiopian Serenaders' Own Book,* p. 10; *Songs for the Democrats,* (n.d., n.p.); Minutes of the Madison Wisconsin Democratic Club, Wisconsin Historical Society, Madison; *Old Guard* 6 (February 1868): 135–38.

[89]*The Lincoln Catechism,* passim. "Our Party Catechism," in *The Campaign Plain Dealer* (Scranton, Pa.: 1862).

[90]Grimsted, *Melodrama Unveiled,* p. 60; *Copperhead Minstrel,* pp. 33, 38; "The Spirit of the Age: To the Voters of the United States," and "Here Sambo Will Soon be White," both in Broadside Collection, Library of Congress; *Christy's Panorama Songster,* p. 80.

Democrats also employed the racial lexicon of popular culture, applying minstrelsy's metonymy "wool" to their Republican opponents. Blackface's set piece, the "Miscegenator's Ball," also emerged as a central metaphor with which to embarrass Republicans. "Heb I de pleasure ob dancing dis set / Wid de President ob the Linkum Club Ball?" inquired Zip Coon in one Democratic caricature, and in other depictions the "gallevating Miss Squash" embraced Lincoln, Sumner, and Stevens. Northerners, attuned to believe in the dissonance of racial mixing, grasped the point, which was reinforced through domestic images: Republicans, Democrats often said, were "wedded" to the Negro, "courted" black voters in the South, and "produced" by way of offspring "illegitimate" programs such as Military Reconstruction, the Civil Rights Acts, and the Fourteenth and Fifteenth Amendments. The party's stubborn fondness for this suggestive metaphor appeared as well in floats portraying black males leading white females into the White House.

The miscegenation theme surfaced during the 1864 campaign when two Democratic editors produced a spurious proamalgamation pamphlet that was, as they intended, attributed to Republicans. As satire of a position even abolitionists rejected, *Miscegenation: The History of the Blending of the Races Applying to the American White Man and the Negro* described racial intermixing as the wave of the future and encouraged Irish males and Negro females to produce a hybrid race superior to either white or black. Playing on images from the popular arts, Democrats David Croly and George Wakeman held that the war must be continued so that white men could marry black women, and they struck several partisan chords in their pamphlet. First, they played on the increasingly topical theme that Republicans were the party of war for the Negro; second, they reinforced fears that any change in the naturally subordinate status of blacks would lead to the destruction of whites, in this case through intermarriage.[91]

An important symbol of Democratic racial views, miscegenation emerged in Congress as the logical result of Republican-sponsored legislation. In a speech on confiscation, a New York Democrat insisted

[91] *New York Day Book*, 8 October 1864; "Miscegenation or the Millennium of Abolitionism," Broadside Collection, Library of Congress; *New York World*, 23 September 1864; [David Croly and George Wakeman], *Miscegenation: The History of the Blending of the Races Applying to the American White Man and the Negro* (New York: Dexter and Hamilton, 1864); J. M. Bloch, *Miscegenation, Maleukation, and Mr. Lincoln's Dog* (New York: Schaum, 1958); "Campaign Broadside No. 1: The Miscegenation Record of the Republican Party," Broadside Collection, New York Public Library.

that any tinkering with the racial rank assigned by God ended at "mulattoism," for which, once begun, there was "no remedy." Ohio Democrat Samuel Cox actually cited the pamphlet *Miscegenation* as evidence of what he called the Republican tendency toward perfect equality of black and white:

> All these things, in connection with the African policies of confiscation and emancipation in their various shapes for the past three years, culminating in this grand plunder scheme of a department for freedmen, ought to convince us that that party is moving steadily forward to perfect social equality of black and white, and can only end in the detestable doctrine of Miscegenation!
>
> Gentlemen may deny that this is the tendency of their party. They used to deny that they favored the doctrine of the political equality of black and white which was once charged upon them and which they are so boldly consummating. The truth will appear. After a year or two some member from New England will come here recognizing the great fact that four million blacks are mixing more or less, and ought to mix more, with the whites of the country, and will advocate a bureau of another kind—a department for the hybrid who are cast upon the care of the government by this system of miscegenation.[92]

Such remarks linked party leaders and followers in shared commitment to a white man's government; hence, when Democrats paraded with signs proclaiming that the "Negro's Elevation means your Degradation," their party served as a vehicle for Northern negrophobia.

Nowhere were the connections between the visible racial opinions of Democratic leaders and the attitudes of the historically voiceless more apparent than in the Negro speech, a form of jeremiad used by Northern Democrats from 1850 to 1880.[93] Unlike the party's random pronouncements on public concerns such as the tariff or currency, the Negro speech was grounded in vernacular expression. Images of blacks imprinted through the popular arts appeared in formulaic warnings of servile wars and impending political chaos. Unmistakably, the Democratic case against public policies from emancipation in the 1860s to the Civil Rights Act of 1875 depended on symbols borrowed from minstrelsy. Democrats not only emphasized the physical differences between whites and blacks and employed suggestive tropes such as wool,

[92]Samuel S. Cox, *Eight Years in Congress, 1857–1865* (New York: D. Appleton, 1865), pp. 367–68.

[93]Sarco Bercovitch believes the jeremiad to be a persistent American form; *The Puritan Origins of the American Self* (New Haven: Yale University Press, 1975).

# THE CONSTITUTIONAL AMENDMENT!

**GEARY**
Is for Negro Suffrage.

**STEVENS**
Advocates it.

**FORNEY**
Howls for it.

**McCLURE**
Speaks for it.

**CAMERON**
Wants it.

**The LEAGUE**
Sustains it.

---

They are rich, and want to make

**The Negro the Equal**

OF THE POOR WHITE MAN,

and then rule them both.

Surely, we did not fight for this!

I thought we fought for the Union!

Come on, my brave boys, you saved the Nation.

Dat's so, Brudder Yank, and you need our votes now. De poor White Trash must stand back.

POLLS

Negroes rule us now

We have no chance here.

**The BLACK Roll**

CANDIDATES FOR CONGRESS
WHO VOTED FOR THIS BILL.

THAD. STEVENS
WM. D. KELLEY
CHAS. O'NEILL
LEONARD MYERS
JNO. M. BROOMALL
GEORGE F. MILLER
STEPHEN F. WILSON
ULYSSES MERCUR
GEO. V. LAWRENCE
GLENNI W. SCHOFIELD
J. K. MOORHEAD
THOMAS WILLIAMS

## THE RADICAL PLATFORM--"NEGRO SUFFRAGE THE ONLY ISSUE!"

**Every man who votes for Geary or for a Radical Candidate for Congress, votes as surely for Negro Suffrage and Negro Equality, as if they were printed on his ballot.**

Political broadside, 1868. Stern Broadside Collection, Library of Congress.

Africans, King of Dahomey, and monkey; they also used Zip Coon, Jim Crow, and Uncle Ned as symbols of a politically retarded race. When Philip Johnson, a Pennsylvania congressman, spoke against the Fourteenth Amendment, he connected his party's essential themes of prorepublicanism and antinegroism. "In the ship of state," claimed Johnson, "a certain class of persons must be set apart as operators of the public will. All are messengers on board the ship of state, but all are not officers in command; yet all are protected by the flag at the mast head."[94] In another version of the Negro speech a Maryland Democrat, speaking against the proposed Fifteenth Amendment, used the same antiblack cues. Said Senator George Vickers:

> It is hardly magnanimous in the Senator from Massachusetts [Charles Sumner] to endeavor to fix this law of suffrage upon those who do not desire it, because the fragrant black rose does not grow well in the frosty soil in New England, nor in the northern latitudes. This District [of Columbia] may be called the botanical political experimental garden. During the heated months of June and July last, when it became necessary for me to take the avenue cars to reach the Capitol, there was a considerable intermixture of this beautiful black flower. I was uncharitable enough to wish the Senator from Massachusetts were present also, that he might inhale the delightful odor. Such proximity in public conveyances is alike offensive to the taste, instinct, and judgment, and olfactories of the citizen.[95]

From 1850 to 1880, missile words and slogans familiar to Northerners through popular culture appeared in the party's cartoons and broadsides, where an iconographic Negro—popeyed, electric-haired, and slack-jawed—was contrasted with a serious-eyed, firm-chinned white. For those who did not grasp the partisan implications, the *Indianapolis Daily Sentinel* offered guidance: "Look at this picture. Elect Lincoln and the Black Republican ticket and you will have Negro Equality."[96]

Because blacks provided the central focus of public policy for this

[94]*Congressional Globe,* 39th Cong., 1st sess., app., p. 55.

[95]Ibid., p. 55. For other examples of the Negro speech in and out of Congress, see Paul Horn to George Paul, 21 May 1861, Horn Family Papers, New Hampshire Historical Society, Concord; *Congressional Globe,* 39th Cong., 1st sess., 64; ibid., 40th Cong., 2d sess., app., pp. 68–70, 264, 407; ibid., 41st Cong., 3d sess., 124; ibid., 38th Cong., 2d sess., 221; ibid., 42d Cong., 1st sess., 15, 21, 74. The names Sambo and Pompey were constantly used by Democratic officeholders. See ibid., 42d Cong., 1st sess., 164.

[96]*Indianapolis Daily Sentinel,* 11 October 1860, 3 October–7 November 1864 (quotation from 1 November); Joel Silbey, *A Respectable Minority: The Democratic Party in the Civil War Era, 1860–1868* (New York: W. W. Norton, 1977), pp. 81, 191–92.

generation, the Negro speech was a natural response of the Democratic minority to Republican-sponsored change. More than in any other period, including the 1960s, blacks were, as one Democrat explained, "brought forth by the times," and to see preoccupation with race solely as manipulation imposed by Democratic leaders anxious for office is to overlook the context, language, and symbols of the message.[97] In the public mind, the Negro had been a preeminent issue in the North for some time, and the transfer between popular culture and racial policy was complete when the blacks' changed circumstances emerged as a partisan symbol of public disorder and civic pollution. This explained why, no matter where they began, Democratic set speeches invariably ended with blacks as the reason for higher taxes and tariffs, the impeachment of Andrew Johnson, inflationary greenbacks, and Republican corruption.[98] The Democrats looked at currency and saw the Negro, reviewed impeachment and ended with the Negro, debated the purchase of Alaska and concluded with the Negro. Logically there was no reason to see black suffrage as installing the African to rule the Anglo-Saxon. But Northern Democrats like Pennsylvania's George Woodward did, as did Samuel J. Tilden, the party's presidential candidate in 1872, who declared in 1866 that his party "rejected black suffrage as we would reject the doctrine that an African or a Negro has a right to marry our daughter without our consent." Logically there was no reason to include blacks in a speech on the Southern Pacific Railroad, but in 1870 Benjamin Biggs did just this in his version of the Negro speech.[99]

Chained to his racially derived characteristics of color and political incompetence, the Negro stood for immutability, and as such synthesized the conservative ethos of this generation of Northern Democrats. By using words to restore order in life and by making blacks the theme of these words, Democrats simultaneously established their own equal-

[97]For a quantitative measure of the importance of racial issues in public policy throughout American history and the links between popular choice and legislation, see Benjamin Ginsberg, "Elections and Public Policy," *American Political Science Review* 70 (March 1976): 41–49. Ginsberg's model reveals the extremely large interparty differences during the 1860s and 1870s in the area of what he calls "universalism," that is, issues regarding "equality of rights and privileges for domestic minorities."

[98]The concept of the speech event is developed in Drew Gilpin Faust, "The Rhetoric and Ritual of Agriculture in Antebellum South Carolina," *Journal of Southern History* 45 (November 1979): 541–68; see also Dell Hymes, *Foundations in Sociolinguistics: An Ethnographic Approach* (Philadelphia: University of Pennsylvania Press, 1974).

[99]*Congressional Globe,* 41st Cong., 3d sess., 124, 129; ibid., 1st sess., 27–29; ibid; 40th Cong., 2d sess., app., pp. 208, 264, 375, 294; quotation from Mohr, *Radical Republicans in the North,* p. 73.

ity as whites and confronted questions that reached beyond the freedman's status into essential issues of government, states' rights, and the nature of their republic. "The Negro element in its formal condition, and its natural relationship to us," wrote one Democrat in 1868, "is the cornerstone of our republican edifice and the fundamental basis of American liberty." A popular party toast, usually delivered after the salute to Union and Constitution, made the same point: "To the light of other days when liberty wore a white face and America wasn't a Negro." Thus the Democratic slogan "the Negroes where they are" combined the remembered past of a white republic with a commitment to keeping the North white; through the image of the politically impaired black man, Democrats saw themselves simultaneously as citizens of a unique nation and as members of a political party.[100]

Eventually the Negro emerged as the characterizing agent of this era in Democratic history, as what Kenneth Burke calls the "causal ancestor of the lot." In the same way that the title of a novel does not name only one of its elements (*Gone with the Wind* is an example) but, according to Kenneth Burke, "sums up the vast complexity of elements that compose it giving its character, essence or general drift,"[101] so the Negro became a code for the despised innovations of Civil War and Reconstruction. Earlier Jackson's war against the United States Bank had done the same thing for the Democracy, and later silver would become the dominant element in party politics. In the middle years of the century, issues that might have remained inchoate—problems involving local government, the centralization of government, military reconstruction, the impeachment of a president, the Ku Klux Klan—moved from the abstract to the concrete through the Northern Democrats' understanding of the Negro as an incurably deficient citizen—an impolitic man whose changed condition had already been the occasion for violating the rules of the republic. Such a view was a powerful sentiment because it drew on pictorial images long established in the Democratic mind. Northerners of that persuasion were accustomed to believing the condition of blacks as unchangeable as nature and as unalterable as God's laws. The

[100]*New York Day Book*, 28 November 1863; quotations from *Old Guard* 6 (June 1868); 470; and *Bergen County New Jersey Democratic Meeting, November 28, 1863* (n.p.), Rutgers University Library, New Brunswick, N.J. See also *Congressional Globe*, 39th Cong., 1st sess., app., pp. 78–82; *Cincinnati Daily Commercial*, 16 June 1865.

[101]Kenneth Burke, *A Grammar of Motives* (New York: George Braziller, 1955), p. xvi; idem, ed., *Language as Symbolic Action: Essays on Life, Literature, and Method* (Berkeley: University of California Press, 1966), p. 361. See also J. David Sapir and J. Christopher Crocker, eds.; *The Social Use of Metaphor: Essays in the Anthropology of Rhetoric* (Philadelphia: University of Pennsylvania Press, 1977).

race became a negative symbol of the good old days; as one Northerner put it, "You can no more convert a Negro into a white man than a loaf of rye bread into one of wheat."[102]

Like the Puritan jeremiads it resembled, the Negro speech emerged from the dark side of the American mind, once described by Arthur Schlesinger as a place of "pervasive self-doubt, this urgent sense of the precariousness of the national existence."[103] Here the buoyant world of American progress and mission was replaced by warnings of chaos, and Democrats of this period referred their disruptions—a civil war, forced military service, direct taxation, and a government-controlled currency—to the black. As with all jeremiads, there was an implicit path to redemption—in this case by the restoration of the white man's republic. A Bush County, Indiana, Democratic convention expressed the point: "We hold resolved that this government was made on the white basis by white men for the benefit of white men and their posterity forever and that whenever the white men and the Negro come into contact in this country the normal condition of the latter is servitude and inferiority."[104]

Several modern nations have provided barbaric versions of how to enforce servitude and inferiority, and it is worth noting that Northern Democrats did not put forward strategies of national segregation, apartheid, removal, and genocide. However pernicious popular culture's image of blacks, it also provided benevolent depictions. Yet the Democratic entitlement that matched popular attitudes to party policy was no partisan smokescreen; had it been, it would have been easier to dissipate.

[102]Quoted in Lorman Ratner, "Northern Concern for Social Order as a Cause for Rejecting Anti-Slavery, 1831–1841," *Historian* 28 (November 1965); 8.

[103]Arthur M. Schlesinger, Jr., "America: Experiment or Destiny," *American Historical Review* 82 (June 1977): 510.

[104]McLaughlin, "Popular Reactions," p. 90.

# Part III

# BEHAVING AS DEMOCRATS

## CHAPTER 7

# *The Meaning of Elections*

Some presidential elections catch the special attention of those who live through them and those who later write about them. A few—1852, 1896, and 1928 are examples—are signposts marking new directions in voting behavior; others, like the presidential elections of 1828 and 1856, signify important moments in a party's history. Still others are memorable for their consequences: Lincoln's election in 1860 led to the South's secession, and Nixon's 1972 campaign initiated the series of events known as Watergate. In every case analysis depends on two types of information: descriptive accounts of platforms, candidates, campaigns, and votes—what constitutes, according to Theodore White, "the making of a president"; and quantitative data based, for the most part, on aggregate election returns and survey data—what Paul Lazarsfeld considered as reflective of "the people's choice." The element common to both is the vote, and the central symbol of American democracy has always been the casting of it in presidential elections.[1]

By such standards the contests of 1864 and 1868 have little status. In technical terms, they are maintaining elections in which issues, appeals, campaign techniques, and, most important, partisan choices stay the same; in Angus Campbell's alliterative summation, "the pattern of partisan attachment in the preceding period persists."[2] National statistics

[1]Angus Campbell et al., *Elections and the Political Order* (New York: John Wiley, 1966); Walter Dean Burnham, *Critical Elections and the Mainsprings of American Politics* (New York: W. W. Norton, 1970); V. O. Key, "A Theory of Critical Elections," *Journal of Politics* 17 (February 1955): 1–18; James Ford Rhodes, *History of the United States from the Compromise of 1850* vol. 6 (New York: Macmillan, 1906), 6: 179, 194–97.

[2]Angus Campbell, "A Classification of Presidential Elections," in Jerome Clubb and Howard Allen, eds., *Electoral Change and Stability in American Political History* (New York: Free Press, 1971) p. 106. Richard Niemi and Herbert F. Weisberg, *Controversies in American Voting Behavior* (San Francisco: W. H. Freeman, 1976).

always mask local shifts, but both the percentages of the Northern Democratic vote—43 percent in 1856, 45 percent in 1860, 45 percent in 1864, and 47 percent in 1868—and the correlations that emerge at the county level suggest that these elections belong in the paradigm established by the realignment of the 1850s.[3] Accordingly, they become illustrative footnotes rather than explanatory material.

It is clear that contemporaries were not particularly excited by either contest, and despite procedures for voting in the field, turnout (the traditional gauge of interest) declined in 1864. Such apathy might be explained by the war, but four years later, as measured by the percentage of eligible voters, the lowest turnout in forty years sent Ulysses Grant to the White House. Nor have historians paid these elections much attention; there seem to be more crucial matters to investigate during these years. Even the traditional presidential synthesis that organizes American history into four-year blocks falters, for Lincoln's death occurred too soon after his reelection to permit any measure of his platforms against his performance, and Grant earned neglect by proving to be an uninteresting military leader-turned-partisan.

Another way of studying presidential elections is to evaluate voting as a symbolic demonstration of the way Americans led their public lives. From this perspective election campaigns become community rituals embodying national values, what Victor Turner calls "a storage unit" into which, over the years, Americans placed information about their political norms, beliefs, sentiments, and roles.[4] As ritual, election campaigns summarize political customs, traditions, and designs, and within this ritual, voting, the master symbol, encompasses a series of public meanings. Elections take place the way they do because of these meanings, and, properly understood, presidential contests display American political culture. Hence all hold equal significance. Such an approach to political history explores the latent function, not the purposive goals of selecting a president and vice-president. To ask, then, how Ameri-

[3]William L. Shade, *Social Change and the Electoral Process* (Gainesville: University of Florida Press, 1973), p. 47. In Shade's complex typology, 1864 is a "restabilizing" election within the larger category of "maintaining." Shade uses the term to refer to presidential elections occurring after a strong third-party challenge in which the electorate "restabilizes" into the traditional two-party system. See also Gerald Pomper, *Elections in America: Control and Influence in Democratic Politics* (New York: Dodd, Mead, 1968), p. 104; idem, "Classification of Presidential Elections," *Journal of Politics* 29 (August, 1967): 535–66. For turnouts, see Robert F. Lane, *Political Life: Why People Get Involved in Politics* (Glencoe, Ill.: Free Press, 1959), p. 21.

[4]Victor Turner, *The Drums of Affliction: A Study of Religious Processes among the Ndembu of Zambia* (Oxford: Clarendon Press, 1968), p. 1.

cans voted in 1864 and 1868 is not so much to inquire into who voted for whom and why, as it is to seek information about the procedures and ceremonies of casting a ballot.

This approach banishes the persistent conundrums that have attached to political history. The issue is not what choices presidential elections offered voters—whether, for example, candidates responded to public opinion and echoed each other, or instead manipulated voters, thereby rendering elections delusive expressions of democracy.[5] Concern shifts to other matters: Where and how did Americans vote? What preparations did they undergo before doing so? What metaphorical language and political iconography did they use? From this perspective, today's controversy over the relative importance of religion, culture, and economics in voter choice gives way to evaluations of what voting meant in a collective sense, and the election results so crucial to aggregate analysis become less important than the preparation for and delivery of the vote. Conventions, mass meetings, and ratification assemblies emerge as better clues than regression analysis. Just as it has never been essential to know how many Balinese participated in cockfights (although who went may be crucial) or to know how many Yankee City residents participated in Memorial Day parades, so rolloffs, turnouts, and turndowns hold less meaning than the messages contained in ritual deportment and the relation between political imagery and its objects. At issue is what public ceremonies reveal about American values.[6]

Of course, presidential campaigns fulfill instrumental extrinsic purposes quite different from communion services, Balinese cockfights, Memorial Day parades, and Trobriand rites of passage. Presidents are chosen; majorities do produce a government. (An exception is the political parade, which has only a loose link with electing candidates.) To the extent that voting provides an observable result, anthropologists designate it rational-technical, purposive behavior and distinguish it from activities associated with magical, supernatural proceedings.[7] Ac-

[5]For a recent review of these issues, see Benjamin I. Page, *Choices and Echoes in Presidential Elections* (Chicago: University of Chicago Press, 1978).

[6]C. Raymond Firth, *Symbols: Public and Private* (Ithaca, N.Y.: Cornell University Press, 1973); Mircea Eliade, *Rites and Symbols of Initiation: The Mysteries of Birth and Rebirth* (New York: Harpers, 1958); Clifford Geertz, *The Interpretation of Cultures: Selected Essays* (New York: Basic Books, 1973); idem, ed., *Myth, Symbol, and Culture* (New York: W. W. Norton, 1971); W. Lloyd Warner, *The Living and the Dead* (New Haven: Yale University Press, 1959).

[7]This classic anthropological distinction, derived from (and therefore more appropriate to) nonliterate societies, excludes the mixed rituals of modern man. Edmund Leach, "Ritualization in Man in Relation to Conceptual and Social Development," *Philosophical Transactions of the Royal Society of London*, ser. B, 251, no. 772, (December, 1966), p. 403.

cordingly most analysts have characterized politics as a form of technical conduct and have assumed that the behavior of participants is logical.[8] Such an approach obscures the symbolic world of electioneering; for, although the rituals and ceremonies of modern societies serve a less obvious role than they do in preliterate societies, nonrational elements nevertheless remain. Public affairs are encrusted with them.

American presidential elections were such rituals. Not only did they involve prescribed behaviors having little to do with their actual function, but they were composed of a series of episodes—party conventions, ratification meetings, serenades, and mass rallies—culminating in the ultimate expression of public life, voting. To paraphrase Victor Turner, presidential elections were periodic restatements of the terms in which men of the United States interacted and produced a coherent social life.[9] What follows is an exploration (not an explanation) of the symbolic meaning of two presidential elections, divided, as any ceremony might be, into preparations for and celebration of the ritual.

By 1864, Americans had elected sixteen presidents, and although the procedures they used had changed (in 1789 Washington's sixty-nine electors had been chosen by state legislatures), the understanding that presidential elections were public occasions in which the people's will cohered into a single collective expression had become, like a well-traveled road, deeply and clearly outlined in the national consciousness. The election of presidents was such a familiar, recursive activity that Americans incessantly gossiped about who might next hold the office, although they gave little attention to a process that had become so routine as to be, like air, translucent in its obviousness. Even during the war—and 1864 was surely a low point for Northerners—no one seriously considered postponing the election; instead, the issue became how to extend voting privileges to Union soldiers in the field.

The belief that presidential elections were enactments of popular sovereignty had been present from the beginning of the republic, and although there was always disagreement about who the people were, James Wilson, a Pennsylvania delegate to the Constitutional Convention, expressed the popular view that "the election of a first magistrate by the people at large is a convenient and successful mode expressing

[8]V. O. Key and Milton Cummings, Jr., *The Responsible Electorate: Rationality in Presidential Voting, 1936–1968* (New York: Random House, 1968); Page, *Choices and Echoes*, pp. 6–7, 281–82; Anthony Downs, *An Economic Theory of Democracy* (New York: Harper, 1957).

[9]Turner, *The Drums of Affliction*, p. 3. For an exception, see Jacob Murray Edelman, *The Symbolic Uses of Politics* (Urbana: University of Illinois Press, 1964).

George Caleb Bingham, *The Verdict of the People, No. 2.* Courtesy of the R. W. Norton Art Gallery, Shreveport, Louisiana.

the sense of the nation." Benjamin Franklin encouraged convention delegates to remember that "returning" to the mass of the people made government officials servants, and the people their superiors; even Alexander Hamilton, usually so distrustful of popular majorities, considered the "chief magistrate" the representative of the "nation"—a kind of concrete symbol of America. Writing in the Constitution's most useful thesaurus, *The Federalist Papers,* he held that "the sense of the people should generate the choice of the person to whom so important a trust was to be confided." Gradually, in a process that helped allay Americans' fears of executive power, the office (though not always its occupant) became a respected authority, representing, according to James Madison, "the genius of the American people," and, in Gouverneur Morris's felicitous phrase, "the people as King." "We are one people in the choice of a president," agreed Andrew Jackson.[10]

There was nothing new about the mechanism used to translate the people's voice. Although nineteenth-century Americans claimed a special kinship to voting and made it the central symbol of their community life, balloting (the word itself is of Italian origin) was an ancient and universal activity, having different meanings in different societies. For centuries the English had used it to delegate authority to sheriffs and vestrymen, and their seventeenth-century descendants in America elected a variety of public officers. The process gained added sanction when revolutionaries accorded legality to their local conventions and to the Continental Congress, on the grounds that the people had transferred their authority to delegates through the vote; hence the power of such assemblies was established through the people's ballot. When Americans explained their revolution in voters' terms ("no taxation without representation") and in the Declaration of Independence, where twenty-seven indictments against King George dealt with violations of pop-

[10]Max Farrand, ed., *The Records of the Federal Convention of 1787,* 4 vols. (New Haven: Yale University Press, 1911–1937), 1: 68, 80; 2: 29, 120; Geoffrey Seed, *James Wilson* (Millwood, N.Y.: KTO Press, 1978); Paul Leicester Ford, ed., *The Federalist Papers* (New York: Henry Holt, 1898), pp. 245, 452, 454, 457; Gouverneur Morris quotation from Richard Morris, "We the People of the United States: The Bicentennial of a People's Revolution," *American Historical Review* 82 (February 1977): 1. For the process by which the presidency came to hold ascendancy within the government, see Arthur M. Schlesinger, Jr., *The Imperial Presidency* (Boston: Houghton Mifflin, 1973). For George Bancroft's version, see his "Oration Delivered at the Commemoration of the Death of Andrew Jackson," in Bancroft, *Literary and Historical Miscellanies* (New York: Harper Brothers, 1855), pp. 461–80. The Jackson quotation is from Arthur Bernon Tourtellot, *The Presidents on the Presidency* (New York: Doubleday, 1964), p. 35; Charles C. Thach, *The Creation of the Presidency, 1775–1789: A Study in Constitutional History* (Baltimore: Johns Hopkins University Press, 1923).

ular sovereignty, they linked the formative event of their republic to the ballot and ensured that elections would be events charged with importance.[11] By the nineteenth century all the artifacts of voting—election parades and campaigns as well as the act itself—had become more than just a means of choosing leaders. Even the slip of paper used to transfer power was transformed, like the flag, into a reverential symbol, protected by law and decorated with images.

Predictably, the vote came to serve as an informal measure of citizenship and was used to define membership in the community. The right to vote was elevated, along with freedom of speech, religion, and the press, into an essential civil liberty; some said a natural right.[12] Sensitive to popular conviction on this point, Noah Webster defined *citizen,* in the 1828 edition of his dictionary, as a "person native or naturalized who has the privilege of exercising the elective franchise or the qualifications which enable him to vote for rulers."[13] By using the categories of landholding, wealth, tax-paying, place of birth, religion, sex, and race as qualifications for what Caleb Cushing called "votership,"[14] Americans needed no further definition of national membership and did not have any until after the Civil War. And, just as voting served as a criterion for citizenship, nonvoting furnished a reason for denying privileges. Chief Justice Taney used just this tautology to deny that blacks were citizens in his *Dred Scott* opinion: voters are citizens, argued Taney; blacks are not voters; therefore blacks are not citizens.[15]

There was political theory to support these exclusions. Voters must have, as Blackstone had written in his well-known paraphrase of Montesquieu, a will of their own and be immune from coercion. "Power over a man's support," agreed Missouri's Thomas Hart Benton, means "power over his will."[16] Thus the ancient measure of independence, the

[11]Marchette Chute, *The First Liberty: A History of the Right to Vote in America, 1619–1850* (New York: E P. Dutton, 1969); Michael Kammen, *A Season of Youth: The American Revolution and the Historical Imagination* (New York: A. A. Knopf, 1968).

[12]For the importance of voting to international liberalism, see Massimo Salvadori, *The Liberal Heresy: Origins and Historical Development* (New York: St. Martin's Press, 1977); Rush Welter, *The Mind of America, 1820–1860* (New York: Columbia University Press, 1975), p. 182.

[13]By the twentieth century this connection had lapsed, and *Webster's New International Dictionary* defines citizens as members of the state or those who give allegiance to it and are therefore entitled to reciprocal protection.

[14]Caleb Cushing, *Speeches on the Amendment of the Constitution of Massachusetts Imposing Disabilities on the Naturalized Citizens of the United States* (Boston: Boston Post, 1859), p. 1.

[15]Don Fehrenbacher, *The Dred Scott Case: Its Significance in American Law and Politics* (New York: Oxford University Press, 1978), p. 342.

[16]Quoted in House, "The Covode Investigation," 36th Cong., lst sess., *House Rept.*, no. 648, p. 2.

freehold, became a logical voting qualification, with those omitted from the franchise—mainly blacks, women, and servants—represented by the property owners within their households. Later, a broader definition of "votership" accommodated economic and familial changes in the new republic; like shareholders in a company, voters had to have a stake in society, the latter made visible in the form of acreage, tax receipts, personal wealth, and residency. What was denied to women, blacks, and members of some religious groups on the grounds of an intellectual and social inferiority predisposing them to dependence and political seduction was at first withheld from the poor on the grounds that they had no attachment to the community. Here two basic strains of political understanding reinforced each other: the republican's fear of a corruptible society (in this case threatened by the infusion of an easily swayed populace) and the liberal's commitment to private property. Only those capable of personal self-government were held responsible enough to vote, and here another double meaning was added to an already ambiguous political vocabulary. "Suffrage," according to one congressman, is "the mechanism by which governments derive their just powers from the consent of the governed. Self-government is natural and inherent; no man confers it upon his fellow. But it is absurd to speak of self-government as belonging to anyone who is denied the ballot, for without the ballot no man governs himself."[17] Only in the twentieth century was self-government—a term first applied to those who could control themselves and who therefore required light governing—applied exclusively to political systems.[18]

There is no need to retell the story in which nonlandowning, nonwealthy, nontaxed, non-Christian, nonnative, nonwhite, and, finally, nonmale Americans were redefined as capable of self-government.[19] What is significant here is the preoccupation with the issue. Discussed before the Civil War at constitutional conventions (assembled in some cases just for that purpose), during election campaigns, at meetings of workingmens' associations, in newspapers and private conversation, the question of who had the vote transfixed mid-century Americans. More than a mechanism by which government derived its just power, voting

[17] *Congressional Globe,* 40th Cong., 3d sess., 95. See also M. A. Richter, *On Self-Government, together with General Plans of a State Constitution and a Constitution for a Confederation of States* (Boston, 1847).

[18] Welter, *The Mind of America,* p. 185.

[19] The classic modern study is Chilton Williamson, *American Suffrage: From Property to Democracy* (Princeton: Princeton University Press, 1960). For an earlier study, see Samuel Jones, *Treatise on the Right of Suffrage* (Boston: Otis, Broaders, 1842).

became a hallowed ceremony, an occasion for manifesting the self-governeds' virtues of restraint as well as a community ritual with prescribed episodes. No more than the Fourth of July or Christmas could it escape symbolic accretions.[20] Like all other humans, Americans possessed an imperative impulse for symbols, deriving much of the form and expression of their political rituals from religion.

It is an unenlightening cliché to call pre–Civil War politics the nation's secular religion. Yet, in an exchange more easily described than understood, public affairs replaced spiritual matters at the center of many a white male's universe. There is no way to measure this conversion, although numbers do reveal a changing commitment. In 1840, when nearly two and a half million American men voted, only 250,000 were enrolled in churches, and throughout most of the nineteenth century, party rallies were better attended than Sunday services or even the meetings of itinerant preachers. In Tennessee, for example, a carpenter explained to his father that he could not describe a recent camp meeting because he had gone instead to a political rally. "We don't do much else but talk politicks nowadays." In New York a farmer physically enacted the transfer from church to party when, in 1860, he actually traded his "Testament for a Political Textbook." On the other hand, a Michigan farmer was still caught between two worlds and confided, "I don't bother about politics. I put a Democratic ticket in the box and leave the rest to God." A Young Men's Democratic Club in Hartford, Connecticut, fused the two institutions by becoming a prayer meeting in nonelection years.[21]

[20]Howard Hastings Martin, "Orations on the Anniversary of American Independence, 1776–1876" (Ph.D. dissertation, Northwestern University, 1955).

[21]William Clebsch, *From Sacred to Profane America: The Role of Religion in American History* (New York: Harper & Row, 1968). Jon Butler, "Magic, Astrology, and the Early American Religious Heritage, 1600–1760," *American Historical Review* 84 (April 1979): 317; Edwin Scott Gaustad, *Historical Atlas of Religion in America* (New York: Harper & Row, 1976), pp. 41–43, 168. Butler calculates that after 1656 even in New England only about one-third of all adults belonged to a church, with the rates in the middle colonies about 15 percent; Diary of Francis W. Squire, entry for 4 August 1860 (Collection of Regional History, Cornell University), cited in Lewis O. Saum, "Whig Beliefs and Democratic Ballots: Political Persuasions of the Unelevated" (Paper delivered at meeting of American Historical Association, 1978); Lewis O. Saum, *The Popular Mood of Pre–Civil War America* (Westport, Conn.: Greenwood Press, 1980), p. 160; Robert Cawardine, *Transatlantic Revivalism* (Westport, Conn.: Greenwood Press, 1978), pp. 28, 30–31. Saum's conclusions differ from mine. Arguing on the basis of his study of the "common man's" diaries that politics was relatively unimportant to this generation, he nevertheless provides a good deal of evidence for the contrary view; his assumption that diaries are revelatory documents opens his results to challenge. Robert Swieringa, ed., *Beyond the Civil War Synthesis: Political Essays of the Civil War Era* (Westport, Conn.: Greenwood Press, 1975), p. 113.

On a more theoretical level, George Camp found strong similarities between the history of religion and "democratic liberty." Considering these resemblances "neither capricious nor fanciful," Camp held in *Democracy*—his 1841 attempt at a native version of Tocqueville's *Democracy in America*—that the "Christian religion tended directly to the institution of democracy." Camp then described the fusing of the sacred and profane into a "happy conviction" that America had become God's paradise, with politics an expression of his earthly will.[22] In this transformation, all America became a political arena; what the French critic Jacques Ellul has protested as the dangerous modern habit of politicizing every aspect of life began in the United States with an innocent partisanship.[23]

Nowhere was the connection between public affairs and God's will more closely drawn than in George Phillips's 1864 *American Republic and Human Liberty Foreshadowed in Scripture.* In the Ohio clergyman's hands, the Old Testament emerged as American history. Phillips discovered in Revelations a disclosure of the Pilgrims' flight from Holland to the New World; in Isaiah's prediction of a nation "born at once," the Declaration of Independence; and in Exodus, a prophecy of the Boston Tea Party. Even Moses' injunction from Deuteronomy—"the cause which is too hard to you bring it unto men and I will hear it"—foretold the Supreme Court. "We were shadowed forth by types and symbols and pointed out by prophecy at different periods from Moses to the Revelator." By reducing the scriptures to national prophecy, Phillips explicitly linked religion and politics.[24]

In this convergence politics played cowbird to religion, appropriating its language, behaviors, and understandings. The term *election* was itself a loan from Protestants who believed that a Supreme Elector chose some individuals (and nations) for salvation. Originally suffrage meant a liturgical petition offered to God, and the first covenants were between God and the ancient Hebrews. Many Northern denominations elected their ministers, thereby delegating temporary authority to these officials in the same kind of process that occurred in public affairs. Nor did Protestants hold exclusive rights to these behaviors. American Catholics participated vicariously in elections whenever the College of Cardinals chose a pope, as it did in 1775, 1800, 1823, 1829, 1831, and 1846. Moreover, the nineteenth-century contests between Catholic lay trust-

[22]George Camp, *Democracy* (New York: Harper Brothers, 1841), pp. 178, 180.

[23]Jacques Ellul, *The Political Illusion* (New York: A. A. Knopf, 1967).

[24]Reverend George S. Phillips, *The American Republic and Human Liberty Foreshadowed in Scripture* (Cincinnati: Poe and Hitchcock, 1864), pp. 154, 95, 54.

ees and priests uncovered similar impulses of popular sovereignty and self-determination. "Democracy," explained Ralph Waldo Emerson, "is better for us because the religious sentiment of the present time accords better with it."[25] Today we call this symmetry a "civil religion," meaning, according to Robert Bellah, a nonsectarian public piety expressed in religion-filled political expressions, symbols, and rhetoric and delineated in the coherence between theological belief and democratic behavior that Abraham Lincoln once described as the "political religion necessary to sustain the American republic."[26]

Aping religious observance, nineteenth-century elections became secular holy days, a time when daily routines were interrupted, work was suspended, and communities observed a public festival. Even the procedures of voting replicated ecclesiastical habits, with communicants approaching a designated window (sometimes even called an altar) demarcated by rail, rope, or board. Preelection rallies also resembled religious services, for they often began with the singing of a patriotic hymn such as "Columbia the Gem of the Ocean," followed by lessons in the form of resolutions, and ended with a sermon based on party principles.[27] Common to religious denominations and parties was a body of doctrine which Democrats often referred to as a "creed"; a catechism and exhortative rhetoric which Kenneth Burke has called "secular prayer";[28] a group of communicants with commitments ranging from occasional participation and contributions of money and time to a collective self-consciousness that inspired members to think of themselves as a church; and, finally, a vocabulary that included the elect, the unwashed, and loaves and fishes. Through the acceptance of their creed, the celebration of their sacrament, and the demonstration of their functions, churches and parties, like most organizations, provided their members with various reassurances: for some, a feeling of renewal, purification, and hope; for others, a sense of fraternal identity.

[25]Ralph Waldo Emerson, "Politics," in *Essays by Ralph Waldo Emerson* (New York: Thomas Y. Crowell, 1951), p. 409. See also Clebsch, *From Sacred to Profane America*, pp. 28, 74.

[26]Robert Bellah, "Civil Religion in America," *Daedalus* 96 (Winter 1967): 1–21; Roderick Hart, *The Political Pulpit* (West Lafayette, Ind.: Purdue University Press, 1977); for a critique see John F. Wilson, "The Status of Civil Religion in America," in *Religion of the Republic*, ed. Elwyn A. Smith (Philadelphia: Fortress Press, 1971), p. 14. Lincoln's phrase is from his "Young Men's Lyceum Address," in *The Collected Works of Abraham Lincoln*, ed. Roy Basler (New Brunswick, N.J.: Rutgers University Press, 1953), 1: 112.

[27]On the similarities between Fourth of July celebrations and religious services, see Martin, "Orations," p. 88.

[28]The phrase is from Kenneth Burke, *A Grammar of Motives* (New York: George Braziller, 1955), p. 393.

George Caleb Bingham, *The County Election*. Collection of the Boatmen's National Bank of St. Louis.

Typical of this overlapping of the spiritual and secular was the election sermon, delivered in colonial times at the opening session of assemblies to delegates soon to choose the governor's council. After the revolution aristocratic councils disappeared, but the election sermon survived, providing Sunday-before-election advice from the pulpit on how to do God's partisan will, and displaying through its persistence a civil religion that could legally separate church and state because in practice the nation itself had become a religion. According to Nathaniel Hawthorne, the intent of the election sermon was to relate "the Deity and the communities of mankind."[29] Eventually even Catholic and Episcopalian clergy spoke on partisan matters, just as the more pietistically inclined Methodists and New School Presbyterians always had. During the Civil War there was a revival of the election sermon, and clergymen delivered policy directives from their pulpits. Some politicians reacted against this practice, although few went as far as the Ohio congressman who in 1863 demanded "a new church organization in which Democrats might enjoy the privilege of having preached the pure gospel."[30]

Usually this convergence of politics and religion is examined from the church's position, and the effect on party of what Horace Bushnell called "a peculiar penetration of the great principles of the gospel into the order of states" is ignored. As a result, secularized churches are seen as entering the common man's world, creating social programs, running schools, and sponsoring associations for moral improvement.[31] Viewed from this perspective, political parties may be seen as reversing this process and absorbing the intangible dimensions of religion. To serve nineteenth-century Americans as religion had, politics had to incorporate nonrational components. Thus what the church lost as it became more worldly was found by political parties, which offered ritual deportment along with their better-known activities. From this nineteenth-century merging of religion and politics came a partisan

[29]Nathaniel Hawthorne, *The Scarlet Letter* (Columbus: Ohio State University Press, 1962), p. 249; Martha Counts, "Political Views of Eighteenth-Century Clergy as Expressed in Election Sermons" (Ph.D. dissertation, Columbia University, 1956); A. W. Plumbstead, ed., *The Wall and the Garden: Selected Massachusetts Election Sermons, 1670–1775* (Minneapolis: University of Minnesota Press, 1968); Hart, *Political Pulpit*. For a Civil War example, see E. J. Stearns, *A Platform for Parties* (Baltimore: J. P. Des Forges, 1860); and, in 1868, Henry Ward Beecher's sermon against Pendleton's greenback plan printed in the *New York World*, 13 July 1868.

[30]George Henry Porter, *Ohio Politics during the Civil War Period* (New York: Longmans, Green, 1911), p. 189.

[31]Quoted in Clebsch, *From Sacred to Profane America*, p. 164.

universe full of dramatic actions. As Jacques Ellul describes the process, "in reality, [man] does not expect to accomplish [his destiny] from politics or from any other person, but from a mysterious and superior power, invested with indefinable qualities such as sovereignty—a power which by a sort of magic transforms the citizens' poor efforts into something good and absolute. As prayer will release transcendental forces, the voting ballot will move the sovereign will."[32]

In a nation that mythologized the people and considered "the public mind" a source of power, it was no sacrilege to transform elections—the means of ascertaining this will—into expressions of God-given commands. George Bancroft thus celebrated "the common mind" as "true Parian marble, fit to be wrought into likeness to a God." A group of militia offered a more succinct version: "Representative democracy is the ordnance of God. Here the right to vote is God-given." So considered, Noah Webster's proposal that ministers be given three votes (the extras presumably were God's proxies) was entirely plausible, as were the admonitions to vote which made ballot-casting the nineteenth-century duty that churchgoing had been for the eighteenth century. No one better understood the connection than humorist David Locke, who, after establishing "a church" of Democrats at Wingert's Corner, installed P. V. Nasby in "sacerdotle" robes as its pastor and made voting the "strait" ticket "a Confeshun uv Faith among the congregation."[33]

Consequently, voting was at the center of the nation's public controversies: in Rhode Island in the 1840s, in Kansas in the 1850s, and in the South in 1860. In each case, differences became more volatile because they were attached to an important national symbol, and issues that might have been settled lost their negotiability because they were entangled with a charged act of community life. In Rhode Island, reformers (historians have had a hard time making them into radicals) fought to extend voting rights limited by that state's seventeenth-century charter to "owners of property worth $134 or renters who paid $7 a year or more." Unable to loosen suffrage requirements by the usual methods of constitutional revision and insistent that they acted under the people's provenance, Thomas W. Dorr and his followers wrote their own con-

32Ellul, *Political Illusion,* p. 187.

33George Bancroft, "The Office of the People in Art, Government, and Religion," in Bancroft, *Literary and Historical Miscellanies,* p. 23; Williamson, *American Suffrage,* p. 227; Clebsch, *From Sacred to Profane America,* p. 164; David Ross Locke, *The Struggle (Social, Financial and Political) of Petroleum V. Nasby* (Boston: Lee and Sheppard, 1888), pp. 69–71, 80.

stitution, christening themselves the People's party.[34] These events foreshadowed the voting boycott that in the name of the people awarded legitimacy to alternative governments sanctified by the use of elections.

In contrast, the conflict concerning the franchise in Kansas developed because too permissive a suffrage violated customary protocols. Among its peculiarities, the Kansas-Nebraska Act had not specified any residency requirements, and the Missourians who flooded Kansas polls in 1854 were technically not illegal voters. But their intrusion (later made illegal by Congress) disrupted habitual electoral behavior, and in the eyes of free-soil Kansans destroyed the authority of the territory's officials. Because residency was an established voting qualification, the number of ballots cast by non-Kansans altered the electoral process sufficiently to encourage a boycott by some citizens of the Pawnee and, later, Lecompton governments. Kansas displayed the revolutionary possibilities of a system that transmitted authority through free elections but had not developed a means to accommodate alienated voters who organized a competing process. Like their predecessors in the late eighteenth century, free-state Kansans argued that conventions, constitutions, and officials were legitimate if they represented the people's will as expressed through elections. As a result, by 1857 Kansans held two sets of elections, delegated authority to two sets of officials, lived under two constitutions, and were governed from two capitals. Both sides justified their abstentions on the grounds of unfair election practices; both sides also believed that their conventions conferred sovereignty. Thus to some Americans the crime against Kansas was not, as Charles Sumner held, slavery, but the sacrilege committed against the much-revered national ceremony of voting.[35]

All this was a preview to the South's adoption of the boycott's more powerful relative, secession. The occasion for the rupture was a presidential election; refusing to accept Lincoln (some Southerners justified their actions by charging that Northern voters no longer exercised "free will," for they were hopelessly brainwashed by abolitionist schools and preachers),[36] most Confederate states initiated their governments

[34]Marvin Gettleman, *The Dorr Rebellion: A Study in American Radicalism, 1833–1849* (New York: Random House, 1973); Jacob Frieze, *A Concise History of the Efforts to Obtain an Extension of Suffrage in Rhode Island from the Years 1811–1842* (Providence: Benjamin Moore, 1842).

[35]James A. Rawley, *Race and Politics: Bleeding Kansas and the Coming of the Civil War* (Philadelphia: Lippincott, 1969), p. 87; "The Covode Investigation"; *Report of the Special Committee,* 34th Cong., 1st sess., H. Rept. 200.

[36]Howard Cecil Perkins, ed., *Northern Editorials on Secession* (New York: D. Appleton, 1942), 1: 53, 99, 158, 163, 186; Allan Nevins, *The Emergence of Lincoln* (New York: Scribner's, 1950), 2: 318–28.

through popularly elected conventions. This process encouraged Southerners to believe that such assemblages were authentic expressions of sovereignty, and hence that the vote canonized a revolutionary transfer of authority. The lesson here was clear, although it would not be used again: revolution required the imprimatur of elected assemblies, and dissidents working outside the party system had only to adopt the expressive symbol of the insiders—elections.

Thus, by the 1860s, presidential voting had become a ceremony that expressed public life, "a thing," as Victor Turner defines symbol, "regarded by general consent as naturally typifying or representing or recalling something by possession of analogous qualities or by association in fact or thought."[37] Not only did balloting recall the nation's beginnings, but, representing the people's will, it became a synecdoche for political values. Americans wrote of "overturning the ballot box," "the sanctity of suffrage," and "speaking out at the ballot box." Europeans noted this preoccupation. Politics was the only pleasure Americans knew, according to Tocqueville: "It penetrated their most trifling habits." Mrs. Trollope, as she did of most things American, complained of "the election fever. . . . This electioneering madness engrosses every conversation, irritates every temper, substitutes party spirit for personal esteem and in fact vitiates the whole system of society." In the 1850s another English visitor, Alfred Bunn, compared election campaigns to "a telegraph or electric chain across the whole land of the republic."[38]

One reason voting had gained such a central place in nineteenth-century political culture was its informality. In anthropological terms, procedures had been desacralized (but not demystified) and had lost the pomp that might have rendered them incongruous in a system dependent on participation. A hallowed ceremony, voting was not a formal occasion. No one dressed in special clothes, not even the judges and inspectors who superintended the process. No one expected reverential silence; election days were noisy affairs filled with the incessant staccato of firecrackers, guns, cries, and yells. This carnival atmosphere reminded a London *Times* correspondent of Derby Day at Epsom; only it

[37]Victor Turner, *The Forest of Symbols: Aspects of Ndembu Ritual* (Ithaca, N.Y.: Cornell University Press, 1967), p. 19.

[38]Alexis de Tocqueville, *Democracy in America* (New York: A. A. Knopf, 1960), 1: 260; Mrs. Trollope, *Domestic Manners of the Americans* (New York: 1832; reprint, A. A. Knopf, 1949), p. 255. Quoted in William E. Chace, "The Descent on Democracy: A Study of American Democracy as Observed by British Travellers, 1815–1860" (Ph.D. dissertation, University of North Carolina, 1941). For the phrases see *Caucasian* (New York), 17 September and 1 October 1864; James Wall, *Address Delivered at Newark July 4, 1863* (Middletown; N.J.: J. F. Warren, 1864), *p. 6.*

was of "a somewhat shabbier character, with a dash of an Italian masquerade and carnival frolic in it. . . . There were huge triumphal cars, heavy boats and pontoons on wheels, . . . with an endless flutter of fluttering flags, monstrous devices, a din of fife, trumpet and drum and the endless firing of light and heavy artillery. . . . It was a fair, a picnic. . . ."[39] A human endeavor, election campaigns existed in a world where there was always an appreciable but comforting gap between the ideal and the real, the theory and the practice. The understanding that elections were not intimidating penetrated the popular imagination, and they emerged as a suitable topic for all forms of mass culture—jokes, songs, ministrel shows, broadsides, fiction, and art. In fact only the War of Independence was a more popular subject, and this was because Americans were so young as a nation that they filled their lack of a collective past by endlessly repeating the story of their creation and its human director—George Washington.

By the Civil War, two basic images had developed in popular culture: the first held elections to be a cherished occasion when independent freemen expressed their will and delegated temporary authority to their leaders. According to one congressman, the ballot fell as

Snowflakes fall upon the sod  
But executes a free man's will  
As lightning does the will of God.

A nonpartisan creation accessible in newspapers and poetry, this romanticized version was represented in a series of paintings completed by George Caleb Bingham in the 1850s: *The County Election, Stump-Speaking or The County Canvass, Canvassing for a Vote or Candidate Electioneering,* and *The Verdict of the People.*[40] Although Bingham did not completely expunge the seamier aspects of elections—the drinking, bribery, and fraudulent counts that often made voting no more than the gain of a dollar and much less than the untrammeled judgment of informed citizens—still the Missouri Democrat (who was also a politician) was respectful. His large canvases portray stock public figures: the earnest candidate intent on defining his positions (or at least his opponent's failings); the attentive citizens (one of whom resembles

[39]Quoted in George Winston Smith and Charles Judah, eds., *Life in the North during the Civil War: A Source History* (Albuquerque: University of New Mexico Press, 1966), p. 112.

[40]*Congressional Globe,* 42d Cong., 1st sess., app., p. 140; E. Maurice Bloch, *George Caleb Bingham: The Evolution of an Artist* (Berkeley: University of California Press, 1967); Albert Christ-Janer, *George Caleb Bingham of Missouri* (New York: Dodd, Mead, 1940).

George Caleb Bingham, *Stump Speaking*. Collection of the Boatmen's National Bank of St. Louis.

Abraham Lincoln) measuring the men who seek their vote; the supposedly incorruptible election judges, inspectors, and clerks who accept the paper tickets; and the orderly congestion of the people as they crowd around the polls. According to Bingham, elections were a popular occasion full of symbolic meaning, a ceremony whereby power was conveyed to public servants by an intelligent electorate.

What Bingham treated beneficently, others parodied; the other image of elections was one of demagogues flimflamming foolish audiences, corrupt officials stuffing ballot boxes, and an ignorant electorate selling ballots to the highest bidder. Later considered either the catalyst of American antipartyism or the response of Whig gentry nudged from power by the Jacksonians, the fraudulent election became a staple in comic literature, in fact its most important subject. From John Pendleton Kennedy to Seba Smith and David Ross Locke, from Artemas Ward to Josh Billings, Americans irreverently satirized voting practices. Elections as farce also appeared in minstrel shows, where endmen declaimed the extravagant bunkum of political aspirants. A typical skit involved a candidate whose parents had been Tories during the revolution but who insisted on sprinkling his speeches with references to his grandfather's patriotic service in Washington's army.[41] Audiences encountered similar themes in the perennial productions of Robert Mumford's eighteenth-century play *The Candidates;* and cartoons and songs ridiculed candidates and voters alike. In one a drunken citizen, hat askew, ballot in hand, shouted to a crowd, "I'm an hindependent Helector. I means to give my vote according to my conscience and him as tips the most."[42]

The underside of elections produced its own stock characters, and Bingham's candidates were transmogrified into bombastic officeseekers more eager for money than for serving an ignorant populace. In Seba Smith's version, the supporters of political aspirant Major Jack Downing have forgotten the issues, if they ever understood them, and instead resolve to use "all fair and honorable means and if necessary dishonora-

[41]Seba Smith, *Letters and Writings of Major Jack Downing* (Boston: Lilly Wart, 1835), p. 102; John Pendleton Kennedy, *Annals of Quodlibet* (Philadelphia: Lippincott, 1860), p. iv; Walter Blair and Hamlin Hill, *From Poor Richard to Doonesbury* (New York: Oxford University Press, 1978); Jennette Tandy, *Crackerbox Philosophers in American Humor and Satire* (New York: Columbia University Press, 1925); David Grimsted, ed., *Notions of Americans, 1820–1860* (New York: George Braziller, 1970), pp. 151–54, 218–20.

[42]Political Cartoon Collection, Smithsonian Institution, Washington, D.C. Puppet theater also dealt with election themes. See Paul McPharlin, *Puppet Theatre in America* (New York: Harper, 1949). For a later version, see Arthur Kaser, *Election Night in Slumpdump, A Riotous Time for Black-Face Comedians* (New York: Fitzgerald, 1932).

ble" to secure the victory of their favorite. Rather than opportunities for free choice, elections have become an occasion to "be shure and vote at lees once. . . . Buckle on yer Armer and go to the Poles. See to it that your neeber is there. See that the Kripples are provided with cannopes. Go to the Poles! To the Poles! and when yar get there vote jest as often as you darn please. . . . This is a privilege we all persess."[43]

Most early nineteenth-century humor seems to have derived from politics. As a source of comic inspiration, elections had become a cliché, and what amused was the association of incongruities. The transcendent event of public life was linked to more earthly behaviors—gambling, cheating, and drinking. Arthur Koestler has described the logic of this humor as "bisociative": we laugh because "two consistent but habitually incompatible reference frames intersect, causing an abrupt transfer of the train of thought from one matrix to another."[44] To create this effect, American humorists relied on travesty and treated a serious subject in an aggressively familiar style.[45] They dressed up elections in their worst clothes (undeniably owned and sometimes worn), and invariably sharpened the incongruity by writing in an incomprehensible, phonetically spelled version of the way prewar Americans talked. Here the comic depended on an ideal, in this case a decorous public occasion when the people's authority was transformed, by means of a contest over issues and statesmen, into the power of government. It was this tension between the real and the ideal that made caricatures such as David Locke's description of elections so amusing to nineteenth-century Americans:

> The returns cumin—Ohio—Linkin! "Good! 'Rah!" shouts I, with great presences uv mind. "Why good?," anxshusly asks the expectants. "Becoz to carry Ohio, the Ablishnists must hev brot votes from New York, which will give us that state, shoor Noo York—Linkin!" "Good Lork!," answers I, promptly; "the Noo York Ablishnists must hev voted in Ohio and hev got home in time to vote agin."[46]

[43] *Vanity Fair,* 4: 13 July 1861.

[44] Arthur Koestler, *The Act of Creation* (New York: Dell, 1964), pp. 35, 95.

[45] John D. Jump, *Burlesque* (London: Methuen, 1972).

[46] Locke, *Nasby,* p. 148. Politics also inspired poetry. For a typical example see Marian Douglas's "Politics," which includes the lines: "The tide of politics ran high / Among the village boys, / And those were truest patriots / Who made the greatest noise. / And who could higher toss his cap / Or louder shout than I? / Till all the mountain echoes learnt / My party battle cry."

There was an element of self-preservation in this humor, for by recognizing the discrepancy between what elections often were and what they ought to be, Americans retained their sense of the ideal.

Overall, the effect was to deflate what might have been a solemn, austere occasion into a popular event in which those with the proper credentials could participate as temporary equals. But plebeian treatment did not erase the charged symbolism of the ceremonies associated with elections. Like many popular images, the comic representation turned back on reality and helped ensure that elections would in fact be a public festival filled with appropriate secular symbols. In the case of presidential elections, the ritual comprised a series of episodes involving two main activities: preparations for and delivery of the ballot.

## *Preparations*

For a small group of Northern Democrats, preparation for the 1864 election began the day after Lincoln's victory in 1860. Even before the inauguration, party managers—particularly New York's August Belmont, Samuel Tilden, Manton Marble, and Samuel Barlow—had remeasured Douglas for 1864, and their preoccupation with the next election survived not only Douglas's death but also the defection of Democratic leaders to the Confederacy. It continued until the final coded telegram from Belmont to Barlow announced McClellan and Pendleton as the party's nominees; and the day after McClellan's defeat, planning for the presidential election of 1868 resumed among these notables who directed, but did not control, the Democracy's national convention.[47] A few participants in this self-perpetuating inner circle were members of the party's national congressional committee, which raised money and circulated party literature. A few were newspapermen, but most were private men who had contributed money to the Democracy.[48] All served as self-appointed members of an informal club

[47]C. Wickcliffe to Manton Marble, 5 September 1864; Peter Cagger to Manton Marble, 8 March 1864; W. Cassiday to Manton Marble, 25 June 1864, Manton Marble Papers, Library of Congress (hereafter cited as Marble Papers); S. L. M. Barlow to Manton Marble, 12 November 1868, Samuel Barlow Papers, Huntington Library, San Marino, Calif.; Charles Wilson, "The Original Chase Organization Meeting and the Next Presidential Election," *Mississippi Valley Historical Review* 23 (June 1936): 61–79; Irving Katz, *August Belmont: A Political Biography* (New York: Columbia University Press, 1968), pp. 124–29, 147–49.

[48]Samuel Cox to Manton Marble, 1 June 1863, 4 January 1864, "Plan of Democratic Campaign," October 1864; Manton Marble to unknown correspondent [1863]; all in

in which president-making was a traditional activity. The recursive nature of presidential elections encouraged such looks to the future, especially among losers, who believed that next time's candidate would make the difference between victory and defeat. Political conversations focused on personnel, enabling the hierarchy to keep in touch, to reflect on one anothers' opinions, and to prepare again.

Never did the inner circle limit its potential candidates to Democrats, and such ecumenism meant that party loyalty was not required for the nomination. In 1864 the Democratic directorate discussed John Frémont, the Republicans' first presidential candidate in 1856; four years later it considered Ulysses Grant and Salmon Chase—the latter closely associated with the Republicans in his role as a cabinet officer.[49] That presidential candidates, like utility infielders, could change teams reflected the need to attract the votes of outsiders. But the fact that men without strong party identifications were attractive candidates and that voters were not shocked by partisan promiscuity suggested too that whereas parties directed and organized campaigns, the American presidency was a national, not a party, symbol: "the echo," as one Democrat put it, "of the voice of the people."[50]

For a larger group of Democrats, the 1864 campaign began early that year with a series of collaborative activities that ended only on election day. For the most part these affairs served to separate Democrats from other Americans, and because they inspired a sense of particularity and specialness, they served as rituals of dissociation. Less than a quarter of the Democratic voting population participated, and usually no more than a tenth had a part in the series of delegate-selection conventions that funneled upward from ward and county district assemblies to state conventions, and finally to the national convention, held in Chicago in 1864 and four years later in New York. Every Northern state did this a little differently. The timing varied, as did specific procedures, but no matter what the variation, the mechanism served on two levels: as purposive behavior that produced a candidate and as part of a symbolic agenda that induced the sense of being a Democrat.

In New Jersey, conventions began in the spring—nature's and the

---

Marble Papers; William F. Zornow, "The Democratic Convention at Chicago in 1864," *Lincoln Herald* 54 (Summer 1952): 2–12.

[49]Martin Mantell, "The Election of 1868: The Response to Congressional Reconstruction" (Ph.D. dissertation, Columbia University, 1969); Charles Coleman, *The Election of 1868: The Democratic Effort to Regain Control* (New York: Octagon Books, 1971), pp. 102–29, 184–86.

[50]*Ohio Statesman* (Columbus), 1 September 1864.

Democracy's time for renewal. At the call of the district's Democratic committee, Hunterdon County partisans met at the courthouse in the county seat of Flemington and, after a Saturday-morning session, selected five delegates for the May meeting of the state Democratic convention.[51] In Trenton, as representatives of their local units, these Democrats chose New Jersey's delegates for the national convention planned for July Fourth but later postponed until August. More than five hundred Hunterdon Democrats (of a voting population of four thousand) participated either in the selection of a delegate or in a parallel process, the choice of the Democratic presidential electors for whom New Jerseyites would vote in November and who, if elected, would travel to Washington to cast their votes for McClellan.

In Baltimore's heavily Irish and German second ward, where over 30 percent of the population was foreign-born, Democrats duplicated this process, with one difference. The Second Ward Club rented an upstairs room in the Pioneer Ladder Firehall, where throughout the summer and fall the faithful gathered to talk politics, drink cider, organize parades and rallies, and read campaign literature (some in German but none in Gaelic). Only in August did the ward select its delegates to the city convention, which in turn picked representatives to the state convention.[52] As in New Jersey, the process was hardly a spontaneous expression of preference, but though arranged by party leaders, it was still sufficiently familiar to require neither written bylaws nor charter. Officers appointed by the ward club committee ran these local meetings, and participants occupied a hierarchy of honorific positions whose titles—from president and vice-president to doorkeeper—provided incentives to serve the party. This was especially important in a presidential election year and in an organization that offered few material benefits. Unlike the Freemasons, Improved Order of Red Men, and even the Know-Nothing lodges of the 1850s, the Democracy did not provide welfare assistance, and patronage jobs were few and uncertain. But even those who were not officers gained what students of organizational behavior call a solidary benefit—the sense of being part of a fellowship.[53] Ward meetings accomplished this by encouraging participants to shout their affirmation to the resolutions written by the platform

[51]*Hunterdon County Democrat,* 21 April 1864.

[52]Eleanor Kress, "Baltimore's Second Ward" (Paper presented at a seminar at Goucher College, 1976).

[53]James Q. Wilson, *Political Organizations* (New York: Basic Books, 1973); Jean H. Baker, *Ambivalent Americans: The Know-Nothing Party in Maryland* (Baltimore: Johns Hopkins University Press, 1978), pp. 113–15.

committees; by offering an opportunity to choose friends as representatives to the city convention; but, most of all, by providing an occasion to assemble. Party songs expanded on this theme of solidarity:

We come as the waves come
When navies are stranded
We come as the winds come
When forests are rended
We come as free men come
When there's Union to serve
We come as true Democrats
With strong Hearts and Brave.[54]

Like performances before opening night, these interlocking conventions provided practice for party activists, who rehearsed the delegation of authority and devolution of power they would enact in November. In Ohio, for example, delegates to the state convention (earlier elected by their counties) immediately discovered the limits of their authority. Most did little to organize the Columbus meeting in 1864; the state's executive committee chose not only the session's permanent chairman but also its vice-presidents and the members of the Committee of Resolutions. A nasty fight over delegate credentials never reached the floor, but was negotiated offstage by another appointed committee. Only on the second day of the convention, when the moment came to offer nominees and to choose among them, did delegates have equal power. And just as the party's national convention would later proceed through a ritual that began in controversy and ended in harmonious support of platform and candidate, so too did Ohio's Democratic convention.[55]

One of the delegates at this Ohio convention was George Morgan, who with other Democrats shouted his affirmation to the six resolutions read to, but not discussed by, the convention. For the rest of the year Morgan would use these resolutions as benchmarks, concentrating on how they distinguished him from his opponents. Three of the resolutions did this especially well: as a Democrat, Morgan was neither an abolitionist nor a miscegenationist, nor was he engaged in subverting free government by enrolling blacks in a white man's army. Later, in

[54]Quotation from Broadside Collection, Smithsonian Institution, Washington, D.C.; Broadside Collection, Pennsylvania Historical Society, Philadelphia: *Proceedings of the Democratic Convention Held at Harrisburg, March 1859*.

[55]*Proceedings of the Democratic State Convention* (Columbus, O., 1864).

Chicago, his party would expand on these themes, offering specific criticism of Lincoln ("the direct interference of military authorities of the United States in recent elections"), general comments assuring commitment to national ideals ("we will adhere unswervingly to the Union under the Constitution"), and broad suggestions for the future ("the aim and object of the Democratic party is to preserve the Federal union and rights of the states unimpaired").[56] Analysts of nineteenth-century politics too often dismiss such statements as manipulative abstractions, arguing that the failure to provide specific programs for the future prevents the electorate from making issue-referenced choices. Such an appraisal misses the mark. Platforms were just that: a special place for Democrats to stand during the campaign.

There were other ways in which Democrats could have nominated a candidate and defined a set of principles. Ward and county leaders could have interviewed members and transmitted their policy and personnel preferences to a national committee. This in fact was the original understanding of a canvass. In eighteenth-century England, candidates presented their views at meetings, and by the end of the campaign one aspirant had usually withdrawn, leaving the election uncontested.[57] Or a group of party leaders could have caucused, as had been the practice in the late eighteenth century. Alternatively, Democratic hopefuls could have campaigned for the nomination, as they do in today's presidential primaries. Transportation and newspaper facilities were sufficiently developed for McClellan and Seymour to have presented themselves and their ideas to the membership. But because the intentions of the nominating process were secondary to its function of denoting Democrats, such procedures were not appropriate. Instead, as a partisan activity designed to detach Democrats from other public personalities they

[56]Porter, *Ohio Politics,* pp. 170–74, 190–97; Eugene Roseboom, *The Civil War Era, 1850–1873* (Columbus: Ohio Historical Society, 1954), pp. 412–14, 419–23; Reginald McGrane, *William Allen* (Columbus, O.; F. J. Heer, 1925); John S. Hare, "Allen G. Thurman" (Ph.D. dissertation, Ohio State University, 1933); quotations from Kirk H. Porter and Donald B. Johnson, ed., *National Party Platforms, 1840–1972* (Urbana: University of Illinois Press, 1956), p. 34; Morgan to McClellan, 4 August, 9 and 13 October 1864, George McClellan Papers, Library of Congress (hereafter cited as McClellan Papers). For McClellan's own uncertainty about the platform, see Charles R. Wilson, "McClellan's Changing Views on the Peace Plan of 1864," *American Historical Review* 38 (April 1933): 498–505.

[57]Robert Worthington Smith, "Political Organization and Canvassing: Yorkshire Elections before the Reform Bill," *American Historical Review* 74 (June 1969): 1538–60; Sir Lewis Namier, *The Structure of Politics at the Accession of George III* (London: Macmillan, 1957), pp. 158–60; Paul F. Burke and Donald de Bets, "Identifiable Voting in Nineteenth-Century America: Toward a Comparison of Britain and the United States before the Secret Ballot," *Perspectives in American History* 2 (1977–1978): 257–88.

might inhabit (in the case of Ohioan George Morgan, his Presbyterianism and membership in the state agricultural society), these interlocking conventions were effective rituals of separation. So viewed, the platforms that accompanied them were political badges, not commitments to public policy.

A second group of supporters learned to behave as Democrats in clubs. Party adjuncts, these informal organizations became the political equivalents of the nineteenth century's much-remarked voluntary associations, affording the same kinds of benefits to their members as did temperance, penal reform, and Hibernian societies. Open to what one charter vaguely described as "members in good standing in the Democratic party" and another termed "full communion with the Democracy of state and nation,"[58] they varied from federated ward and district associations to the group of pamphleteers known as the Society for the Diffusion of Political Knowledge. Like many other American arrangements, clubs followed residential patterns and class lines, although membership was occasionally based on other criteria—age, occupation, or a shared experience such as military service. In 1864 veterans of the Army of the Potomac's peninsular campaign formed McClellan Legions whose remnants, perniciously renamed the White Boys in Blue, reappeared in 1868. That same year, New York Democrats not only organized the Chapultepec Society, which included Mexican-American War veterans and their sons, but also established the elite Manhattan Club, with headquarters on Fifth Avenue and annual dues of fifty dollars. To these the Republicans added the secret Order of the American Knights and Knights of the Golden Circle, but Democrats disclaimed any connection to such supposedly disloyal organizations.[59]

Few clubs were as well established as New York's Tammany Hall or could finance a monthly speaker's program, as did Philadelphia's Democratic Union Association. Certainly few were as powerful as New York's Mozart Association, which sometimes made its own nominations for local offices. Nor could many match the social program of the Morris County, New Jersey, Democracy, whose entertainments included picnics, fireworks, and a "Democratic Ball" at which a brass

[58]Minutes of the Democratic Club, 1863–1864, State Historical Society of Wisconsin, Madison; Morris County (New Jersey) Democratic Club, "Charter and Bylaws, 1863," New Jersey Historical Society, Newark.

[59]William F. Zornow, *Lincoln and the Party Divided* (Norman: University of Oklahoma Press, 1954), p. 181; Frank L. Klement, "Civil War Politics, Nationalism, and Post-War Myths," *Historian* 38 (May 1976): 419–38; Henry Liebeman to George McClellan, 8 October 1864; Hiram Ketchum to McClellan, 5 September 1864; both in McClellan Papers; Henry Watterson, *History of the Manhattan Club* (New York, De Vinne Press, 1915).

band played the McClellan Schottische. On the other hand, none equaled in notoriety and violence Baltimore's Bloody Eights, Butt-Enders, and Eighth Ward Blackguards.[60]

By the late spring and early summer of 1864 and 1868, most Democratic clubs met weekly, usually on Monday nights at 7:30. In other years members assembled on a desultory basis, once a month or, in the case of organizations that provided commutation fees for drafted Democrats, when necessary. But in presidential years, clubs needed extra time to repair torchlights; to order new uniforms, transparencies, and fireworks; to solicit new members; and to establish credit with the firms that specialized, like New York's Charles Becker Company, in such equipment. Some clubs—and not just those of the wealthy—encouraged their members to follow the *New York World*'s injunction "to quit work if you can for the duration of the campaign";[61] several prominent Northern Democrats began lifelong political careers in local clubrooms.

Even in the somnolent reading rooms of the gentry, where, according to one charter, Democrats met "to hold intelligent and agreeable intercourse and conversation, read the latest and most reliable political information, play chess, drafts, and backgammon," the pace quickened during presidential years, and the bonds among members—what a Kansas Democrat called the "democracy in fellowship"—tightened.[62] In the same manner as conventions, clubs set apart, in common cause, a band of partisans who prepared the series of ceremonial occasions that climaxed in November's balloting. By late summer both groups—club members and convention activists—had assumed an identity: they were soldiers in the Democratic army, who after their training would now recruit others. And, as in war, some would make better soldiers than others.

## *The Language of Elections*

As the link between the ideal of popular sovereignty and its practice, elections were an essential American ceremony, with their meaning conveyed through figurative language. And well before the 1860s, war

[60]Morris County Democratic Club, "Minutes and Bylaws," 1864, New Jersey Historical Society; Minutes of the Democratic Club, 1863–1864, State Historical Society of Wisconsin; Baker, *Ambivalent Americans,* pp. 121–22; William Evitts, *A Matter of Allegiances* (Baltimore: Johns Hopkins University Press, 1974), pp. 114–17.

[61]*New York World,* 3 November 1864; *Philadelphia Age,* 16 April 1863, 24 March 1864.

[62]*Constitution and Bylaws of The Central Democratic Club* (Philadelphia: H. G. Leisenning, 1863); *Democratic Rules as Revised* (Philadelphia: H. G. Leissenning, 1867); "Constitution and Bylaws of the Chesapeake Club," Maryland Historical Society; "The Covode Investigation," p. 167.

furnished the master image. Not only did martial terms suffuse political language, but military behaviors were actually reproduced in partisan parades, rallies, and voting "battles." In 1864, the most foreboding year of the Civil War, this application of military terms was especially ironic, for newspapers applied the term *campaign* to the Union Army in Virginia as well as to politics. Today we still speak of electoral campaigns, party rank and file, political strategies and tactics. A loser remains the casualty of a rout or one of the fallen; a winner is a victor. By now commonplace, the metaphors have lost their meaning, and like most clichés are no longer motives for action.

It was not so in the 1860s, when Northern Democrats were exhorted "to close ranks and stand firm." "Falter not before the enemy" went the election-eve incantation. "Use your paper bullets." "Revenons à nos moutons," wrote G. T. Curtis to McClellan before the 1864 election. "Turn all batteries on the enemy." When they marched, Ohio Democrats sang the same battle music as the state's volunteer regiments and shared, with soldiers, the quick tempos of:

> Come rally round the clarion sound,
> The bugle blasts are sounding.
> The marshalling hosts are at their posts
> The enemy surrounding.[63]

In Wisconsin there was a slightly different version: "Stand up to the racket, stand up to the fight. Boys, off with your packets, and in with your might." In Chicago, as they approached Union Square, Democrats chanted "Rally then, with warm hearts, willing hand, and full ranks." In Philadelphia the short speech of George Pendleton was likened to "a big salvo," and, according to a local resident, the popular New Jersey congressman A. J. Rogers had "poured the hot shot of political truth in a continuous volley, annoying Republicans with a frequent 100 lb. shell." A campaign rally in California was "an encampment," and a popular slogan became "a telling hit." In Indiana a defeated candidate was likened to a casualty, the victim of violations of "war codes," because out-of-state Republican soldiers had voted. Congressional contests held in October were portrayed as "a first dash at the enemy," "a skirmish" before the crucial November engagement, after

[63]New York *Caucasian,* 1 October 1864; *New York Times,* 13 and 15 October 1864; Samuel Cox to Manton Marble, 8 October 1864, Marble Papers; G. T. Curtis to McClellan, 12 August 1864, McClellan Papers; Clement L. Vallandigham, *Songbook: Songs for the Times* (Columbus, O.: J. Walter, 1863).

which, like military commanders, party leaders called for more men, money, and materials, acknowledging pamphlets and newspapers as their "sinews of war." On election eve, the New York Democratic committee repeated the traditional call to battle—an electoral rendering of the reasons why the cause was just, honorable, and therefore deserved support. "Act with deliberation, manhood, and courage, so you know your rights and knowing, dare maintain. One more impetuous charge and the battle is won." To a crowd in New York, a Democratic congressman shouted, "We are not only on the war path; we have thrown the heart of Bruce into the ranks of the enemy." And in Maine the words were nearly the same: "Prepare for the conflict at the Ballot Box. We'll welt them with our full divisions and our brave soldiers." One self-proclaimed "Christian soldier" from Boston wrote McClellan: "We will gird up our loins like men with humble prayers to Almighty God."[64]

The apocalyptic note of such rhetoric is similar in tone and purpose to battle-eve oratory. According to one Democrat, "If we falter, it will change history like Caesar halted at the Rubicon or Charles Martel at Tours. It will be an end to the struggle waged for five centuries between liberty and servitude, free institutions and despotism." Other versions were similarly foreboding: "I call you to arms. This is the most vital struggle since the founding of the republic." "By sundown we will know whether the United States will be a Republic." "The results of our battle will reach farther than any engagement fought during this war and will determine whether or not we shall be freemen." "If the enemy prevail on Tuesday their success will encourage them to proceed to disfranchise free men forever." "Now is a time for the end of words and a time for deeds. By their votes the freemen of America will stand or fall."[65]

Persisting after the war because they were independent of it, such martial images continued to reflect the political culture of Northern Democrats. In 1868 the Democrats' most popular campaign song—

[64]*Newark Journal,* 8 October 1864; *New York World,* 5 November 1864; Broadside Collection, 1864, 1868, Smithsonian; "A Soldier of Christ" to George McClellan, 5 September 1864; John Stark to McClellan, 2 November 1864; Ben Ely to McClellan, 5 September 1864, all in McClellan Papers; *Portland* (Ore.) *Weekly Advertiser,* 18 October 1864.

[65]*New York Times,* 13 and 15 October 1864; *New York World,* 3 and 8 November 1864; ibid., 3 November 1868; *Official Proceedings of the Democratic National Convention* (Chicago: Chicago Times Steam Book, 1864), pp. 3–7; *Ohio Statesman,* 1 September 1864; Henry Bradbury to Manton Marble, 4 October 1864, Marble Papers.

"Seymour, Blair, and Liberty"—used the music, tempo, and words of a popular Civil War march:

> Yes, God restore the right through us
> Our captains even these,
> The brave and true shall lead us through
> To victory, power and peace.

As it had been for over three decades, campaign language still abounded with exhortations "to do battle," "man your guns," "hurl salvos," and "take possession of the polls." Party meetings were "demonstrations," ballots "the bullets of war." "You have driven the Republicans to the baggage wagons. You have almost routed them," exhorted a Maryland Democrat, after which the membership sang:

> The Day of Battle draws nigh
> Reverence for your Patriot sires
> And strike for your altars and your sires.

Party iconography repeated battle themes: torchlights were fashioned after gunstocks, with only the light at their end to distinguish them from bayonets. And the capes and caps of Democrats in 1868 were such close replicas of those worn by the Army of the Potomac that many veterans paraded in their old uniforms.[66]

Because this Democratic army was hard pressed (not having won a campaign since 1856), its martial imagery was defensive, like that of a small force that knows itself to be in the right but must acknowledge the superior strength of what one Democrat called the "mercenary legions of the enemy of Republican soldiers and patronage holders." Other appeals echoed this understanding: "Stand firm and hold the line." "Never give up." "Our watchword is BE READY." "BE READY and hold steady." "Organize or the Philistines will be upon you." "No thin Ranks." After defeat, the military idiom also consoled; as a loyal Democrat advised McClellan, the Republicans had violated established political codes and "were too unscrupulous for a yeoman militia to successfully assail them." Democratic ideals, especially the party's opposition to black suffrage and congressional reconstruction, became salients behind which the army could retreat while they prepared for an offensive

[66]Democratic Songbooks, Broadside Collection, Library of Congress; Coleman, *Election of 1868,* p. 357; Baker, *Ambivalent Americans,* pp. 34–36; Saum, *Popular Mood,* p. 154.

in 1872. "Bide your Time," encouraged a Wisconsin Democrat, "in the old Campground of the Democracy."[67]

Although the Democrats portrayed electoral campaigns in military terms, they did not support the soldiers' right to vote in the field. This was ironic but logical, for although a party that claimed most of the Union Army might be expected to work toward a suspension of the residence requirements that made out-of-district voting illegal, a higher consideration prevailed. Holding politics to be war carried on by other means, Democrats believed their army must be trained, and this was difficult to accomplish during the war. As Northern Democrats discovered, their access to soldiers in the field was impeded by distance, by army regulations, and by Republican officers. Not only was it impossible for their recruits to receive party propaganda, but, as one veteran noted, "there are no meetings," a judgment with which the Democratic congressman Samuel Cox agreed. "The soldier's vote," he wrote, "is aloof from all social and political influence. We can't reach it."[68] And because soldiers in the field could not participate in the series of rituals that produced Democrats, the party came to oppose, as one member explained, "voting in camps far away from supervision."[69] In this their partisan intuitions were correct, for in 1864 Lincoln carried the soldier vote three to one.

## *Preelection Ceremonies*

Within weeks of the party's national convention (September in 1864, July in 1868), state central committees organized the first episode in partisan activity—local ratification meetings. There was no effort at this

[67]*Baltimore Sun*, 1 November 1868; *New York Times*, 10 November 1868. Joseph Fraesch to McClellan, 19 November 1864, McClellan Papers; George Smith to "Nat—," 24 September 1868, George Smith Papers, Wisconsin Historical Society, Madison; *Caucasian*, 11 October 1868.

[68]John Phelps to Horatio Seymour, 20 September 1864, Seymour-Fairchild Papers, New York Historical Society, New York (hereafter cited as Seymour-Fairchild Papers); Samuel Cox to Manton Marble, 14 June 1863, Marble Papers. For various interpretations of this issue, see T. Harry Williams, "Voters in Blue: Citizen Soldiers in the Civil War," *Mississippi Valley Historical Review* 31 (September 1944): 187–204; N. Oscar Winther, "The Soldier Vote in the Election of 1864," *New York History* 25 (October 1944): 440–81; Arnold Shankman, "Soldier Votes and Clement L. Vallandigham in the 1863 Ohio Gubernatorial Election," *Ohio History* 82 (Spring 1973): 96; William Louis Young, "Soldier Voting in Ohio during the Civil War" (master's thesis, Ohio State University, 1948); Josiah H. Benton, *Voting in the Field* (Boston: privately published, 1915).

[69]*Cincinnati Convention for the Organization of a Peace Party for States Rights and Jeffersonian Democratic Principles, 18 October 1864* (n.p., n.d.).

point to appeal to outsiders; those who disapproved either organized insurgent conventions (as did Peace Democrats angry with McClellan's letter of acceptance) or stayed home with their discontent.[70] It was a self-selected group that confirmed the party's nominee and agreed to serve in the campaign. Such assemblages of Democrats served no function save to bring members together, but they were popular, well-attended affairs. Hierarchical in structure (the usual panoply of officers determined the agenda and the resolutions), the event was nonetheless informal and plebeian. In Columbus, Ohio, thousands heard out-of-town speakers declaim McClellan's glories and shouted their approval to resolutions declaring the importance of electing "Our Little Napoleon." Four years later a similar ratifying convention approved the nomination of Horatio Seymour in New York's City Hall Park. In both instances, and in ratification meetings held throughout the North, the crowd confirmed what its leaders had already done. Though a matter of form, the ceremony engendered a sense of participation, for in theory the Democracy could refuse to serve under their "general." Once ratified, however, the party ticket deserved support.

Only after ratifying McClellan and Seymour did Northern Democrats organize the next episode of their campaign: the parades in which members became active partisans, enacting the military behaviors of their language. Not every Northern town, county, or city held such a parade in 1864 and 1868; but most did, and they were remarkably similar events, whether in a small Maine town like Portland, a large border-state city like St. Louis, or a rural setting such as Cecil County, Maryland. Again the occasion was more expressive than instrumental, more inspirational than informative, and more directed at promoting internal unity than at generating external propaganda. With their well-ordered rows of Democratic marchers, parades reified the essential concept of American political culture—the people's will—by providing a collective activity that unified diverse individuals. To those who lined the streets and watched the Democrats as they headed for a village center, a city square, or a picnic grove, the message was clear: join our army. It will be the largest and best equipped with ballots, the political weapons of this campaign. It fights for the goals abbreviated on our transparencies, displayed on our wagons, and expressed by our leaders.

Democratic parades were invariably organized like a nineteenth-cen-

[70]*Cincinnati Daily Gazette,* 8 September 1864; Sidney D. Brummer, *Political History of New York* (New York: Longmans, Green, 1911), p. 402. A comic version occurs in Locke, *Nasby,* pp. 544–46; "Ratification Meeting, Burlington, New Jersey, 1 September 1864," McClellan Papers.

Democratic electioneering in New York, 1864: torchlight procession. From the *Illustrated London News,* 15 October 1864.

tury army; their military form dispelled, among participants and observers alike, any sense of a formless mass of individuals. There was order and discipline in these battalions.[71] Led by a commander-in-chief, chosen by the parade's self-appointed organizers, the host was arranged in divisions and subdivided into company units of one hundred, officered by a captain, who as president of a Democratic society usually carried his unit's banner. Dressed in caps and capes resembling army uniforms, paraders met in the early evening and were handed the torches and transparencies they would carry during the march. Each division began on a parallel street, for the intent was to arrive simultaneously at the speakers' stand, thus creating among participants and observers alike the sense of a huge mass of individuals being merged into the single element of the Democracy. Sometimes this effect was difficult to achieve; in larger cities as many as forty thousand Northern Democrats marched, and the gun signaling the beginning of the procession could not be heard above the din. In smaller areas the roads into town were clogged with the wagons of farmers who had come to watch, and there were no parallel streets, only perpendiculars. In some rural communities, Democrats marched from four different directions into squares, creating the effect of a multitude become one. Size was important because popularity was measured by the length of the parade and the time taken to pass by the reviewing stand.

After the paraders had marched below the reviewing stand, they dispersed, awaiting speeches that might last as long as four hours. (This led one Democrat to complain that politics in his community was "all the go hear.") By this time it was dark; the only light was that of torchlights, bonfires, gaslights,fireworks, and the lanterns of those who had not used up their kerosene supply. But even before marchers reached the square, supporters along the way had illuminated their houses in a concrete representation of what party leaders called "lighting the fires of popular support." A correspondent of the *Illustrated London News* found the effect remarkable:

> The whole heavens were illuminated as if by magic and the square was broken into brilliant coruscations of light. Every platform was garlanded by Chinese lanterns and gas lamps beside. At eight o'clock the artillery

[71]This is a composite picture based on newspaper accounts of political parades held in 1864 and 1868. See also Brummer, *Political History of New York*, pp. 419, 423; Harold Hancock, *Delaware during the Civil War* (Wilmington: History Society of Delaware, 1961), p. 165. *New York World*, 9 October 1868; J. Thomas Scharf and Thompson Westcott, *History of Philadelphia* (L. H. Everts, 1884), pp. 818, 1819.

> began to bray. The Star Spangled Banner blended with the waltz from Faust. A big eagle in gas suddenly spread his dazzling wings over the portal of a [restaurant] . . . from the corner of 14th street a blinding ray from a calcium light apparatus shot for many hundred feet a bridge of radiance. There was a display of fireworks before the procession of wards entered the square.[72]

So important was light to these ceremonies that its use became a source of public controversy. When, during the war, Republican mayors and city councils tried to restrict illuminations to military celebrations, Democrats protested this appropriation of an essential feature of their partisanship.[73]

There were regional and rural variations in this political ceremony, for Democratic politics never produced standard arrangements. But most parades depended in one way or another on light. In New York's Union Square, for example, calcium lights played on the equestrian statue of George Washington, producing the shadow of a mounted figure calculated to remind Democrats of General George McClellan. In Portland, Oregon, as Democrats marched into the square chanting "To the Polls, To the Polls," an immense fireworks display bathed the center of the city in light. In Indiana a parade ended in a picnic grove lit by huge bonfires.[74]

Light has always been a symbol of purification, and the illumination used in the Democratic parade conveyed the idea of the party as a purveyor of radiance to the people—a means, as it were, of freeing the nation from darkness and corruption. "It has been dark but there is light ahead," encouraged the *New York World* on the eve of the 1864 election.[75] Democratic speakers in 1864 and 1868 repeatedly linked their party to "the brightness of a public truth" that would, according to one, "set the country on fire." The expressive nature of this theme was obvious in the scheduling of parades that could have been held, like campaign rallies, on Saturday afternoons or after work. But daylight would have destroyed the symbolic interplay between the light of the people's Democracy and the darkness of its opponents' conspiracies. As they marched swinging their torches, Democrats also symbolized

[72]Saum, *Popular Mood*, p. 145; *New York World*, 7 November 1864; *Illustrated London News*, 1 October 1864.

[73]*New York World*, 1 October 1864; C. S. Matloon to Charles Bell, 2 October 1864, Bell Family Papers, Delaware State Archives, Dover.

[74]*Illustrated London News*, 15 October 1864; *Portland Weekly Advertiser*, 8 October 1864.

[75]John Harlan to George McClellan, n.d., McClellan Papers; *New York World*, 2 November 1864; "Political Campaign Torches," *United States National Bulletin*, 1964.

Party rally, New York City, 1864. From the *Illustrated London News,* 1 October 1864.

watchfulness, and this republican theme reappeared in other iconography, notably the silhouette of an all-seeing eye that adorned some party tickets.

Light had other meanings. During the 1850s and 1860s bonfires suggested public atonement for the national disgrace of disunion. In the past, Americans had observed days of humiliation decreed by the president following catastrophes such as the explosion of the *Princeton* in 1844.[76] In the 1860s Democratic affairs, with their luminous stands and brightly lit squares, produced a provocative contrast with the surrounding darkness and suggested a means of expiation. These occasions constituted a partisan message to join up as a Democrat, to serve as a soldier against evil, and to redeem self and nation.

There is no way of knowing how each Democrat felt during these parades; few participants recorded their impressions. Informants to whom such charged events are familiar—whether Catholics at mass or Tikopians at a rite of passage—rarely produce self-conscious commentaries on their state of mind at the time. The sense of enlisting in an army was, however, inescapable, for the smells as well as the sounds of the parade were those of battle. The thick sulfurous odors left by fireworks were reminiscent of gunpowder, and to march in uniform accompanied by a brass band, to be attended by mounted officers who rode alongside shouting "Hurry up there" and "Close up the ranks" must have aroused martial feelings. Only incidentally directed toward winning votes—that traditional but overexamined activity of parties—parades enlisted members in the organization. For those who watched—and thousands did—parades evoked the sensation of an army of light, on its way to battle the enemy.

Two other Democratic affairs, in no particular sequence, also became significant episodes in presidential campaigns. One, the pole-raising competition, originated with the English maypole celebrations, which as expressions of eighteenth-century opposition to the Crown came to symbolize liberty. Later, Democrats of the Jacksonian period made poles of hickory, thereby linking their hero Andrew Jackson to the revolution.[77] By the 1860s, raising and maintaining trees adorned with party emblems had become a ritual. Throughout the North, Democrats

[76]President Tyler and members of the cabinet were aboard the *Princeton,* a steam-propelled warship, in 1844 when it exploded, killing two members of the cabinet.

[77]Arthur M. Schlesinger, "The Liberty Tree: A Genealogy," *New England Quarterly* 25 (December 1952): 435–38; John W. Ward, *Andrew Jackson: Symbol for an Age* (New York: Oxford University Press, 1962), pp. 54–56, 63; Robert Gunderson, *The Log Cabin Campaign* (Lexington: University of Kentucky Press, 1957), pp. 232–33.

erected huge poles, sometimes over a hundred feet but normally no more than twenty, bearing the names of their candidates. Atop these they placed one of their traditional emblems, usually either an eagle holding the American flag between his talons or a banner proclaiming the Democracy. Part of an elaborate ceremony, pole raising was the special province of local Democratic Old (and, after Polk's administration, Young) Hickory Associations. After their installation came partisan speeches and singing. On one occasion Stephen Foster provided New Jersey Democrats with an appropriate ode in which he compared the lifting of the party banner to the expressive behavior it represented—the rising of the people through their votes.[78]

Once a pole was erected, there was no assurance that it would survive the campaign, and parties struggled to have the highest one, believing this a forecast of the election. In 1844 in Ellington, Connecticut, Democrats managed to raise a hickory pole of over a hundred feet only to spend the next four months defending it from the Whigs. By election time the pole had been reduced to thirty feet. The contrived passion of these events suggests that ritual deportment was important. According to one Illinois Democrat: "On Monday night some miserable infamous low-flung narrow-minded ungodly dirt-eating cut-throat hemp-deserving deeply-died double-distilled consecrated miscreant of miscreants sinned against all honor and decency by sawing down two or three poles."[79]

Most communities held pole raisings, but only a few participated in a second type of unscheduled but expressive ritual—the serenade to the standard-bearer. Because most nineteenth-century presidential candidates stayed at home, serenades (which usually required the nominee's presence, but not his words) were rare. They deserve mention as a partisan ceremony, however, because the postures adopted symbolized the ideal relationship between the public and its leaders. Believing their nomination a gift, Democrats considered rhetorical petitions by the candidate a violation of this transaction. Lesser candidates—as well as the party's faithful—could make stump speeches and plead for support, but presidential candidates should stay at home, keep up an active correspondence, and appear mute at occasional serenades. "I would not

[78]Fletcher Hodges, "Stephen A. Foster, Democrat," *Lincoln Herold* 47 (June 1945): 2–30. For a postrevolutionary instance of raising the liberty pole and its association with the rising up of the people, see H. M. Brackenridge, *History of the Insurrection in Western Pennsylvania* (Pittsburgh: W. S. Haven, 1859), p. 128; Charles Lanman to George McClellan, 8 October 1864, McClellan Papers.

[79]Saum, *Popular Mood,* p. 154; *Illinois State Journal,* 4 August 1860.

of course expect you to take the stump," wrote a Pennsylvania organizer to McClellan, "only to show yourself to the people."[80] In keeping with this expectation, McClellan spent most of the fall in New Jersey, and only at the end of the 1868 campaign did a reluctant Seymour deliver any speeches.[81]

When they did venture beyond their homes—in McClellan's case to nearby Trenton and New York—both candidates were saluted in a prescribed ceremony of singing and marching. In New York for an October meeting with the "Delmonico set"—that influential group of party aristocracy who met regularly at Delmonico's restaurant on Park Avenue—McClellan appeared on the balcony of his father-in-law's Manhattan apartment. Saying nothing, he waved and returned the salute, smiling, according to one source, when he heard the popular songs he inspired:

> To Mac, my darling, proud am I
> To hear that you've been nominated.
>
> Little Mac, Little Mac
> You're the man.
>
> Hurrah for Little Mac
> Millions of volunteers my boys
> Our Own George B. McC.
> Little Mac—First in Peace,
> First in War, First in the Hearts
> Of his Countrymen.[82]

Later the *New York World* complimented the candidate on his perseverance, for, eager for political salute as he had not been for battle,

[80]C. Lippincott to McClellan, 5 September 1864; Hedrick Wright to McClellan, 25 October 1864; both in McClellan Papers. In 1864 Manton Marble recommended to McClellan "diligent friendly correspondence with your friends"; Manton Marble to McClellan, 12 September 1864, McClellan Papers. James Russell Lowell considered even letter writing a dangerous activity. "There is nothing a party dreads more than a letter from its candidate: 'Litera scriptament,'" and he hoped that "the candidate could take his position on either side of the fence with entire consistency." *James Russell Lowell's The Biglow Papers: A Critical Edition,* ed. Thomas Wortham (De Kalb: Northern Illinois University Press, 1977), pp. 115, 117–18.

[81]The desultory nature of American campaigning led Grant to describe his 1868 campaign as the pleasantest time he had had since the beginning of the rebellion. U. S. Grant to William Smith, 25 September 1868, Grant Papers, microfilm edition. On the nomination as a gift, see McClellan memoir, n.d., 1864; James Wall to McClellan, 18 July 1864; both in McClellan Papers.

[82]*New York World,* 1 September 1864; *McClellan Songster* (New York, 1864).

McClellan appeared early and could not leave until after midnight when the last song had been chorused by the now-hoarse throng. In 1868 Seymour was also serenaded at a similar occasion in New York when fifty thousand Democratic voices joined together, accompanied by Dodsworth's Brass Band, in "Seymour's March to the White House."[83]

Reenacted in these ceremonies was the expected relationship between leader and follower in a democratic society. Just as they had during parades, party members passed below their leaders (who invariably appeared on balconies or platforms) and, as a military company might its commanding officer, saluted by song or gesture those to whom they would shortly grant authority. These gestures conveyed deference but not servile submissiveness. Democrats stood below McClellan just as they had a few years before as members of the Army of the Potomac. In this sense Little Mac was an ideal candidate, for, as recognized in Democratic song, "the pride of the nation's wars" had become "the hope of the nation's politics." "If [political] campaigns are in fact military affairs," concluded the *Caucasian,* "then generals are the best to lead them." So viewed, the national proclivity for transforming generals into presidential candidates was not so much a search for strong leaders as it was a substitution of icons. Acknowledging this exchange, Democrats produced etchings of McClellan over the legend, "If I cannot have command of my own men, then let me share their fate on the field of battle."[84]

The military metaphors and behaviors in this serenade conveyed the ideals of nineteenth-century militarism: that soldiers would be obedient in order to accomplish a mutual end. An address by the Democratic National Congressional Committee in 1864 described the process: "The great masses of men in a free country can act steadily and usefully only through some organism which combines their power and direction."[85] For Democrats the organism was a political army. Hence no one expected McClellan to speak on the issues, any more than generals analyzed tactics with their men on the eve of battle. But unlike the army, where elected officers were not subject to recall, the Democracy constantly acknowledged the source of its authority. As the faithful sang in Newark:

[83]*New York World,* 2 and 7 November 1864; Brummer, *Political History of New York,* p. 429; Coleman, *Election of 1868,* p. 261.

[84]Sidney Herbert, *McClellan Campaign Melodist* (Boston: Benjamin Russell, 1864); *Caucasian,* 10 September 1864.

[85]Members of the Thirty-eighth Congress, *Congressional Address* (Washington, D.C., 1864), p. 4.

Nothing for the People, but by the People
Nothing about the People, without the People.[86]

Only at the end of October did Democrats organize a more instrumental event—the mass rally. Its intention was to reach beyond the party fraternity and, by presenting complaints against the Republicans, recruit voters—whether apathetic or lapsed Democrats, disaffected Republicans, new voters or independents. The setting of these rallies varied, but of all the preparatory events these had the highest ratio of words to symbols. An Ohio meeting in 1864 was typical. Organized by the state's central committee and well advertised in local newspapers and broadsides, the rally in Columbus began at noon on Saturday with the introduction of a permanent chairman and fifteen vice-presidents nominated by the Committee on Arrangements. For the rest of the afternoon the crowd heard speeches by notables. Four years later a similar affair, marked by the same hierarchical organization, repeated criticism of Republicans and offered nonspecific proposals for the future. The enemy had not changed, although the arena of their transgressions had shifted southward. Whereas Democrats in 1864 charged their opponents (whom they rarely called by name) with trampling the liberties and privileges of white freemen, in 1868 Ohioan Allen Thurman held "black wools" responsible for violating Southern rights, introducing a costly and unnecessary military occupation, turning the white man's government into a black man's anarchy, and disrupting the economy. With the war over and opportunities for tyranny in the North reduced, Democrats focused more on economic affairs, but this shift in emphasis did not change the nature of partisan rallies, which recurred with increasing frequency as election day approached.[87]

Whether in New York's Union Square or a York, Pennsylvania, picnic grove, Democratic rallies transformed elections into issue-preference affairs, with voters encouraged to choose between leaders and platforms. After the martial images and rituals earlier in the campaign, the Democratic party now focused on principles. Yet preoccupation with criticism of the Republicans and haziness about specific programs still made it difficult for voters to choose for the future. Instead speakers reviewed the past, and complained about Lincoln. In 1868 the relationship of former Democrat Andrew Johnson to the Republicans made

[86]*Newark Democrat,* 13 October 1860.

[87]Thomas H. Smith, "The Peace Democratic Movement in Crawford County, Ohio" (Master's Thesis, Ohio State University, 1962); Roseboom, *Civil War Era,* p. 420.

this kind of disapproval difficult, but by substituting Congress and cabinet for president, Democrats attributed national difficulties to the likes of Thaddeus Stevens, Charles Sumner, and Edwin Stanton. These mass rallies, then, attempted to transform elections into a referendum on past policies, and voters were sometimes referred to as "Solomon Sober Second Thoughts."[88]

From this perspective, a campaign became a reaction to what had happened rather than a prospectus for what should. Accordingly, voters on election eve served as a jury about to render political sentence, a role recognized by Iowa Democrat Charles Mason, who concluded that "to refuse to vote would not be unlike a juryman refusing to give any decision in a case pending between two parties."[89] Democrats played on this theme and, in one pamphlet, brought Lincoln to the bar as a defendant charged with tyranny, extravagance, and negrophilism. Washington, Madison, and Clay served as judges, the people were the jury, and the results of the election provided the appropriate sentence: exile to Illinois.[90]

But to review the case against the defendant it was necessary to hear the speakers; rallies were quieter affairs than parades, at which even sharp-eared reporters were reduced to paraphrasing speeches. Separate stands provided a more intimate setting, and listeners interrupted with questions. The nonverbal language of ratification meetings, parades and serenades had encouraged members to think of themselves as a "solid column" ready to go to the polls; rallies provided the reason for the battle. By election eve partisan images disappeared as Old Hickory and Irish lutes gave way to the Stars and Stripes and goddess of liberty, and transparencies depicted the Constitution as an anchor and the Union as a ship. Party buttons, hats, and scarves as well as stiff collars imprinted with the likeness of Washington appeared, to be shared not just by Democrats but by all Americans.

In other nations parties distinguish themselves by emblems, which sometimes become so crucial that insurgent factions fight to control them. For example, when other parties adopted the yoked oxen in 1948, India's Congressional party sued to keep this emblem their exclusive

[88]The term appears in Kennedy, *Annals of Quodlibet,* p. ix; see also *Frank Leslie's Weekly,* 26 November 1864; S. L. M. Barlow to McClellan, 9 November 1864, McClellan Papers.

[89]For use of the expression "the people as a jury," see "Some Letters of Jesse D. Bright to William H. English," *Indiana Magazine of History* 30 (December 1934): 376; Diary of Charles Mason, entry for 9 November 1862, Mason Papers, Library of Congress.

[90]*Caucasian,* 3 September 1864; *The Trial of Abraham Lincoln by Great Statesmen of the Past: A Council of the Past on the Tyranny of the Present* (Baltimore: William Inness, 1864).

property.[91] But there was no such party-specific iconography in nineteenth-century America, and even today the donkey and elephant are more comic signs than charged symbols. Neither Democrats nor Republicans could take out a trademark on the eagle, the ship of state, Washington, or the goddess of liberty, and both parties depended on them in the final stage of their presidential campaigns.

Nor did colors serve to identify a party. Both Republicans and Northern Democrats embossed their envelopes, dyed their party uniforms, and decorated their speakers' stands in red, white, and blue. Neither were costumes nor accoutrements unique; imitating the Republicans, the Democrats held their 1864 national convention in a "wigwam"—an immense structure erected on Chicago's Michigan Avenue. Democrats and Republicans also shared places and tunes; by late October, Masonic and temperance halls, village and picnic groves changed hands nightly. Two days after a Republican rally, Democrats met in Titusville, New Jersey, on the hallowed ground where Washington had massed his troops before attacking the British during the revolution and there sang their version of the Republicans' "Father Abraham."

> Father Abraham we are coming,
> A long Pull, a strong Pull.
> Every Man to the Polls,
> We shall triumph.
>
> We are coming Abraham Lincoln,
> From mountain, wood and glen,
> We are coming Abraham Lincoln,
> With the ghosts of murdered men.[92]

The effect of this sharing was to make both parties into American institutions; whereas clubs, conventions, parades, and serenades isolated adherents, the Democracy's visual symbols were so universal and patriotic, so familiar and commonplace, as to return its members to the nation.

[91] Firth, *Symbols: Public and Private,* pp. 23–24. The best collection of such iconography is in the Smithsonian. For nineteenth-century renderings of the eagle, see Philip Isaacson, *The American Eagle* (Boston: New York Graphics, 1975).

[92] James Van Clef et al. to George McClellan, 15 September 1864, McClellan Papers; *New York World,* 7 November 1864; Albert Emerich, *Songs for the People: National Patriotic, Sentimental, Comic, and Naval Songs* (Philadelphia: J. L. Gibon, 1864); *Caucasian,* 18 October 1864; Earl Schenck Miers, *New Jersey and the Civil War* (Princeton: D. Van Nostrand, 1964), p. 76; Herbert, *McClellan Campaign Melodist,* p. 18.

Even the epithets with which Northern Democrats and Republicans libeled each other became, like the insults of childhood, permissible derogations. Democrats, believing the term *copperhead* an exaggeration that displayed their opponents' fanaticism, proudly used the emblem of a snake on their envelopes and caps. In a few communities Democrats even sent their children to school in butternut-colored clothes (a grayish-blue color associated with the Confederacy) fastened by Copperhead buttons. Democratic jokes turned the image against the Republicans:

> Why are copperheads more than Loyal Leagues?
> Because leaguers aren't worth a copper.

And the insult was incorporated into party song:

> Copperhead, copperhead, where are you going?
> I am climbing a tree to hear the cocks,
> Then tell me copperhead crowing,
> What do you see?
> Butternuts, butternuts thick as can be.
> Whole butternut now is the emblem of those
> Who stand by the Union, any traitor oppose,
> Aye the Treason of Sumner, of Seward and Chase,
> And all who adore the African race.[93]

Only candidates' faces served as exclusive badges. Occasionally Democrats used the rooster, and in 1868 this traditional symbol of watchfulness carried the slogan "No Negro Equality" in its beak. While Republicans countered with images of amputees and "bloody shirts," Democrats played on racial themes and placed black women on their wagons under the sign "The Republicans are fighting for us." In Indiana young girls in white marched under the banner "Save us from nigger husbands," and in 1868 Democrats circulated pictures of the "blacks who govern Louisiana."[94] But these were exceptions to the shared visual ground of flags, stars, stripes, eagles, liberty trees, goddesses of liberty, and the red, white, and blue.

[93]Song from *Caucasian,* 1 October 1864; W. Flogan to John A. Trimble, 2 December 1862, Allan Trimble Papers, Historical Society of Ohio, Columbus.

[94]*Frank Leslie's Weekly,* 17 September 1864; Silbey, *A Respectable Minority* (New York: W. W. Norton, 1977), p. 209; Rawley, *Race and Politics,* p. 167.

## *Delivering the Vote*
## 1864

Presidential politics depended on good weather, not only on election day but throughout the campaign. Repeatedly crowds overflowed town halls and meeting places, and outdoor politics was familiar to all nineteenth-century Americans. By late October most farmers had finished their harvest and could afford a half day or more at the polls. Even city voters who worked indoors sensed, in autumn, the approach of the year's end. November was thus an appropriate time for reviewing the regime and perhaps choosing a new one.

Tuesday, 8 November 1864, was rainy and cold throughout most of the North and Midwest (though not in the far West), weather that nineteenth-century politicians called "stay-at-home times."[95] But it did not keep Baltimorean William Preston away from the polls. A onetime congressional aspirant, Preston had helped organize his party's Saturday-before-election rally, and county Democrats had finished their six-months campaign by singing a cappella:

> Walk up and do your duty,
> As freemen at the polls.
> Victory then will crown your efforts,
> And the Tyrant will be overthrown.
> Cheer up for Little Mac and Pend
> And down with Lincoln's shoddy.

Broadsides on the large oak and elm trees and on the Towson Court House repeated the theme: "Close up Ranks." "Your country calls." "Are you prepared for Battle?" "Rally Freemen."[96] Such appeals demanded action, for Americans could not fulfill their civic functions at home. They must travel to the polls—in Preston's case over ten miles—and an electoral vocabulary full of visceral, active verbs impelled them

[95]Noah Brooks, *Recollections of Washington in Lincoln's Time* (Chicago: Triangle, 1971), p. 195.

[96]The Preston materials are from the William P. Preston Papers, Maryland Historical Society, Baltimore (hereafter cited as Preston Papers); *Baltimore County Advocate* (Towson), 12 October 1864; T. W. Bedford to James S. Morton, 3 August 1864, James Morton Papers, Library of Congress (hereafter cited as Morton Papers); Neal A. Brooks and Eric G. Rockel, *A History of Baltimore County* (Towson, Md.: Friends of the Towson Library, 1979), pp. 253–64. For a British traveler's description of voting, see E. S. Abdy, *Journal of a Residence and Tour in the United States of North America from April 1833 to October 1834* (New York: Negro Universities Press, 1969), 1: 1–4. Song from *Democratic Songs* (Baltimore: Inness, 1864), p. 3.

to do so. Hence Americans "cast" their ballots (never simply gave, placed, yielded, or bestowed them); they "worked" for the cause (did not just help). They "stood" or "lined up" as Democrats (were not or did not merely become Democrats); they "rallied" at the polls (did not just go there or attend an election).

Acting on his own advice, Preston appeared early at Baltimore County's Ninth Election District polls. Arranged on the wide veranda of the Smedley House in Govans, ticket windows would remain open until six in the evening and during that time would serve as the center for a milling, pushing, shouting crowd, far larger than the five hundred who actually voted. The informality of the setting—the roped-off steps, the hastily positioned tables of inspectors and clerks, the glass partition that served as a window, and even the wooden ballot box—was typical of nineteenth-century arrangements. Most Americans voted in the familiar setting of firehouses, markets, schoolhouses, stores, the porticoes of courthouses, and, in the West, where there were fewer public buildings, conveniently located private homes.[97] After the Civil War some reformers urged making district schools the national polling places,[98] but twentieth-century Americans continue to vote in diverse, unceremonious surroundings. Indeed, there could be no permanent temple for an event that, because it encapsulated the abstraction of democracy, depended on the camaraderie of an informal setting.

Like many other Democrats, Preston had already received his ballot from those responsible for distributing the thin, two-by-five-inch slips of white paper which resembled railroad tickets. In most communities a member of the local county or city executive committee with access to a press did the printing, sometimes in exchange for lucrative party contracts. To ensure privacy (and this generation stood somewhere between the colonial practice of viva voce voting and the Progressive ideal of a secret ballot), state law required that election tickets could not be printed on colored paper.[99] Preston knew firsthand the effects of transparent and striped ballots: during the 1850s Democrats and Know-Nothings had used them to identify and then intimidate voters in one-party wards. Laws did not end the practice, and in 1868 the red, white, and blue of the American flag showed through the transparent paper of

[97]*Covode Investigation*, p. 78.

[98]E. J. Ward, *The Schoolhouse as the Polling Place* (Washington, D.C.: U.S. Board of Education, 1913).

[99]Evitts, *A Matter of Allegiances;* Election Tickets, Graphics Collection, Maryland Historical Society; Collection of Political Memorabilia in Nutler's Election House, Political Museum, Fruitland, Md.

A POLLING-PLACE AMONG THE "UPPER TEN."

A POLLING-PLACE AMONG THE "LOWER TWENTY."—SEE PRECEDING PAGE.

Two polling places in New York City, 1864. From the *Illustrated London News*, 3 December 1864.

Republican tickets in many Maryland communities. But in 1864 Preston's ticket was an anonymous white; only when unfolded did it reveal its partisanship and then not by its engraved image—a harassed eagle holding the shield of the United States, the same image used by Republican Unionists. Below this were the legend "the Democratic ticket," the names of the candidates, and the names of the electors who would actually cast Maryland's electoral vote.

Like party members themselves, Democratic tickets were a varied lot. In other Northern communities, some carried the profile of the party's presidential candidates; others included, as would Preston's in 1868, an engraving of Jackson and the tree of liberty. Local circumstances usually dictated the choice of decoration, and because there was no reason to draw attention to McClellan in Maryland (many Democrats believed him responsible for the arrest of the state's legislators in 1861), no ballots were engraved with his image.[100] Preston's ticket, like most, had neither slogan nor motto, for by election day, parties did not need to remind voters of their policies. Like most Americans, Preston carried two separate tickets, one for president and one for congress, and in physical expression of the structure of his government he would deliver both to the election judge. Had he forgotten his tickets, replacements were available either from the hawkers who crowded close to the windows or from the flimsy booths erected nearby.

Preston did not have to wait long to vote. It was still early—the polls had opened at nine o'clock—and, unlike voting districts in larger cities and towns, where as many as four thousand men assembled and were separated into rows by wobbly fences, Preston's district had only seven hundred registered voters. Nor was he forced to take an oath, although there had been rumors that the federal provost marshal would require Democrats to swear that they had never expressed "a desire for the triumph of rebel armies." Three years before, in a local election, Preston had protested such interference and had told friends he would not make any "additional declaration." Earlier in the summer he had presented himself before the registering clerks, and, in a procedure used in most American communities, his name had been entered on an official register, then transferred to a poll book. Now, as he stood below the election judge, he identified himself: William Preston of Pleasant Plains (a designation necessary to differentiate him from another William Preston). At this point election clerks (in Maryland appointed by county commissioners, in other states by police commissioners or boards of elections)

[100] *Proceedings of Democratic National Convention*, pp. 28–33, 39.

checked their poll books. By law officials first marked off the names of voters, then in another column made a straight mark under the candidate's name. "Let your information be accurate,"[101] enjoined election manuals. Because he was listed on the books, Preston did not have to take an oath, administered by the election judge, that he had been born in the United States or had been naturalized and that he had resided six months in the county and twelve in Maryland. Next, as in a commercial transaction, Preston handed his tickets through the window to the election official, who inserted them in the large wooden dry-goods box whose contents, at the end of the day, would represent the public voice of his district.

Designed with considerable ingenuity, nineteenth-century ballot boxes sometimes had false bottoms where ballots could be stored, later to be mixed with legal tickets. To prevent such fraud, New Yorkers used glass cylinders that as they filled with ballots reminded Samuel Cox of "political snowflakes."[102] In a few communities, preelection festivities included a parade in which the ballot box was transported from courthouse to polling place on a wagon attended by city officials, but Baltimore County held no such ceremony.[103]

For Preston—and all the nine million citizens who cast ballots in 1864 and 1868—the process of voting expressed both the limits of their authority and the proper relation of citizens to the regime. Voters acted out a transfer of authority as they stood in line on a first-come, first-served basis, dissevered from party connections, group affiliations, or class status—wheat farmers alongside small town druggists; dry-goods merchants from the county's crossroads; landowners and their tenants; fervent Democrats along with Republicans and Know-Nothings; Lutherans, Methodists, and Catholic beside the unchurched; the rich with the poor. Homogeneity was sexual and racial; social inequalities were temporarily suspended. At the polls an assembly stood whose physical action linked them to their government at the same time that it legitimized the winners.

Suspended on election day was the understanding, cultivated during

[101]Joseph Harris, *The Registration of Voters in the United States* (Washington, D.C.: Brookings Institute, 1929); Baltimore's Registry Law, "An Act to Guard against Fraud," n.d., n.p.; quotation from Register Books, 1848; both in Baltimore City Archives; Poll Lists, Augustus Bradford Papers, 1865, Maryland Historical Society, Baltimore.

[102]*Congressional Globe*, 41st Cong., 2d sess., 398. For a typical nineteenth-century ballot box, see the collection at the Hunterdon County Historical Society, Flemington, N.J. For other descriptions, Allan Blakeley to J. S. Morton, 10 December 1860, Morton Papers.

[103]Ward, *Schoolhouse as Polling Place*.

the campaign, that Democrats were soldiers in an army. Preston had not arrived at the polls with other Democrats, although he had spent the fall with them. At the critical moment he was alone, an individual about to exercise free choice; if his decision was to be the reasoned reflection that classic democratic theory required, Preston must be separated from his party. Thus the procedures of American voting diluted the group solidarity built up during the campaign and reduced post-election tensions among partisans. In casting their vote, the people became the sum of its individuals, not of its groups.

Well before 1864, parties had tamed the practice of voting by controlling nominations, framing issues, and leading campaigns. During the colonial period the less passive, community-oriented system of viva voce balloting prevailed; and for a brief time after the revolution, citizens had written the names of their choices on blank tickets. But gradually parties provided ballots to voters, although at first some election judges considered printed tickets illegal. In Massachusetts, for example, they were challenged in the 1830s as interfering with "private decisions." But a decade later the issue was settled, and Preston, like other voters, stood before the judges with a ballot created and paid for by his political organization.[104] Although he had had more to do with its form than did most Democrats, his participation was limited. So too was the physical act of voting: like most Americans, Preston did not cast his ballot personally, but delivered it to a public official—a surrogate for those who would later govern. This official, after calling his name to the clerk to see if "Preston, William" was on the registry, had the power to decide whether to accept his vote. Preston had no way of knowing whether the official actually placed his ticket in the ballot box and later counted it, but his part in the procedure was now complete. A barrier—in Preston's case rendered tangible both by the voting window and by the election officials who actually placed the ballot in the box—curbed his participation.

Another way to interpret nineteenth-century voting and its symbolic meaning is to consider alternatives. Preston could have met fellow Democrats and marched with them to the polls. He could have stayed home, his vote tallied by traveling canvassers who recorded his political choices as census takers did his address, age, occupation, and wealth. Or

[104]Spencer Albright, *The American Ballot* (Washington, D.C.: American Council on Public Affairs, 1942), pp. 19–20; Michel Brunet, "The Secret Ballot Issue in Massachusetts Politics from 1851 to 1853," *New England Quarterly* 25 (September 1952): 354–62.

he could have inserted his own ballot, thereby achieving a firmer sense of his authority.

Having cast his ballot, Preston joined other voters around the polls, sharing this day with neighbors he sometimes saw only on election days. The hotel's bar was closed, as was the nearby tavern, for it was widely believed in mid-century America that whiskey and free will did not mix. Instead groups of men and boys played cards, wagered on the outcome (although such betting was against Maryland law), ate the special election cakes, and, in Preston's case, served as poll watchers. Most voters had preregistered and were therefore included in the window list, but should an unlisted voter appear, judges examined his qualifications by oath. As a watcher Preston intended to challenge any soldiers who were not residents of the community, for he had read in October that Massachusetts units had voted in Indiana. In this activity he was serving his party's injunction "to stand by the polls until the box is closed." In late afternoon Preston rode into Baltimore, there to join a growing crowd in front of the newspaper offices. No one expected to know the results on election night, and the desultory process of gathering returns—as well as the long hiatus before presidential electors cast their ballots in January and the president took office in March—made it difficult to consider elections as policy referendums. Because they were verdicts on the past—in the words of a party song, "Forget not the past, by it be your votes cast"—there was no need for immediate verification. Voting was a blunt instrument, and victors did not expect prompt reward. As he rode home, Preston did not know who had won, and the nonpartisan songs that accompanied the reading of the results and that helped restore unity gave him no clue.[105]

## 1868

Four years later, William Preston repeated this performance. Although peacetime had dispelled differences over how and whether to fight the South, war-inherited controversies over the Negro and the

[105] *Wingate's Register* (Maryland, 1864); House, 38th Cong., *Cases of Contested Elections in Congress from 1834 to 1865* (Washington, D.C.: Government Printing Office, 1865), p. 153; William Preston to Meg, 10 November 1864; Preston diary, 1864, both in Preston Papers. Maryland House of Delegates, *Committee on Elections in Relation to Contested Elections,* Document Y, February 27, 1860, House Documents; Broadside Collection, Smithsonian; Samuel Barlow to George McClellan, 9 November 1864, McClellan Papers; Herbert, *McClellan Campaign Melodist,* p. 10; Emerich, *Songs for the People; Baltimore Sun,* 9 November 1864. The election cake was a popular form of pound cake usually baked the weekend before the election.

South still focused partisan attention. Northern Democrats in 1868 concentrated on the economy, specifically the issue of how to redeem government war bonds. (The national platform equivocated on the issue, approving the rapid payment of the public debt "where obligations of the government do not expressly state upon their face, or the law under which they were issued does not provide, that they shall be paid in coin" but saying nothing about national bank notes.)[106] Many issues were similar to those in 1864: Democrats criticized their opponents for a costly and unnecessary occupation of the South and repeated their charges (now somewhat attenuated in heavily black areas) that Republicans intended to turn a white man's government into a black-controlled dictatorship of miscegenators. In Maryland there were special circumstances; a new constitution had expunged postwar loyalty oaths, and Preston expected a full turnout of voters to return the state to the Democracy.

Although some concerns had altered, the procedures of presidential voting had not. Democrats repeated the rituals that bound their members into an army soon to do battle for Seymour, Pendleton, and the Democracy. In late fall they "called out the people" through the traditional episodes—ratification meetings, parades, and rallies—referred to as "the people's awakening."[107] Finally, on election day, Democrats participated in the battle of ballots.

Even before he voted, Preston expected that Seymour would lose, not Maryland or Baltimore County, but the nation. Like many Democrats, he had begun a process of reconciliation in late October, when the apocalyptic, end-of-the-republic-if-they-are-elected tone disappeared from his letters and speeches and gave way to practical comments on how to attract votes. Throughout the country, differences essential in reinforcing partisanship and activating the indifferent were deflated, and although early in the campaign Preston had believed the Union depended on a Democratic victory—"we must carry it or perish"—by late October he had found some points of similarity with Republicans, mostly on currency matters. Preston was aided in his retreat by local newspapers, especially the *Baltimore County Advertiser,* which, after highlighting partisan controversy throughout the year, in

[106]*Official Proceedings of the Democratic National Convention* (New York, 1868); Coleman, *Election of 1868,* pp. 200–05.

[107]Clement Vallandigham often used this expression. See Vallandigham to Alexander de Boys, 1 September 1863, Alexander De Boys Papers, Ohio Historical Society, Columbus; N.C. Goodwin to George McClellan, 21 September 1864, McClellan Papers.

early November rediscovered foreign affairs, sentimental fiction, and holiday recipes.[108]

Preston's forecast was correct. Democrats lost their third presidential election in a row, but the party's military idiom softened his disappointment. Like other partisans, he believed that the Democracy had lost a battle, not the war, and that after a break in the fighting, punctuated only by local skirmishes, the contest would resume in 1872. Because victory celebrations were rare, it was easy to forget the election, and although both parties traditionally awarded banners to their strongest wards and districts, the occasion did not perpetuate rivalry. Overnight the physical signs of voting disappeared. After the polls closed, officials carried away its simple accoutrements: the Bibles, registers, poll books, sheets of foolscap, and ballot boxes. Hotel employees promptly removed tables and chairs, ticket window and railings. Even the flimsy booths from which Democratic peddlers had dispensed their ballots were easily dismantled. Ephemeral as the railroad tickets they resembled, ballots were destroyed. Most leases for rented party rooms ended before the election on the last day of October, and for Preston as for other Democrats it was easier to remember what had been shared—the campaign procedures, political leaders, public concern, meeting space and national iconography—than what had divided. Democrats could console themselves by looking forward to 1872, and the recursive nature of voting reduced partisan tensions. "Time," a loyal Democrat wrote to Horatio Seymour, "will give us all we ask and have a right to through Ballot Boxes."[109]

Although voting served as act of consent for most Northern Democrats, a few refused to accept the outcome. Such reactions were largely rhetorical: in 1864 New Jersey congressman A. J. Rogers insisted the returns were "forged" and announced that he would travel to New York for news of McClellan's victory. In Ohio Democrats cheered the mixed metaphors of future congressman Allen Thurman—"We will baptize these ballot boxes in blood." Most of those not ready to accept the results gave fraud as the reason, and charges of unfair elections made it easier for Democrats to accept their loss. As Horatio Seymour explained, "A majority of the people are with us when they can act freely," and Democrats comforted themselves by believing in both 1864 and 1868 that they had a majority of the votes cast by "freemen." Such

[108]Preston diary, 1868; Preston to Meg, 18 October 1868; both in Preston Papers.
[109]Daniel Tieman to Horatio Seymour, 7 January 1863, Seymour-Fairchild Papers.

rationalizations were a time-gathering, face-saving mechanism, and charges of cheating provided a partisan safety-valve. In 1864, after Republican judges had thrown out votes from Baltimore County's second district because Southern sympathizers had voted, Preston insisted that Lincoln's victory was "stolen" and considered himself the victim of federal intimidation. In 1863 he described the invasion of his rights:

> We had not proceeded far before we met a couple of our neighbors who dispirited, disapproving and alarmed were returning from the polls and said that the polls were in possession of the military. . . . the polls were surrounded by armed men, soldiers with weapons and miserable low background, wearing badges designated as U.S. marshals. I at once concluded that to put my name on the poll-books under such circumstances would be to sanction the most flagrant and infamous outrage.

On this occasion military interference replaced what in earlier decades had been explained by other forms of misconduct, and the extensive American vocabulary of election misbehaviors—floaters, repeaters, padded lists, stuffers, and cooping—revealed a habitual need to alibi defeat.[110]

Sometimes elections really were stolen, although it is impossible to measure the extent of illegal voting in 1864, 1868, or in any other presidential contest. Yet the issue remains an important one, for it renders suspicious nineteenth-century voting returns. Certainly both contemporary informants and present-day observers consider bribery a more or less permanent component of American politics; one nineteenth-century Northern Democrat was so discouraged by its extent that when describing his paradise, he offered a national election that was "conducted with harmony and decorum where each elector determined for himself for what candidate to vote." One yardstick of corruption—the contested elections brought before Congress—suggests fraud was not extensive. Of the 16,000 congressional elections held from 1789 through 1916, only 214 were contested as unfair due to bribery and intimidation, and in only 90 of these did the House take action, applying the standard that "nothing but the most unequivocal evidence can destroy the credit of official returns."[111] Elections, like suspects in criminal cases, were innocent until proven otherwise.

[110] *Newark Democrat,* 9 November 1864; *Caucasian,* 9 November 1864; *Proceedings of New Jersey Historical Society* 78 (1969): 25; Brooks and Rockel, *History of Baltimore County;* William Preston to Madge, 1863, Preston Papers.

[111] "Honest Democrats, Read This," Broadside Collection, Flemington County Histor-

The problem of fraudulent voting is partly one of definition. Given the understanding that a coerced vote was an illegal one, any undue influence contaminated the ballot. Therefore, returns from company towns in which employers controlled their workers' votes were as meaningless as those from districts in which free drinks, free rides, and false campaign documents affected voting choice. On one level such fraud emerges as a lapse between theory and practice, intention and reality. On another, it becomes a historical problem aggravated when new groups are assimilated into the political system. But when voting is considered as a master symbol of political values and attitudes, its violation becomes implicit in its exercise. The bias that placed republican citizens on alert promptly produced predators, and the militant behaviors encouraged before election sometimes resulted in election-day contests as bloody as Civil War battles. It was impossible, given the meaning of elections, to prevent this. If voting was to demonstrate the people's will, it could not be too far removed from its plebeian roots. To fashion a formal, controlled performance of civil rectitude, to create special places for its practice, and to provide sufficient policing would have destroyed the fraternal pageantry that made elections popular nineteenth-century rituals. This is what Congressman Cox meant when he referred to "electoral licentiousness" as an "alloy of liberty."[112] For Northern Democrats like William Preston, charges of fraud rationalized the past and provided hope for the future.

Thus presidential elections before, during, and after 1864 and 1868 were more than a constitutional means of delegating authority, picking a national leader, and determining public policies. Because the election process involved a series of expressive actions and hidden agendas, its ceremonies summarized the values, attitudes, postures, and behaviors of nineteenth-century Americans. Like the abstractions that pervaded religious services, concepts like popular sovereignty, legitimate authority, and delegated power came alive for Northern Democrats through campaigning and voting. Central to this process was the militaristic vocabulary; though different from eighteenth-century mechanisms, which instilled deference, the idiom nonetheless transmitted a sense of compliance. Never a seismograph of issue-related choice, voting was feeling, instinct, and behavior, and participation in its nineteenth-cen-

---

ical Society, Flemington, N.J.; *Congressional Globe,* 40th Cong., 2d sess., app., pp. 327, 354; ibid., 41st Cong., 2d sess., app., pp. 397–99; 38th Cong., *Cases of Contested Elections;* Jones, *Right of Suffrage,* p. 212.

[112] *Congressional Globe,* 41st Cong., 2d sess., app., p. 397.

tury rituals was never an act of unrestrained power. Nor was the equality of election day anything more than a temporary condition. But because elections brought Americans together in celebrations that began as a display of difference and ended in consent and the conveyance of power, they provided an adaptive mechanism that proved all the more essential in threatening times.

After presidential elections, partisan differences became less strident but did not disappear. Within the ceremony itself, there was an unresolved counterpoint between the mobilization themes of preelection pole raisings, serenades, rallies, and parades and the passive practices of balloting. The domination of campaigns by a few leaders also contradicted the transient equality of election day, and the ideal of free choice by freemen ran counter to party discipline and the acceptance of fraud and violence. Today, shorn of their symbolic incongruities, presidential elections have lost their nonrational meaning—and hence, it might be argued, most of their appeal.

CHAPTER 8

# *Southern Connections and Party Nationalism*

In the years before the Civil War one way to express nationalism was to be a Democrat. Some Americans still suspected political parties of subversion, but by mid-century the Democracy had emerged as an institution through which citizens could celebrate devotion to their country and at the same time favor particular programs, leaders, and ideals. No longer was partisanship considered antirepublican. On the contrary, its nature tended to evoke sentiment for the Union and thus forced Southern separatists like John Calhoun and William Yancey to attempt a replacement.[1] In the North, however, the Democracy continued to inspire unity. "The Democracy is national: it is America, it embraces the continent. It is universal and catholic," explained the *Democratic Review*. For believers, attending rallies, marching in parades, and voting the ballots of this self-designated "great national party embracing the American people" aroused patriotic sentiment. Party banners made the connection: "Our Democratic party stands for America"; "Our whole country, the Democracy, and the Constitution."[2]

Transforming the Democracy into a patriotic instrument had taken more than official exhortations from leaders to silent listeners. In the mid-nineteenth century, it depended on a fusion of community and party through activities that employed American symbols as objects of Democratic devotion. Not only did Washington's Birthday and July Fourth provide the occasions for turning national spirit into partisan channels; in every state Democrats also chose local holidays such as Defender's Day in Maryland, Fort Duquesne Day in Pittsburgh, and

[1]William Cooper, *The South and the Politics of Slavery, 1828–1856* (Baton Rouge: Louisiana State University Press, 1979), pp. 107, 288.

[2]*United States and Democratic Review* 5 (October 1855): 345 (hereafter cited as *Democratic Review*); James Raymond, *Political; or, The Spirit of the Democracy in '56* (Baltimore: John W. Woods, 1850), p. 72.

Founder's Day in Illinois for party rallies. "Let us meet," advised one regular, "on days clustering with memories sacred to American patriots."[3] Earlier, such events had been arranged by town fathers and militia officers and as a result had no partisan entitlement. But gradually Democrats came to sponsor celebrations that fused loyalty to their organization with devotion to country. By mid-century Americans might never meet an official from Washington, but they could hardly avoid a partisan from the Democracy.

Nowhere was this conjunction of party and nation more evident than in New York's Tammany Hall, where a huge bust of George Washington presided over a meeting room decorated with red, white, and blue bunting, American flags, and the seal of the United States. In a physical setting redolent with Americanism, Democrats began their Fourth of July celebrations with "The Star Spangled Banner," followed by recitations of "An Ode to America" and Drake's popular "Address to the American Flag." Ceremonies usually concluded with a cappella renditions of "Democracy and the Nation" and "The Bonnie Old Flag." Along with party business, members listened to Washington's Farewell Address, the first half of the Declaration of Independence, and toasts to "America the Beautiful," "Constitution—the Sheet Anchor of the Union," and "Our Democracy." On July Fourth in 1858, after adopting resolutions supporting Buchanan and the LeCompton Constitution, Democrats heard Caleb Cushing's hour-long oration on "Our Country—Nature's Whole Heaven on Earth." In this inescapably nationalistic atmosphere, partisans felt like Americans while behaving as Democrats, and such experiences encouraged members to believe, as Marylander William Coad did, "that upon the success of the Democracy depends the preservation of union, liberty, and constitution." As a result, those nineteenth-century Northerners who were exposed to politics came to see parties as natural links between citizen and state, and in time this feeling spawned today's conviction that any decline in party interest signals a faltering national spirit.[4]

In different ways, all nineteenth-century political parties wrapped

[3]David Croly, *Seymour and Blair: Their Lives and Services* (New York: Richardson, 1868), p. 48.

[4]*Tammany Society, or the Columbian Order, Annual Celebration, July 4, 1863* (New York: Baptist and Taylor, 1863), p. 4; Allan Franklin, *The Trail of the Tiger* (n.p., 1928); *Speech of Senator Douglas at the Democratic Celebration at Independence Square, Philadelphia, July 4, 1854; Oration of the Honorable Caleb Cushing, July 4, 1858* (New York: Baptist and Taylor, 1858); Jean H. Baker, *The Politics of Continuity: Maryland Political Parties, 1858–1870* (Baltimore: Johns Hopkins University Press, 1973), p. 13.

themselves in the flag. But in the case of the Democrats, their party's relationship to the South became a means of exhibiting patriotism. Three views of this association emerged during the nineteenth century. At first more attitude than behavior, the prewar Democratic image depicted a Unionist institution that included Southerners long after other institutions had divided on regional issues. To belong to such an organization was one way for all Americans to proclaim devotion to the United States. During the war Democrats established their nationalism as Union soldiers. Although they had special reasons not to, they joined the army to restore the object of their allegiance—the Union. Whereas including Southerners as part of the Democratic (and therefore American) family demonstrated love of country before the war, fighting the Confederacy (Northern Democrats rarely called it the South) served the same function during the war. Thus, despite the Republican effort to divide their opponents into loyal and disloyal factions, the Democrats retained a sense of themselves as patriots because of, not despite, their affiliation, and this understanding helped them survive their years as "copperheads." Finally, after the war, the Democratic conviction that the Southern states should be returned to the Union immediately and unconditionally provided a third expression of the party's nationalism. All three versions were based on the Northern Democracy's relationship to the South, and all three displayed an essential component of the party at mid-century—its Americanness.

Considering themselves nationalists, Democrats invariably portrayed their opponents as particularists, representing not the whole American people, but some special, usually privileged, part of them. In Democratic eyes, first the Federalists and then the Whigs appeared as associations of the rich—"a monopoly," according to one Democrat, "of the old aristocracy promising us roast-beef, but feeding us on the shadow of beef-steak."[5] In the 1840s, when Whigs won two presidential elections and it became necessary to explain how the wellborn few had somehow increased to become a popular majority, Democrats argued that election results demonstrated what they had always suspected—the power of money and influence over the people's choice. Not only had Whigs bought votes, but "moneyed corporations" had used "subtle devices, tricks, pompous exhibitions, pictures, and secret organizations" during elections. Stephen Douglas supposed that the Whigs' political weight had always been found "in the scale adverse to the popular will and those measures approved by public opinion. They

[5]*Democratic Review* 3 (November 1854): 442.

have ever courted the influence of wealth rather than the just appropriation of the people."[6]

Similarly, Democrats condemned workingmen's associations as special-interest groups whose preoccupation with the workplace made them inattentive to general affairs and rendered their supporters deficient as citizens. Such a mentality blinded the Democrats to class interests, although their indifference to the economic and social differences between the middle and working classes (but not between producer and nonproducer, working and leisured, "the People" and the aristocracy) explains the economic diversity of their following.[7] Even the Know-Nothings, who took the official name American party as their claim to patriotism, were accused of favoring a particular religion and birthplace. They were, according to Democrats, "the secret enclave of the Anglo-Saxon race and the Protestant religion."[8] In the 1850s, when the Republicans were their principal opponents, Democrats accused that party of representing one section of the Union—New England; one religion—Puritanism; and one interest group—antislaveryism. Such particularism challenged the Democratic vision of a harmonious society, free of artificial restraint and operating as a political counterpart of the economy.

On the other hand, because the Democracy considered itself to include all Americans, its followers were part of what one Northern Democrat called "the genius of our government and the great body of the people"—the latter a collection of the "industrious, honest, manly, intelligent millions of free men," made up of small landholders, tenant farmers, urban workers, artisans, and proprietors as well as lawyers, bankers, merchants, and manufacturers. This preoccupation with a universal following of atomized individuals in contrast with their opponents' dependence on special-interest groups embodied what the *New York Evening Post* called "the spirit of harmony . . . essential to a republican form of government."[9] Unlike its opponents, the distinctive feature of the Democracy was to have no enemies, and thereby to enact the national motto "out of many, one."

In fact the mid-century Democracy was a collection of ethnic and religious groups as well as a coalition of states, and from today's per-

[6]Robert W. Johannsen, ed., *Letters of Stephen A. Douglas* (Urbana: University of Illinois Press, 1961), p. 44.

[7]For one analysis of this party culture, see Allan Dawley, *Class and Community* (Cambridge, Mass.: Harvard University Press, 1976), pp. 65, 70, 99, 205, 219.

[8]Raymond, *Political,* pp. 30–31, 54–55.

[9]*New York Evening Post,* 20 April 1844; *Democratic Review* 1 (October 1837): 1, 2, 7.

spective its commitment to state authority seems to compromise its nationalism. But before the Civil War few Americans considered nation and state as antagonists. By placing final authority in the people, Democrats could support states rights as a necessary protection of diversity, at the same time that they celebrated the Union as an expression of their holism. Recently students of nationalism have discovered that devotion to the modern state is indeed comprised of layers of affection—to county, to church, and perhaps, according to Morton Grodzins, to pinochle clubs.[10] For nineteenth-century Democrats, this spiral of overlapping loyalties had been installed by the Constitution, the Tenth Amendment, and the Virginia and Kentucky Resolutions. "The fathers of the Constitution," James Buchanan admonished in 1867,

> justly believed that the harmony and efficiency of our system could not be preserved without preserving the recognized powers of the Federal and State governments as distinct and independent of each other. They dreaded lest the vast powers and influence conferred upon the Federal governments from the instinct of all governments to increase their own authority, might be perverted to injure the weaker party and usurp the reserved rights of the states. . . . They knew it would be impossible for one Central Government to provide for the ever-varying wants and interests of separate peoples of different lineage, laws, and customs scattered over many states. Consolidation, they knew, would produce extensive corruption among the hosts of officers and agents necessarily employed in conducting a vast concern, a squandering of the public money, a disregard of economy vital in a Republic, and consequently ever increasing taxation. Hence has proceeded the much and unjustly abused doctrine of state rights which is now and must ever be, an essential principle of the Democratic party.

More succinctly, the *Democratic Review* explained that the party sought "the continuous prosperity of the glorious whole of the glorious parts."[11]

But Northern Democrats did not extend their protection of diversity to what they condemned as the "isms" of abolition, free soil, socialism, women's rights, sectionalism, and vegetarianism.[12] By definition, "one-ideaism" threatened patriotism in a way that loyalty to the states could

[10]Morton Grodzins, *The Loyal and the Disloyal: Social Boundaries of Patriotism and Treason* (Chicago: University of Chicago Press, 1956); David Potter, *The South and Sectional Conflict* (Baton Rouge: Louisiana State University Press, 1956), p. 29.

[11]John Bassett Moore, ed., *The Works of James Buchanan,* vol. II (Philadelphia: Lippincott, 1910), pp. 440–41; *Democratic Review* 5 (October 1855): 345.

[12]For a listing of the "isms," see *Democratic Review* 5 (October 1855): 345, and 3 (November 1854): 386, 442, 443.

not. In the latter case the commitment was a historical condition that, given its physical distinctness, did not threaten the republic because the part was of the whole, whereas the former, neither inherent nor natural, might unite in an artificial organization that eventually controlled the government.

To its geographic inclusiveness (Democrats of the 1850s invariably pledged themselves on behalf of "equality of rights and privileges for all citizens and sections") the party added an expansive nationalism. By the 1850s its local, state, and national platforms contained aggressive statements on Cuba, an interoceanic canal, Canada, and Mexico. At a time when Whigs (and, later, Republicans) viewed the enlargement of the United States as a threat to national integrity, Democrat Daniel Voorhees argued the opposite. "The expansion of the Republic," held the Indianan, "is a natural law of its healthy existence." "The time has come," agreed Democrats in their 1856 national convention, "to apply the nation's moral influence to questions of the foreign policy of this country which are inferior to no domestic policy whatever."[13] Such pledges repeated priorities set in the 1840s, and despite the historical attention paid to the young Americans—a clique of spread-eagling enthusiasts which included John O'Sullivan and Stephen Douglas—most Democrats agreed that Great Britain should abide by the Monroe Doctrine and abandon its outposts in Central and South America and that the United States should attain exclusive control over an interoceanic canal and ascendancy in the Gulf of Mexico. When the party divided in 1860, both the Douglas and Breckinridge factions concurred on the necessity of acquiring Cuba.[14] Whether or not this empire-rattling diverted attention from slavery, it did convey an image of the Democratic party as a patriotic organization.

The merger of party and country was further strengthened by Democratic language and advertisements of its presidential candidates. Throughout the nineteenth century the party stood for "the People," who were Democrats because they were democrats. "It is the logical sequitur of all political reasoning," concluded John O'Sullivan, who aptly named his periodical *The United States Magazine and Democratic Review*.[15] Not only did "standing for the People" distinguish the De-

[13]Daniel W. Voorhees, *The American Citizen* (Terre Haute, Ind.: R. H. Simpson, 1860)p. 32. See also Kirk H. Porter and Donald B. Johnson, ed., *National Party Platforms, 1840–1972* (Urbana: University of Illinois Press, 1956), pp. 11, 16, 24.

[14]Robert W. Johannsen, *Stephen A. Douglas* (New York: Oxford University Press, 1973), p. 216.

[15]*Democratic Review* 5 (December 1855); 468.

mocracy's expansive Americanness from its opponents' sectarianism; Democrats capitalized the noun for two other reasons: first, because they meant by it a mass of individuals who summed to a national entity correctly designated by a proper noun; and second, because they were referring to "sovereigns" who governed themselves and who therefore merited, like any king or president, the distinction of capitalization.[16] And believing themselves the collective embodiment of all, not just some, Americans, they were swift to claim credit for the Union-healing compromises of their past: the New Jersey Plan of 1787, the Missouri Compromise of 1820, and even the Compromise of 1850—although in the last case they exaggerated the contributions of Stephen Douglas and neglected those of Henry Clay.

Not only did the Democracy claim responsibility for the important compromises of American history, but they invariably offered their candidates as national men without special allegiance to section, profession, or economic group. In 1852 Franklin Pierce asked his campaign biographer, Nathaniel Hawthorne, "to make him a man for the whole country," and perhaps only a master of fiction could so successfully have transformed the parochial New Hampshire lawyer into an American Adam. Hawthorne nationalized Pierce by concentrating on the candidate's familial ties to the heroes of the revolution and the War of 1812 as well as Pierce's own service in the Mexican-American War, which, though it lasted only nine months, occupied one-fifth of this biography. Not only was Pierce's "intercourse with Jackson frequent and free," but without loving New England less "he loved the country more . . . because his sentiments [of Americanism] had begun by the hearth."[17] Four years later, election-year biographers had an easier time making Buchanan into a national figure; they focused on his service as a soldier in the Battle of Baltimore in 1814, as a congressman and senator in Washington during the 1830s and 1840s, and as ambassador to Great Britain. In various ways, Democratic candidates were delivered to voters as men of the country who, if they had not been in the public service, nonetheless had a special understanding of the nation. New York's Horatio Seymour, the party's candidate in 1868, had "roamed yearly over the prairies of the far west, penetrated the wilds of the upper and lower Mississippi, and is almost as familiarly known to the hardy

[16]Yehoshua Arieli, *Individualism and Nationalism in American Ideology* (Baltimore: Penguin Books, 1964), p. 38.

[17]Richard Robey, ed., *The Life of Franklin Pierce by Nathaniel Hawthorne* (New York: Garrett Press, 1970), pp. iv, 28, 32; Democratic National Committee, *Sketches of the Lives of Franklin Pierce and Wm. R. King* (n.d., n.p.).

inhabitants of Minnesota, Wisconsin, and Nebraska as to the citizens of his own New York."[18] In contrast, opponents had special ties—Harrison and Taylor to the military, Fillmore to "secret societies," and Lincoln to antislavery organizations and ideas.

Opposition parties did not willingly surrender their own claims to patriotism, and Whigs, Know-Nothings, and especially Republicans charged the Democracy with serving its own version of particularism, specifically with granting the South most-favored-region status. "A geographical party," according to Republicans, the Democrats had abandoned their sectional neutrality in the 1840s and, held hostage by their voting majorities below the Mason-Dixon line, took the Southern position on every issue from Texas annexation to Kansas constitutions. Republicans also noted that Northern and Southern Democrats had close personal ties, and they complained that "fireaters" like Pierre Soulé had the ear of Pierce and that Buchanan appointed a predominantly Southern cabinet. Far from being the impartial institution of American nationalism, Democrats appeared to their opponents as the puppets of the slavocracy, with even Stephen Douglas following a prosouthern course during the Kansas-Nebraska controversy. These charges of favoritism became explicit in the 1860 Republican resolution that "the present Democratic administration has far exceeded our worst apprehensions in its measureless subserviency to the exactions of a sectional interest."[19]

This alleged Southern prejudice of the Democracy has become an enduring (and unexamined) legend. Its accuracy is hard to measure. What is important here is the Democrats' view of themselves as a patriotic organization, no more prosouthern than prowestern or antinorthern. In Caleb Cushing's words, "We are a political association which at both ends of the country, North and South, courageously and conscientiously assumes the burden of nationality in defiance of local jealousies and prejudices and which alone professes a consistent political course and follows a constitutional theory of action."[20]

The South demonstrated Cushing's point. For a time both Whigs and Democrats had drawn roughly equal support from that region, in a

[18]*James Buchanan and John Breckinridge* (Cincinnati: H. W. Derby, 1852), p. 78 and passim; quotation from Croly, *Seymour and Blair,* p. 15; Moore, *Works of Buchanan,* 2: 12, 15–21; Johannsen, *Letters of Douglas,* p. 495.

[19]Quoted in Porter and Johnson, *National Party Platforms,* p. 32; for the boarding assignments of one Congress, see *The Congressional Directory of the Third Session of the Twenty-fifth Congress* (n.p.: 1838) William Allen Papers, Library of Congress.

[20]*Oration of Caleb Cushing,* p. 16.

voting balance that was characteristic of the second-party system. But by the 1850s only the Democrats had substantial followings in every part of the country. In 1860, when nearly four of every ten New Englanders voted Democratic, only two of every ten thousand Southerners supported the Republicans (only in Virginia did Lincoln receive Southern votes). Not only was the Democrats' universalism displayed by less variation in their intraregional vote (during the 1840s and 1850s seldom more than 15 percent, compared with the Republicans' 60 percent); their congressional delegations to Washington also continued to come from all regions.[21] Moreover, from the nomination of Van Buren and Johnson in 1836 to that of Douglas and Johnson and Breckinridge and Lane in 1860, Democrats included both a Northerner and Southerner on their presidential tickets. Throughout the period the party continued to hold its national convention in slave and free states and, by requiring a two-thirds vote for nomination, protected its regional minorities along with its reputation as a national institution.

This national presence appealed to Northerners, who, though unfamiliar with specific campaign issues, nonetheless experienced a sense of Americanness by being part of a countrywide organization. The only ethnic groups to vote Democratic persistently and disproportionately during the second and third quarters of the nineteenth century were urban-dwelling immigrants (and first-generation Americans) from Germany and Ireland and rural Midwesterners from the South who established through their membership in the party a sense of belonging to their new communities. It was not because the Democratic party represented outsiders that uprooted Irish joined it, but rather because it conveyed a sense of nationhood. "I cast my ballot for the Democracy," explained one newly naturalized Baltimorean, "and became an American."[22] In this same city native-born politicians depended on new citizens to turn out at rallies and to carry the party's patriotic slogans—"Constitution and Union"; "No North, South, East and West." Although local circumstances sometimes diluted this identification (not all outsiders voted Democratic), the Democrats inspired feelings of

[21]The above is based on Walter Dean Burnham, *Presidential Ballots, 1836–1892* (Baltimore: Johns Hopkins University Press, 1955); see the *Tribune Almanac* (New York: New York Tribune, 1868) for regional makeup of the Thirty-fifth, -sixth, and -seventh Congresses.

[22]Robert Kelley, *The Cultural Pattern in American Politics: The First Century* (New York: A. A. Knopf, 1979), pp. 192–96, 220–25; Paul Kleppner, *The Cross of Culture: A Social Analysis of Midwestern Politics, 1850–1900* (New York: Free Press, 1970), p. 70; Thomas Courtenay to Robert Gill, 15 October 1858, Frederick Brune Papers, Maryland Historical Society, Baltimore.

nationalism because they continued to have a Southern membership.

Had party culture in the North been less Unionist, the Democracy would not have divided in 1860. But Stephen Douglas believed that he had the support of the Southern "People," if not of its leaders, and, believing that he could get beyond "the Demagogues" and that his party was the only instrument available for saving the Union, he traveled South twice in two months. This he did at a time when presidential candidates usually stayed home mute except for a few letters. Neither Bell nor Lincoln campaigned at all; and Breckinridge, the best speaker in Kentucky, delivered only one brief stump speech.

Douglas, on the other hand, had exhausted his voice and material by early September. Addressing three acres of North Carolinians (Douglas measured his audiences spatially; in this case his vantage point was the pedestal of the huge statue of George Washington in Raleigh's Courthouse Square), he offered the Democracy "as the only historical party now remaining in the country—the only party that has its northern and southern support firmly enough established to preserve this Union."[23] In the North, Douglas used his trips to the South as a demonstration of his nationalism and offered himself to voters as a Union man because he was a Democrat, while denying the Breckinridge faction membership in the "stout-hearted Democracy" on the grounds that they were sectionalists. "I believe," he later said, "I may with confidence appeal to the people of every section of the country to bear testimony that I have been as thoroughly national in my political opinions and action as any man that has lived in my day." Certainly his Southern campaigns displayed his patriotism at a time when, as Douglas told a Boston audience, "our liberties are in peril due to sectional parties, appealing to sectional prejudice and sectional ambitions against the peace and harmony of the whole country."[24] As late as July 1860, Douglas believed he would carry five of the eleven future Confederate states, including Georgia, Texas, and Arkansas, and he considered himself stronger than "the superficial currents" set in motion by politicians. Ironically, his understanding of the 1860 election as the Union's last defense against "the infidels" of sectionalism prevented the merger with

[23] *Illinois State Register* (Springfield), 8 October 1860; quotation from Johannsen, *Stephen A. Douglas,* pp. 789–90; Basil Duke, *Reminiscences* (Garden City, N.Y.: Doubleday Page, 1911), p. 437. For Lincoln's "perilous silence" during the campaign, see David M. Potter, *Lincoln and His Party in the Secession Crisis* (New Haven: Yale University Press, 1942), p. 135.

[24] *New York Herald,* 19 July 1860; *Speech of Senator Douglas before the Legislature of Illinois, April 25, 1861* (n.p.), p. 4.

Bell or Breckinridge that would have defeated Lincoln and postponed secession.[25]

Nationalism, however, was out of season in 1860, though Douglas received more widespread support than any other candidate, including Bell, whose constituency was clustered in the border states. Four days after the election Douglas delivered a fitting epilogue to a New Orleans audience: "Let us lay aside all partisan feeling and let us become patriots and lovers of our country."[26] Given the traditions of his party, Douglas believed Americans could solve their differences through compromise. When war came five months later, Douglas provided a new definition of Americanism, again indexed to the South. In a final speech before his death in June 1861, he warned of the South's "hostile armies and aggression. . . . There is but one course left for the patriot and that is to rally under that flag which has waved over the capital from the days of Washington, Madison, Hamilton, and their compeers."[27]

## *Fighting the South to Restore the Union*

By no means did patriotism require fighting the South, at least not in the days before the draft compelled military service. At first, signing up was a matter of personal choice. Freely willed, it was neither legal obligation nor civic duty, and in April 1861 no one—except Quakers and members of the American Peace Society[28]—had more reason to stay home than Northern Democrats. Unlike Republicans, who heard the sentiment only a few times in Horace Greeley's dictum "Let them go in Peace," Northern Democrats had absorbed a decade of anticoercionist argument that stemmed from their intense pro-Unionism. During the

[25]Johannsen, *Stephen A. Douglas,* pp. 74, 740, 781; Incoming Letters, Stephen A. Douglas Papers, University of Chicago (hereafter cited as Douglas Papers); Ollinger Crenshaw, *The Slave States in the Presidential Election of 1860* (Baltimore: Johns Hopkins University Press, 1945), pp. 20, 76, 80.

[26]Johannsen, *Stephen A. Douglas,* p. 806.

[27]*Speech of Douglas before Legislature of Illinois,* p. 2.

[28]By the 1850s the American Peace Society permitted members to join the organization "regardless of their convictions on the issue of defensive war"; given this liberal interpretation, members had little difficulty, after the firing on Sumter, in accommodating their pacifism to military service. Alice Felt Tyler, *Freedom's Ferment: Phases of American Social History to 1860* (Minneapolis: University of Minnesota Press, 1944), p. 411; Peter Brock, *Pacifism in the United States from the Colonial Era to the First World War* (Princeton: Princeton University Press, 1968); George Frederickson, *The Inner Civil War: Northern Intellectuals and the Crisis of the Union* (New York: Harper Torchbooks, 1965), pp. 56–58.

secession winter of 1861 they heard more: in Iowa, Democrats affirmed the impossibility of defeating the South; in Indiana, after rebuking "madmen" North and South, a party official concluded, "Let them go and peace go with them and be with us"; in Maryland a hastily convened assembly of Democrats resolved, "We are firmly and unalterably opposed to any and every attempt on the part of the government or the people of the North to coerce the Southern states or any one of them into submission to the will of the majority of the North."[29] After Lincoln's election George Pugh, a Democratic congressman from Ohio, furnished an eloquent statement of the party's selective pacifism:

> I am for peace and not for war; and least of all, for a war so unnatural as this would be. I am for conciliation; and therefore . . . will endeavor to keep the door of compromise open as long as possible. . . . War is no remedy. It is always a horrible visitation, horrible when waged for the best and holiest cause but horrible indeed and inexpressibly wicked when waged without any cause, and by one portion of our people against another.[30]

Pugh's message echoed across the nation in local conventions held during the secession winter. In most states Democrats orchestrated these antiwar campaigns; in Ohio Congressman Clement Vallandigham, James J. Faran of the *Cincinnati Enquirer,* and Samuel Medary of the Columbus *Crisis* organized rallies, published peace editorials, and drafted anticoercionist petitions. By March the *Dayton Daily Journal* found antiwar sentiments "everywhere." In Maryland the peace crusade was more spontaneous, although meetings sponsored by Democrats also opposed the use of force. At a large assembly in Baltimore, Severn Teackle Wallis held it to be "slavish and absurd to think the Federal government can coerce into allegiance and brotherhood. You cannot shoot and hang men back into union."[31] Meanwhile Democrats in Congress produced desperate plans to restore the Union—war against a

[29]*Brooklyn Daily Eagle,* 15 April 1861, in Howard Cecil Perkins, ed., *Northern Editorials on Secession* (New York: D. Appleton, 1942), 2: 772; Hubert H. Wubben, *Civil War Iowa and the Copperhead Movement* (Ames: Iowa State University Press, 1980), p. 31; James Ferguson to John Davis, 3 February 1861, John Davis Papers, Illinois Historical Society, Springfield; *Baltimore Sun,* 3 February 1861.

[30]*Congressional Globe,* 36th Cong., 2d sess., app., p. 35; see also Stephen Douglas's speech, ibid., p. 39.

[31]*Dayton Daily Journal,* 28 March 1861; Frank L. Klement, *The Limits of Dissent: Clement L. Vallandigham and the Civil War* (Lexington: University of Kentucky Press, 1970), p. 58; *Baltimore Sun,* 2 February 1861; *The Writings of Severn Teackle Wallis* (Baltimore: John Murphy, 1896), 2: 135.

foreign power, tariff associations with the Confederacy, and even a regional federation of Middle Atlantic, New England, Southern, and Western states.[32]

Throughout the Democratic North the message was the same: Don't fight the South. Secession is illegal, but republican governments cannot compel allegiance. James Buchanan, the party's last president for twenty-five years, explained this point in his farewell to Congress: "No such power [of coercion] has been delegated to Congress or any department of the Federal Government. The power to make war against a State is at variance with the whole spirit and intent of the Constitution. . . . our Union rests upon public opinion and can never be cemented by the blood of its citizens in civil war."[33] At issue was a basic tenet of Democratic faith. If the people formed and controlled the government, they could, for sufficient cause and as state jurisdictions, end it. Secession might be unjustified, but federal coercion was unthinkable. To wage war against the South reminded Democrats of English conduct against the colonists. According to the Washington, D.C. *States and Union,*

> a Republican government has no power whatsoever to protect itself, where the people, for whose benefit it was formed, choose to alter, amend, or even annihilate it. The people are the ruling judges, the States independent sovereigns. Where the people choose to change their political condition, as our own Declaration of Independence first promulgated, they have a right to do so. If the doctrine was good then, it is good now.[34]

Rarely did Northern Democrats vent their irritation at what one described as "the swallowing of dirt for the South." Most Democratic antisouthernism was directed at a small clique of "hotspurs," not at the Southern people.[35] In fact Northern Democrats counted on the latter to return their states to the Union. They themselves inclined to non-

[32]Seward later presented a plan for foreign war to Lincoln; Douglas developed the tariff plan based on a Zollverein, or trade association; and Vallandigham presented the proposal for a quadripartite United States to Congress. See *Congressional Globe,* 36th Cong., 2d sess., app. p. 242.

[33]James Richardson, ed., *Messages and Papers of the Presidents,* 20 vols. (Washington, D.C.: Bureau of National Literature and Art, 1908–1917), 5: 636; Johannsen, *Stephen A. Douglas,* p. 832.

[34]Washington, D.C. *States and Union* 21 March 1861, quoted in Perkins, *Northern Editorials,* 2: 651.

[35]Allan Nevins, *The War for the Union* (New York: Scribners, 1959), 1: 15, 16, 95; *New York Express,* 16 January 1861.

coercion because the South was a symbol of their own nationalism, and consequently war would be an act of self-flagellation.

But overnight a singular change occurred. Antiwar in April, thousands of Northern Democrats were volunteering in May. If supporting the South had been a badge of nationalism in 1860, fighting the Confederacy became one by late 1861. And because joining up involved taking action, it offers a rare measure of the sentiments of voiceless followers, and thus of the attitudes of average Democrats.

Throughout the North, Democratic organizations superintended the process of volunteering. In the New York and Brooklyn wards, where the party controlled public affairs and seven of ten adult males voted Democratic, companies filled with recruits as quickly as in Republican New England. Fernando Wood, the former New York mayor notorious for his Southern sympathies, called upon Democrats "to make one phalanx in this controversy and proceed to conquer a peace." By July his Mozart Hall Regiment was training in Yonkers, its ranks filled up with Irish-born Democrats recruited in Massachusetts. New Jersey's Third Congressional District (one of the Democracy's few safe seats during the Civil War) sent off hundreds of volunteers officered by district leaders, and Joel Parker, the state's wartime governor, compared New Jersey's record in furnishing men favorably with that of Republican states. In Iowa even Republicans agreed that Democrats provided most of the recruits from Dubuque, Davenport, and Des Moines, the state's largest cities. In Illinois, Democrats clamored to sign up for the "Douglas" regiment, and on the West Coast like-minded partisans, singing "Our Tree of Liberty," volunteered as the Douglas Invincibles. In Nebraska neutral observers concluded that Democratic volunteers outnumbered Republicans, and by the time Congress met in July the number of Democratic officers—a group that included George McClellan, Daniel Sickles, John Dix, John Logan, William S. Rosecrans, and Benjamin Butler—alarmed some Republicans. Secretary of the Navy Gideon Welles affirmed the obvious in his diary. "The Democrats are offering themselves to the country as well as the Republicans."[36]

[36]A Committee of the Regiment, *The Story of the Fifty-fifth Illinois Volunteers in the Civil War, 1861–1865* (Clinton, Mass.: W. J. Coulter, 1887); *Roster of Members of Mozart Hall, Fortieth New York Volunteers* (New York: Witt Rowan, 1897); Fred Floyd, *History of the Fortieth (Mozart) Regiment* (Boston: F. H. Gilson, 1909); Charles Knapp, *New Jersey Politics during the Period of Civil War and Reconstruction* (Geneva, N.Y.: W. F. Humphrey, 1924), pp. 54–56; *New York Tribune*, 22 April 1861; Wubben, *Civil War Iowa*, pp. 32, 42, 43, 60; J. M. Stirling to Stirling Morton, 15 April 1861; J. W. Thayer to Stirling Morton, 27 June 1861; both in J. Stirling Morton Papers, Nebraska Historical Society, Lincoln; John T. Morse, ed., *Diary of Gideon Welles* (Boston: Houghton Mifflin, 1911), 1: 89–90.

Thereafter it was the Democrats who made army service a partisan issue. Congressman Cox, for example, twitted the Republican counties in the Western Reserve section of his home state of Ohio "for coming up to patriotism slothfully." Other Democrats claimed that the presence at the front of disproportionate numbers of their followers contributed to election defeats at home. And after the draft began in 1863, Democrats accused wealthy Republicans of organizing relief associations to pay commutation fees, thereby avoiding the patriotic service that Democrats voluntarily rendered to the Union. Republicans considered the war a bipartisan effort, and although they accused Democrats of sins ranging from pro-Confederate sympathies to treason, shirking army service was not included. Nor could Republicans reasonably pin the Democratic label on those border-state residents who left Missouri, Delaware, Maryland, and Kentucky to fight for the Confederacy. In the North when volunteering slackened and war became more than a summer's campaign, most commentators acknowledged a universal war-weariness—not copperhead absenteeism.[37]

This commitment needs explaining because Democrats had options. They could have ignored Lincoln's call for 75,000 troops and let Republicans fight the war some Northern Democrats believed that party had caused. As civilians, Democrats could have spoken out against the war or, as Franklin Pierce predicted, sabotaged Union efforts with the "fire in the rear" that Lincoln feared. Certainly Southerners anticipated such guerrilla activities. "You count without your host," Jefferson Davis's son-in-law had earlier threatened. "When the fighting begins, it will all be north of the Susquehanna."[38] Northern Democrats could have encouraged an armed peace—a kind of nineteenth-century cold war—for even after Fort Sumter fell, all was still quiet on the Potomac.

The nation's history supplied precedents for opposing military action. During the War of 1812 opposition had followed partisan lines and had gone beyond antiwar rhetoric to include acts of sabotage encouraged by political organizations. The famous Federalist blue-lights, hung to guide the British navy to coastal targets, were examples of such resistance. At the 1815 Hartford Convention, Federalists not only encouraged the rewriting of the Constitution, but party leaders developed

[37]For a recent discussion, see Peter Levine, "Draft Evasion in the North during the Civil War," *Journal of American History* 67 (March 1981): 816–34; *Congressional Globe,* 37th Cong., 1st sess., pp. 227, 244; Eugene C. Murdock, *One Million Men: The Civil War Draft in the North* (Madison: State Historical Society of Wisconsin, 1971), pp. 52, 63, 239.

[38]Nevins, *War for the Union,* 1: 15, 16, 95; *New York Express,* 16 January 1861; Franklin Pierce to Jefferson Davis, 6 January 1860, Franklin Pierce Papers, microfilm edition.

a plan to exclude the prowar West from a new union. In the state governments they controlled, Federalists kept militias at home—in one instance refusing to cooperate with national forces even after the British had invaded eastern Maine. During the Mexican-American War the Whigs continued this pattern of party-sponsored resistance, and Lincoln's "spot resolutions" were a part of this tradition. In the state legislatures they controlled during the late 1840s, Whigs passed resolutions challenging the legitimacy of the war and opposing volunteering.[39] Given such a pattern, why did Northern Democrats fight? Why, as one journalist asked, did they "imbue their hands in the blood of family and wage war on friends?" Why, in Douglas's words, did they "rush as one man" to defend their government?[40]

Many Democrats fought because party officials encouraged them to do so, volunteering for war as they had in past years for electoral campaigns. This was not the manipulative process it became in the twentieth century, when the young fought the wars their stay-at-home elders provoked. In 1861 those who raised the regiments led them in battle. At least eight Democratic congressmen were in the field by the summer, as were countless state legislators and ward leaders. For many Democrats personal associations offset noncoercive instincts. As one party member explained, "Democrats are waiting to hear the views of their leaders. I have been asked a hundred times what do Douglas and Cox think of this business. We have safe leaders and the truth is we are willing to follow them anywhere and back up their opinions and action."[41] During the uncertain spring of 1861, Democrats sought such advice, and the correspondence of Douglas, Cox, and Pendleton burgeoned with inquiries about the party's position on the war. Many leaders publicized their views at rallies or in letters printed in party newspapers. Tammany Hall sachem Daniel Delavan was no exception when he called a meeting and exhorted members to sign up and demonstrate their patriotism as Democrats. August Belmont, the party's national chairman, equipped two regiments—one in Missouri and one in New York—and in Illinois David Stuart, after donating his own money to equip a regiment, appealed to party members to honor Douglas's

[39]Samuel Eliot Morison, Frederick Merk, and Frank L. Freidel, *Dissent in Three American Wars* (Cambridge, Mass.: Harvard University Press, 1970).

[40]*Washington Democrat* (Salem, Ind.) 18 April 1861, quoted in Perkins, *Northern Editorials,* 2: 782; *Speech of Douglas before Legislature of Illinois,* p. 8.

[41]G. A. Converse to S. S. Cox, 2 January 1861, Samuel S. Cox Papers, Brown University Library, Providence.

memory by signing up. Another party official found the Illinois senator's "patriot or traitor" distinction "worth battalions."[42]

In some Northern communities a pervasive war fever nudged Democrats toward military service, in much the same way that prewar campaign techniques—so suggestive of military behaviors—had readied the party's faithful to be an army unit. Because the public mind was ardently prowar, volunteering became a neighborhood affair, similar to a religious revival or town meeting. Democrats and Republicans, in meetings held in schoolhouses and courthouses, called for recruits to step forward, and, like revivalists in evangelical assembly, young men converted from civilian to soldier, from Democrat to first Infantry, by signing the muster rolls while neighbors cheered and the band played "America." Stephen Douglas explained the partisan implications of this behavior in one of his last letters: "If we hope to regain and perpetuate the ascendancy of our party, we should never forget that a man cannot be a true Democrat unless he is a loyal patriot."[43]

Some decisions to volunteer took place outside partisan context. Democrat James Hiatt provided a fictional but lifelike rendering in his 1864 novel, *The Test of Loyalty*. Asked by his sister what was bothering him, a young farm boy replied: "Nothing is the matter with me, Dora, but the country, the country. That's what I'm thinking about. . . . To go or not to go. Here's the corn to plant and plow. The wheat soon to cut . . . all the season's work to do . . . nobody here but father. But I want to go and help whip the secesh. Nearly all the rest of the boys are going." A Pennsylvania Democrat pinpointed another reason: "If I could have got work," admitted Elias Hicks to his wife, "I wood [*sic*] not have left you or the children." Another expected the bounty to get him out of debt and into landowning; still others joined up because they were bored with farming and faced uncertain prospects in states like Vermont where their generation was too numerous for economic

[42]Committee, *Story of the Fifty-fifth Illinois;* Samuel S. Cox, "Eulogy of Stephen A. Douglas," in *Eight Years in Congress, 1857–1865* (New York: D. Appleton, 1865), p. 213; Irving Katz, *August Belmont: A Political Biography* (New York: Columbia University Press, 1968), pp. 89–90; Nevins, *War for the Union,* 1: 237; James Custis to Caleb Cushing, 20 June 1861; Governor Andrew to Cushing, 27 April 1861; both in Caleb Cushing Papers, Library of Congress (hereafter cited as Cushing Papers); Felix McCloskey to Stephen Douglas, 17 January 1861, Douglas Papers.

[43]Bell Irvin Wiley, *The Life of Billy Yank, the Common Soldier of the Union* (Indianapolis: Bobbs-Merrill, 1951), p. 19; James Clark, *Life in the Midwest* (Chicago: Advance Publishing, 1916), pp. 44–47; Craig Kautz, "Fodder for Cannon: Immigrant Perceptions of the Civil War in the Old Northwest" (Ph.D. dissertation, University of Nebraska, 1976), p. 32; Johannsen, *Letters of Douglas,* p. 513.

security.[44] For some volunteers, war arrived at a convenient time in the academic calendar, and many colleges financed volunteer units in the summer of 1861. At least two midwestern college presidents, Charles Edward Hovey of Illinois State Normal and Henry Burgess of Eureka, organized companies and led their former students into battle. It must have been difficult to resist the appeals of schoolmasters who ended the school term after Sumter fell and, like a popular Minnesota teacher, urged their older students to enlist. Romance inspired other volunteers, as in the case of the Illinois Democrat whose girlfriend became more attentive after he signed up. And in Iowa, some women announced they would marry only soldiers.[45]

The reversal of Democratic attitudes was not a vertical process of leader indoctrinating follower. Joining up occurred as part of what Robert Kelley has described as an "interactive dialogue between leader and populace, both providing inspiration and setting limits for the other."[46] With little time or inclination for reflection, most Northern Democrats did not explain why they went to war, and because the party's hieararchy provided imposing reasons "to stand by the flag," there has always been a tendency to use the latter to explain the former.[47] As a result the motives of common soldiers are indexed to intellectualized conceptions of Union and Constitution, and the behavior of all Northerners is put forward as an effort to defend the modern state. Actually behind the symbols of flag, Constitution, and Union, there were personal images of the United States as a prosperous magisterial land, worth defending as an exemplar for all mankind. Viewed from a nonpartisan perspective, the decision to fight was an effort, according to one historian, "to uphold government and order against the threat of anarchy. . . . again and again Americans proved to themselves that they were lawmakers . . . that the law and order of their communities was

[44]James Hiatt, *The Test of Loyalty* (Indianapolis: Merrill and Smith, 1864), p. 8; Wiley, *Life of Billy Yank,* pp. 38–40; Enoch T. Baker to his wife, 10 November 1861, Enoch T. Baker Papers, Historical Society of Pennsylvania; Burton Bledstein, *The Culture of Professionalism in the Middle Class and the Development of Higher Education in America* (New York: Oxford University Press, 1976), pp. 205–08.

[45]Wiley, *Life of Billy Yank,* p. 19; Wubben, *Civil War Iowa,* p. 42; Aretas Dayton, "Recruitment and Conscription in Illinois during the Civil War" (Ph.D. dissertation, University of Illinois, 1940).

[46]Robert Kelley, *The Transatlantic Persuasion: The Liberal Democratic Mind in the Age of Gladstone* (New York: A. A. Knopf, 1969), pp. xv–xvi. The process of opinion-making is especially difficult for historians to ascertain. For a succinct presentation of the relation among decision-makers, opinion-makers, and opinion-holders, see James N. Rosenau, *Public Opinion and Foreign Policy* (New York: Random House, 1967).

[47]*Boston Post,* 16 April 1861.

their personal responsibility and depended on their actions and efforts. Their connection with the preservation of that order was intimate, vital, and compelling."[48]

Northern Democrats shared these convictions with Republicans, having learned them at home and in school as well as through their party. "There is no choice between support of the government and anarchy," explained one. According to another, "Every man who reveres the memory of Washington must use his efforts and devote his wealth, his personal services and his life, if necessary, in defending the integrity of the government which the patriots of the revolution handed down as a Perpetual Blessing to their posterity." A Massachusetts Democrat saw the issue as one of preserving the Union and fighting over whether "the stars and stripes must be lowered to give place to Palmettos, Rattlesnakes, and Pelicans." Caleb Cushing, the Massachusetts Democrat who had presided over the Breckinridge campaign, shifted from anti-coercion to fighting the South in order to prevent "the overthrow of the government. Our Dear Country now indeed demonstrates the devotion of all people."[49] To a large degree, quasi-military partisan rituals, nonsectional Unionism, and the compliance techniques of Northern schools had transformed the abstract entity of government into a "dear country" worth defending.

Fort Sumter helped: although its capture posed no threat to national security, still the attack made the South an aggressor. As a result Northern belligerency was rendered "the just cause and honorable conflict" necessary to inspire the service of future soldiers.[50] Even though only one Northerner lay dead for martyrdom—and he the victim of technology, not of the Confederacy, when his cannon misfired—still the flag had been fired on. Southerners had tried to "pull down pillars and prostrate the great temple of freedom." Explained one Democratic

[48]Philip Paludan, "The American Civil War Considered as a Crisis in Law and Order," *American Historical Review* 77 (October 1972): 1019, 1023, 1024.

[49]*Boston Post,* 16 April 1861; *Pittsburgh Post,* 15 April 1861, both in Perkins, *Northern Editorials* 2: 740, 738; W. L. Williams to Caleb Cushing, 15 and 24 April 1861; Cushing to John Andrew, 25 April 1861; "Notes by Mr. Cushing," "Speech at Newburyport, Mass."; all in Cushing Papers.

[50]Michael Walzer, *Just and Unjust Wars: A Moral Argument with Historical Illustrations* (New York: Basic Books, 1977). Walzer is persuasive on the point that moral considerations are a part of individual decisions to fight. Even in the Mexican-American War the U.S. government tried to avoid the charge that it was the aggressor, as did the South in 1861. The expression "just cause and honorable conflict," from Shakespeare's *Henry V,* forms part of that monarch's call to arms before the Battle of Agincourt in Act 4, scene 1. For references to the superior moral position of the North, see *Congressional Globe,* 37th Cong., 1st sess., passim.

paper, "Now none but traitors deserving the gibbet will be found sustaining the cause of Southern rebels.Those who are not for the stars and stripes are against them. There is no middle ground. The great Democratic party which established and has maintained the Union of these states thus far will be found as a unit rallying around the banner handed down to a generation who are taught to reverence Jefferson and worship Washington as the "Father of his country." By firing first, Southerners removed the stigma of aggression from the North, and although some Democrats argued that Lincoln had maneuvered the first shot and that Southerners were only defending themselves as their revolutionary fathers had at Lexington, this case had weakened. Lincoln understood the distinction and accused the South of "making" the war, the North of "accepting it."[51]

For these reasons and many more, Democrats volunteered. Exact numbers are not available, but there were enough to make the war a bipartisan effort and to demonstrate that opposition to it would not be a party-approved activity, as it had been for Federalists in 1812 and Whigs in 1848. There were regional variations in the levels of Democratic support, and some counties in the border states of Kentucky, Missouri, and Maryland sent nearly as many Democrats to the Confederacy as to the Union. But most Americans followed the decision of their state and were considered traitors only if they did not. The most extreme form of this state-dictated loyalty occurred when Maryland-born Captain Franklin Buchanan resigned his commission in the U.S. Navy because he expected Maryland to secede. When his home state did not, he unsuccessfully requested the Department of the Navy to withdraw his resignation and rescind his month-long allegiance to the Confederacy. Overall, the popular slogan of 1861, "We're all a'coming," included Democrats. "The South's attack," exulted the *New York Times,* "has made the North a Union. One intense inspiring sentiment of patriotism has fused all other passions in its fiery heat."[52]

Although Northern Democrats accepted a Republican president's authority to call 75,000 militia to fight the South, they distinguished between the Republican administration, which they rejected and wanted to replace, and the American system of government, which they supported and wanted to continue. "It is our duty to perform the

[51]*Daily Capital City Fact* (Columbus, Ohio), 13 April 1861, quoted in Perkins, *Northern Editorials,* 2: 728. Lincoln's comment appears in his message to the 1861 special session of Congress; Richardson, *Messages and Papers,* 6: 276.

[52]Matthew Page Andrews, *History of Maryland: Province and State* (Hatboro, Pa.: Tradition Press, 1965), p. 535. *New York Times,* 15 April 1861.

obligations of citizens, be obedient to the laws, and be loyal to the constitution," wrote one Democrat; but "our strong outburst of patriotism" is not an "endorsement of the policy and principles of the Republican party." Argued another, "It is not the administration as an administration, but as the embodiment of our institutions which is entitled to obedience."[53]

Not every Northern Democrat separated administration and regime or subscribed to the rapid reversal that made fighting the South an expression of party (and therefore national) loyalty. Those who did not encouraged a no-party-now policy, joined the Republican-sponsored Union party (thereby resolving the personal conflict of behaving as Republicans while remaining Democrats), retired from public affairs, or served the South as soldiers and propagandists.

Among the latter were a handful of Northern Democrats who chose to live in Europe during the war. John O'Sullivan, the former editor of the *United States Magazine and Democratic Review,* was the best known of those exiles who, though they could not bring themselves to live in the South, preferred not to stay in the North.[54] From Portugal, O'Sullivan requested Confederate citizenship and was listed as an agent in official documents of the Richmond government. Unlike most Democrats, who surrendered their anticoercionist principles after Sumter, O'Sullivan retained his; as Buchanan's minister to Portugal he had been overseas in the 1850s, and hence had not absorbed the special devotion that emerged from his party's amalgamation of partisanship and nationalism. A man without a country, O'Sullivan kept his distance in Lisbon and London, urging Northern Democrats first to lay down their arms and then to abandon the organization that divided them from their Confederate brothers. Finally, when the war turned against the South, O'Sullivan advised his Confederate "comrades in arms" to burn Richmond. "Let every man set fire to his own house," retreating southward to become, if necessary, a guerrilla in North Carolina.[55] But most Democratic expatriates took no part in public affairs; some, like

[53]*New York Journal of Commerce,* 6 May 1861; *Daily Chicago Times,* 12 June 1861, both cited in Perkins, *Northern Editorials,* 2: 760–62, 848. See above, Chapter 3, pp. 188–196.

[54]Sheldon H. Harris, "The Public Career of John Louis O'Sullivan" (Ph.D. dissertation, Columbia University, 1958); idem, "John O'Sullivan Serves the Confederacy," *Civil War History* 10 (September 1964); 275–90; John O'Sullivan, *Peace the Sole Chance Left for Reunion* (London: William Brown, 1863)); *Union, Disunion, and Reunion: A Letter to Franklin Pierce* (London: R. Bentley, 1862).

[55]Harris, "O'Sullivan Serves the Confederacy," pp. 283–86. For O'Sullivan's postwar position, see F. R. Shaftner to Andrew Johnson, 17 May 1865, Andrew Johnson Papers, microfilm edition (hereafter cited as Johnson Papers).

Maryland's William W. Glenn, expected to return home; others, like Kentucky's Charles Morehead, Delaware's William Ross, and California's William Gwinn, withdrew into the English country life they had always admired.[56] Drawn together by wartime circumstances and peacetime associations, Northern expatriates gradually surrendered their partisan allegiance. In Europe the Democracy's Unionist creed no longer fitted their prosouthernism.

In the North, party-imbued devotion to the Union deterred acts of prosouthernism; just as Democratic expatriates did not join the Confederacy because they could not entirely renounce their Unionism, so Northern Democrats did not incite desertion, discourage enlistment, obstruct the draft, or otherwise disorganize the army. Individual Democrats did desert and did resist enrollment. Some counseled their friends to leave the army and sold supplies to Confederates. Wrote an Ohio Democrat: "Well, Wesley, my advice to you is this. . . . Come home if you can possibly get home, for to conquer the South is an impossibility and the only hope for you to reach home is to desert." Others gave information to Confederate guerrillas. But so too did Republicans, independents, former Whigs, nonvoters, and Know-Nothings. Overall, disloyal practices were unrelated to partisanship.[57]

Invariably, however, Republicans held Democrats to be at the heart of every act of subversion. In New York, Horatio Seymour's criticism of the conscription act ten days before the attacks on the provost marshal's headquarters served as the Republican explanation of the 1863 draft riots. In smaller communities where draft officials were attacked, charges of copperhead activity linked Democrats to sabotage. Effective propaganda, such accusations transformed spontaneous community responses (usually within ethnically homogeneous neighborhoods) into political subversion and confused local efforts to retain autonomy with disloyalty. Given their backgrounds, immigrants often resisted the draft not because they were Democrats, but because conscription had pro-

[56]Bayly Ellen Marks and Mark Norton Schatz, eds., *Between North and South: A Maryland Journalist Views the Civil War* (Rutherford, N.J.: Fairleigh Dickinson Press, 1976), p. 102.

[57]Civil War Political Prisoners' Records, U.S. State Department Files (hereafter cited as Political Prisoners' Records); Lafayette Baker-Levi Turner Papers, Adjutant General's Records, War Department; both in Record Group 94, National Archives, Washington, D.C.,; Wayne Jordan, "The Hoskinsville Rebellion," *Ohio State Archaeological and Historical Quarterly* 47 (October 1938), 319–54, quotation from p. 320; Eugene Roseboom, "Southern Ohio and the Union," *Mississippi Valley Historical Review* 39 (June 1952): 27–44; Arnold Shankman, "Conflict in the Old Keystone State: Antiwar Sentiment in Pennsylvania, 1860–1865" (Ph.D. dissertation, Emory University, 1972), pp. 195–202.

vided the occasion for leaving the Old World and hence could not be tolerated in the New. On the other hand, native-born Americans whose lives had been untouched by the government opposed conscription on the republican grounds that it was "enslavement." Many Democrats distinguished between opposing the draft and opposing the war. Thus what the Republicans promoted into "the wars" of Hoskinsville, Ohio; Fulton County, Illinois; and Ozaukee, Wisconsin, had little to do with supporting the South, and less to do with the treachery of Democrats. In these communities residents refused to give up army deserters because they disliked the provost marshal and his trespass on their traditional independence. Such affairs enacted a form of "reactionary" violence designed to protect rights once enjoyed but now threatened by the nationalizing effects of war.[58]

In fact the dangerous copperheads of Republican imagination were often among the first to condemn antiwar violence. Fresh from his vote against the 1863 conscription bill, Congressman Daniel Voorhees appeared before an antidraft meeting in Sullivan County, Indiana, to encourage a peaceful enrollment and obedience to the law. Verbal criticism was different from acts of civil disobedience, argued Voorhees, who supported redress at the polls, not at the provost marshal's headquarters. To the crowd's delight, Voorhees used the occasion to accuse Republicans of avoiding the draft by hiring substitutes and by paying commutation fees, while "stout-hearted" Democrats volunteered for the Union. "Who then," he concluded, "are the loyal men?" Another specimen Copperhead, Clement Vallandigham, supported conscription once it became law, and with the same ferocity that accompanied his criticism of the administration argued for observance of the draft. Making clear his opposition, Vallandigham nonetheless held that "the laws of the land must be obeyed" and "the People" must seek redress through the courts and the ballot box.[59]

[58]Stewart Mitchell, *Horatio Seymour of New York* (Cambridge, Mass.: Harvard University Press, 1938), pp. 303–07; Frank L. Klement, *The Copperheads in the Middle West* (Chicago: University of Chicago Press, 1960), pp. 24, 67, 79, 80, 161; Eugene C. Murdock, *Patriotism Limited 1862–1865* (Kent, O.: Kent State University Press, 1967), pp. 52, 63, 239. In Iowa the same process occurred when an unpopular provost marshal overreacted and arrested several Democrats, whom grand juries promptly freed. Kautz, "Fodder for Cannon," pp. 33–93; Wubben, *Civil War Iowa,* p. 52; Levine, "Draft Evasion," p. 824. For an interesting typology of violence, see William F. Holmes, "Moonshining and Collective Violence: Georgia, 1889–1895," *Journal of American History* 67 (December 1980): 589–90.

[59]Leonard Kenworthy, *The Tall Sycamore of the Wabash: Daniel Wolsey Voorhees* (Boston: Bruce Humphries, 1936), pp. 58, 71, 72; Klement, *Limits of Dissent,* p. 142; Dayton *Daily Journal,* 14 March, 1863; U.S. War Department, *The War of the Rebellion: A*

Similar feelings of party-induced patriotism kept most Northern Democrats from joining the Knights of the Golden Circle and the Order of the American Knights. Organized in the South before the war, both associations preached filibustering and expansion into Mexico.[60] Their fictive revival, which occurred mostly in the minds of Republicans and Union commanders, provided a convenient explanation for the slow course of victory. Not only did references to a fifth column justify battle losses; they also furnished an incentive to vote Republican. By creating what one Northerner called "a Democratic elephant with horns,"[61] when in fact the elephants were mice and nonpartisan at that, Republicans embellished the myth of the copperheads, who now became not just treasonous individuals but members of an organized conspiracy. In fact Know-Nothings (who were attracted by its oaths and ritual), paroled Confederates, agent provocateurs, nonpartisans, and, by 1864, secret service agents made up most of the active membership of the Knights.[62] But in the overheated imaginations of army commanders and midwestern Republicans, the discovery of a few Democrats in the ranks of these fellow travelers transformed impotent bands of dissenters into subversive arms of the Democratic party. On investigation, civilian grand juries rarely found any grounds for indictment. According to one, the entire issue was a "diabolical" electioneering scheme, with the Knights of the Golden Circle and Order of American Knights "mere roorbacks of huge dimension."[63]

Eventually the copperhead myth backfired. Although it misled a few voters who connected the Knights of the Golden Circle and the Order of American Knights with the Democracy and who took seriously organizations which intended to fight the war with lances,[64] the fable also encouraged Confederate commanders to believe that a vast prosouthern

---

*Compilation of the Official Records of the Union and Confederate Armies* (Washington, D.C.: Government Printing Office, 1884), 3: 247, 339, 397.

[60]Ollie Crenshaw, "The Knights of the Golden Circle," *American Historical Review* 47 (October 1941): 23–51; Frank L. Klement, "Phineas Wright, the Order of American Knights, and the Sanderson Exposé," *Civil War History* 18 (March 1977): 5–23.

[61]Felix G. Stidger, *Treason: History of the Order of the Sons of Liberty* (Chicago: n.p., 1903), pp. 40, 80, 90.

[62]Ibid., pp. 67, 68, 69, 87; Ben Pittman, *The Trials for Treason at Indianapolis* (Cincinnati: Moore, Wilsatch, 1865). For a fictional version by a Democrat, see Hiatt, *Test of Loyalty*.

[63]Klement, *Copperheads in the Middle West,* pp. 140, 144, 135–70; idem, "Civil War Politics: Nationalism and Post-War Myths," *Historian* 38 (May 1976): 419–38; Wubben, *Civil War Iowa,* pp. 65–68. The word *roorback,* meaning "defamatory falsehood," originated in the 1844 election.

[64]Stidger, *Treason,* p. 50.

league awaited liberation. Actually except in Kentucky, where contacts between Northern civilians and Confederate soldiers were frequent, there was little organized collaboration with the enemy. Instead Southern information about the Union came from the Republican press, whose preoccupation with internal subversion promoted border raids. Thus Confederate General John Morgan expected, according to Basil Duke, his second in command, "that hundreds, perhaps thousands, of the Knights of the Golden Circle and the Sons of Liberty would flock to his standard and endeavor to carry the state to the Confederacy." When Morgan did cross into Ohio and Indiana in 1863, he encountered instead hastily enrolled state forces. Within thirty-six hours, over thirty thousand residents, including many Democrats, had responded to the Republican governor's call to defend Indiana from the Confederacy.[65]

Those few Northern Democrats who became Knights soon abandoned the party, for it was not as Democrats that they had joined. Rather, they had done so as Westerners who wanted a Northwest Confederacy separate from New England and the South, as individuals who enjoyed membership in a secret society, or as friends of its leaders. Democrats like Lambdin Milligan promptly recognized the distance separating them from their former allies and, according to Milligan, who had once been a party official, could no longer represent former colleagues in the Democratic party, for "there is no similarity between us."[66]

When Democrats did attempt to establish a counterpart to the Republican Union Leagues, few regulars joined. The aims of the Sons of Liberty were hardly subversive: it was, according to its midwestern founders, a mutual-protection society organized to defend Democrats harassed at the polls and jailed by the military without charge, hearing, or trial. Sponsors of the Sons of Liberty stated their opposition to secret societies and explicitly condemned the Knights of the Golden Circle. But Republicans overlooked this distinction and included the Sons of Liberty in their list of seditious organizations. Such inaccuracy helped to destroy the Sons' usefulness (for as a result many Democrats were uncertain about its loyalty), but so too did the organization's secrecy. Imbued with republican theory, Democrats considered disguise the tactic of conspirators; hence this effort to organize a defensive arm of their party died of nonsupport in 1864.[67]

[65]Basil Duke, "A Romance of Morgan's Rough Raiders," *Century Magazine* 19 (January 1891): 413.

[66]Stidger, *Treason*, p. 151.

[67]Klement, *Copperheads in the Middle West*, pp. 165–68.

More crucial for the protection of Northern Democrats was the party's militant constitutionalism. Throughout the war, Democrats insisted that the government abide by the legal definition of treason and refused to believe that loyalty could be legislatively defined. This struggle to maintain what Democrats called "established forms and old practices"[68] occurred throughout the North, but its most important arena was Washington, where Republican congressmen pressed for lesser categories of disloyalty and conspiracy. Democrats opposed such changes; given their historical relation to the South, they had special reason to insist that the administration adhere to the constitutional definition of treason as an overt act based on a conscious design to aid and abet the enemy and observed by two witnesses. By this definition all Confederates were guilty of treason. After some confusion, official policy designated them alien enemies of war "who had looked to their own state to determine their action" and who must be treated as foreign enemies.[69]

More problematic was the government's response to Northerners who sympathized in varying degrees with the South. From the beginning of the war Democrats separated deeds from words, arguing, according to James Bayard, that "condemnation for mere opinion apart from acts can never be justice." By insisting that all participants in overt acts against the United States government were principals, they prevented the kind of degradation trials in which associates accused their former colleagues in public testimony. Although Republicans depended on informers during the loyalty investigations of federal employees in 1861, Democratic protest was sharp enough to prevent any repetition. Even some Republicans agreed that testimony regarding disloyalty must not come from those who stood to benefit.[70]

Congressional Democrats began their strictures on loyalty even before the first Battle of Bull Run. At first they defended the patriotism of fellow party members accused of prosouthern sympathies, but in time their concerns ranged from the effect of rumor on the careers of Union generals to the State Department requirement that steamship pas-

[68] *Congressional Globe,* 39th Cong., 1st sess., 60.

[69] J. G. Randall and David Donald, *The Civil War and Reconstruction* (Boston: D. C. Heath, 1961), p. 449; *Congressional Globe,* 37th Cong., 1st sess., 428.

[70] Harold Hyman, *To Try Men's Souls: Loyalty Tests in American History* (Berkeley: University of California Press, 1959); "Loyalty of Clerks and Other Persons," 37th Cong., 2d sess., House Reports, ser. 1166. For modern examples of degradation trials and their significance, see Victor Navasky, *Naming Names* (New York: Viking Press, 1980); quotation from *Congressional Globe,* 37th Cong., 2d sess., 184.

sengers traveling from New York to California carry passports.[71] Throughout the war Democrats held that the government should apply only existing antitreason statutes and thereby avoid favoritism based on personal enmity. On the grounds that the mind becomes "biased in times of high excitement," James Bayard argued that "there can be no protection unless you adhere to forms under such circumstances." Full of English precedents, other Northern Democrats—especially the party's two California senators, Milton Latham and James McDougall—remembered that treason had been used in Britain as a political tool to quiet the opposition. From this historical perspective the Confiscation Acts, which first defined traitors as nonjurors and then penalized them, seemed to repeat the danger to liberty. Said Latham, "I am opposed to laws that will send mercenaries crawling all over Missouri, Virginia, and Maryland to buy a charge of treason to entitle them to half his property."[72] Instead, loyalty to the United States was an indeterminate matter that ironclad oaths of permanent devotion trivialized. "What is a loyal citizen?" asked Senator McDougall in 1863: "What does loyalty mean? It has been said that every man has his own definition. Loyalty is not a term known to law, and questions of loyalty will have to be determined by the caprice, proclivities or inclinations of whoever may be the judge in the case. . . . Loyalty means attachment and there are various levels of it. There may be a certain degree of loyalty or disloyalty united in the same individual's opinion."[73]

McDougall's warning was not always respected during the Civil War. Republicans did redefine treason into lesser categories of conspiracy; local attorney generals did arrest uncounted Northerners for treason, including thirty-six Coloradons who were indicted for drinking Jefferson Davis's health. And although Lincoln is deservedly acclaimed for his restraint, Secretary of State Seward with only hearsay evidence publicly charged former president Pierce with joining a disloyal organization, and Secretary of War Stanton with less cause authorized the arrest of thousands of Northern civilians.[74] However, by insisting on the distinction between deeds and opinions, Northern Democrats limited the range of Republican power.

[71]*Congressional Globe,* 37th Cong., 2d sess., 30, 184, 183; ibid., 3d sess., 175–77.

[72]Ibid., 2d sess., 184.

[73]Ibid., p. 66.

[74]James W. Hurst, *The Law of Treason in the United States* (Westport, Conn.: Greenwood Press, 1970), pp. 126–235; James G. Randall, *Constitutional Problems under Lincoln,* rev. ed. (Urbana: University of Illinois Press, 1964), p. 90; Political Prisoners' Records; R.G. 94; Frank Klement, "Franklin Pierce and the Treason Charges of 1861–1863," *Historian* 23 (August 1961): 436–49.

Northern Democrats were less successful in restraining military efforts to enforce conformity of opinion. Under the ancient sanction of *inter arma silent leges,* army commanders accused, convicted, and jailed Northern civilians. On many occasions military commissions acted even when civilian courts were in session and the writ of habeas corpus was in force. The most dramatic instance occurred in 1864, when a military commission convicted four former Democrats of treason and sentenced one, Indianan Lamdin Milligan, to death. After the war the conviction was reversed on what defense attorney Jeremiah Black called the "exceedingly plain point, that a military commission had no jurisdiction over civilian activities."[75] Black's defense drew on three traditions that informed the Democracy's behavior during the Civil War: first, military government had no place in a republic; second, the devotion to Union that made some Northerners sympathetic to the South was a form of nationalism; and third, those who disputed civilian jurisdiction over matters of loyalty had no faith in the people.

## *Restoring the South to the Union*

No group in the United States celebrated the end of the war more expectantly than did Northern Democrats. After 1862, negotiated peace rather than unconditional surrender had been the aim of only a few purists who opposed the war on the grounds that coercion destroyed the voluntary attachments of American citizens.[76] For these Democrats peace restored not only the physical union but also its spiritual meaning. Party leaders like Manton Marble, August Belmont, and Samuel Barlow observed another benefit: with the white South voting again, the Democracy would return to full strength and would become, with the proper handling this New York establishment expected to provide, the majority party. Because the Democracy's following in the South had always guaranteed the sense of their own patriotism, its repatriation signaled an end to the disorder and anarchy that had afflicted the great republic for more than four years. Given the Democrats' understanding of nationalism as based on the shared elements of what one

[75]William Brigance, *Jeremiah Sullivan Black* (Philadelphia: University of Pennsylvania Press, 1934), p. 151; Pittman, *Trials for Treason.*

[76]Joel Silbey, *A Respectable Minority: The Democratic Party in the Civil War Era, 1860–1868* (New York: W. W. Norton, 1977), pp. 96–99, 106–14. Silbey divides Northern Democrats into purists and legitimists, the former defined as party members who held an uncompromising commitment to limited government, the Constitution, and conservative social policy; the latter as Democrats who shared these ideas but were more likely to compromise principle for party.

called "a common blood, a common language, a common heritage, a common ancestry, a common history, a common glory, and a common faith," patriotism depended on reunion.[77] Still another group of Northern Democrats who disliked Republicans could now exchange an uncomfortable wartime alliance with what one Indiana Democrat called "the sneaking, crouching, pretending New Englanders" for more congenial associations with Southerners. In all cases Northern Democrats continued to establish their identity through the South, and whereas before the war party members had connected love of the Union with a political defense of the South and during the war had established their nationalism by fighting the South, now reunion recreated the harmonious ideal of "no East, no West, no North and South. . . . But all for the Union."[78]

The South's importance to the Northern Democracy ensured that Reconstruction would be neither an exalted constitutional conversation between party notables nor a partisan argument between Washington-based Republican and Democratic congressmen. For the next decade the process was the subject of resolutions in local conventions, speeches in election campaigns, and cartoons in which the South was portrayed as a dignified but tormented goddess of liberty.[79] Maine's Democratic state convention in 1866 was typical. The first order of business was not local, but instead involved a definition of the aims of war and reconstruction. "The people of our South," the convention resolved, "must be subject only to such penalties as the Constitution of our common country and laws passed in pursuance of it may prescribe." A year later, after Congress refused to seat Southern representatives, the Maine Democracy complained that "ten million people who made a full surrender to our victorious arms have been deprived of their full rights."[80] Frequently even Northern candidates for county commissioner or state assemblyman overlooked local concerns to concentrate on the Freedmen's Bureau, the Civil Rights Act, and the Fifteenth Amendment. Thus, because it touched on the Democrats' negrophobia as well as their special relation to the South, Reconstruction transformed what

[77]*Congressional Globe,* 37th Cong., 2d sess., 122.

[78]G. R. Tredway, *Democratic Opposition to the Lincoln Administration in Indiana* (Indianapolis: Indiana Historical Bureau, 1973), p. 4; Kelley, *Cultural Pattern,* pp. 241, 277–78, 301–02.

[79]"Honest Democrats Read This," 1865, Broadside Collection, New York Public Library.

[80]*Appleton's Encyclopedia,* 1866, pp. 404, 408, 461; see also the 1867 edition, pp. 467, 545, 619; Marvin Mantell, "New York and the Elections of 1866" (master's thesis, Columbia University, 1962).

might have been abstract public policy into intimate voter concerns.

Furthermore, the character of congressional debate guaranteed that the Southern problem would stir Northern Democrats. The image of the Negro as an irreparably defective candidate for citizenship had galvanized the party for nearly half a century, and in the eight Northern states where postwar plebiscites decided the issue of black suffrage, Democrats confronted Reconstruction in concrete terms. Amending the Constitution also nationalized politics; a public process undertaken only twice after 1791 was accomplished three times in the period 1864–1872.

Reconstructing the South concerned many party members because Republican behavior reenacted what Democrats had long considered their opponents' original sin—antirepublican meddling in the economy. As one Democrat reminded Alexander Stephens:

> The Yankee idea of Republican sovereignty is to have a central sovereignty to foster sectional interests of a business character: to give grants of public lands to incorporated companies in perpetuity, demolishing the people by partial legislation. The Constitution doesn't authorize the federal government to overthrow the internal domestic institutions of any of the states nor to pass laws for the benefit of any number of the states for the profit and gain of some states.[81]

With the treatment of the South serving as their litmus paper for testing states' rights and the health of the republic, Democrats accused Republicans of interfering not only with entrenched racial customs but also with economic arrangements. "The North," wrote Horatio Seymour, "wants to remake the South until its ideas of business and industry, money-making spindles and looms are those of New England." To accomplish their goal, according to Northern Democrats, Republicans sought to repeople the section with carpetbaggers and avaricious speculators, just as before the war they had sent Yankee and antislavery missionaries to Kansas.[82]

Even before the war ended, Northern Democrats had formulated the constitutional argument that, though developed to challenge Lincoln's specific arrangements for Louisiana, Arkansas, Tennessee, and North Carolina, continued to underwrite their objections to Reconstruction

[81]F. I. Byrdsall to Alexander Stephens, 12 November 1872, Alexander Stephens Papers, microfilm edition (hereafter cited as Stephens Papers).

[82]Quoted in Kelley, *Cultural Pattern,* p. 242; *Congressional Globe,* 39th Cong., 1st sess., app., p. 48.

policies. According to Northern Democrats, secession by states was illegal but not treasonous. Only individuals committed acts of treason against the government; if they followed the "corporate decision" of their state, they were innocent of disloyalty.[83] In the Democrats' view, only the illegitimacy of secession justified the North's coercion of the South, and because the war had resulted from a partial insurrection (some Northern Democrats referred to it as the War of the Confederate Rebellion, not the Civil War, or, as Southerners preferred, the War of the Northern Invasion) and not from an uprising of all the people, once resistance ended, states automatically retrieved their prewar status. As the nation's original political communities, they did not have to wait for either a congressional or presidential mandate. For Northern Democrats, the purpose of the war was to maintain the Union, not to redesign it; hence reunion should imitate the Whiskey and Shays rebellions. In these instances once those in arms had surrendered, communities had resumed their formal allegiance, like a lung reinflating. "When the war is over," explained Indiana Democrat Joseph Edgerton shortly before it was, "the Southern states are in the Union because they are a part of the nation's life, body and soul. The states have a vital power to restore themselves."[84] Accordingly, Northern Democrats supported reconvening Confederate state legislatures when it appeared that the federal government might follow the minimal procedures of the Sherman-Johnston agreement: soldiers to lay down their arms, the army to disband, and the people to resume their identity as citizens of state and Union.[85]

If the political advantages of such peace conditions were obvious, the ideological basis for the idea was also familiar. Prewar Northern Democrats had resolutely acknowledged the states as retaining certain powers on the assumption that they were closer to the people than was the national government. After the war the party's notion of a perpetual union based on popular sovereignty was transformed into a theory of reconstruction. Both concepts were based on the same sentimental view of the people's authority within their local jurisdictions, and both represented the Democrats' ideal of republican government as self-govern-

[83]This argument would have been used to defend Jefferson Davis, although the former president of the Confederacy was never brought to trial. See Jeremiah Black Papers, 28 May and 6 July 1865, Black Papers, Library of Congress.

[84]*Congressional Globe,* 38th Cong., 2d sess., app., pp. 75–77; ibid., 39th Cong., 1st sess., app., p. 63.

[85]Jonathan Dorris, *Pardon and Amnesty under Lincoln and Johnson* (Chapel Hill: University of North Carolina Press, 1953), p. 98.

ment by the states.[86] To be sure, this position clashed with various theories of the Republicans, who argued that the seceding states had committed suicide, that their rights were temporarily suspended, and that the Confederacy should be treated as a conquered province. Republicans used these interpretations to establish minimal protections for Southern blacks and based their policy of nationalizing civil liberties on the guarantee clause of the Constitution.[87]

Democrats offered instead the exclusive nationalism of a white man's government. Their sole program consisted of immediate pardon for Confederates and conferring, in the phrase that became a party slogan, "the mantle of oblivion over the past." In May 1865 and again in December 1867, President Johnson did grant general amnesty to former Confederates, but he excluded large landholders and permitted the special pardons that Democrats believed encouraged favoritism. Even Johnson's third proclamation of amnesty (after which only Jefferson Davis remained unforgiven) did not end Democratic concern, and at their 1868 national convention, party leaders favored "amnesty for all past political offenses and the regulation of the elective franchise in the states by their citizens."[88] Besides the immediate restoration of Southern states to their prewar status, Northern Democrats offered no proposals. Both their emphasis on state authority and their minority status absolved them from the need to do so.

Nor did Democrats provide a consistent economic program; even George Pendleton's compromise plan to redeem war bonds with greenbacks rather than gold divided the party. James Bayard had predicted as much. "We will," he had written in 1868, "disagree on currency and financial matters. Therefore we should confine ourselves to things we agree on."[89]

Nor, to the surprise of some observers, did Northern Democrats agree on slavery any more than they had before the war. They continued to consider the institution to be a local matter. "Slavery," ac-

[86]Herman Belz, *A New Birth of Freedom: The Republican Party and Freedmen's Rights, 1861–1866* (Westport, Conn.: Greenwood Press, 1976).

[87]Philip Paludan, *A Covenant with Death: The Constitution, Law, and Equality in the Civil War Era* (Urbana: University of Illinois Press, 1975), pp. 34–36. For Democratic interpretations of this "elastic" guarantee, see *Congressional Globe,* 38th Cong., 2d sess., app., pp. 55–60, 79.

[88]Dorris, *Pardon and Amnesty,* pp. xvii, 117, 354; *Congressional Globe,* 39th Cong., 1st sess., app., 26; Porter and Johnson, *National Party Platforms,* p. 37.

[89]James Bayard to Samuel L. Barlow, 20 January 1868, Samuel Barlow Papers, Huntington Library, San Marino, Calif. For disagreement about Pendleton's Ohio Plan, see Seymour's "Address to the New York Democracy," *New York Herald,* 26 June 1868.

cording to Indiana's Edgerton, "is not the issue for the Democracy which has subordinated the question of Negro slavery and all kindred questions to stand by the Union. We should leave to states the issue of Negro slavery." In 1865, fifty-six of seventy-nine Democratic congressmen opposed the Thirteenth Amendment as an invasion of local prerogatives, but a growing minority—including the fifteen congressmen who voted yes—believed the issue a dead one. "Its removal," argued Samuel Cox, "would be the wisest counsel of conservatism and would assure the ascendance of Democrats." Cox meant, of course, that once blacks were freed, his Republican opponents would be revealed as the sponsors of black equality.[90]

What Northern Democrats did agree on was the theory of perpetual union and its engrossment in two policies: amnesty for white Southerners and the restoration of Southern states. Some party regulars were concerned that their organization offered no alternatives and instead fought, as Richard Vaux alleged, "on its enemies' battlefield." According to the Philadelphia congressman, "We always wait till the Republicans act and then pick up the odds and ends."[91] But other Northern Democrats found the notion of an indissoluble Union sufficient to accommodate the multiple legislative settings of Reconstruction. Accordingly, Democrats held the Freedmen's Bureau, the Civil Rights Act, the Military Reconstruction Acts of 1867, and the Fourteenth and Fifteenth Amendments, in the words of New Yorker Joseph Chanler, "unconstitutional, usurpatious, fatal to representative government, partisan, interfering, violating the checks and balances, overriding state laws, unnatural, and antisouthern."[92] Northern Democrats said nothing about the noxious black codes that Southern legislatures established in 1865 and 1866, and when white vigilante groups sponsored antiblack rioting in Memphis and New Orleans, Northern Democrats presumed this to be the natural result of the government's persistent interference in local affairs. Later, party members denied the existence of even the Ku Klux Klan, which they explained as a local association exaggerated into a conspiracy by Republicans.[93]

[90]LaWanda Cox and John H. Cox, *Politics, Principle, and Prejudice, 1865–1866: Dilemma of Reconstruction America* (Glencoe, Ill.: Free Press, 1963), pp. 20–21, 238; *Congressional Globe,* 38th Cong., 2d sess., app. p. 75.

[91]Quoted in William Gillette, *Retreat from Reconstruction, 1869–1879* (Baton Rouge: Louisiana State University Press, 1979), p. 60.

[92]*Congressional Globe,* 39th Cong., 1st sess., 82.

[93]Charles Tansill, *The Congressional Career of Thomas Francis Bayard, 1869–1885* (Washington, D.C.: Georgetown University Press, 1946), pp. 68–70; *Congressional Globe,* 42d Cong., 2d sess., app., pp. 452–69.

White Southerners agreed, for they too held the theory of perpetual union and supported state authority over reconstruction. But this concurrence did not ensure the immediate reunification of the party's Northern and Southern wings, for Southerners, who sometimes misgauged their own power to negotiate Reconstruction, resented what they considered the betrayal of their interests by former allies. Four years outside the party increased what one Georgia Democrat described as "expressions of distrust of Northern Democrats."[94] Even after the 1868 presidential election, when 58 percent of the vote in the previously Confederate states went to Seymour and F. P. Blair, Southern Democrats worked for a new conservative coalition. Having lost the sense of themselves as Americans, former Confederates no longer shared their Northern colleagues' belief in the Democracy as an eternal association that would survive every man-made challenge. Thus former Southern Democrats were among the first to predict that the Democracy's minority status would lead, as it had with the Federalists and Whigs, to its disappearance. "Is not the Democratic party effectively dead as a national organ," inquired W. C. Oathes after its defeat in 1872, "or if not, a mere shell?"[95] Few of the South's leaders in the late 1860s had ties with the prewar Democracy: many were former Whigs, others were elected because they had stayed outside secessionist politics, and a third group that included former slaves had never been in politics.[96] Gone too were the intimate associations that had brought Northern and Southern leaders together in Washington and continued to link them through correspondence.

Nor were Northern Democratic tactics always congenial to Southerners; in fact, the party impaired its standing by frequently reversing itself. Northern Democrats had never spoken with one voice, but during Reconstruction partisan atrophy in the South required a single expression of opinion. Often the legislative pace was so swift that re-

[94]Edward Gambill, "Northern Democrats and Reconstruction, 1865–1868" (Ph.D. dissertation, University of Iowa, 1969); Martin Mantell, *Johnson, Grant, and the Politics of Reconstruction* (New York: Columbia University Press, 1973), pp. 6–8; Marcellus Emory to Manton Marble, 1 June 1867, Manton Marble Papers, Library of Congress (hereafter cited as Marble Papers). See also George Stearns to Andrew Johnson, 17 May 1865, Johnson Papers.

[95]W. C. Oathes to Alexander Stephens, 14 November 1872, Stephens Papers; Michael Perman, *Reunion without Compromise: The South and Reconstruction, 1865–1868* (Cambridge: At the University Press, 1973), pp. 168, 173, 249.

[96]Richard Hume, "The Black and Tan Constitutional Conventions of 1867–1869 in Ten Former Confederate States: A Study of Their Membership" (Ph.D. dissertation, University of Washington, 1969).

quirements for readmission remained unclear even in the 1870s, and Southerners sniffed political expediency in the conflicting advice from Northern Democrats. When the influential *New York World* at first encouraged Southerners to accept the Fourteenth Amendment so that they could participate in the presidential elections of 1868 and then, a few months later, argued for noncompliance, the *Richmond Times* complained that Northern Democrats were using the South for their own election purposes.[97]

Locked into a minority position (the Democracy did not win the House until 1871, the Senate until 1879, and the White House until 1884), Northern Democrats wooed Andrew Johnson, seeking reunion through a Southern president who had been a Democrat longer than he had been a Republican. In 1865 and 1866 Jeremiah Black, Joseph Wright, and Charles Mason haunted the president's anterooms, and August Belmont, the party's titular leader, spent several afternoons alongside equally expectant Republican officials. But, as Samuel Cox acknowledged, there was "no bridge" through the president, and although Democrats attended the 1866 Johnson-sponsored Union Party convention in Philadelphia, their participation was not, according to Belmont, "a repudiation of the Democracy."[98] Rather the three-day event served as an occasion for renewing personal contacts.

Two years later, a more important reunion took place at Tammany Hall on 4 July 1868, when Northern Democrats welcomed to their national convention 172 delegates from the former Confederate states. Although the electoral votes of Virginia, Mississippi, and Texas would not be counted in the November election, Democrats revived their sense of nationalism through this partisan reconciliation. Reunification—not the twenty-two ballots necessary to nominate a presidential ticket—was the hidden agenda of this meeting, as Northern and Southern Democrats celebrated what one called "our pedigree and ancestry." Said another, "We are the spontaneous instinct of the average national character always imbued with intense national feeling." And so it appeared within the hall, where South Carolina palmettos and Alabama camellias waved alongside the Stars and Stripes. Despite the political dangers (for the South remained a barbed political opportunity), dele-

[97]Eric McKitrick, *Andrew Johnson and Reconstruction* (Chicago: University of Chicago Press, 1960), pp. 465–67; Katz, *August Belmont,* p. 90; Perman, *Reunion without Compromise,* pp. 248, 320.

[98]Cox to Marble, October 1866, Marble Papers; Katz, *August Belmont;* Mantell, "New York and Elections of 1866"; Gambill, "Northern Democrats and Reconstruction," pp. 147–65.

gates desectionalized the army and claimed for all soldiers—Confederate and Union—a devotion "to cause and country."[99]

So convinced were Northern Democrats of the loyalty of their Southern colleagues that they reinstated the two-thirds rule for nomination, thereby restoring sectional privilege. But no Southern bloc emerged, although there were differences between the two regions, with Southerners at first supporting Andrew Johnson and then switching to the Pennsylvania conservative General Winfield Scott Hancock. Finally, however, they accepted, and campaigned for, the convention's choice of Horatio Seymour and Francis Blair. In the North the return of the South to the Democracy provided a concrete expression of reunion, and even during a losing political campaign Northern Democrats expressed their patriotism—again through their relationship with the South. Said August Belmont in an address that fused party, nation, and military service: "Our ranks are unbroken; our courage is unabated. Once more to the breach, this time victory."[100]

[99]*New York World,* 4–10 July 1868; [Democratic National Committee], *The Official Proceedings of the National Convention* (Boston: Rockwell and Rollins, 1868); Homer A. Stebbins, *The Political History of the State of New York,* Columbia University Studies in History, Economics, and Public Law, no. 55 (New York: Columbia University Press, 1913), pp. 333–50.

[100]Quoted in Charles Coleman, *The Election of 1868: The Democratic Effort to Regain Control* (New York: Octagon, 1971), p. 355.

CONCLUSION

# *The Democracy as Imitator and Shaper*

The preceding chapters have discussed the ways in which the Democratic party shaped the behavior and attitudes of its adherents, a group whose selection of the party had been influenced by family, personality, and community. Once established, this choice in turn shaped subsequent orientations to public affairs. As its self-awareness increased, the party provided an authentic subculture that influenced the way its followers felt and acted; at the same time, these Democrats, more certain than earlier Americans had been of the uses of party, made the Democracy into an active agent of national persuasion. Thus it was through the instrument of party that millions of Northerners received information not only about public issues but also about the appropriate attitudes and behaviors expected of them as American citizens.

By mid-century, when these Northern Democrats reached political maturity, they participated in a series of recurring rituals and ceremonies that separated them from other Americans. Notwithstanding significant areas of policy agreement and extensive sharing of political symbols by all Americans, the Democracy was just different enough from other organizations to convey a sense of autonomy. But at the same time that the party furnished its supporters with a separate public identity, it also returned them to the nation as Americans. The primary contribution of the party during the critical years of the Civil War was to channel loyalty to the party into support for the nation. On the one hand, Democratic solidarity was accomplished through preelection activities, when members paraded, chose and ratified their leaders, and cast their party's tickets at the polls. On the other hand, party members distinguished themselves from opponents through their commitment to "the Union as it was, the Constitution as it is, and the Negro where he is." This commitment to a white man's republic was sufficiently distinct from the Republican doctrine of "free men, free soil and free labor" to underwrite the ideological differentiation necessary for electoral competition. In turn, party rivalry inspired civic participation consistent with national values.

Party leaders displayed both the ideas and the behavior of Northern Democrats, and Democratic notables in and out of office talked, wrote, and voted to maintain their blueprint of continuity. But the popular attitudes of the Democratic rank and file (the term a legacy of the party's military language) were reinforced through other mediums—especially the minstrel shows of popular culture. Just as the effect of the party's pronounced Americanism appeared in mass behavior such as volunteering for the Union army, so the impact of minstrelsy was readily observable in the Democrats' antiblack activities, which ranged from race riots to discrimination.

By 1876 an organization once judged subversive was serving to Americanize its followers, instructing them in two ways. The first was the creation of internal mechanisms that replicated the external political culture. The delegation of power to representatives in conventions, the division of authority between state and national organizations, the emphásis on participation, the allocation of limited resources, and the rotation of offices provided training in the active passivity required of American citizens. The party also instructed its members by means of a nationalistic rhetoric that sometimes made its name a synonym for the country. In these two ways, the Democracy both formed a part of, and actively shaped, the very thing it imitated.

When a later generation of Democrats—Northern and Southern—came to power, the party was less anxious about the Republic's survival and more influenced by other agencies such as labor unions and trade associations. After the 1880s these Democrats generated a new partisan subculture less concerned with patriotic pageantry and symbolism. Such a transformation was a slow process. Although the Democracy continued to define what its members did and thought, the affective sense of its affairs that earlier transformed love of the Democracy into love of the United States diminished.

# *Bibliographic Notes*

Primary sources are cited in the footnotes. What follows is a brief, general assessment of the secondary literature, arranged by topic.

## *Political Culture and Socialization*

The notion of culture as a customary set of patterns and orientations is a modern one, and not until the mid-twentieth century has the term been applied to public life in such comparative studies as Lucien Pye and Sidney Verba, *Political Culture and Political Development* (Princeton: Princeton University Press, 1965), and Gabriel Almond and Sidney Verba, *The Civic Culture: Political Attitudes and Democracy in Five Nations* (Princeton: Princeton University Press, 1963). Proceeding from the premise that politics is a deeply rooted cultural activity, these studies depend on questionnaires and cross-national analysis. Two important efforts at defining political culture are Gabriel Almond, "Comparative Political Systems," *Journal of Politics* 18 (August 1956): 319–409; and Robert C. Tucker, "Culture, Political Culture, and Communist Society," *Political Science Quarterly* 88 (June 1973): 173–91. More recent studies separate ideology and behavior into two components; see, for example, Archie Brown and Jack Gray, eds., *Political Culture and Political Change in Communist States* (New York: Holmes and Meier, 1977). Applying the concept to the United States are Donald J. Devine, *The Political Culture of the United States: The Influence of Member Values on Regime Maintenance* (Boston: Little, Brown, 1972). Devine emphasizes the "value continuity" of liberal consensus which persists within what he calls a "discontinuous social structure." More specialized and topical are Edgar Litt, *The Political Culture of Massachusetts* (Cambridge, Mass.: M.I.T. Press, 1965); Daniel Howe, *The Political Culture of the American Whigs* (Chicago: University of Chicago Press, 1979); and John Blum's effort to limn from wartime politics the elements of American culture, *V was for Victory: Politics and American Culture* (New York: Harcourt Brace Jovanovich, 1976).

Implicit in the concept of political culture is the establishment of orientations to political action. This concept of political socialization in society is covered in contemporary studies such as David Easton and Jack Dennis, *Children in the Political System: Origins of Political Legitimacy* (New York: McGraw-Hill, 1969); M. Kent Jennings and Richard Niemi, *The Political Character of Adolescence* (Princeton: Princeton University Press, 1974); Kenneth Langton, *Political Socialization* (New York: Oxford University Press, 1969); Stanley Renshon, *Handbook of Political Socialization Theory and Research* (New York: Free Press, 1977); and Judith Torney, A. N. Oppenheim, and Russell F. Farner, *Civic Education in Ten Countries* (New York: John Wiley, 1975). For a review of the issues in the field, see Jack Dennis, "Major Problems of Political Socialization Research," *Midwestern Journal of Politics* 12 (February 1968): 85–114. For a modern study of the child's identification with a leader, see Fred Greenstein, "The Benevolent Leader," *American Political Science Review* 54 (December 1960): 934–43.

Particularly useful for understanding symbols as social facts and rituals as generalized attitudes are Clifford Geertz, ed., *Myth, Symbol, and Culture* (New York: W. W. Norton, 1971); Geertz, *The Interpretation of Cultures: Selected Essays* (New York: Basic Books, 1973); and his most recent study, *Negara: The Theatre State in Nineteenth-Century Bali* (Princeton: Princeton University Press, 1980). See also Victor Turner's *The Drums of Affliction: A Study of Religious Processes among the Ndembu of Zambia* (Oxford: Clarendon Press, 1968) and *The Forest of Symbols: Aspects of Ndembu Ritual* (Ithaca, N.Y.: Cornell University Press, 1967). For applications to American politics, see W. Lloyd Warner, *The Living and the Dead* (New Haven: Yale University Press, 1959), and Jacob Murray Edelman's evocative *The Symbolic Uses of Politics: Mass Arousal and Quiescence* (Urbana: University of Illinois Press, 1964); also Marc J. Swartz, Victor Turner, and Arthur Tuden, *Political Anthropology* (Chicago: Aldine, 1966).

## *Nineteenth-Century Education*

Until recently the history of American education treated the external components of the system and concentrated on the evolution of formal institutions of instruction. Schools (and especially the public high school) emerged as self-contained entities only distantly related to American culture. The standard works of this genre are Ellwood Cubberly, *Public Education in the United States* (Boston: Houghton Mifflin, 1919); Edwin Dexter, *A History of Education in the United States* (New York: Macmillan, 1904); and Lawrence Cremin, *The American Common School* (New York: Columbia University Press, 1951). In the 1960s education was redefined as what Bernard Bailyn, in *Education in the Forming of American Society* (New York: Vintage Books, 1960), termed "a transfer of culture which both affected and reflected society." By the 1970s education had entered social (and economic) history in studies such as Samuel Bowles and Herbert Gintis, *Schooling in Capitalist America: Educational Reform and the Contradictions of Economic Life* (New York: Basic Books, 1976). Other works that consider schools as dedicated to preserving social peace and prosperity are Carl

Kaestle, *The Evolution of an Urban School System: New York, 1750–1850* (Cambridge, Mass.: Harvard University Press, 1973); Carl Kaestle and Maris Vinovskis, *Education and Social Change in Nineteenth-Century Massachusetts* (New York: Cambridge University Press, 1980); David Nasaw, *Schooled to Order: A Social History of Public Schooling in the United States* (New York: Oxford University Press, 1979); Michael Katz, *Bureaucracy and Schools: The Illusion of Educational Change* (New York: Praeger, 1971); Michael Katz, *The Irony of Early School Reform: Educational Innovation in Mid-Nineteenth-Century Massachusetts* (Cambridge, Mass.: Harvard University Press, 1968); and David Tyack, *The One Best System: A History of American Urban Education* (Cambridge, Mass.: Harvard University Press, 1974). For an introduction to the literature, see John A. Hague and Diane E. Lea, "Revolution in American Education: A Bibliographic Essay," *American Quarterly* supplement, 13 (1974): 11–20.

The standard histories of higher education are Frederick Rudolph, *The American College and University: A History* (New York: A. A. Knopf, 1962), and Laurence Veysey, *The Emergence of the American University* (Chicago: University of Chicago Press, 1965). Almost all the early Northern colleges have celebratory, in-house accounts of their early years. Two recent monographs do for colleges what the "Harvard school" has done for schools. They are Stephen Novak, *The Rights of Youth: American Colleges and Student Revolts* (Cambridge, Mass.: Harvard University Press, 1977), and Burton Bledstein, *The Culture of Professionalism: The Middle Class and the Development of Higher Education* (New York: W. W. Norton, 1976).

For the concept of the hidden curriculum, see Philip W. Jackson, *Life in the Classrooms* (New York: Holt, Rinehart and Winston, 1968); Michael W. Apple, "The Hidden Curriculum and the Nature of Conflict," *Interchange* 2 (1971): 27–40; Ivan Illich, *Deschooling Society* (New York: Harper & Row, 1971); and Alan Gartner, Colin Greer, and Frank Reissman, eds., *After Deschooling, What?* (New York: Harper & Row, 1973). The most important application of the hidden curriculum to nineteenth-century schooling appears in Barbara Finkelstein, "Governing the Young: Teacher Behavior in American Primary Schools: A Documentary History" (Ph.D. dissertation, Columbia University, 1970) and "Pedagogy as Intrusion: Teaching Values in Popular Primary Schools in Nineteenth-Century America," *History of Childhood Quarterly* 2 (Winter 1975): 361–66.

## *The Democratic Party*

Traditional narratives of the nineteenth-century Democratic party include Frank R. Kent's anecdotal *The Democratic Party: A History* (New York: Century, 1928); David L. Cohn, *The Fabulous Democrats* (New York: Putnam, 1956); and Ralph M. Goldman's *Search for Consensus: The Story of the Democratic Party* (Philadelphia: Temple University Press, 1979), which traces the history of the party since its formal organization in 1832. For an account of its Jefferson-

Jackson Day celebrations, see Ronald F. Stinnett, *Democrats, Dinners, and Dollars: A History of the Democratic Party, Its Dinners, Its Ritual* (Ames: Iowa State University Press, 1967. Essential documents appear in William Nisbet Chambers, *The Democrats, 1789–1864: A Short History of a Popular Party* (Princeton: D. Van Nostrand, 1964), and Michael Holt and Paolo Colletta have provided succinct introductions in *History of U.S. Political Parties,* ed. Arthur M. Schlesinger, Jr., 5 vol. (New York: Chelsea House, 1973). Jerome Mushkat's *The Reconstruction of the New York Democracy, 1861–1874* (Rutherford, N.J.: Fairleigh Dickinson University Press, 1981) treats the decline and regeneration of the New York party at mid-century. Robert Kelley sets the party in a cross-national context in *The Transatlantic Persuasion: The Liberal Democratic Mind in the Age of Gladstone* (New York: A. A. Knopf, 1969). For the Civil War period see Joel Silbey, *A Respectable Minority: The Democratic Party in the Civil War Era, 1860–1868* (New York: W. W. Norton, 1977); Leonard Curry, "Congressional Democrats," *Civil War History* 12 (September 1966): 23–29; and Christopher Dell, *Lincoln and the War Democrats* (Cranbury, N.J.: Associated University Press, 1978). Dell argues that Lincoln successfully lured Democratic voters into the Republican party and that both the story of the wartime Democrats and the resulting erosion of American conservatism have been neglected. For the prewar era, see Roy F. Nichols's Pulitzer-Prize-winning *The Disruption of the American Democracy* (New York: Macmillan, 1948). David Meerse concentrates on patronage in his excellent dissertation, "James Buchanan, the Patronage, and the Northern Democratic Party, 1857–1858" (University of Illinois, 1969). Other important unpublished studies of the mid-century party are Edward L. Gambill, "Northern Democrats and Reconstruction, 1865–1868" (Ph.D. dissertation, University of Iowa, 1969), and Van M. Davis, "Individualism on Trial: The Ideology of the Northern Democracy During the Civil War and Reconstruction" (Ph.D. dissertation, University of Virginia, 1972).

For the Democrats as "disloyal copperheads," see George Fort Milton, *Abraham Lincoln and the Fifth Column* (New York: Vanguard, 1942); Wood Gray, *The Hidden Civil War; The Story of the Copperheads* (New York: Viking Press, 1942); Frank L. Klement, *The Copperheads in the Middle West* (Chicago: University of Chicago Press, 1960). For the corrective, see Richard Curry, "The Union as It Was: A Critique of Recent Interpretations of the Copperheads," *Civil War History* 20 (September 1974): 215–38; and Frank L. Klement, "Civil War Politics, Nationalism, and Postwar Myths," *Historian* 38 (May 1976): 419–38, and "Middle Western Copperheadism and the Genesis of the Granger Movement," *Mississippi Valley Historical Review* 38 (March 1952): 679–94.

On the nature of parties and politics, see Samuel P. Hays, *American Political History as Social History: Essays* (Knoxville: University of Tennessee Press, 1980); Benjamin Page, *Choices and Echoes in Presidential Elections* (Chicago: University of Chicago Press, 1978); William L. Shade, *Social Change and the Electoral Process* (Gainesville: University of Florida Press, 1973).

Recent studies have emphasized parties as elements in a system, and much of the current literature treats the Democrats from this perspective. See Richard

McCormick, *The Second American Party System: Party Formation in the Jacksonian Era* (Chapel Hill: University of North Carolina Press, 1966); Michael F. Holt, *The Political Crisis of the 1850s* (New York: Wiley, 1978); Paul Kleppner's *The Cross of Culture: A Social Analysis of Midwestern Politics, 1850–1900* (New York: Free Press, 1970) and *Third Electoral System, 1853–1892: Parties, Voters, and Political Cultures* (Chapel Hill: University of North Carolina Press, 1979) place the Democratic electorate in ethnic and religious categories. For the party in Congress, see Thomas Alexander, *Sectional Stress and Party Strength: A Computer Analysis of Roll-Call Voting Patterns in the United States House of Representatives, 1836–1860* (Nashville: Vanderbilt University Press, 1967); Joel Silbey, *Shrine of Party: Congressional Voting Behavior, 1841–1852* (Pittsburgh: University of Pittsburgh Press, 1967); Glenn Linden, *Politics or Principle: Congressional Voting on the Civil War Amendments and Pro-Negro Measures* (Seattle: University of Washington Press, 1976).

## *General Studies of Mid-Nineteenth-Century Politics*

The most comprehensive introduction to the period remains Allan Nevins's magisterial *Ordeal of the Union*, 8 vols. (New York: Scribner's, 1947–71). David Donald's *Liberty and Union* (Boston: Little, Brown, 1978) provides comprehensive coverage of national affairs, as does his standard text, J. G. Randall and David Donald, *The Civil War and Reconstruction*, (Boston: D. C. Heath, 1961). A number of recent studies cover various aspects of Northern public life. They include Philip Paludan, *A Covenant with Death: The Constitution, Law, and Equality in the Civil War* (Urbana: University of Illinois Press, 1975); James A. Rawley, *The Politics of Union: Northern Politics during the Civil War* (Hinsdale, Ill.: Dryden Press, 1974); Herman Belz, *Emancipation and Equal Rights: Politics and Constitutionalism in the Civil War Era* (New York: W. W. Norton, 1978); Leonard Curry, *Blueprint for Modern America: Non-Military Legislation of the First Civil War Congress* (Nashville: Vanderbilt University Press, 1968); and Eric Foner's idea-oriented *Politics and Ideology in the Age of the Civil War* (New York: Oxford University Press, 1980). Extremely helpful in understanding civic attitudes during the period is Rush Welter, *The Mind of America, 1830–1860* (New York: Columbia University Press, 1975). The classic study of civil rights remains James G. Randall, *Constitutional Problems under Lincoln*, rev. ed. (Urbana: University of Illinois Press, 1964). A number of studies cover aspects of Northern politics. Particularly useful for the Democrats of this period are LaWanda Cox and John H. Cox, *Politics, Principle, and Prejudice, 1865–1866: Dilemma of Reconstruction America* (New York: Free Press, 1963); Martin Mantell, *Johnson, Grant, and the Politics of Reconstruction* (New York: Columbia University Press, 1973); William Gillette, *The Right to Vote: Politics and the Passage of the Fifteenth Amendment* (Baltimore: Johns Hopkins University Press, 1965); and Gillette's massive new study, *Retreat from Reconstruction, 1869–1879* (Baton Rouge: Louisiana State University Press, 1979). In a different vein, Jacques Ellul, *The Politi-*

*cal Illusion* (New York: A. A. Knopf, 1967), identifies the process of politicizing public issues.

For the concept of republicanism see J. G. A. Pocock, *The Machiavellian Moment: Florentine Political Thought and the Atlantic Tradition* (Princeton: Princeton University Press, 1975) and idem, *Politics, Language, and Time: Essays on Political Thought and History* (New York: Atheneum, 1971). Gordon Wood's article "Rhetoric and Reality in the American Revolution," *William and Mary Quarterly* 3d ser., 23 (January 1966), is indispensable, as is his delineation of republicanism in *The Creation of the American Republic, 1776–1787* (Chapel Hill: University of North Carolina Press, 1969). Robert Shallhope has placed this ruling ideology within its historiographic framework in "Toward a Republican Synthesis: The Emergence of an Understanding of Republicanism in American Historiography", *William and Mary Quarterly*, 3d ser. 29 (January 1972): 49–80.

Very little work has been done on the "sense of party." The most important introductions are Franklyn George Bonn, "The Idea of Political Party in the Thought of Thomas Jefferson and James Madison" (Ph.D. dissertation, University of Minnesota, 1946), and Richard Hofstadter, *The Idea of a Party System: The Rise of Legitimate Opposition in the United States, 1789–1840* (Berkeley: University of California Press, 1969). The concept of antipartyism is convincingly treated in Ronald P. Formisano, *The Birth of Mass Political Parties, Michigan, 1827–1861* (Princeton: Princeton University Press, 1971).

# Index

*Library of Congress Cataloging in Publication Data*

Baker, Jean H.
Affairs of party.

Bibliography: p.
Includes index.
1. Democratic Party (U.S.)—History. 2. Political socialization—United States—History. 3. United States—Politics and government—1849–1877.
I. Title.
JK2316.B34 1983 324.2736'09 82-14283
ISBN 0-8014-1513-6
ISBN 0-8014-9883-X (pbk.)